Stigma

About the author

Imogen Tyler is a Professor of Sociology at Lancaster University and a Fellow of the Academy of Social Science. A teacher, writer and social activist, she is a member of the Morecambe Bay Poverty Truth Commission and a trustee of the UK Poverty Truth Network. She has published widely on issues of social inequality and injustice, and her critically acclaimed book *Revolting Subjects* (2013) was shortlisted for the Bread and Roses Award for Radical Publishing.

Stigma

The Machinery
of Inequality

Imogen Tyler

BLOOMSBURY ACADEMIC
LONDON • NEW YORK • OXFORD • NEW DELHI • SYDNEY

BLOOMSBURY ACADEMIC
Bloomsbury Publishing Plc
50 Bedford Square, London, WC1B 3DP, UK
1385 Broadway, New York, NY 10018, USA
29 Earlsfort Terrace, Dublin 2, Ireland

BLOOMSBURY, BLOOMSBURY ACADEMIC and the Diana logo are trademarks
of Bloomsbury Publishing Plc

First published in Great Britain by ZED BOOKS 2020
Paperback Edition Published 2021
Reprinted in 2021
This edition published by Bloomsbury Academic 2022

An earlier version of Chapter 2 was published in the Sociological Review, and an earlier
version of Chapter 3 was published in Ethnic and Racial Studies.

Some names and details have been changed to protect the privacy of those involved.

The author and publisher are grateful to the Elizabeth Roberts Working Class Oral
History Archive at the Regional History Centre, Lancaster University for permission to
quote from interview data from the archive.

For legal purposes the Acknowledgments on pp. 352–4 constitute an extension
of this copyright page.

Cover design by Steve Leard
Cover photo © Shutterstock

ISBN: PB: 978-1-3503-7927-5
ePDF: 978-1-7869-9331-1
eBook: 978-1-7869-9332-8

Typeset by seagulls.net
Index by John Barker
Printed and bound in Great Britain

To find out more about our authors and books visit www.bloomsbury.com
and sign up for our newsletters.

This book is dedicated to the Morecambe Bay Poverty Truth Commission whose humanity and practices of social solidarity fill me with hope for the future

Contents

List of illustrations

The mantle of liberalism has been discarded and the most disgusting despotism in all its nakedness is disclosed to the eyes of the whole world. ... It is a truth which ... teaches us to recognize the emptiness of our patriotism and the abnormity of our state system, and makes us hide our faces in shame. You look at me with a smile and ask: What is gained by that? No revolution is made out of shame. I reply: Shame is already a revolution of a kind. ... Shame is a kind of anger which is turned inward. And if a whole nation really experienced a sense of shame, it would be like a lion, crouching ready to spring.

Letter from Karl Marx to Arnold Ruge, March 1843

Introduction

Stigma, the machinery of inequality

Stigma, noun. Figurative. A mark of disgrace or infamy;
a sign of severe censure or condemnation, regarded as
impressed on a person or thing; a 'brand'.

Oxford English Dictionary

Every news bulletin seemed to be calling me scrounger,
fraud, cheat or scum. I began self-harming, carving the
words 'failure', 'freak' and 'waste of space' into my arms,
legs and stomach.

Stephanie, 2019

March 2019. I am sitting with my friend Stephanie in the corner
of a bar in Lancaster, the small city in North West England where
I live and work.[1] Stephanie is a former schoolteacher and a single
mum whom I have got to know through our work together on
the Morecambe Bay Poverty Truth Commission, one of thirteen
such commissions currently running across the UK, which bring
together people living in poverty with local decision makers to try
to find ways to ameliorate the destitution which has followed in
the wake of austerity – a programme of government reforms which
have eviscerated the British welfare state since 2010. When I told
Stephanie that I was writing a book about stigma, she asked if she
could tell me her stigma story, so I could share it with others, with

you, the readers of this book. She asked to meet in this bar because her wounds are raw and she feels a public setting will allow her to retain some composure, some dignity, while she speaks. So here we are, two middle-aged women drinking coffee in a city centre bar; late afternoon sunlight streams in from the window behind the table where we sit, casting shadows over Stephanie's face, as she explains how she reached a point where she began carving stigma words into her arms, stomach, thighs with a razor blade.

'The only way I can describe it', she says, 'is if you watch a washing machine go through its cycle, you have worries and then they calm down, more worries, then they calm down. Then the machine goes into the spin cycle, and you get to that point when it feel like it's not going to stop, and the only way to get that out is to attack yourself because there is nobody else left. You have to cut that spin cycle. It's as harsh as pulling the plug. That's what you are doing, but it only works for a little while … for seconds … then you feel even more shame for having done it.'

The story Stephanie tells me begins over a decade ago, when her mum was diagnosed with terminal cancer, the same day her husband told her that he was leaving. Stephanie and her daughter, Isla, moved into her mum's house so she could care for her. After her mum died, Stephanie got a temporary job as a teaching assistant and started to build a better life. Not long afterwards, she had a serious accident at work which left her immobilised and in chronic pain. A cycle of medical interventions and operations began, which finally culminated in a knee replacement. When she was back on her feet, Stephanie secured a new teaching post, but then Isla became seriously ill and she had to take time off work to care for her. Stephanie's employer lost patience with the periods of parental leave, and she was forced to quit her job.

There is a familiar story here, about women's unpaid labour, the care they provide for elderly relatives and children, and how this care work can make it difficult, sometimes impossible, to sustain waged work. During these years of difficult, if ordinary, life events, Stephanie sold her home at a loss to prevent repossession. Then austerity cuts to school budgets meant that the teaching supply work she had been getting by on dried up. Before long she had sold everything of value she owned.

'The shame', Stephanie says, 'is building' throughout these years: 'Every time the card was declined when I was shopping. I'd be standing there with £6 of shopping but it wouldn't go through and everybody in the queue is … you know … every little thing that happens piles on more stigma and shame.' Stephanie was really struggling now to keep a roof over her head. She was increasingly relying on charitable foodbanks to survive. In desperation, she took out a high interest payday loan and a rapid spiral into debt followed. Before long, she says, 'We started getting letters to evict us'. The dry mouth each time the phone rings. Her heart beating faster in her chest each time a letter drops on the door mat. The rush of anxiety that accompanies every unexpected knock at the door. Stephanie couldn't see a way out of her situation, so she sought advice and was told she should qualify for unemployment benefit and housing benefit. She applied for the relief to which she was entitled, during the exact period when the British government's austerity programme of welfare reform was beginning.

In February 2008, in the midst of the global banking crisis, the Shadow Chancellor George Osborne gave a speech to the Conservative Party with the title 'There Is a Dependency Culture'. This was the period leading up to the 2010 general election, which would see Osborne installed as 'the austerity Chancellor'. Osborne used this speech as an opportunity to outline the Conservative Party's economic response to the financial crisis, which centred on plans to implement 'the most far-reaching programme [of] welfare reform for a generation'.[2] There was no evidence for the claims Osborne made in this speech that an overly generous system of welfare provisions was responsible for the national economic outlook, which he variously described as indebted, stagnant, inflexible, vulnerable and exposed. Yet he confidently identified 'millions of people' who were 'languishing on out of work benefits' as a central challenge facing the British economy: an 'unproductive' residuum of people 'persistently playing the system' and deceitfully milking the rewards of what he termed a 'something for nothing culture'. Osborne announced that cuts in benefits, services and provisions, a deterrent welfare system spiked with conditions and sanctions, and punitive workfare programmes outsourced to 'private and voluntary sectors' was the 'tough' medicine required to move people 'off benefits and into work'.[3] He promised that these austerity reforms would end what he described as a 'shameful' 'dependency culture in Britain', 'free up supply' (of capital and labour), 'unleash billions of pounds', 'restore the health of the public finances', liberate those 'stuck on benefits' and 'transform' the 'life chances of millions of families'. In fact, as I examine in Chapter 4 of this book, what followed in the wake of austerity is what can only be described as a planned social catastrophe.

When the Conservative Party came to power in a coalition government in 2010, their programme of welfare reform began in earnest. A former job centre advisor has described how her job changed overnight from one of helping people to 'the persecution of vulnerable people'.[4] 'The pressure was incredible', she says, as frontline staff became subject 'to constant and aggressive pressure to meet and exceed targets' to get people off benefits by imposing conditions and sanctions. It was, she says, 'like "getting brownie points" for cruelty'.[5]

What Stephanie experienced when she applied for benefits was a welfare system in chaos, as it was being redesigned in ways which sought to deter people from making claims. As we will see, the stigma Stephanie encountered when interacting with frontline workers and welfare agencies was shocking. However, this was only one element of what she describes as an 'overwhelmingly hostile environment'. For what accompanied the implementation of these welfare reforms was an extraordinary political and media propaganda campaign which sought to manufacture public consent for austerity by stigmatising those in receipt of relief.

Stories about 'benefits cheats' seeped incessantly into Stephanie's world; every time she turned on the radio or television or brushed past a rack of newspapers in a shop, she would come across 'things like these people are stealing your taxes', which left her 'thinking that is me they're talking about'. This 'welfare stigma machine' needled Stephanie from every direction: 'It keeps coming, it's relentless, one constant cycle of judgement, like a knife being stuck repeatedly into you.' This unremitting stigma slowly eroded Stephanie's self-esteem. She began to feel that her daughter would be better off without her. She started to regularly self-harm. She became suicidal: 'I stockpiled tablets waiting for the right moment.'

In 2015, a letter arrived alleging that Stephanie had erroneously claimed income in the form of child tax credit to which she wasn't entitled, and that this benefit was being stopped while an investigation took place.[6] This stream of regular income (circa £250 a month) was essential to service the interest on her debts. When Stephanie read this letter, she broke down: 'I was in a state. I completely lost it. I was absolutely distraught. I was hitting myself with things. I was scraping my skin off.'

That same day she was supposed to attend an appointment at the job centre, so she rang and explained to them that she was 'in terrible distress', but they told her that a failure to attend would be taken as evidence she was unwilling to work, and that she would be sanctioned, potentially losing her right to claim benefits for up to three years. 'So, I just got in the car. I parked illegally in the middle of the street outside the job centre. I was hysterical. I was bleeding. The security guard looked at me and said I couldn't go inside. Eventually the man I was supposed to be signing on with came outside of the building with the form.'

The job coach didn't speak to Stephanie; he simply handed her a pen, and she signed on in the street. 'As I signed it, blood dripped all over the paper. I will never forget it.' Nobody expressed concern or worry for Stephanie as she stood outside the job centre with blood dripping from her wrists and arms. Nobody attempted to sooth her, to calm her. Nobody called for medical assistance. When I ask her why nobody did any of these things, she says: 'Nobody cared.' 'You end up not feeling human, like you don't have the right to be part of that society.' In the end, you are 'so dehumanised' that you begin to perceive yourself as an object, a thing, 'just scum'.

While Stephanie is describing this to me, her voice is breaking and her body is shaking. I stop her and say, 'I'm worried that recalling this trauma is repeating the harm'.

She replies, 'At one point a psychotherapist said to me that sometimes it helps to write down negative thoughts rather than keep them in your head, so what I ended up doing was writing a list of descriptors of myself'; and she recalls them:

waste of space
failure
freak
useless
burden
scrounger
waste of oxygen …
A whole list of negative things.

She continues: 'Then one day I started to cut the words from the list into my body. I'd think to myself, I'll do this one this time. I was writing on myself to say to the rest of the world, who you perceive as looking at you like that: "I know, you don't have to tell me, I already know. I know what you're thinking, but don't think I don't know that as well. Look."'

When I arrived home after my conversation with Stephanie, I lay down on my bed and wept for a long time.

A vigorous and relentless assault upon human dignity

In the foreword to the 2016/2017 Amnesty International Report on the state of the world's human rights, Amnesty's Secretary General Salil Shetty warned that we are witnessing 'a global trend towards angrier and more divisive politics' in which 'the idea of human dignity' is 'under vigorous and relentless assault from powerful narratives of blame, fear and scapegoating, propagated by those who sought to take or cling on to power'.[7] 'Across the world', he writes, 'leaders and politicians wagered their future power on narratives of fear and disunity, pinning blame on the "other" for the real or manufactured grievances of the electorate.'[8]

It is the thesis of *Stigma* that in order to counter the 'vigorous and relentless assault' upon human dignity that is a major characteristic of the current global authoritarian turn, we require a better understanding of how stigma is propagated as a governmental technology of division and dehumanisation. We need to track the role played by 'stigma politics' in producing the toxic climate of fear and hatred that is enveloping and dividing societies and communities. We need to examine how 'stigma power' is crafted and cultivated as a means of leveraging political capital. We also need a better understanding of the ways in which this divisive politics gets under the skin of those it subjugates; how this state-cultivated stigma changes the ways in which people think about themselves and others – corroding compassion, crushing hope, weakening social solidarity.

Stigma seeks to enrich sociological understandings of stigma as a concept, idea, material force and practice. It hopes also to enliven wider public debates about what stigma is, where stigma comes from, how and by whom stigma is produced and for what purposes. *Stigma* is concerned with what social scientific accounts of stigma frequently neglect, namely an understanding of stigma as embedded within the social relations of capitalism, and as a form of power entangled with histories of capitalism, colonialism and patriarchy. *Stigma* stretches the frameworks within which we ordinarily think about stigma. It aims to dislodge stigma from the settled meanings it acquired within twentieth-century social sciences, and to disrupt the individualistic, ahistorical and politically anaesthetised conceptualisations of stigma inherited from this tradition. *Stigma* is concerned with undisciplining stigma, with decolonising stigma, and with thinking about stigma within a distinctly political register.

This introduction is a précis of key themes and concepts in this book, and also a guide to the chapters that follow.

What is stigma?

In *Historical Ontology*, Ian Hacking reminds us that all 'concepts have their being in historical sites'.[9] The word 'stigma', as the *Oxford English Dictionary* defines it, is a figurative noun that means a 'distinguishing mark or characteristic (of a bad or objectionable kind)' and a 'mark of disgrace or infamy; a sign of severe censure or condemnation, regarded as impressed on a person or thing'. Everyday uses of the word 'stigma' draw on both these definitions; we employ 'stigma' to describe the degrading marks that are affixed to particular bodies, people, conditions and places within humiliating social interactions.

These two definitions of 'stigma' were composed by lexicographers at the *Oxford English Dictionary* in 1916, and they don't reflect the ways in which the word acquired an increasingly psychological meaning from the mid-twentieth century onwards. As we saw in Stephanie's story, when people use the term 'stigma' today, they also tend to use it experientially, to describe the debilitating psychological effects of being stigmatised, with a particular emphasis on how the shame induced by stigma corrodes well-being and damages your sense of self. However, psychological understandings of stigma often focus on individual experiences of being stigmatised in ways that occlude an understanding of stigma as a material force, a structural and structuring form of power. *Stigma* develops a more psycho-political understanding of stigma, reconceptualising stigma as a form of power that is written on the body and gets under the skin.

The *Oxford English Dictionary* also defines stigma as 'a mark made upon the skin by burning with a hot iron (rarely, by cutting or pricking), as a token of infamy or subjection'. This literal definition emphasises stigma as a material practice of bodily marking and subordination. Indeed, it is difficult for us to imagine activities that involve burning somebody with 'a hot iron', or cutting or pricking their skin for the purposes of indicating 'infamy' and 'subjection', as actions that aren't saturated with power.

To illustrate this definition, the *Oxford English Dictionary* includes a phrase penned by the nineteenth-century London *Times* journalist William Howard in *My Diary North and South* (1863), a book composed from diary entries and letters written while he travelled in North America during the American Civil War. The phrase reads: 'advertisements for runaway negroes ... the description of the stigmata on their persons – whippings and brandings, scars and cuts'.[10] This use of 'stigmata' to describe the marks left by torture on the skin of runaway slaves furnishes stigma with a vicious and bloody meaning, binding the etymology of stigma to the 400-year history of chattel slavery.

The legal right of English people to own human beings as 'goods and chattel' was first established by English colonialists in the *Barbados Slave Code*: 'An Act for Better Ordering and Governing of Negroes' (1661). This Act mandated that if a slave 'shall offer any violence to any Christian ... he shall be severely whipped, his nose slit, and be burned in some part of his face with a hot iron. And being brutish slaves, [they] deserve not, for the baseness of their condition, to be tried by the legal trial of twelve men of their peers, as the subjects of England are'.[11] It seems likely that the *Oxford English Dictionary* definition of stigma as 'a mark made upon the skin by burning with a hot iron' derives in part from these seventeenth-century legislative codes.[12] Other histories of stigma unfurl from this submerged etymology, histories of torture and slave labour, but also histories of British citizenship, for in legalising torture what these slave codes legislated is that chattel slaves and their descendants were not citizens; indeed, they were not considered human at all.

A mark made upon the skin by burning with a hot iron

In *Black Reconstruction in America* (1935), the sociologist W.E.B. Du Bois (1863–1963) described the Atlantic slave trade as 'the transportation of ten million human beings out of the dark beauty of their mother continent into the new-found Eldorado of the West. They descended into Hell'.[13] From the beginning of this trade in the sixteenth century, 'Europeans took control of slave bodies by branding them, burning symbols of European ownership into the flesh', permanently stigmatising people as chattels.[14] In 1527, Nzingna Mbemba Affonso, then ruler of the African Kongo Kingdom, wrote to the King of Portugal asking him to cease the trade.[15] Describing how his 'black free subjects' were being kidnapped en masse, he wrote that 'as soon as [they] are in the hands of white men they are branded with a red-hot iron'.[16] Once stigmatised, people were stored in prison hulks, barracoons and factories (the terms used for the barracks and pens used to temporarily hold the enslaved) on the coast of West Africa, before they were shipped across the Atlantic. Those who survived the terrors of this factory complex, and the death ships of the Middle Passage, were often further branded or tattooed when they were auctioned in Caribbean and North American slave markets. Violent stigmatisation continued in the 'psychopathic' plantation regime in the Americas, where 'the technology of the whip' was employed to turn 'sweat, blood, and flesh into gold'.[17]

To understand what the literal definition of stigma adds to our understanding of the meaning of this word, let's consider a fuller example of a runaway slave announcement. The following is an advertisement posted in *The London Gazette*, seeking the return of a young woman called Sabinah, who has escaped the ship *Hannah* while it was docked in London on 6 June 1743, at the height of British involvement in the Atlantic slave trade:

> A Black Negro Woman, about nineteen Years old, with two Letters on her Breast and Shoulder, made her Escape out of the Ship Hannah, Capt. Fowler, for Jamaica, the 6th inst. goes by the Name of Sabinah, is suppos'd to be deluded away by some other Black about Whitechapel, Rag-Fair, or Rotherhith. Whoever brings her to the late Mr. Neale's, on Lawrence-Pountney-Hill, shall have three Guineas Reward; or if put on board the Ship again any time between this and next Tuesday, Ten Shillings more.[18]

This advertisement is one of 800 similar advertisements published in English and Scottish newspapers between 1700 and 1780, and recently collected in the Runaway Slaves in Britain database.[19]

When reading the descriptions of runaway slaves like Sabinah, branded with 'two Letters on her Breast and Shoulder', we can begin to ascertain how stigma marks functioned as a visual form of identification; that is, as technologies of surveillance and mechanisms of capture.[20] We might also consider the stigmatising gaze these advertisements seek to inculcate in the public they address. The readers of eighteenth-century London newspapers are being solicited to search for identifying stigmata on the bodies of those they encounter; encouraged, with the inducement of financial rewards, to apprehend and return this lost property. The US-based Freedom on the Move database has amassed over 20,000 runway advertisements, many of which are similarly 'festooned with descriptions of scars, burns, mutilations, brands, and wounds'.[21] Stigma is certainly not metaphorical in these examples: these are marks that have quite literally been impressed on people.

The coining of blood into capital

In 1663, the Royal Mint in London began striking a new gold coin 'in the name and for the use of the Company of Royal Adventurers of England trading with Africa'.[22] Impressed with the figure of an elephant, these coins were originally made of gold from Guinea in West Africa and were designed for use in 'the Guinea trade'. As Sukhdev Sandhu writes: 'Not for nothing did a coin – the guinea – derive its etymology from the West African region of that name, the area from which hundreds of thousands of indigenous people were seized against their will. For traders in 17th and 18th-century Britain, the stigmatised African was quite literally a unit of currency.'[23] Slaves were an extremely valuable commodity. Identifying Sabinah by the letters impressed on her breast and shoulder, and returning her to Captain Fowler on his slave ship bound for the Jamaican market, would have netted you as a reward the equivalent of £260 in guineas.

The tattoos, brands and whip marks inscribed on the bodies of the enslaved and the reproduction of these stigmata in the publicity produced by slave traders reveal the extent to which stigma was an integral part of the machinery of 'the Guinea trade'. As Simone Browne argues, 'branding was a measure of slavery, an act of making the body legible as property that was put to work in the production of the slave as object that could be bought, sold and traded'.[24] The violence of stigmatisation was part of 'the work of commodification, of "producing" slaves'.[25]

An example of the branding irons used in barracoons and plantations can be seen at the Liverpool Museum of Slavery, while the Metropolitan Museum of Art in New York has in its collection an 1863 photograph of a freed slave called Wilson Chinn, who is branded on his forehead with the letters 'V.B.M.', the initials of his owner, a sugar planter called Volsey B. Marmillion. This stigma archive reminds us of the ways in which the catastrophe of slavery was written on the skin – with stigmata that transformed human beings into property, into things, into commodities and into guineas. A stigma practice captured in Karl Marx's phrase 'the coining of blood into capital'.[26]

This other etymology of stigma is entangled with the history of the small city of Lancaster, in which I live. In 1754, a Lancaster-born slaver called Miles Barber established one of the most significant commercial slaving hubs in the history of British involvement in the Atlantic slave trade. This place of horror was called 'Factory Island', and was located on one of the Îles de Los, a group of islands off the African coast of Guinea, at the mouth of the Sierra Leone River. Over the course of the following decades Barber developed and managed an estimated eleven slave factories and barracoons along this stretch of West African coast, and by 1776 was being described by his contemporaries as the owner of 'the greatest Guinea House in Europe'.[27]

In the eighteenth century, Lancaster was heavily involved in the Atlantic slave trade. It was the fourth largest slave-trading centre in England, and Lancaster slavers developed extensive commercial networks in the West Indies and Americas, importing slave-produced goods such as mahogany, sugar, dyes, spices, coffee and rum, and later cotton for Lancashire's mills, from plantations, and exporting fine furniture, gunpowder, woollen and cotton garments. Young men from Lancaster slave-trading families worked as agents and factors across the West Indies. Over generations these families accumulated land and property, plantations and slaves. As Eric Williams details in *Capitalism and Slavery* (1944), slave traders and their descendants dominated local political life in towns such as Lancaster 'as aldermen, mayors and councillors'.[28] Some invested their inherited fortunes in the development of local mills and businesses.[29] It was the profits from slavery that financed the industrialisation of England and the development of its civic infrastructure and welfare estate. The history of slavery is the history of capitalism, and it remains, as the American novelist and essayist James Baldwin put it, 'literally present in all that we do'.[30]

Letters of blood and fire

Situating stigma within the historical scenography of chattel slavery foregrounds the violence within the more passive conceptualisation of stigma that we have inherited from twentieth-century social sciences. It binds stigma to practices of bodily marking, and emphasises the role of stigmatisation in systems of social discipline and punishment. When we use the word stigma today we don't tend to use it to mean the literal acts of inscription that this definition suggests. In supplementing the meaning of stigma with this other etymology, I am aware that I am already asking you to think about stigma from a strange perspective. You probably already associate stigma with suffering and cruelty. Certainly, we know from contemporary social scientific literature that stigma often has devastating effects on people's health and well-being. You might even imagine stigma as a form of subjection which is socially embroidered, pressed and needled upon people through hurtful words or degrading looks. However, we don't ordinarily associate stigma with physical violence, use the word stigma to describe physical wounds or scars, relate stigma to the branding iron, or associate it with the 'whipping-machines' of plantation labour.[31]

If we imagine stigma as a form of violence at all, we tend to think of it as a more nuanced form of persecution. For example, in 1970 the sociologist Robert Pinker argued that what distinguishes stigma from other forms of violence is that it is often 'slow' and 'unobtrusive': 'a highly-sophisticated form of violence which can best be compared to those forms of psychological torture in which the victim is broken psychically and physically but left to all outward appearances unmarked'.[32] Pinker is correct: in liberal democratic societies the violence of stigma is often symbolic, diffuse, slow and indirect – but not always. *Stigma* argues that recoupling the concept of stigma to economic and materialist histories of bodily marking deepens our understanding of the social, political and economic function of stigmatisation. As Michel Foucault suggests, even when systems of government 'do not make use of violent or bloody punishment, even when they use "lenient" methods involving confinement or correction, it is always the body that is at issue – the body and its forces, their utility and their docility, their distribution and their submission'.[33] Stigma marks people out: 'it is intended either by the scar it leaves on the body, or by the spectacle that accompanies it, to brand the victim with infamy'.[34]

Of the source materials drawn on by the lexicographers at the *Oxford English Dictionary* to build a definitional picture of stigma, the use of the term 'stigmata' to describe the marks on the bodies of runaway chattel slaves is the most instructive for understanding the 'historical being' of the concept of stigma. Critically, this other etymology emphasises the ways in which stigma is bound to 'the voraciousness of capital, the capitalization of human misery, and the profits of immiseration'.[35]

In Chapter 1, 'The Penal Tattoo', I examine in more detail the harrowing practices that unfold from histories of stigma. As you will discover, we cannot disentangle stigma power from histories of slavery, colonialism, empire, capitalism, the history of enclosures, the Industrial Revolution, and the formation of the liberal democratic state. The history of stigma 'is written in the annals of mankind in letters of blood and fire'.[36]

Stigma power

What is 'stigma power'? Robert Pinker argued that 'stigma is the commonest form of violence used within democratic societies', and yet it is rarely theorised either as a violent practice, or as a form of power.[37] Indeed, scholarly research on stigma has, until recently, remained largely impervious to what Stuart Hall termed 'the radical expansion of the notion of power' in the wake of the mass social upheavals and freedom movements of the mid-twentieth century.[38] It is this gap in our understanding of how stigma functions as a form of power that this book seeks to address. In short, *Stigma* seeks to make it impossible to think of stigma separately from power. In this endeavour, this book builds on a new body of social scientific research.

Over the last decade there has been a growing recognition of the constraints of the existing 'excessively individualistic focus' of twentieth-century social scientific research on stigma.[39] This has led to attempts to 'expand and reorient stigma's theoretical lens to focus on meso and macro socio-cultural structures'.[40] Most significant for this book is Bruce Link and Jo Phelan's concept of 'stigma power', a term they coined to describe the role played by stigma in the 'exploitation, control or exclusion of others'.[41] There is an important recognition in this term that 'stigma arises and stigmatisation takes shape in specific contexts of culture and power', and in particular that sigma is deployed in ways that seek to amplify 'existing inequalities of class, race, gender and sexuality'.[42] This recent focus on 'stigma power' suggests an emergent cross-disciplinary social scientific consensus on the pivotal significance of stigma in the reproduction and distribution of social inequalities. *Stigma* extends this work, but also departs from some of its disciplinary constraints – for example, I draw more on history than social science in reconceptualising stigma as power in this book.

Stigmatisation, as I reconceptualise it, is a practice that, while experienced intimately through stigmatising looks, comments, slights, remarks made in face-to-face or digitally mediated encounters, is always enmeshed with wider capitalist structures of expropriation, domination, discipline and social control. Stigma is a more *productive* form of power than that currently understood in the contemporary social scientific literature.

I opened the introduction with the stigma Stephanie carved into her skin, as her scars testify to the entangled relationship between stigma as experience and the governmental exercise of stigma power, the consideration of which lies at the heart of this book. Indeed, when listening to people's 'stigma stories', I grew increasingly frustrated with the weak understanding of stigma that underpins much social scientific writing on stigma – particularly research in which stigma is conceived of as being a social problem that can be ameliorated through education, by changing individual attitudes, and/or by teaching the stigmatised how to better manage the stigma pinned on them (see Chapter 2). I grew tired of hearing the claim – frequently made in charitable anti-stigma campaigns – that challenging the stigma associated with particular conditions – from poverty to mental ill health – can overcome 'barriers to help-seeking', without an acknowledgement of the ways in which stigma is deliberately designed into systems of social provision in ways that make help-seeking a desperate task (see Conclusion).

In short, much existing research on stigma, and social action around stigma, brackets off from consideration the ways in which stigma is purposefully crafted as a strategy of government, in ways that often deliberately seek to foment and accentuate inequalities and injustices. While people like my friend Stephanie might not always be able to successfully defend themselves against the cycles of stigma and shame in which they become ensnarled, they understand that the crushing stigma they endure is not simply an unfortunate outcome of illiberal social interactions. That is, people who are stigmatised are cognisant of the ways in which the 'stigma machines' in which they find themselves entangled have been *engineered*.

When we begin with an understanding of stigma as power, we can also begin to perceive stigma as a site of intensive social and political struggle – and to track often occluded histories of anti-stigma resistance. Indeed, people's experiences of being stigmatised are a critical source of 'sociological imagination' (see Chapter 6) and a vital resource in collective struggles against the capture of human lives in the exploitative, dehumanising machineries of capitalism.

Neoliberal stigma power – looking up

Stigma: The Machinery of Inequality is a sister project to my book *Revolting Subjects: Social Abjection and Resistance in Neoliberal Britain* (2013), which developed a theoretical account of 'social abjection' as a means of critically engaging with the politics of disposability that characterises neoliberalism. In the wake of the 2008 global financial crisis, and the fracturing of neoliberal hegemony this precipitated, many national governments have tipped increasingly towards authoritarian rule.[43] As neoliberal capitalism bares its authoritarian teeth, the practices of social abjection I tracked in *Revolting Subjects* have accelerated. We are currently witnessing the intensification of what the criminologist David Garland describes as a 'new punitiveness' characterised by 'disproportionate punishments' and 'brutalizing and wasteful' forms of social control.[44] This 'new punitiveness' is evident in a vast range of social practices and phenomena, such as rising prison and migrant detention populations, the intensification of discriminatory policing and surveillance measures, the design of ever more exclusionary citizenship and deportation regimes, and the workfare and sanctions meted out to discipline welfare claimants.

Drawing on research in the US judicial system, Mona Lynch describes this as 'waste management' government that transforms people 'from sociologically and psychologically rich human beings into a kind of untouchable toxic waste that need only be securely contained until its final disposal'.[45] At the twilight of neoliberal capitalism, practices of 'waste management' government are accelerating, and borders, cages, camps and walls are proliferating across the face of the earth.[46] One argument of this book is that the exercise of stigma power is an integral component of this punitive authoritarian shift.

Stigma builds on a small body of research that has tracked empirical links between the amplification of social stigma and extractive forms of neoliberal capitalism, in processes as diverse as welfare retrenchment, labour precarity, eviction, displacement, social cleansing and gentrification, anti-migrant politics and punitive citizenship regimes, the proliferation of internal borders and violent bordering practices. For example, Graham Scambler argues that governmental 'weaponizations of stigma' cannot be disentangled from the imperatives of financial capitalism; while Kirsteen Paton urges us to 'gaze up' and examine the 'processes of power and profit' that motivate the manufacture of stigma.[47]

'Looking up' allows us to ascertain how stigma is designed, crafted and activated to govern populations on multiple scales, as state-led stigma campaigns and cultural stigma production cascade into our everyday interactions with each other.

Genealogies of stigma power – looking back

The governmental exercise of stigma power is entangled with histories of oppression, and with the forms of inequality required by different modalities of capitalist exploitation and economic discipline. What I mean by this is that institutional, economic and social policies intent on the production of grotesque inequalities require diverse, state-sanctioned stigma strategies that often involve the reactivation of stigma along historical lines. As Michel-Rolph Trouillot argues: 'tracking power requires a richer view of historical production than most theorists acknowledge'.[48] In short, to understand the intensification of stigma power in the current conjuncture we need to both 'look up' and 'look back'. To these ends, the chapters in *Stigma* cut a series of historical slices through stigma power, tracing the ways in which stigma has been exercised in the past to govern populations through degrading forms of marking. As Foucault puts it, bodies manifest 'the stigmata of past experience'; the task is to expose how bodies are 'totally imprinted by history'.[49]

The feminist theorist Donna Haraway describes her genealogical methods as akin to untangling a ball of yarn.[50] She notes: 'I think of these balls of yarn as gravity wells, as points of intense implosion or as knots. They lead out to worlds, you can explode them, you can untangle them, you can somehow loosen them up.'[51] In *Stigma* my approach involves unravelling particular constellations of stigma power, tracing threads of connection, examining how and why particular stigma figures emerge in specific historical and geopolitical contexts, and in the process making tangible relations between often seemingly unrelated forms and practices of stigmatisation.

Genealogy is not about comparison; rather, as William Walter argues, it is a method of 're-serialisation' which is concerned with 'the retrieval of forgotten struggles and subjugated knowledges'.[52] It is an interdisciplinary method that seeks to lessen our 'perspectival captivity' in the present.[53] Genealogical methods allow for new insights into the increased velocity of stigma as a modality of governance in the current moment of authoritarian neoliberal capitalism. Indeed, it is the argument of *Stigma* that the knowledge garnered through histories of stigma power is critical for understanding how inequalities are reproduced and, further, that histories of stigma power and anti-stigma struggles might inform resistance to the authoritarian turn that characterises the current conjuncture.

This genealogical approach is also inspired by the recent work of scholars such as Jenna Loyd and Anne Bonds, whose research on the territorial stigmatisation of particular black neighbourhoods in the US (their study focuses on Milwaukee) reminds us that practices of stigmatisation are always enmeshed with much longer histories and spatial geographies of 'racial capitalism', and the research of scholars such as Joe Feagin and Zinobia Bennefield, whose work on the systematic structural racism of US healthcare details how 'centuries of slavery, segregation, and contemporary white oppression severely limit and restrict access of many Americans of color to adequate socioeconomic resources – and to adequate health care and health outcomes'.[54]

Stigma and racism

Stigma is one of the foundational concepts of twentieth-century sociology and the wider social sciences. This introductory chapter has already strayed some distance from the conventional under-standings of stigma inherited from this tradition. In Chapter 2, 'From Stigma Power to Black Power', I will attend in greater detail to more familiar understandings of stigma. In the social sciences, stigma is most often associated with the work of the North American sociologist Erving Goffman (1922–1982). One of the most widely read and cited sociologists in history, Goffman was already famous when his short book *Stigma: Notes on the Management of a Spoiled Identity* was first published in 1963. His previous books *The Presentation of Self in Everyday Life* (1956), and *Asylums: Essays on the Social Situation of Mental Patients and Other Inmates* (1961) were best-selling titles, an unusual achieve-ment for academic texts.[55] Goffman's *Stigma* alone has sold an astonishing 800,000 copies in the fifty years since its publication. Indeed, my reason for returning to Goffman is that despite many refinements of his account, his book is widely considered the foun-dational text on stigma, and his definition of stigma continues to buttress contemporary understandings.

In the opening pages of *Stigma: Notes on the Management of a Spoiled Identity*, Goffman notes that his study was motivated by the fact that there has been 'little effort to describe the structural preconditions of stigma, or even provide a definition of the concept itself'.[56] Despite this concern with 'structural preconditions', one of the striking features of Goffman's account is that he unplugs the concept of stigma from power: both the power-inflected micro-aggressions of the everyday social interactions that he was osten-sibly interested in, and the larger structural and structuring power relations which shape the societies in which we live. In order to address this strange absence of power, Chapter 3 resituates *Stigma: Notes on the Management of a Spoiled Identity* within the historical context of the explosive political movements against the 'humilia-tions of racial discrimination' taking place while Goffman wrote his book.[57] Indeed, it is the contention of this chapter that the 1960s US civil rights and black power movements invite critical revision of Goffman's decidedly apolitical account of stigma.

This chapter reads Goffman's stigma concept through the lens of black sociology, a field of knowledge which here designates not only formal sociological scholarship, but political manifestos, journalism, creative writing, oral histories and memoirs. As we shall see, the contrast between Goffman's powerless stigma concept, and the account of racial stigma which emerged out of black activist and sociological writing in the same period couldn't be more striking. This black stigma archive offers a radically alternative theory of stigma as power, allowing for a reconceptualisation of the social and political function of stigma as a governmental technology of racial capitalism.

The liberal and normative understanding of stigma inherited from twentieth-century social sciences has significantly contracted the purchase of stigma as an analytic concept. *Stigma: The Machinery of Inequality* insists that bringing racism to the front and centre of our understandings of stigma transforms a weak concept into a powerful one.

Decolonising stigma

This historical revision of Goffman's stigma concept builds on a growing body of research on 'the relationship between race, segregation and the epistemology of sociology'.[58] Satnam Virdee, Professor of Sociology at the University of Glasgow, argues that sociology is replete with origin myths about its own radical, critical and leftist orientations, myths that obscure the 'Social Darwinian, cultural evolutionary and eugenicist perspectives' of many of this discipline's founding thinkers and practitioners.[59] This is particularly evident, he writes, when we consider the ways in which 'the liberal white gatekeepers of the discipline actively marginalized that contraflow of emancipatory African American thought emergent within the discipline'.[60] For example, despite the sophisticated understanding of racial stigma (racism and racialisation) developed over a hundred years of black sociological thought, the conceptualisation of stigma within the white sociological canon has largely ignored or marginalised this body of knowledge.

Stigma: The Machinery of Inequality responds to Gurminder Bhambra's call for what she terms 'connected sociologies' which challenge and reconstruct 'the historical narratives that inform sociological conceptions of the contemporary world'.[61] This requires developing a 'deep historical consciousness', a commitment to 'unlearning' the epistemological foundations of disciplinary knowledges, and a candid examination of 'the myriad of effects and consequences' of the concepts, vocabularies and methods that have shaped the discourses and practices of sociology since its invention as a science in the mid-nineteenth century.[62]

Stigma contributes to this decolonising project by reconceptualising stigma through existing minority knowledges of stigma within the black sociological tradition, critical race scholarship, social history, postcolonial histories and decolonial theory, feminist and disability studies. These *other* epistemologies of stigma are particularly instructive because they emerge out of long and collective struggles against stigma; that is, they are concerned with challenging the oppressive and restrictive social norms and ideals which stigma proscribes, and stigma power inculcates. My hope is that the understanding of stigma that emerges out of these rich submerged seams of stigma knowledge might be used by others to unsettle permanently the individualistic, ahistorical and apolitical understandings of this concept. Together, the chapters in this book seek to demonstrate that stigmatisation is a technology of government which is embedded in the history of racial capitalism.

Borders, walls and fences

Stigma: The Machinery of Inequality is particularly concerned with stigma as a form of statecraft, including the role of stigma politics in fomenting ethno-nationalist hatreds, and legitimating punitive regimes of citizenship and violent practices of deportation and detention.[63] In Chapter 3, 'The Stigma Machine of the Border', I examine this through the lens of the epidemic of state racism that followed in the wake of the 2015 so-called refugee crisis in Europe. This chapter focuses on events in Central and Eastern Europe, and the responses of the Czech and Hungarian governments to the arrival of refugees at their borders. It examines how the humanitarian crisis triggered by refugee arrivals mutated into a 'racist crisis' as migrants were made the focal point for anxieties about national identity and security. This racist crisis splintered liberal tolerance and social solidarity across the region on a scale unprecedented since the 1930s.

One argument of Chapter 3 is that the current authoritarian re-turn requires a better understanding of the historical relationship between statecraft and what Karen Fields and Barbara Fields term racecraft.[64] To this end, the chapter examines how racist understandings of human difference forged in twentieth-century practices of European colonialism in Africa and Nazi-era colonial fascism re-emerged and converged in public responses to the 2015 refugee crisis, as the racially stigmatised bodies of refugees were employed, both literally (through their incarceration in camps) and metaphorically (in political propaganda and public speech), to mark out the borders of the white nation.

Stigma is the fuel that lubricates far-right nationalist politics; it shapes the propaganda that characterises neoliberal authoritarian forms of rule; it legitimates what the sociologist Zygmunt Bauman terms 'human waste-production' within states and at their borders.[65]

In short, the propagation of divisive stigma politics is corroding what remains of the progressive egalitarian and internationalist democratic consensus forged within (and between) twentieth-century freedom movements (see Conclusion).

Alongside the global growth of profitable carceral, policing and 'welfare' industries designed to silo waste populations – from refugees caged at borders (Chapter 2) to disabled people trapped in their homes (see Chapter 4) – the punitive and dehumanising character of late neoliberalism has become ever more culturally entrenched. Throughout, *Stigma* seeks to capture some of the cultural practices that characterise the intensification of stigma politics in the current conjuncture, including the ascendance of stigmatising media and cultural genres: 'stigmatainments' in which the public are called upon to perform roles as angry and outraged citizens.

The political economy of stigma

We are currently living through a period of capitalist enclosure and extraction, of dispossession and displacement, as turbulent as that which accompanied the world transition to capitalism some 500 years ago – a period with which, as we shall see, the current conjuncture shares some significant features. As Silvia Federici writes: 'A return of the most violent aspects of primitive accumulation has accompanied every phase of capitalist globalization, including the present one, and is realized with the maximum of violence and state intervention.'[66]

Stigma is concerned with what I term 'the political economy of stigma' in this process, namely the role played by stigma power in the distribution of material resources and the transformation of cultural values, the crafting of stigma in the service of governmental and corporate policy goals, and the cultivation of stigma to extract political and economic capital. Indeed, stigma production from above accelerates in periods of political and economic turmoil, as a means of initiating new rounds of capitalist accumulation and as a means of containing class struggles.

Stigma is a form of classificatory violence 'from above' which devalues people, places and communities. Devaluation creates new opportunities for capital – a process David Harvey terms 'accumulation by dispossession'.[67] As Jessica Perera details in her study of the mass clearances of 'low value' people from London, capitalism accumulates value 'through dispossessing the poor of public (state-owned) assets, land and wealth which are sold off to private ownership'.[68] Indeed, 'the corporatization, commodification, and privatization of hitherto public assets' has been a signal feature of the neoliberal project, which has sought 'to open up new fields for capital accumulation in domains formerly regarded off-limits to the calculus of profitability'.[69] *Stigma* is concerned with the role of stigma in opening up new fields of capital accumulation. What I mean by this is that when we begin to theorise stigma as a form of power embedded within political economies, we can begin to understand how stigma functions to devalue entire groups of people with the purpose of both fortifying existing social hierarchies and creating new opportunities for the redistribution of wealth upwards.[70] The intensification of stigma production, and the 'degradation ceremonies' this involves, services capital accumulation.[71] We might usefully think of this as akin to the shorting practices employed by stockbrokers to devalue stock and destabilise markets deliberately in order to create conditions for profiteering.[72] What stigma devalues are people and the places where they live. What stigma destabilises are local communities and social bonds. What stigma shortens is lives.

In Chapter 4, 'The Stigma Machine of Austerity', I draw on my experiences of working as part of the Morecambe Bay Poverty Truth Commission as a guide for thinking about the break that austerity signals from welfare to post-welfare capitalism in the British state. 'Force', as Marx reminds us, 'is the midwife of every old society pregnant with a new one. It is itself an economic power'.[73] In the case of the welfare state, stigma is the force that is driving the break from the old to the new.

This chapter is a case study in the political economy of stigma. It examines how austerity was implemented through state-crafted stigma, a 'welfare stigma machine' that churned a corrosive path through society, settling in institutional forms, embedded in the design of social policies, and infecting the culture, practices and attitudes of welfare workers. It considers how welfare stigma changed the ways in which the public made evaluative judgements about inequality, welfare, poverty and need. That is, how stigma was crafted to tutor the public into believing that people living in poverty had chosen their fates, and how the disenfranchisement and distress which have followed in the wake of cuts to social provision were deserved: a consequence of people's poor behaviours, indiscipline and shamelessness. It argues that this 'stigma-optics' is altering ways of seeing poverty, hardening people's feelings towards the suffering of those around them – those queuing outside the food banks now installed in every British town and city, for instance, and the homeless gathering on street corners and in doorways. Social movements from below, such as the Poverty Truth Movement, are fiercely contesting the stigma politics of austerity, and this chapter considers both the limits and possibilities of resistance.

Understanding stigma as entangled with economic forms of de/ valuation and capitalist movements of enclosure and extraction enables us to draw parallels between neoliberal projects, such as austerity, in the global North and the kinds of fiscal discipline and structural adjustment programmes long imposed upon the global South by Western governments and global institutions of financial capitalism in the wake of decolonisation.[74] As Silvia Federici reminds us, every phase of capitalist crisis resembles the next, inasmuch as it is the web of sexual and racial inequalities built within global capitalism itself that enables it to reproduce itself. The difference today is that 'the conquistadors are the officers of the World Bank and the International Monetary Fund'.[75]

Fighting shame

The overarching aim of *Stigma* is to deepen the understanding of stigma as a governmental technology of exploitation; to draw new lines of connection between people's dehumanising experiences of stigmatisation and the socio-political machining of stigma in service of extractive forms of capitalism. In recalibrating our understanding of stigma as an exploitative apparatus, this book seeks to make stigma into a more useful concept: a device for thinking more deeply about how power etches itself into us and 'take[s] up residence within us'.[76] While stigma is a disabling force, a form of power that is inscribed in bodies, places and communities in ways that often leave profound and permanent scars, understanding the wounds of stigma as social and political injuries can assist in the forging of networks of care and solidarity. As women from Leeds Poverty Truth Commission put it in *Fighting Shame* (2019), their film about living with the stigma of poverty in austerity Britain: 'It's important that people hear about the shame. It's about living the shame, feeling it, living on, inspiring people through that shame.'[77] Stigma has always been resisted by those it is pressed upon.

It is the argument of *Stigma* that the knowledge garnered through histories of struggle against stigma 'has important implications for emancipatory politics', informing strategies of resistance to authoritarian forms of government today and improving our capacity to understand and resist the divisions which stigma politics are designed to cultivate.[78] This is a task to which we urgently need to attend, with all the imagination and tools at our disposal.

Reconceptualising stigma has involved the development of a new lexicon of stigma, a grammar with which to prise open the different modalities and operations of stigma power. Alongside deepening the concept of 'stigma power', this book experiments with minor concepts such as 'stigma politics', 'stigma machines', 'stigma-optics' and 'stigmacraft'. My hope is that some of these concepts are useful, have traction and take flight, and that you, the readers of this book, become students of stigma power, adding your own vocabulary to the language of stigma power that I have begun to develop in these pages.

Chapter 1

The penal tattoo

Every power, including the power of law, is written first of all on the backs of its subjects. … The law constantly writes itself on bodies. It engraves itself on parchments made from the skin of its subjects. … It makes its book out of them.

Michel de Certeau, *The Practice of Everyday Life*[1]

Even after two decades, the sound of a needle gun painfully scribbling Jeb Katri on my forehead is something that still haunts me and wakes me up in the middle of the night.

Parmeshri Devi, a Sansi woman tortured by the Punjabi police[2]

On 8 December 1993, five women were arrested near the Harmandir Sahib (the Golden Temple) in the city of Amritsar, Punjab, India. They were accused of a stealing a purse.[3] The women, Gurdev Kaur, Parmeshri Devi, Mohinder Kaur, Hamir Kaur and Surjit Kaur, were imprisoned for eight days before being released on bail. A few days later Surjit was picked up again, and police garlanded her with shoes and paraded her through a local market.[4] After Surjit had been publicly shamed in the marketplace, she and the other four women were taken to a police station in the Rambagh area of Amritsar where they were physically restrained by being tied to chairs. The police then sent for 'a handheld needle gun, meant for marking utensils' and proceeded to engrave the words *Jeb Katri* (pickpocket) on their foreheads.[5] As Parmeshri recalls 'as we writhed in pain, there was a power cut', so the police chief 'ordered his men to bring the battery of their official Gypsy [a police SUV vehicle], which they used to turn the machine back on and complete the permanent marking'.[6]

The penal tattooing of the women came to light when they were presented in court some days later on charges of theft. The police brought the women into the courtroom with their foreheads covered with dupattas (head scarves), but Parmeshri Devi defiantly unveiled her penal tattoo in front of the judge. At the time, nobody in the court seemed concerned by Devi's revelation, however a newspaper report on the case in the Punjabi paper *Ajit* – crucially accompanied by a photograph of three of the women outside the court – later made the pages of two national newspapers.[7]

The women petitioned the Punjab and Haryana High Court for compensation for the torture and humiliation they had suffered and for plastic surgery to remove the tattoos. Responding to the newspaper coverage of the case, the Indian National Human Rights Commission of India intervened and in 1994 the court awarded costs for the removal of the tattoos.[8] However, the treatment offered to the women at a local hospital didn't involve the removal of the tattoos but only their over-writing. In desperation, the five resorted to borrowing money for a course of laser treatment at a private clinic. One of the women, Hamir, died before her tattoo had been fully removed.[9]

The police officers denied that they had tattooed the women, blaming others in the local community 'fed up by their habit of pickpocketing' who desired to 'publicly shame them'.[10] However, the surviving women continued in their struggle to bring the perpetrators to justice, and after a staggering twenty-three years an investigation by India's Central Bureau of Investigation eventually led to some prosecutions. In October 2016, three of the policemen involved received prison sentences for forcibly tattooing the words *Jeb Katri* on the women's foreheads.

Interviewed by journalists after the conviction of the police, the women and their families explained how they had suffered years of police harassment: 'the police slapped many cases on all of us to pressurise us to not to give statement in court'.[11] Mohinder Kaur's son Pappu described how he had been taunted at school as a consequence of his mother's tattoo: schoolmates would stick paper notes with the words *Mein jeb katri da beta han* (I am the son of a pickpocket) on his back.[12] Parmeshri Devi's son committed suicide by self-immolation, a consequence, she vehemently believes, of the social stigma and years of police harassment provoked by the case.

In Hindi, the closest word to the English word stigma is *godna* – a word meaning 'to prick, puncture, to dot, to mark the skin with dots, to tattoo' and 'to wound or lacerate a person's feelings'.[13] This dual meaning of *godna* as designating psychological and/or bodily inscription resonates in the women's accounts of their torture at the hands of the police. As Devi told a journalist: 'we had to undergo torture for the past 23 years'.[14]

Stigma as inscription

In *The Practice of Everyday Life*, Michel de Certeau reminds us that every power 'is written on the backs of its subjects', and that this inscription involves mediating instruments. As he writes:

> In order for the law to be written on bodies, an *apparatus* is required that can *mediate* the relation between the former and the latter. From the instruments of scarification, tattooing, and primitive initiation to those of penal justice, tools work on the body. Formerly the tool was a flint knife or a needle. Today the

instruments range from the policeman's billyclub to handcuffs and the box reserved for the accused in the courtroom. These tools compose a series of objects whose purpose is to inscribe the force of the law on its subject, to *tattoo* him in order to make him demonstrate the rule, to produce a 'copy' that makes the norm legible.[15]

As de Certeau suggests, power is inscribed in bodies in ways that demonstrate the force of law – be that within more formal judicial contexts, or in broader social and cultural contexts of policing, discipline and control.

It is the argument of *Stigma* that the historical name for practices which describe these impressions of power is stigmatisation. Further, when we think of stigmata as literal inscriptions of power on the body, our attention is immediately drawn to the writing implements, to *who* is doing the marking, and for *what purpose*. The instruments used to impress stigma on the other extend from bloody implements of state violence to more symbolic forms of public shaming, including stigmatising visual and textual representations in popular media. This chapter draws on the long history of the penal tattoo, and associated violent practices of marking and public shaming to add depth to an understanding of stigma as a form of power written on the body. What emerges is an incredibly rich and expansive history of stigma as an inscriptive form of power.

The ancient penal history of stigma

The modern word 'stigma' originates in a clutch of Ancient Greek words, derived from the root *stig-*, meaning to prick or to puncture.[16] In the essays 'Stigma: Tattooing and Branding in Graeco-Roman Antiquity' (1984) and 'Stigma and Tattoo' (2000), classics scholar Christopher Jones transformed received understanding of the meaning of stigma in the Graeco-Roman world. Through meticulous research, Jones uncovered that in Ancient Greece the verb *stizo* was used to describe ink tattooing with needles or other sharp implements on human skin, and stigma described the resulting mark. In short, a stigma was an ink tattoo, an involuntary tattoo, pricked into human skin for 'penal and property purposes'.[17] As Jones and other classics scholars have revealed, penal stigmatisation was 'routine' and 'entrenched' in these ancient empires.

One of the first recorded uses of the word 'stigma' appears in a fragment of sixth-century BC poetry written by Asius of Samos, who uses the word *stigmatias* to describe 'a marked slave'; and slaves are henceforth regularly and scornfully referred to with words such as *literati* (lettered), *stigmatici* (tattooed), *inscripti* (inscribed) and *graptoi* (written upon). Indeed, in the Graeco-Roman world, penal tattooing was a punishment reserved exclusively for non-citizens: slaves, indentured labourers, prisoners of war, other resident aliens or religious minorities. As Plato wrote in *The Laws*, a dialogue on the ethics of government, 'if anyone is caught committing sacrilege, if he be a slave or a stranger, let his offence be written on his face and his hands'.[18]

Penal tattooing involved the inscription of words, symbols, and sometimes full sentences into the skin. These tattoos 'usually consisted of the name of a crime' inked into the face.[19] Records of common stigmas include 'Thief' or 'Stop me, I'm a runaway', tattooed on the forehead.[20] If you survived the torture of being tattooed (without antiseptic) you would never be free of the stigma, the 'disgrace, humiliation and exclusion' remaining 'indelibly written on one's face for all to see'.[21] As Mark Gustafson reflects, 'the effects of a penal tattoo forcibly applied to the face' must have been 'deeply felt, devastating even'.[22] Certainly, a tattoo on the face would have been difficult to conceal: 'the gaze of the onlooker is virtually inescapable; there is little defence against it'.[23]

Penal stigmatisation was intentionally visible, a public form of inscription designed to humiliate and inculcate shame. The Greek philosopher Bion (c. 325–c. 250BC) described how his father had 'in place of his face ... a document [*syngraphen*] on his face, the mark of his master's harshness'.[24] The Byzantine chronicler Zonaras records a case from the eighth century of two brothers, Christian monks, whose religious worship of icons led to them having twelve lines of 'execrable poetry' tattooed on their faces.[25] Later sainted as Theodorus and Theophanes, these brothers came to be known by the surname *Grapti*, from the Greek '*graptoi*', meaning written upon. Penal stigmatisation was a form of bodily inscription which, as the Roman emperor Valerius Maximus (AD 14–37) put it, turned the stigmatised into the 'image of his own penalty'.[26]

Page duBois draws our attention to a play written by Herondas in the third century BC, in which 'a slave is tattooed on the forehead with the proverbial words "know thyself"'.[27] This tattooing was a punishment meted out by a mistress upon a slave who is her lover, but who 'has lost sight of his position as a slave' by cheating on her.[28] The choice of the Delphic maxim 'know thyself' underscores the way in which a penal stigmatisation functioned as an injunction to a particular kind of self-knowledge: a mortifying punishment through which you were taught to 'know yourself' by 'knowing your place' in a highly stratified social order.[29] Stigmatisation was thus an act of pedagogical violence through which a person was tutored back into a place of unfreedom, and a means through which domestic slaves, indentured miners, soldiers, roadbuilders, munitions workers could be 'marked for life with the insignia of their professions' – stigmata signalled that your labour (and body) was owned by another.[30]

This Graeco-Roman practice of writing a crime or criminal sentence into the skin adds a literal dimension to the practice of being sentenced. As Steven Connor suggests, in 'the mark incised or pricked or burned upon the body of the criminal, the law precipitates a lasting sign of its action, the letter of the law made actual and present'.[31] As a 'running advertisement of one's guilt and subjugation', stigmatisation was designed to permanently lower your social status.[32] For example, in Ancient Rome, where slaves could theoretically earn their freedom, a Roman law from the fourth century AD details that slaves who had been tattooed on account of a crime should never be allowed to become free citizens. If a tattooed slave later earned their freedom they were consigned 'to the lowest possible category of free non-citizens'.[33] A penal tattoo (a stigma) relegated the stigmatised to a bottom rung in the extant social hierarchy. The letters on your body marked your exclusion from citizenship (and rights).

The Ancient Greeks associated voluntary tattooing, undertaken as an aesthetic and/or a religious practice, with 'barbarians' and in particular with their despised northern neighbours, the Thracians.[34] Surviving Greek pottery portrays Thracian women as marked with decorative tattoos.[35] Indeed, within the iconography of vase painting, Greek artists employed tattoos to visually differentiate Thracian women, other foreigners and enslaved people from their *unmarked* Greek superiors. In 'Stigma and Tattoo', Christopher Jones suggests that it was most likely because of this abject cultural association between tattoos and feminised foreign others that the Greeks developed the practice of tattooing slaves as a humiliating punishment. As we shall see, the association between voluntarily acquired tattoos and 'barbarians' was revived in eugenicist social scientific discourses in the nineteenth century, when the tattoo became foundational to the development of the discipline of criminology, and its ancient connotations of 'barbarianism' were viciously reworked as a means of classifying the 'lower orders' within both the European interior and its imperial outposts – including India.[36]

Penal stigmatisation was so entrenched a practice in antiquity that it began to be used metaphorically as a term of disgrace. The

Greek orator and writer Aelius Aristides (117–181 BC) attacks Plato for slander with the words 'you never tattooed any of your own slaves but you have as good as tattooed the most honoured of the Greeks'.[37] The Roman poet Martial (circa AD 38–104) also employs stigma as a metaphor, writing that 'whatever the heat of my anger burns into you will remain for good and be read throughout the world, and Cinnamus [an acclaimed historian] with his cunning skill will not erase the tattoos'.[38] The Roman writer known as Nicanor Stigmatias (in the early second century) was given the name Stigmatias as a teasing reference to his work as a grammatician, a labour which involved punctuating text; the joke being that it was unimaginable that a citizen, especially one of such high standing, would actually be stigmatised. It is in these ancient allegorical uses of the term stigma that the modern understanding of stigma as a symbolic mark of disgrace was forged. Indeed, these metaphorical uses mark the beginning of a traffic in the meaning of stigma, between stigma as a literal punishment, and the more psychological meanings that stigma subsequently acquired.

Capturing labour

In the ancient Graeco-Roman world, penal stigmas had a specific economic function as a mechanism for the systematic exploitation of specific classes of people. That is, stigmatisation was a way of marking bodies in order to secure an indentured or slave labour force. Over time, the economic efficacy of penal tattooing intensified as 'the sentence of exile and, most likely, hard labour' became 'part of the total package of which the penal tattoo [was] the sign'.[39] Indeed, the Romans extended practices of penal stigmatisation to 'all classes virtually indentured to the state' employing stigma en masse to generate new sources of slave labour for the vast economies and infrastructures of expanding empires.[40]

In the Roman period, while a penal stigma might still record the name of a specific crime or infraction, it was as likely to spell out the type and length of the criminal sentence handed out by a court of law, or the name of the emperor under whose jurisdiction a sentence of hard labour was enforced. As the classics scholar Mark Gustafson details, there is extensive evidence in late antiquity of the words *metallicae damnationis* (condemned to the mines) being tattooed on the foreheads of those convicted in Roman courts. People marked in this way were called the metallic. They were tattooed, 'beaten with clubs' and chained, before being transported, by land and sea, to imperial outposts, where they would be lucky indeed to survive their sentence of hard labour.[41] The Romans also regularly tattooed captured enemy soldiers during border skirmishes and expropriation of territory, and tattooed army recruits (evidence suggests mainly on the wrists) so they could be 'recognised if they go into hiding'.[42]

As the classics scholarship suggests, the meaning of stigma is entwined with slavery, with the punishment of the enslaved and with the capture of people as unfree labour. In *Metamorphoses* (*The Golden Ass*), the Roman writer Apuleius (c. AD 124–170) describes an utterly abject scene of labourers working in a public flour mill. Whip marks have left their skin 'painted with livid welts', their heads are half-shaven, and their feet are chained together.[43] Their tattooed foreheads (*frontes litterati*) mark out these mill workers as slaves who have been sentenced to indentured labour.

Graeco-Roman economies were 'slave economies': 'slaves were essential in mining, worked on the rural estates and in the workshops and businesses of the wealthy, and served them in their homes'.[44] There is a tendency to 'forget' that slavery was the economic structure which underpinned these often venerated cradles of European civilisation and democracy. Or rather, ancient systems of slavery have been mystified and romanticised in ways that disguise the material realities of enslavement, including the fact that 'the ancient Greeks and Romans routinely tortured slaves'.[45] As Page duBois suggests, the 'torturability' of slaves and their susceptibility to being written upon marked 'the boundary between slaves and free beings'.[46]

Penal stigmatisation was particularly associated with people's attempts to escape enslavement. Indeed, a penal stigma was often a record of an escape attempt. In some cases, slaves who had previously tried to escape would be collared rather than tattooed. These slave collars were iron neck rings which would have been riveted in place, and the inscriptions on them 'often provide the owner's name, status, occupation, and the address to which the slave should be returned'.[47] Several Roman slave collars 'have been found in funerary contexts, suggesting that, for some slaves at least, a metal neck collar was permanent'.[48] One surviving fourth- or fifth-century Roman slave collar has a bronze tag that reads: 'I have run away; hold me. When you have brought me back to my master Zoninus, you will receive a gold coin.'[49] Like the advertisements for runaway chattel slaves posted in British and North American newspapers more than 1,000 years later, these penal forms of stigmatisation signalled commodification and ownership, and were a means of identification, capture and retrieval.

Threads of racism

In *Black and British: A Forgotten History* (2016), David Olusoga details a similar fashion for slave collars in eighteenth-century Britain: 'usually brass or copper, occasionally silver', these collars 'were riveted or padlocked around the neck and could not be removed'.[50] A runaway advertisement posted in *The Edinburgh Evening Courant* in 1727 reads:

RUN away on the 7th Instant from Dr. Gustavus Brown's Lodgings in Glasgow, a Negro Woman, named Ann, being about 18 Years of Age, with a green Gown and a Brass Collar about her Neck, on which are engraved these Words 'Gustavus Brown in Dalkieth his Negro, 1726.' Whoever apprehends her, so as she may be recovered, shall have two Guineas Reward, and necessary Charges allowed by Laurance Dinwiddie Junior Merchant in Glasgow, or by James Mitchelson, Jeweller in Edinburgh.

People like Ann who were collared in Georgian Britain were evidentially unfree and considered property.[51] Just as in Ancient Rome, these slave collars demand 'the reader's attention on behalf of the absent owner' and 'assert the owner's control of the slave'.[52] In so doing, they stigmatise the collared person as a possession, an object – *a Negro*. That those stigmatised in this way were not considered fully human is underscored by eighteenth-century English paintings such as Bartholomew Dandridge's portrait *A Young Girl with an Enslaved Servant and a Dog* (c. 1725), in which both the servant and dog are collared. Olusoga directs us to a 1726 advertisement for 'Matthew Dyer, a goldsmith on Duck Lane in Westminster', who specialises in making silver collars and padlocks 'for Blacks or Dogs'.[53]

The similarities between the tattooing, branding and collaring of slaves in the ancient Graeco-Roman empires and in Georgian Britain at the dawn of another European empire is striking. In *The Invention of Racism in Classical Antiquity* (2004), Benjamin Isaac argues that we can trace 'red threads' of connection between 'proto-racisms' in the Graeco-Roman world and modern scientific racisms. As Isaac argues, 'racism is a phenomenon that can assume many apparently different shapes and forms while preserving a remarkable element of continuity which is undeniable, once it is traced over the centuries'.[54] Similarly, Cedric Robinson argues that the 'template' for modern racism, 'its ordering principle, its organizing structure, its moral authority, its economy of justice, commerce, and power', can be found in the writing of Aristotle, and other 'aristocratic apologists' for slavery in the ancient world.[55] This racialised understanding of slavery in the ancient world is highly contested, raising questions about the changing meaning of 'race' and whether systems of slavery are always racialised. Amongst critical race scholars, the general consensus is that modern epistemologies of race emerged during the European Renaissance with European colonisation of the Americas. Scholars such as Sylvia Wynter, C.L.R. James and Aimé Césarie suggest that modern racism is coincident with Columbus' discovery of the West Indies in 1492, the expansion of the West into the New World and the racial genocides that followed.

What we can say with certainty is that penal tattooing forms part of a long and expansive European tradition of social classification through degrading forms of bodily marking, and is linked especially to the stigmatisation of slaves. Robinson makes the further point that 'slave labor persisted within European agrarian production up to the modern era'.[56] We also know that the penal tattooing of slaves, serfs and indentured workers continued within Europe 'through late antiquity and the Byzantine Empire into the Middle Ages and into the modern period'.[57] With the advent of the colonial capitalist world order from the fifteenth century, distinctions between citizens and slaves, civilised and barbarian, capital and labour, and between the propertied and unpropertied classes sedimented in the creation of new classed, gendered and racialised social hierarchies. The European men who placed themselves at the top of this new global racial order exported and innovated penal stigmatisation as technologies of classification and subjugation.

In summary, stigma is an Ancient Greek word which originated to describe forced tattooing – words, marks and images etched into the skin against your will, in ways designed to permanently lower your social status and curtail your mobility. In a world before identity cards, passports, finger-printing, biometric forms of marking, penal tattooing was an important technology of identification, surveillance and social control, innovated and expanded to aid colonial expansion. Seeing the tattooed faces of slaves and indentured labourers doubtless functioned as a terrorising warning to others, assisting with the task of imposing order on the variously dispossessed and disenfranchised multi-ethnic classes of slaves and non-citizens who lived within the vast territories of these ancient empires, and quelling the freedom dreams of conquered and subjugated peoples. Stigma was also, then, an important form of political publicity.

Misogyny and stigma

Penal stigma also has a gendered history. In *Women and Power: A Manifesto* (2017), Mary Beard teaches us that women of all social classes were barred from (full) citizenship in the Graeco-Roman world. Even elite women had no independent legal personhood, but existed in a property relationship to male heads of households, and the wider patriarchal state. Oratory was the 'defining attribute' of elite masculinity.[58] Citizenship was in effect demarcated by those who had the right to speak in public (and in so doing could partici-pate in politics), and those who did not. Only free male citizens could exercise this right. The mothers, wives and daughters of citizens, along with slaves and foreigners, were prohibited from public speech.

If the exclusion of slaves from citizenship was distinguished by their vulnerability to being written upon, women were identified by their muteness.[59] Beard quotes a second-century AD writer who notes that, 'a woman should as modestly guard against exposing her voice to outsiders as she would guard against stripping off her clothes'.[60] There is a relationship, then, between the social position of women of all social classes and that of slaves of both sexes – inasmuch as they all existed in a property relationship to men. Page duBois highlights how women were 'sometimes likened to a writing tablet, a surface to be "ploughed", inscribed by the hand, the plough, the penis of her husband and master'.[61]

It is not only, as Beard argues, that women's voices were absent from the public sphere, but that this prohibition on women's speech was trumpeted, flaunted and enjoyed by male citizens. Greek and Roman literature is replete with examples of women actively being silenced. The muzzling of women was publicised in every genre of cultural production – in legal documents, in philosophy and liter-ature and in comic and tragic plays. Women's attempts to speak were laughed at and mocked; they are transformed into wordless statutes, animals, nymphs, echoes, and they are more violently 'shut up' – raped, mutilated, their tongues cut out.

The parading of gagged and silenced women in antiquity has cast a long shadow. As Beard writes, 'this is not the peculiar ideology of some distant culture. Distant in time it may be. But I want to underline that this is a tradition of gendered speaking – and the theorising of gendered speaking – to which we are directly or indirectly heirs'.[62] The ancient genealogy of misogyny is instruc-tive, she argues, in understanding the machinations of contempo-rary practices that seek to 'quiet women' within spheres of public debate today, 'from the front bench to the shop floor'.[63] What is the relationship, Beard enquires, between 'Twitter threats of rape and decapitation', and ancient practices of gagging women?[64] As she reflects, even when women are 'not silenced' they still 'pay a very high price for being heard'.[65] Beard's prescient examination of the shade cast by ancient forms of misogyny deepens our under-standing of how we might learn from antiquity.

Figure 1.1 'Ann Bidlestone being ridden through
the streets of Newcastle by an officer of the city',
Ralph Gardiner, *England's Grievance Discovered* (1655).

'Muzzled like dogs and paraded through the streets'

The public exhibition of silenced and gagged women continued in Europe for millennia. In medieval England practices of 'scolding' insubordinate women were recorded in court records from the thirteenth century. The scolding of garrulous women was also represented (often in comic guises) in church woodcarvings and stained-glass windows, in which the women are often depicted with gorgets (bands of linen) pressed over their mouths.[66] This practice of gagging women is most dramatically illustrated by 'the scold's bridle' or 'brank', which was employed in Britain (and its colonies) from the sixteenth until the mid-nineteenth century to torture and publicly humiliate women whose speech was deemed unruly, rowdy or otherwise troublesome (see Figure 1.1, an engraving based on a 1655 witness account).[67] The brank was particularly used to punish 'older women such as widows and paupers' who were perceived as 'a drain on the parish' or as not under the appropriate control of a male head of household.[68]

Branks consisted of an 'iron framework to enclose the head, having a sharp metal gag or bit which entered the mouth and restrained the tongue'.[69] Surviving branks reveal that the bit was sometimes spiked with pins, which would have pierced the tongue and the roof of the mouth. Women sentenced to the brank were 'ridden' through the town by a male 'rider'. The motion of being jerked along would have continually disturbed the bit in the woman's mouth, 'threatening to break her teeth, shatter her jawbone, or lacerate her tongue'.[70]

The riding of the branked woman was a form of street theatre. E.P. Thompson describes the noise of jeering and clattering that accompanied these kinds of 'rough music' processionals as 'ritualised expressions of hostility'.[71] At the end of this mocking parade, the branked woman would have been made to stand in a market square or village green and subjected to verbal scorn, and had mud, stones, urine, faeces and rotten food thrown at her. In 1686, one Dr Plott writes that the brank was not removed 'till after the party begins to show all external signs imaginable of humiliation'.[72]

There is only one known surviving first-hand account of the experience of being branked, which was written by Dorothy Waugh, a servant from Preston in Lancashire. Waugh, a radical Quaker, was branked by the mayor of Carlisle for preaching in the town in 1655. Waugh's account was later published in a pamphlet, which was intended to stir sympathy and support for the persecution of the Quakers, and it begins with her arrest at the marketplace in Carlisle, before her removal to prison and questioning by the town's mayor.

[The mayor was] so violent & full of passion that he scarce asked me any more questions, but called to one of his followers to bring the bridle as he called it to put upon me, and was to be on three hours, and that which they called so was like a steel cap and my hat being violently plucked off which was pinned to my head whereby they tore my clothes to put on their bridle as they called it, which was a stone weight of Iron and three bars of Iron to come over my face, and a peece of it was put in my mouth, which was so unreasonable big a thing for that place as cannot be well related, which was locked to my head. And so I stood their time with my hands bound behind me with the stone weight of Iron upon my head and the bitt in my mouth to keep me from speaking. And the Mayor said he would make me an example to all that should come in that name. And the people to see me so violently abused were broken to tears ... And that man that kept the prison door demanded two pence of everyone who came to see me while their bridle remained. After a while ... the Mayor ... sent me out of the city with it on, and gave me very vile and unsavoury words, which were not fit to proceed out of any man's mouth, and charged the officer to whip me out of the town, from constable to constable to send me, till I came to my own home.[73]

Silvia Federici argues that it is significant that it was during the 'Age of Reason', and at the dawn of capitalist societies, 'that women accused of being scolds were muzzled like dogs and paraded through the streets'.[74] The branking and scolding of woman was part and parcel, Federici suggests, of a broader movement of capitalist accumulation through enclosure. As we shall see, this process was characterised in England by the enclosure of land but also involved *the enclosure of social relations*. As Federici argues, the European witch-hunts of the sixteenth and seventeenth centuries were part of this project, 'a war against women … a concerted attempt to degrade them, demonize them, and destroy their social power'.[75] The stigmatising punishments meted out to outspoken, unruly women was, then, part of a deeper and wider political project (of capitalist enclosure) which signalled the hardening of a gendered social contract in which women were understood as the property of men.

This enclosure of women within the new social relations of the patriarchal capitalist state was supported by mass propaganda, including 'countless misogynistic plays and tracts'.[76] As Federici notes, 'Shakespeare's *The Taming of the Shrew* (1593) was the manifesto of the age'.[77] Indeed, *publicity* was a central function of these ritual stigmatising punishments. The scolding of women functioned as a warning to other women to hold their tongues. More than this, the riding of branked women, the piercing of tongues, the whippings and public scorn, and 'the stakes on which the witches perished' were sites through which new ideals of obedient domestic womanhood were forged.[78]

Branking in the twenty-first century

More than traces of this history persist in the misogynistic violence regularly employed to stigmatise women today in practices of public scolding which seek to silence and deter women from political and public speech. For example, as numerous feminist scholars have detailed, the rise of social media platforms has seen a significant intensification of misogynist vitriol and threats of violence directed against women.[79] The scolding of women in virtual public spaces extends from practices involving the use of humiliating, sexist and often sexualised epitaphs (cunt, bitch, whore), to physical threats (most frequently threats of sexual violence and rape)[80] – speech which, as Dorothy Waugh described it, is characterised by 'vile and unsavoury words, which were not fit to proceed out of any man's mouth'.

These virtual branking campaigns escalate and move offline when sustained trolling campaigns are accompanied by the release of identifying information, such as women's home addresses or phone numbers, sometimes leading to stalking or physical acts of harm. This 'technology-facilitated sexual violence' is frequently triggered when women speak out in public, often when they raise issues of inequality, but also when they participate more generally in political or public debate – as many women politicians and public figures have discovered to their cost.[81] Indeed, Mary Beard was prompted to write *Women and Power: A Manifesto* after becoming subject to misogynistic trolling campaigns. After I published my book *Revolting Subjects*, I received death threats, including a suggestion I should be cremated in a gas oven. For many women, communication technologies which have ostensibly been designed to enhance, facilitate and democratise public speech are also experienced as stigma machines – spiked with threats of violence.

In short, men continue to use stigmatising devices to brank women – that is, to humiliate them in order to deter them from public speech and terrorise them into silence. As in the seventeenth century, these twenty-first-century practices of branking weaponise stigma to inculcate fear and curtail women's freedom.

While *Stigma* focuses on developing an account of stigma as an inscriptive form of power which operates through the axis of race–class, the penal history of stigma reminds us that stigma is also a mechanism of patriarchal power. It stresses also how ritual forms of humiliation are elements within the wider systems of stigmatising classifications which accompanied the emergence of a new capitalist world order. Just as the scolding of women intensified with the emergence of the capitalist state, other stigmatising punishments were devised to mark out, discipline and control and mark the criminalised 'lower orders' within Europe and her overseas dominions. Indeed, it is important to note that branking devices were employed in exactly the same historical period to muzzle enslaved people on colonial plantations (see Figure 1.2).

Slave masks

Historical evidence suggest that slave masks were sometimes used to subdue resistance when people were captured and transported in coffles (lines of people fasted together with wooden planks, ropes or chains) from the African interior to the coast, and during the holding of people in slave factories and slave ships. Slave masks were employed more often as a punishment for insubordination or escape attempts on colonial plantations in the West Indies and Americas, and as a means of preventing the enslaved from eating crops, or soil – 'dirt eating' was a documented method of self-harm and suicide amongst the enslaved.[82]

In *Plantation Memories: Episodes of Everyday Racism* (2008), the Portuguese artist and academic Grada Kilomba explores the historical dynamics of contemporary racisms in Europe through the cultural archive of plantation-era violence. Kilomba introduces us to a figure from her childhood, the popular Brazilian saint 'Escrava Anastácia' – an enslaved woman of African descent who is usually depicted wearing a muzzle over her mouth and an iron collar around her neck. Anastácia has been muzzled, one version of the legend has it, to stop her speaking of her sexual torture and rape by a plantation owner. Kilomba argues that the muzzling of enslaved women 'represents colonialism as a whole ... It symbolizes the sadistic politics of conquest and its cruel regimes of silencing'.[83]

In 1968, an illustration of a masked and collared woman made by the French artist Jacques Arago, circa 1817, was discovered in a church in Brazil, and was displayed in Rio's black museum (Museo de Negro) (see Figure 1.2). This image was interpreted by many black Brazilians as evidence for the existence of the mythical

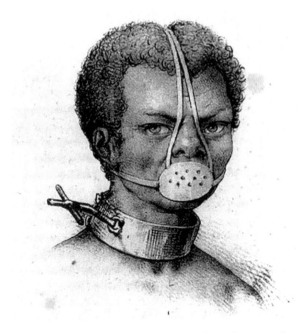

Figure 1.2 'Escrava Anastácia', engraving of an enslaved woman by Jacques Arago, whom he describes as wearing a 'Máscara de flandres', originally printed in *Souvenirs d'un aveugle: voyage autour du monde* (Paris: H. Lebrun, 1868).

Anastácia.[84] Indeed, the display of this single image saw the cult of Escrava Anastácia grip Brazil. For many descendants of the enslaved, Escrava Anastácia remains a venerated figure – a defiant rebellious symbol of the resistance of black women. As Kilomba suggests, the veneration of Escrava Anastácia, the making of shrines and icons in her image, is a means of *speaking* the history of slavery and colonialism, and of making visible its enduring legacies of anti-black racism and misogynoir sexual violence.

The changing meanings of tattoos

While the word stigma has its roots in practices of penal tattooing and slavery in the ancient world, we don't ordinarily associate practices of tattooing with the word stigma today – although interestingly one of the most popular brands of ink-tattooing machines is called Stigma. One of the likely reasons for the obfuscation of the etymological associations between the word stigma and practices of penal tattooing is due to the introduction of the word 'tattoo' into the English language in the eighteenth century, a word which is primarily used to denote voluntary bodily inscriptions for aesthetic or cultural reasons. In a ground-breaking collection of essays, *Written on the Body: The Tattoo in European and American History* (2000), Jane Caplan explains that the Western history of tattooing 'remains barely researched and widely misunderstood'.[85]

The first documented appearance of the word 'tattoo' appears in English explorer and cartographer James Cook's journal in 1769 when his ship HMS *Endeavour* arrived at the Pacific Island group of Tahiti and he witnessed Tahitians 'tattowing' their skin with pieces of sharp bone or shell and a black ink derived from candle nuts 'in such a manner as to be indelible'.[86] Contemporary historiographies of tattooing often begin with heroic accounts of Cook's expeditions in the Pacific. Frequently mentioned is a young tattooed Polynesian man called Mai (Omai) who had worked as an interpreter for Cook, and who was brought to England in 1774. On his arrival, Mai was exhibited to paying customers in a 'Museum of Curiosities', and was taken under the wing of Cook's celebrated botanist Joseph Banks. During his two-year stay in Britain, Mai was examined by scientists, presented at the court of George III and to scholars at the University of Cambridge, was toured around country estates, and was drawn and painted by the most celebrated artists of the day.

Polynesian tattoos entered British visual and literary culture through paintings, drawings, engravings, prints and stories about Mai. The most famous visual depiction of Mai was *Portrait of Omai* (1776) by the fashionable London portrait painter Joshua Reynolds, which was exhibited at the Royal Academy Exhibition.

Reynolds portrays Mai in a classical idiom, turbaned and draped in toga-like robes, with the distinctive tattoos which so fascinated eighteenth-century London society clearly visible on his hands and arms. Mai would be the first of many tattooed people displayed as exotic objects of curiosity in Europe.

Conventional chronologies of tattooing in Europe describe how European sailors adopted and adapted practices of Polynesian tattooing, and began inking themselves as a means of recording their travels and marking their identities on their skin. Certainly, by the nineteenth century, voluntary tattooing was widely practised amongst the working classes, particularly those who lived and worked on the social margins, such as sailors and travelling labourers. However, a focus on fashions for voluntarily acquired tattoos occludes the fact that practices of penal tattooing coexisted within Europe in the same period. In medieval and early modern Europe, up to and including eighteenth-century England, into which the word 'tattoo' was imported, the penal tattooing and/or branding of convicted criminals was an established practice.

As Caplan details, 'the relative absence of institutions of confinement' 'made branding and tattooing valuable public markers of criminal identity'.[87] In France, up until 1832, 'offenders were branded or tattooed on the arm with letters denoting their criminal status' and sentence. The letter G or GAL was tattooed on those sentenced to indentured labour on galleys, and TP (short for *travaux publics*) for those condemned to hard labour in public works, which might well involve transportation to a penal colony. Similarly, in England 'all kinds of alphabetic marks, from the V for vagrant, to thumb-brands of "M" for murderer, or "T" for thief', were used to stigmatise criminals and the indigent poor.[88] Judicial practices of penal tattooing and branding continued well into the nineteenth century. For example, the penal tattooing of serfs (unfree indentured peasant labourers), was not abolished in Russia until 1863.[89] In the Siberian penal system 'public serfs' who were convicted of a crime had the letters KAT (for *katorsh-niki*, meaning 'public slave') tattooed into their cheeks or forehead before 'gunpowder was rubbed into the wounds'.[90]

While I was writing *Stigma* I undertook jury service at the Crown Court in Lancaster, which is housed inside the medieval Lancaster Castle – the museum in the castle also houses a scold's bridle. This is one of the oldest courts in England, and in the dock there still hangs 'a metal holdfast designed to immobilise the wrist and fingers' and a 'branding iron embossed with the letter M' which was heated and applied to the brawn of the thumb, identifying the convicted prisoner as a 'malefactor'.[91] It was from this practice of branding convicted prisoners that the custom arose of requiring those on trial to raise their hand while they swore on the bible, so judge and jury could see whether they bore the mark of a previous conviction. The last recorded use of this branding iron was in 1811.

Lancaster was one of the major judicial centres for the sentencing to transportation of convicts to colonial outposts during the eighteenth and nineteenth centuries. As I noted in the Introduction, eighteenth-century Lancaster was also the fourth largest slave-trading port in England. While Lancaster slave traders shipped branded Africans as chattel across the Atlantic, Lancaster's judicial elites branded and transported the English poor to North America, the West Indies, and, after the American War of Independence, to Australia. For a period, then, Lancaster was a small but significant global headquarters for the forced movement of unfree labour across the world.

For the hundred years between 1700 and 1800 at least 122 ships sailed from Lancaster to the coast of Africa, sealing their signs of ownership on captured Africans. Lancaster merchants were involved in the capture and selling of an estimated 30,000 people. We can now scrutinise the records of Lancaster ships in the transatlantic slave ship database.[92] For example, the slave ship *Thomas and John*, captained by Thomas Paley, purchased 152 people in the Sierra Leone estuary in 1768 and delivered 130 survivors to the slave market in Savanna-la-Mar in Jamaica, before returning with a cargo of sugar, rum, cotton, pimento, logwood and thirty-six planks of mahogany to Lancaster Quay.[93] This ship was owned by Thomas Hinde, a former slave ship captain, come slave ship owner, merchant and plantation investor, and twice a mayor of Lancaster. Indeed, it would be difficult to find a Lancaster elite from this period whose wealth and power wasn't derived from what is often euphemistically referred to as the West Indies trade.[94]

This mixed traffic and trade in stigmatised bodies underscores the extent to which the tattoo (and brand mark) was 'a promiscuously travelling sign' in the seventeenth and eighteenth centuries, 'moving literally on the homeless bodies of slaves, criminals, pilgrims, sailors, soldiers and transported convicts'.[95] However, there are crucial differences in the meaning and function of these bodily inscriptions. For example, those convicted in the Lancaster Assizes who were deported from England with the indelible brand of a criminal class on their thumb travelled as human beings, not as property. The conditions they endured on board prison hulks and ships were wretched, dangerous and sometimes deadly. Nevertheless, transported people kept their names, and their conviction and forced emigration was recorded – a difference underscored by the fact that Australian citizens can today use court archives to trace histories of transportation in their family trees, an impossibility for the descendants of enslaved Africans whose relatives travelled as chattel (and whose owners christened them with new names). Transported African men, women and children 'were stripped of all specificity, including their names'; only their 'financial value' was 'recorded and preserved for insurance purposes'.[96] As Saidiya Hartman reflects, for the descendants of enslaved Africans genealogical research involves encountering 'a past that has been obliterated so that even traces aren't left. ... Life worlds disappeared and destroyed; the names of places that would never be remembered and all the names of persons that would never be uttered again'.[97] In contrast, after completing a sentence of forced labour, deported convicts were able to earn (or buy) their freedom. Indeed, those convicts shipped to Virginia from England in the seventeenth and eighteenth centuries sometimes used their freedom to purchase slaves.[98]

The differential meaning of tattooed bodies in the eighteenth century is exemplified by the fact that advertisements for public exhibitions of drawings and etchings of Mai, whose tattoos were an object of intense public curiosity,[99] appeared in mid-eighteenth-century British newspapers at the same time as newspaper advertisements seeking the return of branded, tattooed, lettered, numbered and collared chattel slaves. In 1743, the year before the tattooed Mai arrived in England, celebrity artist and satirist William Hogarth painted *The Inspection*, which depicted the young syphilitic mistress of a viscount with the letters 'FC' tattooed on her breast: a penal tattoo which most likely meant 'Female Convict'.

These genealogies of penal tattooing reveal that practices of bodily marking are continually shifting, and have multifarious meanings and functions. One argument of *Stigma* is that by considering penal stigmatisation as a dehumanising classificatory technology, we can trace links between what at first glance may seem unconnected practices. In so doing, we can begin to map the role of penal stigma in the formation of the figure that Sylvia Wynter terms 'Man-as-human'.[100] Wynter uses this phrase to refer to the ways in which over many centuries European Enlightenment man emerges as the unmarked universal category of humanity, against and through which other categories and forms of human life are marked and measured, valued and judged.

The enclosure of land

To deepen our understanding of the relationship between practices of penal stigmatisation and what Beverley Skeggs terms 'the entangled vine of gender, race and class', it is helpful to turn our attention to the history of enclosures.[101] In the sixteenth century, merchant capitalism, namely the trade in and export of goods, including enslaved people, by entrepreneurial merchants (which from the outset also involved the expropriation of foreign land) began to combine with the power of the state. That is, what began as the private enterprise of individuals and companies developed into state-sponsored and state-governed systems of commerce and colonial occupation. The financial institutions, banks, insurance companies, legal systems and the like, which developed to support overseas trade in goods and people, reshaped the government of English society.

As E.P. Thompson details in *The Making of the English Working Class* (1963), the transformation of feudal, agricultural England into a capitalist state was characterised by the mass enclosure of land, a practice that began in the fifteenth century but continued over many centuries.[102] Land enclosures were most intensive during the eighteenth century, and between '1760 and 1810' alone it is estimated that 'five million acres of common fields' were enclosed.[103] This mass privatisation of land saw the 'open field' system (in which land was divided and shared amongst a community) transformed into a tenant farm system, in which land became the property of individual landowners, and was worked by wage labourers. As Robert Allen has argued, in terms of productivity, land enclosures brought few if any benefits, but greatly enriched landowners.[104] Critically, these enclosures cut off people's rights of access to the common wealth of the land – freedoms to graze animals, grow crops, gather firewood and hunt for food. The enclosures also eroded long-established customs and moral codes of social provision, by transforming those who could work into precarious waged worker and tenants, and making those who couldn't, such as the sick, elderly or disabled, vulnerable to the whims of aristocratic landowners and their tenant farmers. (Jim Crace's wonderful novel *Harvest* imagines land enclosures from the perspective of dispossessed villagers.)[105]

As the poet Robert Crowley reflected in 1550, working people were held to ransom by 'the great farmers … the men of law, the merchants, the gentlemen, the knights, the lords'. These men, Crowley laments, 'take our houses over our heads, they buy our grounds out of our hands, they raise our rents, they levy (yea unreasonable) fines, they enclose our commons'.[106]

> Men without conscience. Men utterly devoid of God's fear. Yea, men that live as though there were no God at all! Men that would have all in their hands; men that would leave nothing for others. … Cormorants, greedy gulls; yea, men that would eat up men, women and children.[107]

In short, the transformation of England into a capitalist society was a form of internal colonisation in as much as it involved the theft of land, and the systemic destruction of people's customary access to independent means of subsistence. This massive act of state-legislated theft was implemented through forced evictions, the use of bloody penal codes, the innovation of stigmatising Poor Laws, the introduction of new policing and surveillance measures, the incarceration of people in workhouses and prisons, mass transportation (forced emigration to the colonies) and the use of hunger as a weapon.

Enclosure propagandists

In the eighteenth century, utilitarian arguments about the need for greater efficiency in systems of agricultural production were used by the social elites to justify the enclosure of land. Economic arguments were supported by the construction of what E.P. Thompson terms 'a moral machinery'.[108] Indeed, in the eighteenth century a panoply of 'enclosure propagandists', aristocrats, politicians, journalists and a new middle class of social policy gurus argued that land enclosures were a moral and civilising mission.[109] Enclosure propaganda painted the commons 'as a dangerous centre of indiscipline' and a 'breeding-ground for barbarians'.[110] For example, Arthur Young (1741–1820), an influential writer on agricultural improvements, described the commons as 'nursing up a mischievous race of people'.[111] As Thompson puts it, 'Ideology was added to self-interest' and 'it became a matter of public-spirited policy for the gentleman to remove cottagers from the commons, reduce his labourers to dependence, pare away at supplementary earnings, drive out the smallholder'.[112]

Within this new moral schemata, the village poor were transformed from entitled and rights-bearing subjects into undeserving populations, 'designing rogues, who, under various pretences, attempt to cheat the parish' and whose 'whole abilities are exerted in the execution of deceit which may procure from the parish officers an allowance of money for idle and profligate purposes'.[113] Indeed, there was a growing consensus amongst the propertied elites that 'it was essential to restore in the poor a proper sense of degradation'.[114] It was considered essential not only because the existing systems of poor relief were perceived as unaffordable (poor rates had inevitability increased as common land was enclosed) but because the very idea of relief was increasingly perceived as incompatible with the new capitalist doctrine of laissez-faire, an ideology which sought to enhance the rights and increase the wealth of the propertied classes by encouraging self-sufficiency, resilience and rugged individualism amongst the unpropertied masses. What this meant in practice was the devastation of people's access to a measure of security and the basic resources they required to sustain the lives of themselves and their dependants. Enclosures were a 'revolution of the rich against the poor'.[115]

As Thompson documents, resistance to enclosures was fierce and sustained. Faced with this catastrophe, people gathered to plan how to resist the violence wrought upon them. Popular radical movements emerged and people furiously debated the pros and cons of continuous agitation, riots, large-scale organised revolts (including the bearing of arms), and softer tactics of democratic enfranchisement and moral persuasion. Mass campaigns of direct action saw the levelling of the ditches and walls which had enclosed common land, machine breaking, rioting, the destruction of private property and bread riots: as Thompson notes, there were repeated food riots, 'in almost every town and county' up until the 1840s.[116]

Branding the vagabond, badging the poor

Karl Marx summarises the history of the English enclosures in *Capital*, describing how 'agricultural people [were] first forcibly expropriated from the soil, driven from their homes, turned into vagabonds, and then whipped, branded, tortured by laws grotesquely terrible, into the discipline necessary for the wage system'.[117] As this reference to branding suggests, penal stigmatisation was a pivotal technology in these processes of enclosure, deployed to manage the massive social upheavals and class conflicts that followed in the wake of the destruction of people's customary access to the means of subsistence.

In a chapter of *Capital* titled 'Bloody Legislation Against the Expropriated, from the End of the 15th Century', Marx details how new criminal codes and poor laws were devised to apprehend 'masterless' men and women within systems of indentured, coerced or low-paid labour such as the Elizabethan Roundsman System, which involved the public auctioning of unemployed men – an early form of workfare. Marx gives the example of a late Tudor law, the Vagabonds Act of 1547, which ordained that anyone in England who refuses to work 'shall be condemned as a slave to the person who has denounced him as an idler'.[118] This act mandated a series of stigmatising punishments, notably the use of branding irons to mark the skin of offenders: V for vagabond, S for slave. A subsequent act ordered that 'incorrigible and dangerous rogues are to be branded with an R on the left shoulder and set to hard labour, and if they are caught begging again, to be executed without mercy'.[119] The use of penal stigmatisation and other bloody practices to *mark out* the wayward, displaced, marginal and unemployed continued over the centuries that followed. What I want to emphasise here is that stigma statutes and stigmatising practices were introduced, as Marx puts it, to 'shorten the transition' to a society in which people would have nothing left 'to sell but their own skins'.[120]

The word pauper, a deeply stigmatising term for an 'unproductive' person – 'a person having no property or means of livelihood; a person dependent on the charity of others' – came into everyday use in the eighteenth century to describe the mass impoverishment which followed in the wake of enclosures.[121] 'Look at England', cried the Member of Parliament William Cobbett in 1816, 'swarming with paupers, and convulsed in every limb of her body'.[122]

Experiments in the stigmatisation of the poor intensified as social elites sought to find ways to deter people from making claims on the parish for relief. During the seventeenth century, violent physical practices of stigmatisation, such as branding, were supplemented with less permanent but still visible penal stigmas, such as the wearing of cloth badges and humiliating forms of dress. For example, a 1697 Poor Law decreed that paupers in receipt of alms were compelled to at all times display a cloth badge with the letter P and 'the first letter of the name of the parish or place where they lived' upon their right sleeve.[123] These impermanent stigmas allowed the possibility of reform if you were willing to adopt new forms of work discipline.[124]

While practices of badging of the poor were formally repealed in England in 1810, badging continued in other similar practices of social stigmatisation and public shaming. Practices of badging emerged in concert with new workhouse experiments, for example. Like badging, these houses of correction sought to use stigma, incarceration and hard labour to deter people from seeking relief from the parish – those who had no option but to enter a workhouse were stripped of their remaining worldly possessions, forced to wear humiliating uniforms, and had to undertake demeaning and often backbreaking work in return for their keep. 'I dread the workhouse for the workhouse coat is a slothful, degrading badge. After a man has had one on his back, he's never the same', a blind tailor told journalist and social reformer Henry Mayhew in 1851.[125] As Vivienne Richmond details, up until the early twentieth century men from workhouses in the North of England were forced to work in public 'with a large P stamped on the seat of their trousers'.[126] These practices of badging the poor continue in the government of welfare today – for example, through stigmatising media depictions of benefits claimants as 'designing rogues' (see Chapter 4).

In *The Great Transformation: The Political and Economic Origins of our Time* (1944), the political economist Karl Polanyi argued that the stigmatised figure of the pauper and the market economy 'appear in history together'.[127] As Marx writes, 'it is already contained in the concept of the free labourer, that he is a pauper, virtual pauper'.[128] What Marx meant by this is that for ordinary people the institution of capitalist systems of government made people radically vulnerable to poverty – a system of dependence in which only work for the profit of others could secure some measure of freedom.

Bentham's panoptical welfare stigma machine

In the late eighteenth century, near famine conditions, and revolts and uprisings, saw the problem of paupers become central to social and political debate. Thomas Malthus (1766–1834), famously concerned about population growth, argued that hunger, disease (and war) were checks on population size which shouldn't be interfered with. Hence he proposed the total abolition of poor relief, with workhouses used as a place of last resort, arguing that 'survival of the fittest' policies combined with moral restraints, such as limitations on marriages amongst the poor, would naturally curtail population growth.

Another popular suggestion was that paupers should be encouraged (or forced) to migrate to colonies, to release taxpayers from the burden of relief. Edward Wakefield (1796–1862), a major player in the British colonisation of New Zealand and Canada, argued that the new 'misery of the bulk of the people' could be ameliorated through 'systematic colonization'.[129] What Wakefield meant is that forced emigration and settler colonialism might solve the problem of growing pauperisation in England.[130] Of course this implied the seizure and enclosure of overseas land and the displacement, and pauperisation and murder of indigenous populations.

In contrast, one-man social policy think tank Jeremy Bentham (1748–1882) argued that deporting paupers to the colonies was an expensive and uncertain enterprise. The American War of Independence from 1775 to 1783 had stalled transportation of British convicts to North American colonies, which had created a prison population crisis: prison hulks (prison ships) were periodically overflowing with people sentenced to transportation. Bentham advocated instead for internal colonisation, by which he meant the building of a vast carceral welfare state within England in which paupers could be 'farmed' for profit.[131] Bentham's extensive proposals, the first detailed plans for a fully comprehensive system of state welfare in Britain, was a panoptical stigma machine.

The enclosure of the poor

In *Outline of a Work Entitled Pauper Management Improved*, first published in serial form in the *Annuals of Agriculture* in 1798, Jeremy Bentham outlined 'the most radical and comprehensive revision of the poor law ever proposed'.[132] An extraordinary and terrifying work of utilitarian speculative fiction, Bentham's scheme for farming paupers involved transforming what he called 'that part of the national live stock which has no feathers to it and walks with two legs' into a profitable captive labour force.[133] Bentham's proposals for the management of paupers called for mass privatisation of welfare, including the abolishment of all existing practices and institutions of poor relief, the ending of all outdoor relief, especially cash payments and wage supplements (as in the Speenhamland system),[134] the rescinding of all existing poor laws and the closure of all existing prisons, bridle houses, asylums, hospitals, workhouses and orphanages. In the place of this uneven patchwork of welfare institutions and provisions, Bentham proposed the setting up of a National Charity Company: 'The management of the concerns of the poor throughout South Britain to be vested in one authority, and the expense to be charged upon one fund. This Authority, that of a Joint-Stock Company under some such name as that of the National Charity Company.'[135]

Bentham argued that his scheme would rid the government once and for all of 'the whole body of the burdensome poor': the disabled, the elderly, widows, orphans, felons, vagabonds, beggars, any and all who might be a drain on the public purse.[136] His charity was to be state subsidised (a public–private partnership), funded through the existing systems of poor relief (local taxation), but this tax booty would now be transferred directly to Bentham's company, which would have 'responsibility for the entire management and distribution of relief, having at its disposal the entire sum available for relief, and functioning solely through the medium of industry-houses'.[137] This income would be supplemented by funds derived from private shareholders in the company – Bentham particularly hoped to encourage small-scale investments from middle-class shareholders.[138]

The setting up of this company would involve the building of an 'unprecedented multitude of establishments' to be known as 'industry-houses'.[139] These industry houses were modelled on Bentham's famous panoptical prison plans, which he had initially designed (in response to a newspaper competition to design a new prison) to incarcerate 3,000 people in a single building. In *Pauper Management*, Bentham scaled up these plans, proposing the building of 500 industry houses, which together would form a massive prison-like estate within England, initially housing 500,000 people and rising to a million within twenty-one years. Bentham estimated that the resident population in England and Wales was 9 million, so his plan was to forcibly incarcerate one in nine people, targeting those who were reliant (or were at risk thereof) on poor relief; a million people interned to undertake forced labour.

The National Charity Company was to be granted legal powers to compulsorily enclose land, and the industry houses would be spread across the entirety of southern England, their location determined by mathematical division of land to produce 'an exact equality of distribution', the 'Average distance accordingly between house and house 10 2/3 miles'.[140] Every ten miles, then, a panoptical workhouse with an accompanying farm (or what he sometimes and significantly refers to as a plantation), in which to segregate, incarcerate, breed and farm England's paupers.

While the clientele of Bentham's original panoptical prisons (if they had been built) would have been convicted criminals supplied by the courts, these mixed welfare institutions would receive a vast and diverse clientele rounded up by the company itself. For this purpose, Bentham stated that his company would be granted unlimited legal powers for 'apprehending all persons, able-bodied or otherwise, having neither visible or assignable property, nor honest and sufficient means of livelihood, and detaining and employing them'.[141] Indeed, Bentham's new privatised welfare state involved the creation of a private police force – one of the first proposals for a national police force. It is significant in this regard that Bentham argued that his scheme would remove the fiscal burden of paupers from hardworking taxpayers *and* contain the insurrectionary threat to property (and the propertied classes) posed by the indigent poor. State welfare was imagined from the outset as a system for policing the poor.

Bentham's proposals were not without precedent, he drew on existing practices of identification and surveillance, such as the registration and badging of the poor. He also drew on existing workhouse experiments in England, notably the Relief of the Poor Act 1782 (Gilbert's Act), which allowed neighbouring parishes to join together to develop regional workhouses. Bentham's friend, the philanthropist Jonas Hanway, was experimenting with similar systems of carceral work discipline in his Magdalen Hospital for Penitent Prostitutes (opened in 1758).[142] However, the proposed National Charity Company was on a totally different scale, proposing the enserfment of the entirety of England's poor in a system which would combine the panoptical prison factory with the colonial plantation system to form what Bentham termed 'a domestic colony'.[143]

Colonise at home

Bentham's entire scheme was dedicated to the proposition, 'Colonize at home!', and he imagined it as a pauper empire.[144] He argued that his industry houses and plantations would provide all the advantages of colonisation without the risks which came with the management of foreign colonies.[145] Further, his charitable company was to run on the mercantilist principles of the East India Company, and managed, like the East India Company, by a Board of Directors elected by the shareholders.[146] Indeed, Bentham argued that 'the government of such a concern as that of the proposed National Charity Company would be like child's play to a Director of the East India Company', writing that in India 'you see twenty or thirty millions under the management, and much more absolute government of one Board, and those spread over a surface of country several times as large as South Britain'.[147] Bentham himself was to be director of this charitable company, a role he described as 'Sub-Regulus of the Poor'.[148]

It is notable that Bentham proposed introducing a system of what he termed 'identity washing' (using chemical dyes to mark the faces of inmates) as a surveillance technology for managing the pauper labour force in his proposed domestic colony of industry houses.[149]

Bentham's plans drew extensively on the new tools of accountancy and labour management (forms of punishment and discipline) innovated in colonial plantations in India, the West Indies and North America.[150] Bentham and his brother Samuel had previously spent time (1786–1787) experimenting with new systems of labour discipline on a Russian colonial estate – where Samuel managed a serf labour force.[151] Indeed, it was on this Russian colony that Bentham had first devised his famous panoptical prison design. Bentham wanted to refine these management techniques to transform England's waste populations into work machines. As he wrote, 'Not one in a hundred is absolutely incapable of all employment. Not the motion of a finger – not a step – not a wink – not a whisper – but might be turned to account in the way of profit in a system of such magnitude'.[152]

This marked and captive population would labour for their keep on a debt-bondage model. Breeding was to be encouraged by the company, and children would be held as collateral and security – with child labour used to pay off any inherited debts owed to the company. He imagined paupers (and crucially their offspring) as an untapped treasure trove whose capture and exploitation would yield dividends for investors in his scheme, calculating that within a short number of years his company would become profit making. Bentham's lengthy proposals are best understood as both a policy document and a business proposal. He described his colonial-style welfare scheme as 'my Utopia'.[153]

Bentham's utopia was never realised in his lifetime. He blamed the government and the king for not adopting his plans, as he lamented: 'But for George the Third, all the paupers in the country would, long ago, have been under my management'.[154] However, his proposals deeply influenced the draconian Poor Law Amendment Act 1834 (also known as the New Poor Law) passed into law the year of Bentham's death. The 1834 Poor Laws were composed by Bentham's devoted former secretary and acolyte Edwin Chadwick.

Indeed, Bentham's vision of panoptical houses of industry spread across the land was effectively a blueprint for the 1834 Act, which legislated for the abolishment of all outdoor relief and the building of pauper workhouses across England. This Act was, as E.P. Thompson describes it, 'the most sustained attempt to impose an ideological dogma, in defiance of the evidence of human need, in English history'.[155]

Bentham's panoptical workfare scheme has continued to cast a long shadow over welfare policy making in Britain (and further afield). Indeed, Bentham's legacy weighs heavily on the ongoing austerity enclosures of the twentieth-century welfare commons, and the rise of what Virginia Eubanks has described as 'digital poor houses', namely the development of high-tech tools to mark out, survey, profile, police and govern the poor.[156]

'Flogged, fettered and tortured in the most exquisite refinement of cruelty'

As Karl Marx, Karl Polanyi and other many influential political economists have highlighted, the stigmatised figure of the pauper, and the constellation of stigma practices innovated to mark out and govern populations pauperised by capitalism 'stands at the centre of a political and epistemic complex' from which the British state emerged.[157] However, it is no coincidence that the stigmatising laws and terrorising punishments employed in England from the fifteenth century to transform (and sort) agricultural peasants into waged labourers and paupers bear resemblances to the English slave codes devised in colonial plantation economies in the Caribbean and North America; laws which sought to transform chattel slaves and their descendants into 'Negros' – 'a marginally human group ... fit only for slavery'.[158] Indeed, the proposals of people like Wakefield for 'systematic colonisation', and the schemes of people like Bentham for an internal colony of pauper industry houses and plantations within England, underscores the extent to which 'the enclosure movement in England [was] continuous with colonial dispossession and possession in the "New World"'.[159] It is imperative to consider the operations of this stigma politics, not least as it highlights the ways in which racial capitalism operates through the production of race–class distinctions – classificatory distinctions which differentially function to enclose and exploit those dispossessed by the advocates and beneficiaries of colonial capitalism.

In *Slavery and Capitalism*, Eric Williams notes that by '1750 there was hardly a trading or a manufacturing town in England which was not in some way connected with the triangular or direct colonial trade. The profits obtained provided one of the main streams of that accumulation of capital in England which financed the Industrial Revolution'.[160] Once again the eighteenth-century history of Lancaster is instructive in this regard. The first cotton mills in the Lancaster district were established in a village called Caton in 1783 by a man called Thomas Hodgson (1738–1817). Thomas Hodgson and his brother John worked as slave traders for over thirty years. Between 1763 and 1791 they were involved in the capture and selling of an estimated 14,000 people. Thomas began his slaving career working for the Lancaster-born slaver Miles Barber; indeed, records suggest that the Hodgson brothers took over the running of 'Factory Island' from Barber in 1793 – a decade after they opened their first cotton mill (see Introduction on Barber). For a period, then, these Lancashire brothers owned and managed these two factory complexes simultaneously.

The Hodgson cotton mills in Caton specialised in the exploitation of pauper child labourers, transporting children from urban centres across England to work in their mills – primarily from Liverpool but also from London.[161] As Karl Marx details, alongside colonial plantation slavery, it is child factory labour which characterised 'the infancy of Modern Industry'.[162] Marx quotes from Fredrick Eden's *The State of the Poor* (1797), which describes how the 'small and nimble fingers of little children' were procured by men like the Hodgsons from parish workhouses and orphanages to be 'flogged, fettered and tortured in the most exquisite refinement of cruelty' to work 'the newly-invented machinery' of Lancashire's cotton mills.[163]

During the same period, John Bond (1778–1856), another Lancaster man who would twice be appointed as mayor of the town, inherited several plantations and over 700 enslaved people in British Guiana and Grenada from his slave-trading uncle Thomas Bond.[164] His inheritance included a cotton plantation in Guiana called Lancaster.[165] The Lancaster cotton plantation was visited in the mid-eighteenth century by an English physician, Dr George Pinckard, who described it as 'distinguished' by 'the inhuman treatment of the slaves'.[166] This is a place, Pinckard wrote, where 'cruelty had become contagious' and the plantation manager 'hardened in savage conduct' and 'diabolical cruelty'.[167]

During Pinckard's visit an enslaved husband and wife from the Lancaster plantation escaped. They were recaptured and flogged. Pinckard describes how he is called on to offer medical assistance. When he arrives the man has already died of his wounds, 'an iron collar' still fastened around his neck and heavy chains binding his body to that of his 'almost murdered' wife.[168] She is in a condition so 'horrid and distressing can scarcely be conceived', her 'flesh' is 'so torn as to exhibit one extensive sore, from the loins almost down to her hams'.[169] Pinckard calls this episode 'the most shocking' instance of 'barbarity' he witnessed during his journey through the West Indies and South America. His published letters were later used to support the political case for the abolition of slavery.

The cotton that connects, the cloth that binds

Cotton is one of the threads which connects and binds together the lives of those who 'built the wealth of the European machine' over centuries.[170] Manufactured woollen and cotton goods were sometimes used by slave traders to purchase people on the West African coast. The raw cotton, picked by the enslaved in plantations in the Americas, was weighed and baled, before being shipped to the same quaysides from which slave ships had formerly departed; 'Negro Cloth' – a coarse material sometimes made by grinding up the rags of factory workers – was sent back across the Atlantic as clothing for plantation slaves: an industry of recycling waste cloth which was known as the shoddy trade.[171]

In an artwork called *Cotton.com* (2002), installed inside a former cotton mill in Manchester, the artist Lubaina Himid brings the ghosts of mill workers and plantation workers into dialogue through the medium of cotton, paint and words. As Himid describes this project in an interview with the historian Alan Rice:

[I] imagined the cotton workers in these buildings taking the cotton off the barges that had come up the ship canal and finding little bits of fabric, perhaps finding a bit of cloth, or a bit of hair, some kind of thing that had accidently found its way from the cotton picker's body or clothes or field … into these bales and managed to find its way back across the Atlantic, up the Manchester Ship Canal, there you get this whole bale of cotton off and you have to card it and thin it … imagine all the thoughts you might have had.[172]

We cannot understand the history of industrial capitalism separately from the history of slavery and colonialism. We cannot separate Lancashire's cotton mills from the Lancashire-owned slave factories on the African coast, and the Lancashire-owned cotton plantations – they form part of the same archipelago of enclosure and exploitation. As the economic, judicial, political, architectural and welfare histories of cities like Lancaster attest, the unpaid labour of the enslaved was the source of surplus value which structured the 'free' but exploited waged labour of the English working class. That is, the ability of the 'freeborn' English man to sell 'his own skin' was grounded in the radical unfreedom of others.

In 1862, a 'cotton famine', precipitated by the American Civil War, saw the threads of connection between enslaved cotton pickers in the American South and Lancashire mill workers become visible in people's everyday lives in industrial England, with many mill workers, unions and co-operative organisations expressing their solidarity with the enslaved through an embargo on Southern-picked cotton, and waves of strike action.[173] These acts of transatlantic solidarity testify to the fact that we cannot disentangle class struggles in England – the machine breakers, the levellers and strikers of Britain's multi-ethnic working class – from the freedom struggles of those enslaved in factories, ships and plantations. As Marx reflected on the tumultuous events of the Lancashire cotton famine, 'Labour cannot emancipate itself in the white skin where in the black it is branded'.[174]

Plantation slaves, enserfed agricultural workers, indentured 'coolie' workers, child labourers, waged factory workers and workhouse paupers are 'concretely intertwined and ideologically symbiotic elements of a larger unified though internally diversified structure of exploitation'.[175] Indeed, chattel slavery and plantation labour were as influential in the formation and structuring of English class society as the enclosure of common land and the exploitations attendant with the growth of industrial capitalism in factories and mills. We cannot disentangle the history of the development of the English welfare state and its 'charitable institutions' of orphanages and workhouses from the history of slavery and colonial capitalism.[176] As Robbie Shilliam writes, 'the working class was constitutionalized though empire and its aftermaths; and in this respect, class is race', by which he means that 'there is no politics of class which is not already racialised'.[177]

Many excellent histories of colonial capitalism have been written by others, such as Eric Williams, Catherine Hall, Sven Beckert and Edward Baptist. What *Stigma* seeks to contribute here is an understanding of how penal practices of stigmatisation which devalued and dehumanised people underpinned the emergence of capitalism as a world system. I want to turn briefly to a final twist in the history of the penal tattoo, the moment when the tattoo becomes a building block within the classist and racist eugenicist epistemologies of social scientific knowledge, before finally returning to India and the stigma machine of caste.

Eugenic epistemologies of tattooing

In 1864, the Italian scientist Cesare Lombroso, who is often called 'the father of criminology', developed a highly influential theory of 'the born criminal'. As Lombroso explains, the idea of 'the born criminal' came to him in 1864, when he worked as an army doctor and was 'struck by a characteristic that distinguished the honest soldier from his vicious comrade: the extent to which the latter was tattooed'.[178] From this initial association between tattoos and violent behavioural traits, Lombroso penned a Darwin-inspired thesis, which argued that criminality was a hereditary trait which linked low-class Europeans to savage primitive races. He developed a classificatory system through which, he claimed, criminality could be read off the body, through the identification of physical traits, such as small skulls, and secondary traits, most especially *tattoos*.

In his best-selling book *Criminal Man* (1876), Lombroso argued that the (voluntary) tattoo is a strange relic of 'a former state', a practice of 'atavistic origin' undertaken by the lower classes – peasants, sailors, workers, shepherds, soldiers, and especially criminals.[179] In short, if the penal tattoo had long been used by social elites to criminalise the bodies of the poor, now voluntarily acquired tattoos were employed as a means of identifying the 'congenital criminal'. By the mid-nineteenth century, tattoos were 'routinely included in physical descriptions of suspects, convicts and prisoners and they continued to figure in the more elaborate anthropometric descriptions that were developed in the later nineteenth century, which by then also incorporated the more modern technologies of photography and fingerprinting'.[180]

In 'Criminal Skins' (2005), Jimena Canales and Andrew Herscher detail how Lombroso's eugenicist stigma thesis deeply influenced the twentieth-century modernist movement. This influence is evident in the writing of the Czech architect Adolf Loos, whose essay, 'Ornament and Crime' (1913) utilised the Italian school of eugenicist social science to argue that 'the evolution of culture is synonymous with the removal of ornamentation from objects of everyday use'.[181] For Loos the tattoo was a symbol of degenerate ornamentation *par excellence*, 'a sign of the survival or recurrence of primitive savagery in the bosom of civilisation'.[182] Loos argues that 'primitive people', such as Papuans (people from or originating from Papua New Guinea and the Pacific region, like Mai whom we met earlier), criminals and women (women of all social classes), 'are seized with an inescapable urge to ornament themselves and their surroundings'.[183]

> A modern person who is tattooed is either a criminal or a degenerate. There are prisons in which eighty per cent of the prisoners are tattooed. Tattooed men who are not behind bars are either latent criminals or degenerate aristocrats. If someone dies in freedom, then he does so a few years before he would have committed a murder.[184]

What Lombroso and his followers such as Loos inspired was a eugenicist classificatory gaze, the foundation for a *stigma science* which extended from reading the tattooed bodies of individuals to the entire 'degenerate culture' of 'lower order social classes': an atavistic underclass who could now be identified through their 'tattooed environments', such as the graffiti which ornamented the buildings in areas in which they lived, and the use of jargon in their speech and writing. The tattoo comes then to function as a device which authorises particular ideological, spatial and aesthetic practices of social cleansing.

We can still see this eugenicist classificatory gaze at work today in the ways in which practices of gentrification operate through 'territorial stigmatisation'.[185] Indeed, we can begin to trace here the ways in which the material histories of places (architecture, built environment, the zoning and policing of urban spaces) are shaped by the development of eugenicist race–class distinctions. Indeed, Canales and Herscher argue that the history of architectural modernism and modernist architectural practices pivot on the tattooed body of the race–class other, giving rise to an aesthetic of the unmarked, unornamented building, and 'the white abstraction of "less is more" architecture'.[186] While the implications of these insights are beyond the scope of this book, what I want to underscore here are the ways in which the penal tattoo not only informs modernist aesthetics and values, but underpins the policies and practices of urbanisation, and its attendant culture industries (such as the white cube of the art world).[187] In short, this stigma history is inscribed into the everyday material infrastructures of the built environments and material cultures in which we live.

Following the history of penal tattooing as a literal practice employed by slave traders and propertied elites to mark out the bodies of those they wished to humiliate, devalue, capture and exploit, the voluntary tattoo is now used to compose a science and practice of social classification. This in turn informs new ways of seeing and knowing, and leads to the development of new punitive practices of classification, criminalisation, policing and social control. These two genealogies of stigma dramatically combine in the British colonisation of India.

Penal stigma in India

In the mid-eighteenth century the British East India Company was morphing from trading company into a colonial power – 'the Corporate Raj'. In this period, the British East India company was 'a dangerously unregulated private company headquartered in one small office, five windows wide, in London, and managed in India by an unstable sociopath' – a British army officer and privateer called Robert Clive.[188] Clive drew on the resources of the East India Company to fund a vast private army with which to assume administrative control over large swathes of the Indian subcontinent. This campaign for the political and economic domination of India began in wealthy Bengal. As Thomas Paine wrote in 1775: 'fear and terror march like pioneers before [Clive's] camp, murder and rapine accompany it, famine and wretchedness follow in the rear'.[189] The Great Bengal Famine (1769–1773) killed an estimated one-third of the population in Bengal, around 10 million people. It was the largest of a series of eighteenth-century famines in areas of India under the yoke of the corporate Raj as it enclosed land and people, bleeding the region dry.

Paine wasn't alone amongst his contemporaries in decrying the murderous exploits of the British in India as 'an extermination of mankind'.[190] Reports about the Bengal famine caused such disconcertion amongst the British newspaper-reading public that an investigation into the East India Company was undertaken by the British government. In April 1773, a damning report by a House of Commons select committee was prefaced by the statement 'that the reports contained accounts shocking to human nature, that the most infamous designs had been carried into execution by perfidy and murder'.[191] In actuality, the East India Company was a private–public partnership between state actors and business elites – indeed one-quarter of British MPs 'owned stock in the East India Company' in this period.[192] The policy guru Jeremey Bentham, who, as detailed above, proposed to base the government of his new panoptical welfare state on the East India Company, was also a shareholder.[193]

In 1797, the corporate Raj introduced penal tattooing within its judicial systems of punishment in Bengal, a practice it later extended to other areas in Southern India under company control.[194] From this period onwards life convicts in Bengal 'had their name, crime, dates of sentence and court by which convicted' tattooed on their foreheads.[195] It seems quite likely that a shortage of labour in the wake of famines in Bengal contributed to the decision of the corporate Raj to introduce penal tattooing. Certainly, as the historian Claire Anderson details, colonial control and expansion necessitated 'a cheap and, preferably controllable labour force' to build the infrastructures of empire, and 'convicts had their identity as a prison labour force literally inscribed upon their person'.[196] This tattooed labour force was also transported overseas to other East India Company territories and British-owned plantations as 'coolie' labour.[197] Being tattooed or branded in India in this period effectively turned you into the property of the company.

Penal tattooing wasn't unheard of in pre-colonial India, where 'the use of tattooing as a punishment' was bound up with other caste sanctions 'of shame and humiliation': including mutilation (amputation of nose, ears or hands) and public shaming (head shaving and face blackening). The introduction of penal tattooing by the British was also differentiated along caste lines. For example, serious offenders from high-caste groups, such as Brahmins, might be tattooed in place of execution.[198] These penal tattoos were of course deeply humiliating and a source of shame. Anderson notes how strategies emerged to conceal penal tattoos: 'turbans were worn low to hide godna [tattoo] marks', hair was fashioned to conceal them, and practices of tattoo defacement and removal (through scarification) proliferated.[199]

By the time the British government took direct control of India (the British Raj, 1858–1947), penal tattooing was falling out of favour, as it was perceived as at odds with the British governments stated civilising colonial mission, and there was a new emphasis on reform in penal systems (led in part by utilitarian thinkers such as Jeremey Bentham). As Anderson notes, a debate took place in colonial India over the efficacy of flogging convicts, as the scars left by whip marks on offenders' bodies were a stigmata which made it harder for them to find gainful employment after their release.[200] Despite this new emphasis on reform (through indentured labour), as we have seen throughout this chapter, the suppression of one form of penal stigma is often accompanied by emergence of new stigmatising forms of classification and stigma practices. The British continued to exploit and innovate shaming punishments, legal sanctions and surveillance technologies, particularly by exploiting existing caste hierarchies in India, to which they added their own stigmatising 'prejudices and value judgements'.[201]

The stigma of genetic criminality

In 1871, the British Raj passed the 'Criminal Tribes Act', which saw the introduction of punitive laws for 'the registration, surveillance and control' of Indian's indigenous and traditionally nomadic tribal populations – often known today by the collective term Adivasi.[202] Under the terms of this act, 'criminality was viewed as hereditary', and many Adivasi found themselves classified as 'janam churas (criminals-by-birth)'.[203] To assist in the implementation of this act a nationwide survey and census of India's castes and tribal groups was undertaken. Herbert Risley (1851–1911), a British civil servant, anthropologist and race science enthusiast, was appointed Census Commissioner for India in 1899, and undertook an ethnographic survey of the population of Bengal.[204] Inspired by the new European eugenicist social sciences, Risley employed phrenology, finger-printing and photography as methods for classifying criminal castes and tribes. Risley's field workers were particularly instructed to document tattoos, as tattoos were understood, in the wake of Lombroso's 1876 thesis, as evidence of 'hereditary criminality'.[205]

Once registered as 'criminals by birth', the Adivasi became subject to punitive systems of administration and policing, which included the introduction of a pass system to control their movements. Under this pass system people were forced to register, sometimes daily, at local police stations and were frequently confined to specific villages. These forms of social and spatial segregation bore resemblances to the Jim Crow laws in the United States (introduced in 1877) and the pass systems developed in colonial South Africa to control black labour (for example, in 1896 black African men were required by law to wear on their upper arm a metal badge stamped with a number in order to enter labour districts in the Cape).

In India, those found in breach of pass laws were subject to fines, beatings and imprisonment in reformatories – places of confinement which, as the criminologist Preeti Nijhar argues, bore a strong resemblance to English workhouses.[206]

In his research on the policing of 'criminal tribes' in Punjab, the historian Andrew Major reveals that in the early twentieth century large agricultural and industrial reformatories were established to intern, reform and skill Adivasi for the labour market, including cotton mills.[207] In 1919, a reformatory prison factory established at the site of Amritsar prison held 860 Adivasi men, women and children, mainly from the so-called criminal tribe Sansi. During the First World War this prison-factory complex effectively functioned as a sweatshop. Jeremy Bentham would probably have described this carceral workplace as a utopia.

The political scientist Gopul Guru describes how caste was 'chalked' on people as a means of enabling and legitimating colonial-era rule, including the enclosure of land, resources and labour.[208] Certainly, it is no coincidence that stigmatising punishments, punitive policing and internment measures employed against the Adivasi intensified during the same period when the British were actively enclosing the lands in which Adivasi had traditionally lived. For example, the passing of multiple Forest Acts saw the British government declare ownership over all forested land – as a means, amongst other things, to harvest wood for use in the manufacture of railway sleepers. These land enclosures saw Adivasi deprived of traditional 'grazing, hunting and gathering rights'.[209] As with the enclosures of common land in England, the innovation of new penal systems of classification and surveillance were employed as technologies of colonial capitalist enclosure.

Indian democracy

When British rule ended in 1947, India became the largest democratic nation state in the world. The Constitution of India (1950) was explicit in prohibiting discrimination on grounds of religion, race, caste, sex or place of birth. Untouchability became a criminal offence and Dalits were reclassified as Scheduled Castes, while Adivasi were reclassified as Scheduled Tribes. Ostensibly these new governmental classifications sought to de-stigmatise the caste system, and to enable those disadvantaged by colonial-era social hierarchies to benefit from new redistributive social policies and legal protections, including programmes of 'affirmative action' which promised to offset generations of subordination.[210] However, in the context of historically 'entrenched social, economic, and political inequalities created and justified by the caste-based hierarchical social order', and given the many elite interests invested in the maintenance of this order, these constitutional doctrines remained 'paper principles'.[211] As the Dalit Panthers (inspired by the US Black Panthers) stated in their 1973 manifesto:

> Under pressure of the masses [the Indian government] passed many laws but it cannot implement them. Because the entire state machinery is dominated by ... the same hands who, for thousands of years, under religious sanctions, controlled all the wealth and power, today own most of the agricultural land, industry, economic resources and all other instruments of power.[212]

The Criminal Tribes Act wasn't repealed until 31 August 1952. From this date those registered as 'born criminals' were ostensibly freed 'from their 80-year-old bondage'.[213] However, as Sarah Gandee notes, the act was replaced 'by a series of provincial Habitual Offenders legislation which effectively reproduced the colonial frameworks of surveillance and control'.[214] The very same government officers and police forces who had supervised the 'criminal tribes' were now 'responsible for implementing the ostensibly liberalised agenda of the postcolonial state'.[215] Indeed these groups are still listed as criminal tribes in police training manuals.[216]

As the researcher and activist C.J. Bijoy notes, the spectre of the so-called criminal tribes continues to haunt Adivasi people – the Sansi, Pardhi, Kanjar, Gujjar, Bawaria, Banjara and others – who 'are still considered as the first natural suspects of all petty and sundry crimes'.[217] In their encounters with police and other state actors, Adivasi still endure ritual humiliations, unfounded accusations, and threats against their family and friends.[218]

Public humiliation remains a signal feature of the treatment of both Adivasi and Dalit populations. Social boycotts and sanctions against them extend from restricting access to drinking water, through destruction of property, beatings, sexual harassment, rape and lynchings. Particular kinds of violence are reserved for Adivasi and Dalit women, including 'extreme filthy verbal abuse and sexual epithets, naked parading, dismemberment, being forced to drink urine and eat faeces, branding, pulling out of teeth, tongue and nails, and violence including murder after proclaiming witchcraft'.[219] Feminist scholars have detailed how extreme caste violence, rape and public shaming rituals are often targeted at Dalit women in order to demonstrate caste control over Dalit men.[220] Through practices of gender-based violence, women's bodies are effectively made depositories of the stigmatising violence of the caste system itself. This echoes the long gendered history of penal stigma explored in this chapter, and the ways in which misogyny combines with classism, casteism and racism. The history of racial capitalism cannot be separated from regimes of patriarchy – stigma power functions intersectionally.

The stigma machine of caste

In 2016, a new annotated edition of Bhimrao Ramji Ambedkar's seminal 1935 *The Annihilation of Caste* was published. Ambedkar (1891–1956) was India's first Law and Justice Minister following Independence, and in this role was largely responsible for drafting the new Constitution. Ambedkar was born into an untouchable Dalit caste. Extraordinarily, considering his background and the period, Ambedkar was university educated. In 1916, he began a PhD at the London School of Economics (completed in 1922). He also undertook his formative legal training in London. An economist, politician, lawyer and social reformer, Ambedkar was a prolific writer and campaigner on Dalit rights and other issues of social justice.

In a long essay that prefaces the new edition of *The Annihilation of Caste*, Arundhati Roy asks why caste, unlike other 'contemporary abominations like apartheid, racism, sexism, economic imperialism and religious fundamentalism', hasn't been 'politically and intellectually challenged in intellectual forums'.[221] As Roy argues, despite being 'one of the most brutal modes of hierarchical social organisation that human society has known', the Indian caste system still eludes 'scrutiny and censure'.[222]

Roy reflects on growing up as the daughter of a high-caste Hindu father and a Christian mother in post-imperial India with 'the fissures and cracks of caste' all around her, a social context in which caste was implied and practised but rarely overtly stated. Recollecting her childhood, Roy describes caste as everywhere, in 'people's names, in the way people referred to each other, in the work they did, in the clothes they wore, in the marriages that were arranged, in the language they spoke', and yet, she says, 'I never encountered the notion of caste in a single school textbook'.[223] It is not only that caste 'is not colour-coded' and is therefore 'not easy to see', especially to untrained eyes, but rather that this erasure of the lived realities of caste discrimination is an integral element of post-imperial India's narrative of political modernity: a nationalist project which Roy describes as a 'Project of Unseeing'.[224]

From an outsider's perspective (such as my own), understanding caste, its origins, changing historical meanings and forms seems a dauntingly complex task; however, the 'organising principles' of caste are not difficult to grasp.[225] At its simplest, we can understand the Indian caste system as 'graded inequality' grounded in an 'ascending scale of reverence and a descending scale of contempt'.[226] As Roy puts it, the 'top of the caste pyramid is considered pure and has plenty of entitlements. The bottom is considered polluted and has no entitlements but plenty of duties. The pollution–purity matrix is correlated to an elaborate system of caste-based, ancestral occupation'.[227]

Ambedkar captures Indian social hierarchy in a 'chilling metaphor', as 'a multi-storeyed tower with no staircase and no entrance' in which everybody is doomed 'to die in the storey they were born in'.[228] To keep people in their allotted place in this 'hierarchical, sliding scale of entitlements and duties', the caste system relies upon an 'elaborate enforcement network in which everybody polices everybody else' – the daily grinding of the stigma machine of caste.[229]

This chapter on the penal genealogy of stigma opened with five Adivasi women tortured and tattooed by police with the words *Jeb Katri*. These women were all from a denotified tribe called Sansi, classified as a 'hereditary thieving race' under the British Criminal Tribes Act.[230] Recalling the *Jeb Katri* case, Justice Singhvi, one of High Court Judges who initially awarded the women (inadequate) compensation for their torture, stated: 'It appears that the poor in this country are born with different tags on their heads while the law bends for the rich'.[231] However, we cannot understand this story wholly through the lens of economic injustice and the inequalities of class. What these women were engraved with was the violent signature of caste. To borrow Arundhati Roy's words, 'for a court to acknowledge that caste prejudice continues to be a horrific reality in India would have counted as a gesture towards justice'.[232] Instead, here, as in so many other cases of caste violence in contemporary India, the judge 'airbrushed caste out of the picture'.[233]

In the context of ongoing state, police and Hindu caste violence against Adivasi and Dalit people in India, what is remarkable about the *Jeb Katri* case wasn't that it took twenty-three years for the policemen to be convicted, but that there was any measure of justice at all.[234] That this case was prosecuted is a testament to the courage of these Sansi women, and particularly that of Parmeshri Devi, who unveiled her penal tattoo before the judge's bench. As Devi told journalists in 2016: 'Let us assume that I was a thief. But the police had no right to brand me as *Jeb Katri*'.[235]

Hindu supremacy

I began this chapter with the *Jeb Katri* case because the word stigma has its ancient roots in practices of penal tattooing which so clearly resonate with the humiliation and torture of these women at the hands of the police. Violent material practices of stigmatisation are not only historically entrenched forms of race–class–caste dehumanisation but are 'live' practices in the contemporary world. I particularly wanted to stress that the stigmatising classificatory systems which undergird the Indian social hierarchies are 'not based on the self-representation of the castes in question' but are derived 'from the worldview of native elites and colonial ethnographers'.[236] The stigma politics of caste is particularly instructive for understanding the entanglement of stigma power within histories of colonial capitalism.

The caste system continues to have 'buoyant admirers in high places', who now argue that caste describes not discrimination but rather *cultural differences* that form a 'social glue that binds as well as separates people and communities in interesting and, on the whole, positive ways'.[237] For example, when Dalits 'tried to raise caste as an issue at the 2001 World Conference against Racism in Durban', the Indian establishment 'insisted that caste was an "internal matter"', criticising 'international do-gooders' for 'misconceptions' and for interfering in Indian affairs.[238] In a statement to the BBC, India's junior foreign minister, Omar Abdullah, was quoted as saying that 'condemning the caste system would equate casteism with racism, which makes India a racist country, which we are not'.[239] In defence of caste, the Indian government showcased 'theses by well-known sociologists who argued at length that the practice of caste was not the same as racial discrimination, and that caste was not the same as race'.[240] The 'cultural thesis' of caste continues to be employed by Indian elites, who argue that condemnations of the caste system are 'political correctness gone mad'.

In 2014, Hindu-nationalist Prime Minister Narendra Modi (2014–present) and the right-wing Bharatiya Janata Party (BJP) assumed control of the Indian government. Modi was re-elected in a landslide victory in 2019. The power base of BJP is firmly anchored in upper-caste Hindu support, and pursues purist caste Hindu policies, an ideology of *Hindutva* (Hindu-ness). It is in effect the political arm of a proto-fascistic paramilitary organisation called the Rashtriya Swayamsevak Sangh (RSS).[241] As Priyamvada Gopal notes, 'Modi was a leading activist' for the 'secretive and militaristic' RSS: an organisation that 'on a good day, looks like the British National party but can operate more like Nazi militias'.[242] In ways akin to other twenty-first-century far-right and ethno-nationalist movements in Europe and North America, this stigma politics exploits and generates divisions between different factions of Indian's poorest communities; this includes both ritual performances of Dalit inclusion in the project of Hindu nationalism, and the vilification of Muslims (and other non-Hindus). It is well documented, for example, that the RSS 'is responsible for vicious attacks on Christians, murdering missionaries and calling for Muslims to choose between Pakistan and the graveyard'.[243]

Since Modi came to power, incidents of communal violence (violence across caste, religious or ethnic lines) have increased exponentially, especially against Muslims.[244] Notably, Modi was the Chief Minister of Gujarat in 2002, when widespread riots against Muslims broke out in the region, which saw the mass beatings, rapes and killings of Muslims by Hindu extremists. It is estimated that 2,000 people died and many more were injured in this violence.[245] Evidence of the involvement of police and government officials in these riots has led to claims that this was a state-sponsored pogrom against Muslims. Both RSS and BJP members were named in reports filed by eyewitnesses after the riots.

As I completed this chapter, the Modi-led Indian government was busy further tearing up the promises and protections enshrined in the Indian Constitution of 1947. In August 2019, the Indian government took direct administrative control over the predominately Muslim states of Jammu and Kashmir, a process which has seen 7 million people effectively caged into the region, with all communications with the outside world cut off.[246] In short, a massive new state-led colonial capitalist enclosure of land and people is underway. The long history of Hindu-supremacist caste stigma politics cemented under British rule continues to play a pivotal role in legitimating violence and dispossession in the India.

Connected histories of stigma power

Stigma is an ancient practice, and the word originated to describe tattooing for penal purposes, words, marks and images etched into the skin against your will to denote an offence or crime and to signify a permanently degraded social status. By unpicking some threads from the vast global history of penal stigma, my aim in this chapter has been to underscore the ways in which ancient Graeco-Roman practices of penal stigmatisation have not only persisted but have been deployed, over many centuries, as terrorising governmental technologies. One argument of *Stigma* is that the penal function of stigma persists not only within the etymology of the word, but within contemporary forms of social discipline and exploitation.

Understanding stigma as a socio-political calligraphy of subjection is central to the reconceptualisation of stigma in this book. Of course, the meaning and purpose of penal tattooing and related practices of stigmatising marking, and the violence with which these marks are inscribed, changes over time and in place. The class-based systems of indentured pauper labour in eighteenth-century England, caste-based penal labour systems in eighteenth-century colonial India, and the racialised dehumanisation of enslaved people in eighteenth-century colonial plantations are not equivalent phenomena, but they are nevertheless connected systems of oppression and exploitation.

Jeremy Bentham's eighteenth-century proposals to 'colonise at home' through the enclosure of land and the development of a prison-plantation system for farming England's paupers, plans he first hatched while managing a serf labour force on a Russian colonial estate, is one amongst many examples of the ways in which the emergence of capitalism as a world system saw, over many centuries, a global traffic in stigmatising practices, policies, laws for the expropriation (and reproduction) of labour power.[247]

Through a focus on penal stigma, the intention has been to draw out threads of connection between some of the practices of dehumanisation which were central to the constitution of colonial capitalist modernity. Indeed, one of my motivations for reconceptualising stigma as a form of power is a concern with thinking about the *intersections* between different forms of stigmatisation. To develop a new understanding of stigma as 'a conglomerate of sociopolitical relations that discipline humanity into full humans, not-quite-humans and nonhumans' in order to trouble the naturalised hierarchies of person value upon which patriarchal, capitalist, racist and disablist systems of exploitation depend.[248] What is at stake in stigma is how, as Stuart Hall puts it, 'systems of classification become the objects of the disposition of power'.[249]

Holding to a reading of stigma as punitive practices of bodily inscription is instructive, for these genealogies allows us to rethink stigma from the outside in, retraining our gaze upwards, onto the social, political and economic function of practices of stigmatisation. Certainly, in re-coupling the concept of stigma to histories of capitalism and colonialism, what we gain sight of is stigmacraft: the mechanisms through which stigma is produced, and the processes through which it becomes attached to bodies (and places), by whom, and for whose gain. What emerges from this chapter is a new understanding of stigma as a technique of social classification, a governmental strategy of social sorting, a mechanism through which inequalities are inscribed and materialised – a process Frantz Fanon termed the 'epidermalization' of inferiority.[250] In the following chapters I will further unwind some of these threads of connection.

Chapter 2

From stigma power
to black power

Long we've borne the nation's shame.

John Thompson, 'Exhortation', 1933[1]

*I am black. I know that. I also know that while I am black
I am a human being, and therefore I have the right to go into
any public place.*

Stokely Carmichael, *Black Power*, Berkeley, 1966[2]

In January 1960, a black teenager called Joseph McNeil travelled back from a Christmas visit with his family in New York to North Carolina Agricultural and Technical State University (known as A&T) in Greensboro.[3] When McNeil got back to campus he described the bus journey to his friends: 'In Philadelphia, I could eat anywhere in the bus station. By Maryland, that had changed; by the time I arrived in Richmond, Virginia I was refused a hotdog at a food counter reserved for whites … It was a degrading experience; three hours ago I was a human being … three hours later … some kind of pariah.'[4] Travelling from the Northern to the Southern states in 1960 meant crossing, in Erving Goffman's terms, from one social interaction order into another.[5] Arriving in the South in

1960 meant immersion in the spatial politics of white supremacy, manifest in the Jim Crow signs that segregated social spaces, and in the unspoken 'customs', rules, rituals and codes 'designed to degrade and divide'.[6]

Jim Crow originated as a stigma term for African Americans, and evolved into a shorthand for state-level and local laws which enforced racial segregation in the Southern states of the US after the civil war and the formal end of slavery in 1865.[7] By 1960 the Jim Crow era 'of institutionalized violence' had lasted for close to a century.[8]

McNeil and three teenage friends, Franklin McCain, David Richmond and Jibreel Khazan,[9] had spent the evenings of their first term at university talking long into the night about their heroes, Gandhi, Langston Hughes and Martin Luther King, about the failures of the civil rights movement to effect meaningful change and about the quotidian humiliations of living under white supremacy. Furious after his degrading bus journey, McNeil persuaded his friends to action.

On 1 February, the four went into the Woolworth's store on South Elm Street in Greensboro and sat down at the 'Whites only' lunch counter.[10] They asked for coffee. The waitress refused to serve them, saying, 'We don't serve Negroes here'.[11] The police were called, an officer arrived: 'He took his knife stick out. He took his billy club and began to hit it on his hand.'[12] Taking their place in a long history of Southern freedom fighters, the four refused to move from their seats.

The Greensboro four returned to Woolworths lunch counter every day that week, accompanied by growing numbers of students from A&T, Bennett College (a black liberal arts college for women) and Dudley High School (then a segregated black school). By 6 February, 1,000 students were sitting in at Greensboro Woolworths lunch counter. These initially small-scale challenges to segregation escalated into the largest black resistance movement in the history of the United States.

The protests garnered extensive national television news coverage. By 1958, over 80 per cent of American homes had a television set, and by 1960 the use of 16mm film and the development of wireless audio recorders transformed the ability of television journalists 'to capture volatile demonstrations as they unfolded'.[13] As a consequence of this rapidly growing television audience, and technical advances in shooting news footage, 'the sit-ins provided the nation with a unique experiment in moral theatre, where black protestors (at times with white allies) non-violently withstood verbal and physical abuse'.[14] Anne Moody, then a sociology student at Tougaloo College, described the scene at a sit-in at a Woolworth's lunch counter in Jackson, Mississippi:

> The white students started chanting all kinds of anti-Negro slogans. We were called a little bit of everything. The rest of the seats except the three we were occupying had been roped off to prevent others from sitting down. A couple of the boys took one end of the rope and made it into a hangman's noose. Several attempts were made to put it around our necks. The mob started smearing us with ketchup, mustard, sugar, pies, and everything on the counter. [...] a Negro high school boy sat down next to me. [...] the word 'nigger' was written on his back with red spray paint.[15]

Being black in the United States in 1960 was to be 'smeared with the stigma of "racial inferiority"'.[16] By putting their bodies in white-only spaces, these young people sought to dramatise 'the studied humiliations' of Jim Crow.[17] Protesting against the political and economic terrorism of white supremacy came at a price; people were heckled, intimidated, beaten, arrested and expelled from schools, colleges and jobs. As then student activist (and later sociology professor) Joyce Ladner notes: 'It was very, very difficult to continue because the local police and all the towns had almost crushed us. ... They murdered people, they beat people.'[18] What motivated young people to participate in the face of these 'terrible beatings, brutalities' was often a deeply personal need to express the anguish of living with anti-black racism.[19] These 'subversive demands for a dignified life free from harassment' were acts of resistance against what Malcolm X described as the 'psychological and physical mutilation that is an everyday occurrence in our lives'.[20] As McCain reflects: 'It really started out as a personal thing ... we didn't like the idea of not having dignity and respect ... and decided it was really up to us to find a solution to this thing we were suffering with.'[21] McCain described the Woolworths protest as a reparative act: 'Almost instantaneously after sitting down on a simple dumb stool, I felt so relieved, I felt so clean ... a feeling of total freedom.'[22] Similarly, when Jibreel Khazan was asked what moved him to act, he replied: 'Something had to be done to remove the stigma.'[23]

Two months after Greensboro electrified the civil rights movement from below, the formation of the Student Nonviolent Coordinating Committee (SNCC) saw young people's actions against racial segregation extended to 'Freedom Rides' which challenged segregation on interstate travel, and staged kneel-ins at segregated churches, sleep-ins at segregated motels, swim-ins at segregated pools, wade-ins at segregated beaches, read-ins at segregated libraries, play-ins at segregated parks, watch-ins at segregated cinemas and theatres, wait-ins at housing developments, chain-ins at city halls and rent strikes. By the spring of 1960 it was estimated that 50,000 people had participated. By 1963, 'the southern struggle had grown from a modest group of black students demonstrating at one lunch-counter to the largest mass movement for racial reform and civil rights in the 20th century'.[24]

Struggles in the interaction order

In the midst of this burst of political resistance against the violent regimes of racial stigma and segregation of Jim Crow, Erving Goffman wrote his influential book *Stigma: Notes on the Management of a Spoiled Identity* (1963).

What distinguishes Erving Goffman's contribution to sociology is his career-long focus on 'social interaction', which he defined as 'social situations ... in which two or more individuals are physically in one another's response presence'.[25] In 'The Interaction Order' (1982), his posthumously published Presidential Address to the American Sociology Association, Goffman lists the kinds of everyday places he was interested in studying: 'a local bar, a small shop floor, a domestic kitchen ... factories, airports, hospitals, and public thoroughfares'.[26] Goffman's approach involved observing how people interact with each other in these spaces and what this revealed about the rules, norms and conventions of social life. Those familiar with Goffman's oeuvre will be reminded of his dramaturgical understanding of the interaction order as 'a natural theater', with a front and back stage, in which people perform social roles.[27]

Given his lifelong interest in studying how society works and coheres through social interactions, one might have thought that Goffman would have been interested in the direct and open challenges to (racist) laws, rules and norms of social interaction instigated by young people like the Greensboro Four which were taking place in bars and cafes, buses, shops, schools, universities, workplaces and public streets across the US in the 1960s. After all, the grassroots struggles that characterised this period were taking place within the very kinds of behavioural settings and involved conflicts in the very kinds of service transactions which were, ostensibly, at the centre of his sociological interest. Black citizens were refusing to 'go along with current interaction arrangements' and were revolting against the stigmatised 'social roles' they had been assigned.[28] However, while Goffman acknowledges that 'questions do arise when we consider the fact that there are categories of persons – in our own society very broad ones – whose members constantly pay a very considerable price for their interactional existence',[29] he states that his approach is not 'informed by a concern over the plight of disadvantaged groups'.[30] What is so striking about this statement is that Goffman's career as a sociologist spanned some of the most tumultuous decades of resistance by 'disadvantaged groups' to the dominant social order in US history – including black people, women, disabled people, so-called 'mad' people, lesbian women and gay men.

Between 1960 and 1963 Goffman was teaching a course called 'Deviance and Social Control' at the University of Berkeley in California, Goffman's book on stigma was composed in part from the lectures he wrote for this course. While teaching at Berkeley, Goffman would have been acutely aware of the black freedom struggles that were exploding all around in 'sit-ins, marches, protest rallies and urban upheavals'.[31] As indicated, television footage of 'chanting demonstrators being sprayed by fire hoses and attacked by dogs, freedom riders being abused, sit-in participants being taunted or beaten, and small black children requiring military escorts to enter public schools' made for powerful viewing in this period.[32] Further, in solidarity with Southern sit-in movements, the 'pernicious de facto segregation of the Urban North' was being openly contested in states like California.[33] From the spring of 1960, Berkeley students were picketing hotels and shops which were known to practise racial discrimination in their employment practices.[34] This anti-racist politics leaked into Goffman's classroom, as Gary Marx, a student in Goffman's 1961 'Deviance and Social Control' class recalls:

At the end of the last class session a black student said, 'This is all very interesting Professor Goffman, but what's the use of it for changing the conditions you describe?' Goffman was visibly shaken. He stood up, slammed shut the book he had open on the desk and said, 'I'm not in that business' and stormed out of the room.[35]

In what follows, I examine what happens to Goffman's account of stigma when we take seriously the question of this unnamed black student: what's the use of it for changing the conditions you describe?[36] I am guided also by Jibreel Khazan's clarion call for something 'to be done to remove the stigma'.[37]

Social relations without power relations

In the opening pages of *Stigma: Notes on the Management of a Spoiled Identity*, Goffman offers a working definition of stigma as: 'an attribute that is deeply discrediting' and 'the situation of the individual who is disqualified from full social acceptance'.[38] Goffman roots his definition of stigma in his existing understanding of social identities as 'perspectives' produced in interactional settings. What he means by this is that people acquire stigma in their exchanges with other people – be this a look, a glance, a comment or a more overt form of discrimination such as name-calling. So while stigma might appear to be 'natural', as emanating from the body of the stigmatised, and while stigma might be experienced as an automatic response (for example to somebody who is physically disfigured), for Goffman stigma describes a social relation between people. In short, stigma is not a fixed property of a person, but is produced between people in social settings. The attribution of stigma is a socially conditioned response to somebody who is perceived to deviate, whether through their appearance or their behaviour, from accepted social norms, standards and ideals.

This is much like a classically liberal nineteenth-century definition of stigma. For example, in his *English Synonyms Explained* (1816), George Crabb defines stigma as follows: 'A stigma is what falls upon a person in the judgement of others; it is the black mark which is set upon a person by the public, and is consequently the strongest of all *marks*, which everyone most dreads and every good man seeks least to observe.'[39]

What Goffman adds to this nineteenth-century definition of stigma is a distinctly twentieth-century social scientific understanding of social norms. For Goffman, a stigma arises (or is attributed) when an individual fails to realise 'a particular norm'. This understanding of stigma pivots on the existence of a social consensus about what is 'normal'. That is, what is or isn't stigmatising is determined by prevailing social norms and attitudes.

For Goffman, society 'coheres' to the extent that members of a given society implicitly understand and share the norms in operation in a given social context. So, in our social interactions, Goffman argues, 'there is some expectation on all sides that those in a given category should not only support a particular norm but also realize it'.[40] We generally understand, for example, how we are supposed to interact with a shopkeeper or a taxi driver. A child quickly learns how they are expected to interact with others in a school classroom. We implicitly understand the social roles in place in a given setting, and what role we are supposed to play therein.

Stigma not only describes a relation between people, but also a relation of self to self. Goffman suggests that it is through processes of socialisation that an individual 'learns and incorporates the stand-point of the normal' and in so doing learns how they are likely to be placed in a stratified social order of normal–

stigma positionalities; for example, a person with an attribute which is stigmatising, such as a speech impediment, most likely knows in advance of an interaction how they might be perceived by others. That is, people judge themselves against an incorporated norm and come to anticipate 'the standards against which they fall short'.[41]

Where do these norms come from? Again, Goffman anticipates but glosses over this question, stating in the opening pages of *Stigma: Notes on the Management of a Spoiled Identity* that: 'Society establishes the means of categorizing persons and the complement of attributes felt to be ordinary and natural for members of these categories'.[42] Towards the end of his book, he admits that stigmatisation is historically specific in the forms it takes, notes that 'shifts have occurred in the kinds of disgrace that arouse concern' and implicitly acknowledges that stigma can also function 'as a means of formal social control'.[43] However, he expresses little curiosity about how social norms might be challenged or transformed. Rather, he is concerned with detailing the more abstract operations of the system within which face-to-face interactions take place, in smooth or disordered ways. That is, his interest is in *how* social rules work rather than in *what* they proscribe. Hence the challenging question posed to Goffman by his student: how can we use this knowledge to change things?

So while a relational understanding of stigma is at the core of Goffman's account, his understanding of normal–stigma relations is divorced from power relations – both the macro-level structural power relations of, for example, patriarchy, and the power-inflected micro-aggressions of everyday interactions. The critical point is that Goffman's theorisation of stigma as 'a language of relationships' excludes the fact that social relations are always already structured through histories of power (and resistance).

The erasure of the history of penal stigma

It is worth noting at this juncture that Goffman opens *Stigma: Notes on the Management of a Spoiled Identity* with a reference to the ancient penal etymology of stigma, but only in order to swiftly diminish its contemporary relevance. He writes:

> The Greeks, who were apparently strong on visual aids, originated the term stigma to refer to bodily signs designed to expose something unusual and bad about the moral status of the signifier. The signs were cut or burnt into the body and advertised that the bearer was a slave, a criminal, or a traitor – a blemished person, ritually polluted, to be avoided, especially in public places.
>
> Today the term is ... applied more to the disgrace itself than to the bodily evidence of it. Furthermore, shifts have occurred in the kinds of disgrace that arouse concern.[44]

Goffman is right that today the meaning of stigma tends to be used to refer to the state of 'disgrace itself', and to experiences of being stigmatised, rather than the literal violent acts of inscription that the longer etymology suggests. What I want to underscore here is how Goffman contributes to this more passive meaning. For example, if you read the passage above again, you will see how Goffman already diverts attention away from those *doing* the stigmatising – here the slaveholders and tattooists of Ancient Greece. What Goffman obscures, from the very first page of his book on stigma, is an understanding of stigma as a relation of power. In doing so, he conceals the more active purpose that stigmatising classifications serve, namely the function of stigma in the subjugation, exploitation and control of others. That Goffman produced a stigma concept so toothless, and so emptied of power, is, given the history of this concept, an astounding achievement. The sociology of stigma remains caught within this torpid perspective – it is that flat, ahistorical, powerless understanding of stigma which this book seeks to change.

Fredric Jameson suggests that Goffman's suspension of questions of power is deliberate, for his ambition is 'to evolve abstractions which hold for all social situations', rather than to develop an understanding which is 'concrete and historically determinate'.[45] It is possible to read power back into Goffman, and indeed this is what many social science scholars who draw on his stigma concept have subsequently done, for example by thinking about stigma more explicitly as a form of oppression or discrimination. However, it is the contention of this chapter that interrogating Goffman's account in more detail is important if we are to decolonise the stigma concept, and in doing so push past some of the prevailing limitations in research and social action around stigma.

Atrocity tales: Goffman's methods

Despite his career-long concern with social interaction, *Stigma: Notes on the Management of a Spoiled Identity* is not grounded in empirical research, as are some of Goffman's earlier studies such as *Asylums* (1961), or his PhD research in a Shetland Islands community which formed the basis of *Presentation of Self in Everyday Life* (1956).[46] Indeed, despite being recognised as 'one of the founding figures of microsociology', and despite his self-presentation as a pioneer of observational methods, his 'links to both ethnography and empiricism are rather tenuous, since he rarely engaged in traditional fieldwork and drew on both fictional literary texts and fabricated anecdotes for his evidence'.[47]

Goffman states that his objective in *Stigma: Notes on the Management of a Spoiled Identity* is to explore what a burgeoning psychological literature on stigma – but 'especially popular work' –

might 'yield for sociology'.[48] As Heather Love details, it transpires from his footnotes and references that what Goffman means by 'popular work' is memoirs and biographies, letters and newspaper articles, 'lightly fictionalized [medical] case histories, human interest stories, and counterfactuals'.[49] Indeed, *Stigma* opens with an epigraph, a fictional letter from a sixteen-year-old girl who was 'born without a nose' to a newspaper 'agony aunt', which Goffman has taken from Nathanael West's dark comic depression-era novel *Miss Lonelyhearts* (1933). Goffman's use of this fictional epigraph has been interpreted as signalling compassion.[50] However, given West's 'ironic' and 'dispassionate' treatment of 'emotionally and politically charged material' in this novel, it seems more likely that Goffman is making a playful statement about his own cool and detached approach to stigma.[51] Indeed, I would argue that his use of this epigraph is best understood as a dry joke: the punchline being, as Goffman will reveal at the end of his book, that 'we normals' (as he calls his readers) might, just like the antihero in West's novel, find ourselves switched into the role of the stigmatised.

Stigma: Notes on the Management of a Spoiled Identity draws together a heterogeneous and eclectic archive of writing about blindness, facial deformities, cripples, amputees, alcoholics, gentleman criminals, ex-cons, prostitutes, homosexuals, the 'mentally deficient', 'the mad', anti-Semitism and anti-black racism. Goffman describes his reading method as 'an exercise' in 'marking off the material on stigma from neighbouring facts' and 'showing how this material can be economically described within a singular conceptual schema'.[52] Love argues that this 'marking off' of context produces what she approvingly calls 'thin description'.[53] What this amounts to in practice is that there often no discernible difference in how Goffman deploys, for example, an extract from a clinical account of a facial disfigurement, or a personal memoir or fictional account on the same topic. Certainly, he rarely introduces the authors of the materials he quotes from, but rather substitutes particular accounts of stigma in his text with abstract 'stigma figures', such as 'a blind writer', 'a cripple', 'a prostitute', 'a homosexual', 'a Negro' or 'a Jew', an abstraction which, as Susan Schweik argues, produces an effect of 'impartial realism'.[54]

What is veiled through this method of abstraction are the textual techniques, the particular genres and aesthetics of the writing he draws upon, and the multiple perspectives encoded within these texts. Most significantly, in suppressing 'neighbouring facts' Goffman erases the original intentions which might have motivated what is often confessional writing about lived experiences of stigma. This point is underlined by his acerbic characterisation of some of the literature he draws upon as 'atrocity tales' written by 'heroes of adjustment' and 'stigma professionals' who seek to 'present the case for the stigmatised'.[55]

In short, Goffman draws on the writing of people who have experienced stigma but fails to engage with the authors of these literatures as knowledge producers. Kristie Dotson describes this method of abstraction as 'an active practice of unknowing' which appropriates, erases and silences the other, committing what she terms an epistemic violence[56] (a theme I will return to in Chapter 5).

It is important to note at this juncture that Goffman's *Stigma* was written during a resurgence in confessional writing in US and wider European culture. Indeed, this 'confessional turn' was central to social and political struggles of the period, beginning with the civil rights movement and extending to feminist, queer, disability and anti-psychiatry movements (Goffman's book *Asylums* played a central role in the latter). Goffman acknowledges the 'current literary fashion' for confessional writing, self-help literature and 'advice to the stigmatised' in which 'deeply hidden sores are touched upon and examined'.[57] He cites the writing of James Baldwin in a footnote as an example of 'good material of this kind in regard to

Negroes' but side-lines any of the reformist, consciousness-raising and/or political intentions of these 'atrocity tales'.[58]

More than this, by transforming the authors of stigma experiences into abstract figures – such as 'Negroes' in the aforementioned footnote – Goffman mimics the dehumanising practices which the concept of stigmatisation describes. This nicely illustrates how stigma is actually a relation characterised by the relative power of 'the normal' to silence, constrain and misrepresent 'the other' through the attribution of stigma. The argument I am signalling here is that reconceptualising stigma as a political economy of dehumanisation and devaluation requires critical methods which are rooted not in the imagined 'neutral' and 'detached' observational methods of the social scientist, but in people's knowledge of and struggles against the social structures that, as Du Bois puts it, produce them as 'markedly inferior'.[59]

The stigma of disability

While this chapter focuses on racial stigma (racism), I want to note at this juncture the understanding of stigma developed by disabled people in the early 1960s. In particular, I want to draw attention to the ground-breaking collection *Stigma: The Experience of Disability* (1966), a series of autobiographical essays written by physically disabled people and edited by activist and writer Paul Hunt. What Hunt develops, through the curation and editing of this collection of essays, is a multi-perspectival account of stigma from below. Indeed, in his contribution to this collection, 'A Critical Condition', Hunt argues, in a thinly veiled critique of Goffman, that stigma should not be theorised from the perspective of so-called normals but from 'the uncomfortable, subversive position from which we act as a living reproach to any scale of values that puts attributes or possessions before the person'.[60]

In this essay, Hunt develops an understanding of stigma as a technology of disablement which stratifies people along a differential axis of in/humanity. Hunt's concept of stigma emerged from his concern with the ways in which stigma legitimated the segregation of disabled people from mainstream society. It is stigma, he argues, which allows disabled people to be perceived as 'unfortunate', 'useless', 'tragic' and 'abnormal' and thus undeserving of the rights or considerations of 'normal' able-bodied citizens. Indeed, Hunt composed *Stigma: The Experience of Disability* in a residential home in England where he was incarcerated against his will.

> All my adult life has been spent in institutions amongst people who, like myself, have severe and often progressive physical disabilities. We are paralysed and deformed, most of us in wheelchairs, either as the result of accident or of diseases like rheumatoid arthritis, multiple sclerosis, muscular dystrophy, cerebral palsy and polio.[61]

Hunt's understanding of stigma as a political economy of disability resonates with the longer penal history of stigma, as cruel systems of classification which mark out categories of people in order to impede their freedom and mobility. Further, his understanding of the relationship between stigma and segregation – for his was an anti-segregationist abolitionist disability politics – was directly inspired by the US Civil Rights Movement. Hunt notes that the 'injustice and brutality suffered by so many because of racial tension makes our troubles as disabled people look very small', yet the dehumanisation of disabled people 'stirs in me a little of the same anger' which 'James Baldwin reveals in *The Fire Next Time*': a rather different reading of Baldwin and his centrality to freedom struggles against stigma than that suggested by Goffman.[62]

James Baldwin's *The Fire Next Time* was, like Goffman's *Stigma*, first published in 1963. It is a defining, personal and passionate account of the psycho-social impact of living with anti-black racism in mid-twentieth-century America; 'the indescribable struggle to defeat the stratagems that white Americans have used, and use to deny him his humanity'.[63] You can hear the influence of Baldwin throughout Hunt's *Stigma: The Experience of Disability*. As Hunt concludes: 'we who are disabled are deeply affected by the assumptions of our uselessness that surround us. But it is vital that we should not accept this devaluation of ourselves'.[64]

While I cannot do justice to Hunt's pivotal contribution to disability activism and scholarship here, it is important to note the foundational role his conceptualisation of stigma as a pivotal force in the social segregation of disabled people played in the subsequent social movements of disabled people. Hunt was central to the development of the 'social model' of disability: in which disability is understood as a social problem, rather than a consequence of individual impairments. The policy and attitudinal changes which followed in the wake of disabled people's movements for equality have transformed millions of lives across the world. Sadly, it is Goffman's and not Hunt's book which is the most cited text in disability studies today.[65]

Professor normal

The problems I have identified with Goffman's methods, his suppression of questions of power, and his silencing of the perspectives of the 'stigma knowers' he draws upon are embedded within the very structure of his stigma concept. To further illustrate this, I want to return briefly to the status of norms in *Stigma: Notes on the Management of a Spoiled Identity*. As feminist, queer and critical race theorists have variously elaborated, it is often by unpacking norms that we get to the crux of the problem, the problem here being how Goffman's 'neutral' sociological account of stigma in 1963 reproduces what Du Bois described as the 'National Stigma' of racism.[66]

Goffman uses the terms 'norms', 'normal' and those he designates as 'we normals' in multiple ways. At some points norms seem to designate ideals 'and standards'; at others norms refer to foundational social rules that precede all social interactions; and at others, norms are imagined as more akin to perceptual frames – the social optics – through which we perceive others. In all these cases, norms describe accepted rules, conventions and ways of seeing. Indeed, Goffman is emphatic that 'a necessary condition for social life is the sharing of a single set of normative expectations by all participants'.[67]

The normal human being is also used to mark the authorial position of Goffman, the 'neutral' sociological observer, in the text, while 'we normals' is employed several times to address the imagined readers of his book. What 'we', his readers, are invited to imagine we have in common with the authorial 'I' is a shared normality. So while, as noted above, Goffman's account of stigma draws on the experiential knowledge of stigmatised people, he mediates this stigma knowledge through the perspective of 'we normals'. As he writes, 'norms regarding social identity pertain to the kinds of role repertoires or profiles *we feel* it permissible for any given individual to sustain'.[68]

Goffman justifies grounding his definition of stigma in 'the notion of the "normal human being"' by arguing, firstly, that this is 'the basic imaginary' through which 'laymen currently conceive of themselves', and secondly, that we live in rational societies characterised by 'the tendency of large-scale bureaucratic organizations, such as the nation state, to treat all members in some respects as equal'.[69] Yet as he wrote this, millions of American citizens were explicitly contesting 'the facts' of this equality, and 'the forms' that 'a normal human being' could take. As we have established,

Goffman was aware of ongoing social and political challenges to white normativity (white supremacy), but refused to dwell on the politics of stigma.

Unsurprisingly, and perhaps accurately in the context of the United States in the early 1960s, Goffman reveals that the singular norm he is writing about (and from the perspective of) is 'that of the young, married, white, urban, northern' male: 'There is only one complete unblushing male in America', he argues, and '[e]very American male tends to look out upon the world' from the perspective of heterosexual able-bodied white masculinity.[70] Goffman describes this white male norm as the 'general identity-values' of American society, adding that this ideal identity casts a 'shadow on the encounters encountered everywhere in daily living'.[71]

Goffman doesn't reveal the figure of heterosexual able-bodied white masculinity as the measure of 'general identity-values' until the reader reaches the final chapters of *Stigma*. However, once the abstract normal collapses into the particularity of this figure, he grants us a key with which to unravel 'the normal perspective' through and from which he has produced his account of stigma. Given the strictures of this ideal human, people's potential to fail this norm, and be stigmatised as a consequence, is extensive. Goffman's cast of 'stigma figures' includes the physically disabled, people with 'blemishes of individual character' such as 'weak will, domineering or unnatural passions, treacherous, mental disorder, imprisonment, addiction, alcoholism, homosexuality, unemployment, suicidal attempts', and extending to 'radical political behavior' and those tainted by what he terms 'tribal stigma of race, nation, and religion'.[72] Perhaps Goffman was reflecting on his own Jewish ethnicity, but it seems more likely he was reflecting on the stigma of being black in the United States, when he added that 'tribal stigma ... can be transmitted through lineages and equally contaminate all members of a family'.[73]

Goffman's figures for the racially stigmatised include the 'educated northern Negro' who finds themselves mistaken for a Southern negro, 'urban lower class Negroes', 'an apprehended Negro', 'black skinned Negroes who have never passed publicly' (it is unclear here if Goffman means people who fail to pass as white, or as white enough to be considered fully human) and 'a passing Negro and the white girl he wants to marry'.[74] Goffman also comments on how skin-lightening products are fraudulently sold as a remedy for the stigma of black skin, and reflects on the ambivalent social position of 'the light-skinned Negro' who 'can never be sure what the attitude of a new acquaintance will be'.[75]

While Goffman suggests that many stigmas can be successfully concealed or managed, he reflects on the fact that visibly racialised minorities and members of the lower class 'who quite noticeably bear the mark of their status in their speech, appearance, and manner, and who, relative to the public institutions of our society find they are second class citizens' are 'all likely on occasion to find themselves functioning as stigmatized individuals'.[76]

For sure, the version of white normativity which Goffman depicts tallies with accounts such as that of W.E.B. Du Bois, who had argued two decades earlier in *Dusk of Dawn: An Essay Toward an Autobiography of a Race Concept* that being black in America is to be 'badged' by colour, to be marked out 'for discrimination and insult'.[77] However, as Angela Davis argues, living as a person racialised as black in the early 1960s didn't mean being stigmatised 'on occasion'; it meant daily confrontation 'with the realities of racism, not simply as individual acts dictated by attitudinal bias' but with an entire society organised through 'racial terrorism'.[78] Further, unlike his black sociological elders and peers, Goffman offers no account of why 'to be unconditionally "American" is to be white, and to be black is a misfortune', or how historical norms of white supremacy were being challenged as he wrote his book.[79]

Moreover, we reach a major contradiction in Goffman's account of racial stigma when he suggests that there is a natural difference between what he terms the 'congenital' sign of skin colour and imposed social signs such as 'a brand mark or maiming'.[80] Goffman is here not only illustrating existing racism in US society but also normalising racial difference as a 'fact' – a consequence of deeper genetic human difference, rather than an outcome of histories of slavery and colonialism; a history which included, as we have seen, the penal stigmatisation of black bodies through 'branding and maiming', physical stigmata which were later displaced by the stigma of the colour line. Indeed, Goffman's argument that the 'congenital' fact of blackness is 'a permanent part of the person' seems to contradict his argument that 'the normal' and 'the stigmatized' are social roles – and that anybody might find themselves in either role in a given (interactional) context.[81]

It seems that, for Goffman, blackness is a stigma which is impossible to erase; an understanding of blackness which Patricia Williams describes as 'stigma of inferiority that resides not merely in the label or designation of race', but is imagined as 'embodied in black presence'.[82] In this regard, Goffman's figure of the normal human not only describes existing social norms but reproduces what Lewis Gordon describes as 'the in-advance claim of the white world to human status'.[83] Indeed if, as Goffman argues, 'we believe the person with a stigma is not quite human', then black readers of this book will find that they are 'not structurally regarded as human beings' in the context of white society, and further that this dehumanised positionality is their permanent fate.[84]

For many sociologists, what is appealing about Goffman's conceptualisation of stigma is precisely that it is relational, contextual, contingent and historically malleable. However, by taking Goffman 'at his word', I have demonstrated that one of the limitations of his account is that he uses norms to obfuscate and naturalise historical arrangements of power. Further, while Goffman stresses that the 'psychological price' of stigmatisation is 'living a life that can be collapsed at any moment', he offers neither compassion nor space for imagining alternatives to the system of confining and discriminating norms he describes.[85] Rather, he argues that normal and stigmatised people should 'accept' social norms. As he tersely puts it, 'Not doing so, one could hardly get on with the business at hand; one could hardly have any business at hand'.[86] That this is a political recommendation is most evident in one of the final sections of his book, when Goffman makes a series of proposals about how individuals might manage living with stigma. This is one of the few places in the book that Goffman addresses the stigmatised rather than 'we normals'. His proposals to those suffering with stigma are conservative, pragmatic and, given the relational character of his theory of stigma, oddly individualistic.

'Normals', Goffman reassures the stigmatised, 'really mean no harm', and 'should therefore be tactfully helped to act nicely'.[87] He argues that the stigmatised should not contest the norms that produce stigma, but instead develop strategies of stigma management in social settings where stigma might arise. Goffman's proposals for the stigmatised include 'information management', 'the arts of impression management', employing strategies of 'passing and covering', adopting a position of 'tolerance' and refraining 'from pushing claims for acceptance much past the point normals find comfortable'.[88] As he writes, 'When the stigmatized person finds that normals have difficulty in ignoring his failing, he should try to help them and the social situation by conscious efforts to reduce tension'.[89] In the context of Goffman's larger oeuvre, we might understand these proposals on the management of stigma as dramaturgical – in the sense that they offer suggestions to the stigmatised about how to play an assigned social role which minimises the discomfort of 'normals', and in doing so support, rather than challenge, the relations of power inscribed in social norms.

Further, while Goffman cautions that the stigmatised should not 'ingratiatingly act out before normals the full dance of bad qualities imputed to his kind', he also advises they should play the parts society has assigned to them.[90] To this end he quotes the Norwegian writer Finn Carling who, reflecting on his own experience of living with cerebral palsy, notes: 'the cripple has to play the part of the cripple, just as many women have to be what the men expect them to be, just women; and the Negroes often have to act like clowns in front of the "superior" white race, so that the white man shall not be frightened by his black brother'.[91]

What Goffman suggests is that people racialised as black should act in white society in ways which protect white people from what Patricia Williams terms 'the ferocious mythology of blackness ... as the embodiment of inferiority'.[92] In order to decolonise Goffman's stigma concept, it is imperative that we question why he is seemingly so invested in maintaining an arrangement of normal–stigma relations in which only people who are socially marked as white can be normal. We also have to question why Goffman remained so empathically silent about the struggles against anti-black racism which sought to challenge white normativity by disrupting racist norms of social interaction; struggles which were unfolding all around him, including in his own classroom.

'A black boy hacked into a murderous lesson'

Reading Goffman's *Stigma* through the lens of black freedom struggles, it is possible to discern 'the strategies of power that are immanent' within his stigma theory.[93] In effect, by arguing for the management of stigma – that is, for its pacification – Goffman normalises stigma and conceals 'its violent underpinning and periodic atrocities'.[94] From this perspective, Goffman's stigma concept 'is not innocent of politics, but on the contrary, provides epistemic authority' for the suppression of black humanity.[95]

To take just one example, the Greensboro Four and many others amongst the black students, who would follow them in staging sit-in protests across the segregated Southern states, were haunted by the lynching of fourteen-year-old Emmett Till in Mississippi in 1955; indeed, Joyce Ladner coined this generation of civil rights activists 'the Emmett Till generation'.[96] Born and raised in Chicago, Till was visiting relatives in the small town of Money, when he allegedly wolf-whistled at a white woman in a grocery store.[97] Seemingly unaware of racist social norms and conventions, 'the subtleties of the Jim Crow Mississippi code of racial etiquette', for this crime of flirtation he was abducted, tortured, maimed and shot.[98] His body was later recovered from the Tallahatchie River.

Till's mother insisted her son's mutilated corpse be displayed in an open coffin in order, in her words, to 'rip the sheets off the state of Mississippi'.[99] However, the terrible violent truth exposed by the circulation of photographs of Till's disfigured body, and the later acquittal of his killers by an all-white jury, left many black teenagers feeling fearful, vulnerable, angry and despairing. For this generation of young black citizens, images of Till's body functioned as both an image of injustice and, as Audre Lorde put it, as a 'veiled warning' – a 'black boy hacked into a murderous lesson'.[100]

The death of Till, the publicity surrounding his death and the acquittal of his killers exposed how the violence of white normativity cast a long shadow over black lives in the 1960s. Franklin McCain described Till's death as a revelation which left his fifteen-year-old self in a suicidal depression: 'there seemed no prospect for dignity or respect as a young black man'.[101] This was a context in which black people daily negotiated interactional settings where not playing your socially assigned role as a racially stigmatised person, failing to manage your racial stigma appropriately by reducing tensions in your interactions with white people, could lead to your death. As Jibreel Khazan recalled, this murder revealed 'what happened if we broke the code. If we spoke out of turn, we too could die like Emmett Till'.[102] The haunting of this generation by the lynching of Emmett Till illustrates how stigma functions to confine, segregate and subjugate black lives. However, it also reveals how the violence of being stigmatised can become politicised and act as a catalyst for social change.

Joyce Ladner, a leading civil rights activist, describes how as a teenager she kept a scrapbook of cuttings about Emmett Till which she would regularly weep over in her bedroom. As she states: 'That was the image for our generation that galvanised our generation, we all saw that image on the front cover of *Jet* magazine ... Every black southerner for sure had seen that photograph and it was like the clarion call for action ... when we got older we were going to avenge his death.'[103] Ladner would later bring this activism to bear on the discipline of sociology itself, laying bare, in her edited volume *The Death of White Sociology* (1973), the white norms and racial bias at the heart of sociological knowledge.[104]

Stigma as struggle

Jodi Melamed has detailed the ways in which seemingly neutral or objective forms of liberal knowledge production, typified by mid-twentieth-century social science, operate to naturalise and institutionalise existing relations of power.[105] These epistemologies work through producing and classifying human differences in ways which secure particular hierarchies of human value. By way of contrast, black sociologists of stigma, from Du Bois onwards, developed historical and contingent understanding of racial differences as forged within histories of slavery and colonialism, and cemented by the monstrous *abnormality* of ideologies of white supremacy.

Resituating Goffman's stigma concept within the context of black freedom struggles against 'the legal stigma of second class citizenship' has revealed how his understanding of stigma proceeds from what was then, as now, a deeply contested understanding of white proto-typicality and black inhumanity.[106] While Goffman's stigma concept uncouples the perception of black skin as a stigma from histories of slavery, black freedom struggles remind us that racism is an historical practice 'centuries in the making';[107] a regime of seeing, a 'stigma-optics', crafted in order to deny black people personhood.

The sociologist Karen Fields and the historian Barbara Fields describe this process as 'racecraft' – namely the 'trick of transforming racism into race, leaving black persons in view while removing white persons from the stage. To spectators deceived by the trick, segregation seemed to be a property of black people, not something white people imposed on them'.[108] By insisting on their *equal humanity*, the freedom fighters of the 1960s sought to denaturalise stigma, expose the race trick, and in so doing 'win recognition as human outside of the restrictive terms set by the racial order'.[109] As Stokely Carmichael put it in his 'Black Power' speech to students at Berkeley in October 1966, 'we are now engaged in a psychological struggle in this country … The question is, "How can white society begin to move to see black people as human beings?"'[110]

By targeting the interaction order, the black power movement made visible the concrete ways in which white supremacy invaded 'the lives of Black people on an infinite variety of levels'.[111] As the civil rights activist James Boggs noted, this was unlike the preceding Civil Rights Movement of the 1950s in that 'it aimed at creating the issue, provoking it'.[112] In order to challenge what Du Bois termed 'the stigmata of degradation', young people broke the social rules around segregation and refused to play the roles assigned to them.[113] Reflecting on what motivated him to join the sit-in movement as a teenager in 1960, Stokely Carmichael recalls how: 'when I saw those kids on TV, getting back up on the lunch counter stools after being knocked off them, sugar in their eyes, catsup in their hair – well, something happened to me. Suddenly I was burning'.[114] As Abdelmalek Sayad notes: 'Black American sociology and colonial sociology teach that, as a general rule, one form of revolt, and undoubtedly the primary form of revolt against stigmatization … consists in reclaiming the stigma, which then becomes an emblem of [resistance].'[115] Through acts of stigma dramaturgy, the Civil Rights Movement publicised, revolted against and transformed the stigma of blackness into black power.

Stigma after Goffman

In 1963, the year Goffman's *Stigma* was published, the pioneering black sociologist and activist W.E.B. Du Bois died in exile in Accra, Ghana – the US government had confiscated his passport. After Du Bois' death, 'Maya Angelou led a group of Americans and Ghanaians to the U.S. embassy in Accra, carrying torches and placards reading "Down with American Apartheid" and "America, a White Man's Heaven and a Black Man's Hell"'.[116] A day later, at the March on Washington, Roy Wilkins, leader of the National Association for the Advancement of Colored People (NAACP), led a minute's silence in remembrance of Du Bois. As he stated to the hundreds of thousands of marchers, 'his was the voice that was calling to you to gather here today in this cause. If you want to read something that applies to 1963 go back and get a volume of *The Souls of Black Folk* by Du Bois, published in 1903'.[117] While Goffman didn't reference him, Du Bois was the first theorist of stigma power, identifying not only 'the problem of the Twentieth Century as the problem of the color-line', but detailing how this line was enforced, reproduced and legitimated by the 'systematic humiliation' of black lives.[118]

As Les Back and Maggie Tate have argued, 'Sociological segregation weakens the field as a whole, not only for those to whom it offers a racially unequal place at the table of ideas. It diminishes the intellectual lifeblood of the discipline itself and its capacity to comprehend the key problems of the twenty-first century'.[119] When Goffman was teaching at Berkeley, this segregation was challenged by black students (and this challenge to the racial segregation of knowledge continues today in the global 'Why is My Curriculum White?' movement). In the spring of 1961, a group of Berkeley students formed a reading group, the Afro-American Association, which crafted an alternative 'Black Curriculum' featuring the work of scholars such as Du Bois, Frantz Fanon, James Baldwin, E. Franklin Frazier and Kwame Nkrumah.[120]

This reading group soon extended its activities into the wider community, running a weekly radio programme that attracted other Bay area college and university students, including Huey Newton and Bobby Seale, who went on to form the Black Panthers. At the same time, in segregated black universities in the Southern states, such as Tougaloo College in Mississippi, sociology students like Anne Moody, Joyce Ladner and their professors became active participants in the sit-in movements. Indeed, Jibreel Khazan of the Greensboro Four was also a sociology major. Together these students, activists and scholars were busy producing sociological knowledge about stigma, and developing anti-racist strategies, which included the psychologically reparative work of protest itself.

Of central importance to these black freedom struggles was Carmichael and Hamilton's anti-stigma concept of 'Black Power', which reconfigured racial stigma into 'a revolutionary emotion': 'We aim to define and encourage a new consciousness among black people', they wrote, and facilitate 'a sense of peoplehood: pride, rather than shame, in blackness'.[121] The contemporary Black Lives Matter movement marks another resurgent moment in the long history of resistance against the stigma politics of racial capitalism in the United States – a period Michelle Alexander has coined as 'The New Jim Crow'.[122]

Despite the sophisticated understanding of racial stigma developed over a hundred years of black sociological thought, the conceptualisation of stigma in the social sciences has largely ignored this body of knowledge.[123] In seeking to historically resituate Goffman's original account, this chapter has drawn on a wide range of interlocutors working in a black sociological tradition, including Mario Biondi, James Boggs, Stokely Carmichael, Patricia Hill Collins, Angela Davis, Kimberley Dotson, W.E.B. Du Bois, Roderick Ferguson, Frantz Fanon, the Greensboro Four, Paul Gilroy, Lewis Gordon, Charles Hamilton, Harry Haywood, Robin Kelley, Joyce Lamont, Manning Marable, Zine Magubane, Anne Moody, Cedric Robinson, Hortense Spillers, Cornel West, Patricia Williams and Gary Younge. The account of stigma that emerges through this black genealogy of thinking about stigma challenges the individualism of psychological approaches to social problems, exposes the limits of Goffman's white normative perspective, and troubles 'race neutral' forms of interactional analysis. What this scholarship offers in place of a Goffman-esque approach are rich historical, political and economic conceptualisations of stigma as technologies of dehumanisation, and stigma as a form of power that has been collectively resisted from below.

It is the argument of this chapter that bringing racism and anti-racist scholarship to the front and centre of sociological understandings of stigma enriches its utility as an analytic for understanding other forms of 'dehumanisation' – such as casteist, classist, disablist and misogynist practices – which are also grounded in eugenicist and/or essentialist ideologies of human difference.

Chapter 3

The stigma machine of the border

People no more fasten the stigma of race upon themselves than cattle sear the brand into their own flesh.

Barbara Fields and Karen Fields, 2012[1]

Why they put a number on me? Why they call me by a number? We are humans. We have names. Even they wrote numbers on small children's arms.

M., refugee from Syria, 2015.[2]

During 2015, an unprecedented 1.3 million people applied for asylum in the twenty-eight member states of the European Union, Norway and Switzerland. This was 'nearly double the previous high-water mark of approximately 700,000 [asylum] applications in 1992, after the fall of the Iron Curtain and the collapse of the Soviet Union'.[3] Those seeking protection in Europe were largely fleeing wars, conflicts and political oppression in Syria (over 50 per cent), Iraq, Afghanistan and Eritrea. Some arrived via Balkan land routes, but these borders were soon blocked and the vast majority made treacherous Mediterranean Sea crossings. An estimated 3,771 people drowned in the Mediterranean in 2015 alone, evidence of the life-and-death stakes of this journey. In the summer of 2015, newspapers and news websites across the world were filled with photographs of drowned children and people desperately paddling towards shore on overloaded dinghies.

In response to the growing humanitarian crisis in the Mediterranean, the German Office for Migration and Refugees announced on the social media site Twitter on 25 August 2015 that it was 'no longer enforcing #Dublin procedures for Syrian citizens'.[4] What this meant for Syrian refugees on the ground was that if they could navigate a route to Germany, they would be guaranteed at least temporary leave to remain. This triggered 'a million-man march through Europe', as hundreds of thousands of people caught in dire conditions at camps and transit zones across Europe's southern borders made their way north by foot, car, bus and train.[5] It was amidst this intensifying human and political drama that, shortly after midnight on 1 September 2015, two trains drew to a halt in Břeclav, a town in Czechia (the Czech Republic) close to the border with Austria and Slovakia.

Scene one: Břeclav railway station, Břeclav, South Moravia, Czechia, 1 September 2015

At midnight on 1 September 2015, a squad of Czech Alien Police boarded two trains in Břeclav and forcibly removed 214 people (115 men, 38 women and 61 children). The first train had arrived from Vienna shortly before midnight, the second shortly after midnight from Budapest, both bound for Germany. Czech government officials described the passengers it removed from these two trains as '214 illegal migrants'. The vast majority, over 90 per cent, were refugees from Syria. Many of them had survived treacherous sea crossings from Turkey to Greek islands and were just hours away from their German destination when the trains were

Figure 3.1 'Inking refugees': refugees being numbered by Czech border police at Břeclav train station, South Moravia, Czech Republic, 1 September 2015, reprinted with copyright permission.

intercepted by police, who moved through the carriages checking people's documents. All of those without an EU passport or a travel visa that allowed them to be on Czech territory were removed. The state-owned Czech Railways had informed the Czech Alien Police that large numbers of 'migrants' were on the train, which is why the police were waiting for them in such numbers at Břeclav – along with journalists, for as we shall see this was a politically orchestrated event. After escorting people from the trains, some in handcuffs, the police assembled people on the platforms and proceeded to use indelible pens to ink numbers on their arms and wrists.

Kateřina Rendlová, a spokeswoman for the Czech Alien Police, stated that the inking of refugees was a means of keeping a record of family members. 'We also write the code of the train they have arrived on so that we know which country we should return them to within the readmission system', she said, adding, 'We used to put the numbers on a piece of paper but they kept throwing them away'.[6] The refugees were then packed onto buses destined for temporary camps in local school gymnasiums in south Moravia, where officials said they would be processed, before being transferred to remote rural detention centres in Zastávka near Brno, Vyšní Lhoty, north Moravia, and Bělá-Jezová, central Bohemia.

Events at Břeclav were captured by a Czech News Agency photojournalist, Igor Zehl, and were posted on the Associated Press website. There was one photograph in particular which caught the attention of international news editors, an image of a small child sitting on his mother's lap, his face folded into her body, while a Czech policewoman wearing blue plastic gloves writes numbers on his arm. This image was printed in newspapers, published on news websites and shared across social media platforms around the world (see Figure 3.1). This photograph and the news stories that accompanied it aroused an international outcry from human rights organisations for the disturbing associations it elicited with the badging and tattooing of Jews during the Second World War. As Ruth Dureghello, a Jewish community leader in Rome, explained: 'It is an image we cannot bear, which recalls to mind the procedure at the entrance of Nazi extermination camps, when millions of men, women and children were marked with a number, like animals, and they were sent to die.'[7] These allusions to the Nazi holocaust were not lost on far-right activists. Adam Bartoš, the leader of the fascistic Czech National Democracy Movement (český nacionalista), used Facebook to call for 'the Břeclav intruders' to 'be concentrated in Theresienstadt', a former Nazi labour and concentration camp near Prague.[8] As Jan Čulík, editor of the independent Czech news website *Britské listy* and a scholar of Czech society, detailed, these views were symptomatic of rising anti-refugee sentiments in the Czech public sphere in this period.[9] Indeed, it was not just extremist minorities but establishment figures, such as the Czech President Miloš Zeman, who crafted 'mendacious anti-refugee narratives'.[10] As Zeman stated in September 2015: 'I am profoundly convinced that we are facing an organised invasion and not a spontaneous movement of refugees.'[11] Zeman warned the Czech public that refugees were 'Muslim invaders' who might bring infectious diseases into the nation and could harbour sleeper cells of Islamic terrorists.[12] The fear these kinds of official political statements generated was apparent in local responses to the detention of refugees in Břeclav.

On 8 September, 350 people from Břeclav attended a meeting convened by police, the mayor and representatives from the Ministry of the Interior.[13] This meeting was called to allay the fears of local citizens in the face of 'the refugee invasion'. So many turned up to the public meeting that officials had relocate it from the town hall to a local cinema. Officials reassured locals that migrants would be segregated from any contact from local people and policing measures would be robust. 'The conversation', reported a local journalist, 'was refined and quiet. Only occasionally did the audience shout out statements such as: "It's too late. Europe has turned black."'[14]

'Migrants are like cockroaches'

I have researched issues of asylum, detention and immigration for over a decade, but began working on this chapter during the 2015 refugee crisis in Europe. In the years which have immediately followed, state practices of bordering, detention, incarceration have intensified around the world. Indeed, the concentration of people in prisons, cages and camps, and the expulsion of people from state borders, is a signal feature of the current global authoritarian turn

– a turn which has irrevocably shredded post-Second World War international-level agreements around human rights and particularly the rights of people with uncertain legal status, stateless people and refugees. This shift has been most visible in the United States where since 2017 there has been a significant increase in 'mass illegal pushbacks of asylum-seekers at the US–Mexico border', with many 'thousands of illegal family separations', the deliberate and purposeful infliction of extreme suffering and ill-treatment, including torture, and the 'arbitrary and indefinite detention of asylum-seekers, without parole, constituting cruel, inhuman or degrading treatment or punishment (ill-treatment) which is absolutely prohibited in international law'.[15] The flagrant disregard for international law in ostensibly liberal democratic states has arguably legitimated abhorrent and inhuman practices of detention, torture and expulsion elsewhere in the world.

Citizenship regimes around the world are becoming more punitive and exclusionary; for example, it is estimated that 12 million people are currently stateless, one-third of whom are children. People without citizenship live in a state of non-personhood without recourse to basic human rights or governmental protections. Globally, the number of refuges is also rising, in 2017 it was estimated that 65.6 million people were living in contexts of forced displacement, as a consequence of violence and persecution, wars and conflicts and human rights violations.

It is in this broader context that this chapter examines the amplification of stigma politics which accompanies the current authoritarian turn. The mass breaching of international law and human rights regimes we are currently witnessing across the world operates in tandem with, and is lubricated by, stigmatising representational practices which involve the extreme dehumanisation of people; for it is only when publics no longer see those seeking refuge as human beings that state governments can openly and unashamedly engage in practices of segregation, incarceration, expulsion and torture. The forms of dehumanisation this requires pivot on racism: that is, on the radical devaluation of human lives through racist representations of non-citizens and unwanted people as less than human – as waste populations. What I mean by this is that the institution of policies in places such as Europe which, for example, have now made it illegal for humanitarian groups to aid and rescue those drowning in the Mediterranean Sea, requires the activation of stigma power. This involves the crafting, and the accumulation over time, of stories and visual depictions which transform flesh and blood humans into objects and things. For example, in response to desperate scenes of overcrowded boats in the Mediterranean Sea in 2015, the British far-right journalist and media celebrity Katie Hopkins published a newspaper column titled 'Rescue Boats? I'd Use Gunships to Stop Migrants', stating that 'migrants are like cockroaches ... I don't care. Show me pictures of coffins show me bodies floating in water, play violins and show me skinny people looking sad. I still don't care'.[16]

The resurgence of public racism on the scale witnessed in Europe during the 2015 refugee crisis doesn't emerge from nowhere. Racism is historical: that is, it draws its 'narrative energies' from existing grids of associations, from 'semantic and iconic folds' that are deeply etched in the collective memories of people and places.[17] As UN High Commissioner for Human Rights Zeid Ra'ad Al Hussein noted in 2015, the use by commentators like Hopkins of words such as 'cockroaches' to describe refugees arriving in Europe invokes past racial genocides. As Hussein reminded us, the term cockroach was widely employed by the Nazi regime in mid-twentieth-century Europe to dehumanise Jews, and was also used by the perpetrators of the Rwandan genocide in 1994. In short, this choice of word was a deliberate incitement to racial hatred which invoked previous rituals of dehumanisation that had been employed as precursors to ethnic and racial genocide.

This chapter unfolds from the scene at Břeclav in 2015. In what follows, I dig into this event in order to understand better 'the rush of past racial "debris"' it provoked, and what we can learn from this about the states we are in and the fascistic return we face.[18] One argument of this chapter is that much longer genealogies of penal stigma haunt the images of refugees being written upon at Břeclav train station. As Stuart Hall put it, racism is 'a badge, a token, a sign', a political practice of classification.[19] As we saw in the previous chapters, the badge of race has long been employed as an othering practice, a colouring device, to dehumanise slaves, colonial subjects, non-citizens, refugees and migrants.[20] Racism is 'a system of marks', a mechanism which 'outlines space in order to assign forced residence or to close off borders'.[21] In what follows, I hold to a reading of stigma as material practices of dehumanisation to further examine the relationship between stigmatisation, racism and practices of enclosure and expulsion.

Europe's racist crisis

This chapter focuses on events in Czechia in 2015. Czechia is a nation of 10.5 million people which joined the European Union (EU) in 2004 as part of a group of former communist states, Hungary, Poland and Slovakia, which are known collectively as the Visegrád group. From the early 1990s the Visegrád states transitioned from Soviet-style command economies to neoliberal market economies. This process involved the implementation of the 1993 Copenhagen criteria, a policy package involving rapid privatisation of state-owned infrastructure and assets and the liberalisation of labour and financial markets.[22] This 'shock treatment' injected economic inequality into the region: wage levels collapsed, workers' rights and welfare provisions were eroded, public services and infrastructures were privatised.[23]

While the availability of cheap credit initially cushioned the impact of neoliberal social and economic reforms, there has been increasing public disillusionment with the 'so-called "freedom" and capitalism' promised by EU membership.[24] This disenchantment 'with the ascetic catching-up ideology' intensified in the wake of the North Atlantic financial crisis in 2008, and there was a political shift away from democratic pro-EU parties which embraced neoliberal reforms towards nationalist right-wing parties. As Jodi Dean argues, the inequalities and insecurities introduced by 'globalized neoliberal capitalism' are managed politically through 'racist, nationalist ethnocentrism'.[25] Visegrád politicians harnessed the animosities generated by growing economic inequalities in the region to nationalist fantasies of 'ethnic security' through 'border security'. As Hungarian Prime Minister Victor Orbán announced in 2014, 'the new state that we are building is an illiberal state, a non-liberal state'.[26]

As the humanitarian crisis at Europe's borders deepened in 2015, right-wing Visegrád politicians and public commentators began to craft a special geopolitical role for the region as a buffer zone by which (Western) Europe could be protected against what was characterised as an unstoppable catastrophic flood of (Muslim) migrants entering Europe. A rush of fence-building began on eastern borders, the opening of new camps to detain migrants, the formation by neo-Nazis of 'human walls' against refugees on state borders and the formation of armed citizen militia groups, such as Hungary's state-funded 'border hunters' and a 2,500-strong Czech vigilante border militia. In 2015 alone, the Hungarian government 'invested more than 100 million euros on razor-wire fencing and border controls', transforming itself into what Amnesty International described as 'a refugee protection free zone'.[27] Explicit in these regional securitisation programmes was the idea that misguided liberal Western European political leaders failed to see the 'genocidal' consequences of granting refuge to Middle Eastern, African and/or Muslim refugees. As former Czech President Václav Klaus stated, as he launched a national online petition titled 'Against Immigration' in 2015: 'if Europe wants to commit suicide by accepting an unlimited number of refugees, let them do it but not with our consent'.[28]

'A genocide against white people'

In Czechia, a populist narrative emerged which, drawing on histories of German and communist occupation, imagined the Czech people as engaged in an existential struggle against invading 'foreign hordes'. This struggle was explicitly framed as a race war. For example, a news headline on 3 September 2015 quoted Czech sociologist Petr Hampl stating: 'We have the right to deal with the refugees as though they were aggressors. The traitors of the Czech nation are helping them to exterminate us like the whites have exterminated the Red Indians.'[29] An editorial in the Czech broadsheet newspaper *Lidové Noviny*, penned by 'expert ethnologist' Mnislav Zelený-Atapana and titled 'Is a Genocide against Whites Next for Europe?', argued that: 'Mrs Merkel and those like her are basically undertaking an artificial mixing of the races in which the white race will be gradually liquidated and we Europeans will become black or brown. This is a genocide against white people.'[30] These ethno-nationalist sentiments spilled onto the streets.

On 12 September 2015, thousands gathered in Prague to protest against refugee arrivals, one of many such demonstrations across the country and wider Visegrád region that year. Video footage of the Prague protest captures a carnival atmosphere, with young people and families with children carrying Czech flags and holding up banners with the demands 'Send them back!' and 'Protect the borders'. Many wore T-shirts and face paint adorned with anti-

Islamic and anti-refugee slogans, and crowds chanted in unison, 'Fuck off, Islam'.

While there were also pro-refugee marches and campaigns in Czechia, sustained and organised resistance to the rise of populist proto-fascist politics has proved difficult. The Visegrád states have no significantly large non-white or migrant populations, except for a highly persecuted Roma minority. The once substantial and vibrant Jewish communities in the Visegrád region either emigrated or were murdered in the Nazi holocaust. For example, there were only an estimated 2,000 Muslims living in the Czechia in 2015 – a fact which led Selma Muhič Dizdarevič, an assistant professor at Charles University in Prague, to describe the alarming increase in levels of anti-Muslim racism in the country as 'Islamophobia without Muslims'.[31]

'No camp, no camp'

It is also important to note that Visegrád states are transition rather than destination countries for refugees. For example, in 2015 Czechia granted refugee protection to a mere seventy-one people, out of a total of only 1,525 asylum applications. Indeed, these are states that habitually record negative net migration rates, as young people seeking higher wages migrate west. National policies in the region are designed to deter refugees and migrant workers, despite growing labour shortages. The small numbers of refugees straying onto Czech territory in the summer of 2015 were seeking only to cross the border. In practical terms, refugees and migrants are unlikely to be able to speak Czech or to have family, friends or other contacts to induce them to remain.

What this tells us is that the inking and detention of the refugees at Břeclav was orchestrated political theatre. The refusal to let refugees continue unmolested on their journeys was an opportunity to demonstrate control over national borders. In particular, the timing of the detention of the refugees at Břeclav was designed to add weight to a Visegrád-wide negotiating position on a proposed EU quota system that would require states to accept an agreed number of Syrian refugees. A matter of hours after the detention of refugees at Břeclav, the Czech Interior Minister stated to journalists that he was interested in negotiating a 'simplified procedure' with Berlin, which might allow refugees to travel unmolested across Czech territory on the understanding that any quota scheme would be 'unacceptable to the Czech government'.[32]

That events in Břeclav on 1 September 2015 were political theatre was underscored by similar events on a much larger scale in neighbouring Hungary when, on 3 September, the Hungarian government abruptly cancelled all international train services to Western Europe. Thousands of refugees heading for Germany were trapped at central Keleti train station in Budapest, effectively held hostage by Viktor Orbán's government. International journalists and news crews captured the scenes of despair at Keleti; people left with useless train tickets, families sleeping on the streets, and a lack of food, water and sanitary provisions.

The chaos at Keleti train station saw several hundred people set off on foot to Austria, a walk of 110 miles. Another group of approximately 500 people were eventually herded onto a single train which they were told was heading to Germany, indeed it 'prominently featured a German flag'.[33] In actuality this train was destined for a migrant detention camp near the town of Bicske, a mere twenty miles from Budapest. In scenes, again recorded by international journalists, hundreds of riot police boarded the train at Bicske and attempted to force people to disembark. British journalist James Mates described how the refugees pleaded with journalists and television crews not to leave Bicske train station, and chanted 'no camp, no camp' from the train windows.[34] A siege ensued, in which hundreds of people attempted to break through police blockades at the train station in order to avoid detention and walk to the Austrian border. Some refugees succeeded in fleeing Bicske train station, but a fifty-year-old man died in one escape attempt when he fell and hit his head on the train tracks.

Genealogies of racism in Europe

As Magdalena Nowicka argues, 'Eastern Europe remains a blind spot in theorizing racism in Europe'.[35] Even though the worst atrocities of the Second World War took place on Nazi-occupied Central and Eastern European soil (often with the collaboration of local populations), under communist rule there was no acknowledgement of historical state racisms. Even while the material remnants of a more multicultural past were hidden in plain sight – for example in formerly Jewish neighbourhoods and empty synagogues – neither the genocides that took place during the Nazi occupation, nor the racial classification of Eastern Europeans as 'Slavs', nor the expulsion of German-speaking citizens after the war, were understood through the lens of racism. Further, while, under post-war state socialism, racism continued to be practised against minorities, notably Roma populations, racism wasn't acknowledged as a social problem.

While the occlusion of Nazi-era racial genocide from official histories of Eastern European states has been partially revised since the fall of the Iron Curtain, this process of remembering has been complicated by the ways in which ethnic forms of nationalism became associated with liberation from communist totalitarianism (Soviet-era controls suppressed nationalism through ideologies of a supranational union). Furthermore, it is not only that state racism has been historically repressed, but that racism per se as a topic of debate and concern continues to be marginalised within the Visegrád public sphere, including within academic scholarship. As Nowicka remarks on the Polish context, 'the popular opinion, common also among Polish scholars [is] that "the racial problem has never existed in Poland"'.[36] In short, racism is imagined as a problem imported from Western Europe, and a consequence of Western European colonialism and migration. As the aforementioned 'expert ethnologist' and Czech public figure Zelený-Atapana puts it vis-à-vis the 2015 refugee crisis: 'They [Western European states] started in the distant past colonialist division of the world and after WWII began to reap the rotten fruit as they opened borders to people of former colonies. We, however, did not participate in [colonialism] and therefore we have no moral obligation to accept refugees.'[37]

In 2015 racism emerged 'starkly into the open' in the Visegrád public sphere but was imagined as a 'new' problem which originates from 'outside'.[38] It is important to note also that race is still understood in much of Eastern Europe through the lens of scientific racism.[39] This was evident in political and other public responses to the refugee crisis, where racist views about refugees were expressed not only in terms of religious and cultural differences (for example as Islamophobia), but also in terms of biological differences (see for example Zelený-Atapana's comments above on race mixing as racial genocide).

The persistence of these older forms of racist thinking trouble liberal understandings of race and racism. In Western Europe, scientific theories of race have been incrementally discredited since the Second World War and there has been some official acknowledgement of state racism through the memorialisation of (some) past genocides, albeit primarily Nazi-era atrocities that took place on European soil. However, as Alana Lentin has argued, this commemoration of racist crimes occludes 'the foundational relationship between the liberal political project and the racial-colonial domination within and despite which it developed'.[40] Indeed, as Lentin notes, in Western Europe 'real racism' is imagined as something which was overcome (with Nazi-era fascism), and eruptions of racism are thus imagined and legislated against as the aberrant beliefs and behaviour of a minority of deviant, uneducated individual racists. In the process, actually existing forms of institutional and state racism, including the ongoing exclusion of racialised citizens from the full rights and protections of citizenship, are occluded.

The clash of post-communist and liberal regimes of racism was apparent in liberal Western European commentary around the refugee crisis, where explicit expressions of racism in the East – in political commentary and anti-refugee protests – were storied in the West as a conflict between 'backward' Eastern European racism and a 'superior moral stance of humanitarianism'.[41] By situating racism geographically in the East, state racism against refugees and other racialised minorities was in effect orientalised as a symptom of underdevelopment – a further sign of the distance 'they' must travel 'to become liberal, humanitarian and modern Europeans'.[42]

This chapter does not seek to contribute to the stigmatisation of Eastern Europeans as 'more racist' than their Western neighbours, or to diminish the central role of Western European powers in enabling mass internments and deaths at the borders. It is, however, interested in what we might learn from the conjunction of these different genealogies of racism, not least in terms of what these overlapping regimes of racism might teach us about the dramatic blossoming of neo-fascist politics in Western Europe in the same period; for it was not only right-wing Visegrád politicians who crafted and mobilised populist racisms against refugees as a means to make political capital.

In the UK Brexit campaign in 2016, for example, the two key themes of the Leave campaign, namely that immigration is ripping apart the nation and that 'anything foreign, except investment, is abhorrent', not only granted 'a fillip to popular racism' but allowed 'fully fledged state racism' to emerge.[43] Indeed, while Hungary undertook a state-sponsored propaganda campaign against migrants in October 2016 (see below), the far-right United Kingdom Independence Party (working in conjunction with the official Leave campaign led by high-profile politicians), used almost identical tactics and messages in its campaign to leave the EU. One of the most notorious posters in the Brexit campaign, titled 'Breaking Point', and subtitled 'We must break free of the EU and take back control of our borders', employed a doctored photograph of refugees crossing the Croatia–Slovenia border (taken in 2015) as evidence that white Europe was being 'invaded' by brown migrants (indeed the most visibly white person in the photograph was obscured by a text box in the poster).

A matter of hours after this anti-refugee poster campaign was launched, Jo Cox, a pro-EU Labour MP for Batley and Speen in Yorkshire and a high-profile political advocate for the human rights of migrants and refugees, was assassinated in the street by a white supremacist nationalist. Cox was shot and stabbed repeatedly; as she was slaughtered her killer shouted 'Britain first, keep Britain independent, Britain will always come first', before finally yelling, 'This is for Britain'.

What indelibly connects the two regimes of racism briefly outlined here, namely scientific racism in which race is understood as a consequence of genetic differences in a stratified global hierarchy of human life, and liberal regimes of racism in which race is understood through the lens of cultural and religious differences in which (Western) European society is imagined as more progressive and more 'developed', are white supremacist ideologies. In short, liberal or illiberal, these overlapping regimes of racism are rooted in the same histories and epistemologies of European modernity.

Fascism as a connecting thread

In 2015 different genealogies of racism cross-pollinate and coalesce in anti-migrant racism but they all draw energy from twentieth-century European fascism and ideologies of white supremacy. Indeed, it is precisely fascist tropes of 'racial self-defence', 'self-cleansing', 'political hygiene' and programmes of 'total dehumanization' which characterised the responses of right-wing politicians, pundits and publics across Europe to refugee arrivals in 2015.[44]

In *Modernity and the Holocaust*, Zygmunt Bauman warned us that 'antisemitism survived the populations it had ostensibly been targeted against'.[45] As he writes, 'in countries where the Jews have all but disappeared, antisemitism ... continues abated', albeit, he adds, often against different populations, most notably Muslims.[46] Bauman describes this phenomenon as 'antisemitism without Jews', describing the proliferation and diffusion of fascistic forms of racism in post-war Europe as 'a game without frontiers'.[47]

In Europe, the resurgence and amplification of fascist ideologies, practices and policies is evident on every scale and in every sphere of social life: in the resurgence of far-right, white supremacist nationalistic political parties and the election of charismatic right-wing politicians on anti-immigration platforms; in the unashamed embrace of racist ideologies across the entire political spectrum; in state-led propaganda campaigns against refugees and migrants; in a rush of fence-building and the erection of checkpoints; in the opening of ever more prisons to detain migrants, in the formal and informal dispersal of border enforcement roles to state officials, medical authorities, schools and universities, welfare agencies, employers and landlords; in the incessant production of racial stigma and hate speech in news reporting, social media and everyday speech; and in rising levels of hate crime and everyday racist violence. While explicitly anti-foreigner in orientation, the explosion of public racisms across Europe has also legitimatised racial hatred and violence towards existing racialised citizens, especially Muslims, Jews, Roma, Gypsies and Travellers, and other black and brown ethnic minorities.

The stigma machine of fascism

To understand the current return of fascistic nationalistic politics, it is helpful to examine Europe's still obfuscated colonial reign of terror on the African continent in the late nineteenth and early twentieth century. As Hannah Arendt reminds us, 'the seeds of [Nazi] totalitarianism can be found in the period of colonial rule in Africa'.[48]

German south-west Africa, modern-day Namibia, was a colony of the German empire from 1884 until 1915. Within areas under German control, all Africans over the age of eight had to wear metal passes around their necks, which were embossed with the imperial crown, the magisterial district and a number. As in other pass systems, such as those developed in India, the US and South Africa, this badging was a form of penal stigmatisation that was intended both to humiliate and to facilitate control over captive labour. When people resisted this badging, for example by ridding themselves of the metal tags during escape attempts, a system of ink tattooing was proposed.[49]

In 1904, uprisings by the Herero (and Nama) people against the colonial administration led to the adoption of an extermination policy in the region. What followed was described by the then commander of German forces in south-west Africa, Colonial General Lothar Von Trotha, as 'a racial war'.[50] By 1906, the German colonists had murdered 65,000 Herero people out of a total population of 80,000, many dying of thirst when, encircled by German troops, they were forced to flee into the Kalahari Desert.

Some of those who surrendered were tattooed or branded with the letters 'GH' (*Gefangene Herero*, meaning 'imprisoned Herero'), before being dispersed as slave labour on the farms of German settlers.[51] Alongside the use of penal tattoos, this genocide saw the development of concentration camps in the region. German scientists used the camps to gather evidence to support the now blossoming field of 'racial sciences' (inspired by men like Cesare Lombroso).

Thousands of Herero body parts were collected in the concentration camps, and shipped to the Germany. It is estimated that '3,000 Herero skulls were sent to Berlin for German scientists to examine for signs that they were of racially inferior peoples'.[52] Many of the experiments on Herero and Nama body parts were overseen by Eugen Fischer. Fischer had spent time undertaking field research on mixed race children in German south-west Africa, and his research led to a 1912 ban on interracial marriages in the German colonies. Adolf Hitler was an admirer of Fischer's research, and drew on his book *Principles of Human Heredity and Race Hygiene* (1921) in his vision of a 'purified' Aryan race in *Mein Kampf* (1925).

The genocidal activities of the Germans in Africa in the early twentieth century were not hidden. These events were debated in parliament, reported in newspapers, and a popular German postcard from this period depicted soldiers posing with the skulls of Herero (which the army forced captives to clean before they were sent to German universities). In 1906, the German socialist satirical magazine *Der Wahre Jacob* published a cartoon depicting the skeletonised remains of Herero spread across an expanse of the Kalahari Desert; the caption reads: 'Even if it hasn't brought in much profit and there are no better quality goods on offer, at least we can use it to set up a bone-grinding plant.'[53] As Hortense Spillers notes, 'if the twentieth century would witness, at the midpoint, the terrifying spectacle of the totalitarian regime' then its technologies of terror were 'adumbrated in the long centuries of unregulated violence against black people', and specifically Africans.[54]

German colonial methods of racial classification were further innovated when, as Frantz Fanon puts it, 'Nazism transformed the whole of Europe into a veritable colony'.[55] Indeed, the Nazi drive to 'build an empire in the East' was classically colonial in that it was characterised by 'imperial expansion, settler colonialism and racial genocide'.[56] The Nazi project to 'cleanse and colonise' Europe involved the creation of a vast, bureaucratic stigma machine for the classification of 'racial enemies' (i.e. Jews, Gypsies and Slavs), 'asocial' elements (i.e. the 'work-shy', criminals, sexual deviants) and 'useless eaters' (disabled people and the mentally ill). The identification of these 'aliens to the community' and 'pests harmful to the nation' was the first step in the implementation of the 'racial hygiene' project envisaged by Eugen Fischer and his colleagues. Indeed, Fischer's experiments on the bodies of slaughtered Herero and Nama people was the 'evidence base' which underpinned the 1935 Nuremberg laws (for 'the Protection of German Blood' and 'the Protection of German Honour'), which banned interracial marriages and removed German citizenship from Jews (and later Roma and African Germans).

During the Nazi regime, Fischer and his colleagues continued to experiment on body parts as they sought to evidence their eugenic theory of racial hierarchy, but now they used the dead bodies of Jews, Roma Gypsies and African Germans. Some of the human research material for Fischer's laboratory was supplied by his former student, Josef Mengele, from Auschwitz.

In order to distinguish 'racial enemies', the Nazi regime introduced laws that forced Jews to wear distinguishing badges, most often a yellow star, in public places.[57] At labour and extermination camps, an elaborate system of badging was developed to distinguish different classes of prisoners. Those designated for slave labour at camps, rather than immediate death, were often stamped with ink signs on their forehead, and labour numbers were also frequently inked on the skin. At the Auschwitz complex, stigmatisation extended to the ink tattooing of serial numbers on Jewish inmates selected for work. The first experiments in tattooing used a metal stamp, which perforated the skin (on the left breast), and ink was rubbed into the wound. This developed into a more sophisticated system of needle tattooing (on the left arm). At least 400,000 people were tattooed in this way. The Czech holocaust survivor Ruth Elias recalls how she survived near-starvation in the Jewish ghetto of Theresienstadt near Prague, but it was only when she lined up to be tattooed at Auschwitz that she understood that she was no longer considered a human being: 'The numbers on our forearms marked our depersonalization.'[58]

As Primo Levi describes in *If This Is a Man* (1947), the replacement of your name with a tattooed number was your 'initiation' into a 'great machine' which sought 'to reduce us to beasts'.[59] Bauman terms this 'categorical murder' a process through which 'the concrete individual' is erased, and people are made into 'an abstraction'.[60] The abstraction of people into things through stigmatising classifications underpinned the operations of the entire fascist machine. Indeed, it was the cumulation of practices of dehumanisation which enabled the stigma machine of the slave labour camps to be transformed into 'gigantic death machines'.[61]

Public humiliation and pillory

These penal technologies of dehumanisation were prefigured by a debate amongst prominent legal experts about the efficacy of penal stigma as a judicial punishment. In the 1930s leading Nazi legal scholars, such as Georg Dahm, proposed the reintroduction of 'shame sanctions' as part of the establishment of a new authoritarian legal system. Dahm's basic argument was 'that where liberty had been the highest good of the old liberal order, honour was now the highest good of the new Nazi order. Shame sanctions, which deprived offenders of honour, should accordingly be the Nazi punishment of choice'.[62] In short, he called for a redesign of the German judicial system to support the implementation of the illiberal racial order of the Nazi regime.

While Dahm's proposals for an overhaul of the German legal system were not implemented in full, by the mid-1930s the Sturmabteilung (the Nazi Party's first paramilitary arm) had already reintroduced pillory and other public shame sanctions as part of a Nazification project. These stigma practices involved subjecting people to public humiliations such as sign-wearing, head-shaving, public beatings and lynchings. For example, photographs from Austria during the Anschluss in 1938 depict Jewish women being exhibited in a public square with signs hung around their necks which read 'I have been excluded from the national community (*Volksgemeinschaft*)' (see Figure 3.2). These stigma practices proliferated and intensified as the Nazis colonised Eastern Europe.

The use of stigma punishments was accompanied by massive state propaganda campaigns primarily targeting Jews but also other individuals and groups designated as racial and/or political enemies of the Aryan state, including disabled people, prostitutes and the mentally ill. This Nazification movement included poster campaigns, anti-Semitic newspapers (such as *Der Stürmer*), films, theatre, radio broadcasts and 'degenerate art' exhibitions. For example, the anti-Semitic 'Eternal Jew' exhibition, which opened in the German Museum in Munich on 8 November 1937, and was then toured in Vienna and Berlin, consisted of hundreds of artworks, photographs and objects designed to represent the sub-humanity of Jews. This touring exhibition was accompanied by a catalogue, a lecture series and theatre performances. In 1940,

Figure 3.2 'Kristallnacht shame': Jewish women in Linz, Austria are exhibited in public with a cardboard sign stating: 'I have been excluded from the national community (Volksgemeinschaft)', during the anti-Jewish pogrom known as Kristallnacht, November 1938.

the pseudo-documentary film *Der Ewige Jude* (1940, dir. Fritz Hippler), was one of a collection of fascist films toured across Germany, and later compulsorily screened in occupied cities and towns across Europe. Nazi police reports approvingly note a correlation in anti-Semitic feeling, street harassment and violence in the wake of these propaganda art exhibitions, screenings and cultural events.

Der Ewige Jude was made 'mandatory viewing for police and SS-units, special units of the Wehrmacht, and guards at concentration and extermination camps, since it was thought that the film would ward off any scruples people might feel about the merciless persecution and annihilation of the Jews'.[63]

The death of the scaffold?

In *Discipline and Punish*, Foucault famously argued that the introduction of more 'subtle' punishments, such as imprisonment in place of physical torture, reflects a broader historical shift away from the 'visible intensity' and 'horrifying spectacle of public punishment'. As he writes, 'the spectacle of the tortured, dismembered, amputated, symbolically branded on face and shoulder, exposed dead or alive to public view', begins to die out in Europe at the end of the eighteenth century.[64] There is historical evidence in support of arguments that technologies and mechanisms of social discipline and punishment are transformed *within* Europe in this period. There is a shift, for example, from the spectacle of public executions, to judicial sentences which involve hard labour, including imprisonment and transportation – the last public execution in Lancaster took place in 1865.

However, Foucault's claim that 'the body as the major target of penal repression disappeared' is significantly overstated.[65] It wasn't that 'the spectacle of the scaffold' vanished; rather it was outsourced, as European colonialism spread its 'arsenal of horrors' and penal practices across the world (indeed, public lynchings increased in the US after the emancipation of the enslaved in 1863).[66] Public exhibitions of punishment spectacularly blew back into Europe with the rise of fascism, which inaugurated a new European dawn of public spectacles of violence. This was the mid-twentieth-century Nazi regime under which Foucault grew up in Vichy France: a regime of badging, public pillory and shaming rituals, torture and deportations which, it seems, he couldn't bear to look upon closely.

The use of penal stigma erupted across Europe in post-war backlashes against Nazi collaborators, as seen in shaming punishments meted out to women alleged to have slept with German soldiers. Over 2,000 women are thought to have been subject

Figure 3.3 'Post-war shaming punishments': women being paraded in a Paris street in August 1944, barefoot, their heads shaved, and their foreheads and cheeks marked with swastikas.

to these public humiliations in post-war France, which involved head-shaving, face-marking, being stripped, spat on, jeered at and being paraded through the streets, in ways which echo 'the riding of scolds' centuries earlier (see Figure 3.3). It is significant that, once more, it is women who are targeted for these humiliations, and that women's bodies are made to bear the stigma of the wider community (here the public shame of collaboration with the Nazi occupiers), underscoring once more that we can rarely, if ever, disentangle stigma power from regimes of patriarchy.

One argument of *Stigma* is that in order to understand the periodic intensification of judicial and wider social and cultural practices of public stigmatisation and shaming practices, it is critical that we approach these phenomena not as the appearance of something 'new', but rather as the 'reappearance of something very old'.[67] For example, the lines of argument advanced by Nazi shame advocates in the 1930s resonate with those taking place amongst 'shame advocates' in legal scholarship and wider public culture today. Public shaming and pillory is on the return, and is a central feature of the current global authoritarian turn.

The return of shame sanctions

Since the 1990s, the United States has witnessed the proliferation of legal shaming penalties, as part of a broader regime of 'alternative sanctions' which seek, in the words of one US judge, to 'inflict disgrace and contumely in a dramatic and spectacular manner'.[68] Stigmatising penalties are now widely employed by US federal judges in lieu of prison sentences. These shame sanctions include practices such as forcing convicted petty criminals to hold placards stating 'I am a thief' outside shopping malls and county courts, the enforced use of automobile bumper stickers to declare a driving infraction, being compelled to place newspaper advertisements or billboards detailing your crime, being made to wear a T-shirt pronouncing your guilt, and the public broadcasting of the names of convicted offenders on community-access television channels (Figure 3.4).[69] As the legal scholar David Skeel explains, these shaming punishments are 'designed to elicit moral disapproval from the offenders' fellow citizens'; in short, they employ stigma in order to advertise and reinforce social norms.[70]

James Whitman argues that these kinds of shaming sanctions are cruel, violate human dignity and are dangerous as they cultivate

Figure 3.4 'I stole from Walmart': found photograph of a woman undertaking a shaming punishment in the US in 2007.

'lynch-mob mentalities'.[71] Certainly, there are instructive lessons in the recent fascist history of penal stigma for those concerned about the resurrection of stigma penalties in ostensibly liberal judicial systems across Europe and the US today. Others argue that while stigmatising individuals should be discouraged, shame should be cultivated as a practice with respect to corporations – such as companies that evade tax or pollute the environment. This argument is taken up and developed by Jessica Jacquet in *Is Shame Necessary? New Uses for an Old Tool* (2016), which advocates for the efficacy of shame sanctions as a mechanism through which to nudge corporations into acting with more social responsibility.[72] However, the extensive debate amongst 'shaming enthusiasts' and 'shame detractors' is beyond the scope of this book. Where these debates overlap with the concerns of this book is in terms of what these practices reveals about the persistence of punitive practices of social stigmatisation, and in particular what this renewed intensity of stigma production reveals vis-à-vis wider regimes of state power, and mutating regimes of racial capitalism.

The current intensification of penal stigma isn't restricted to formal systems of punishment but, as Loïc Wacquant has argued, is symptomatic of a much broader 'theatricalization of penality' in neoliberal societies. As he argues:

> In the past quarter-century, a whole galaxy of novel cultural and social forms, indeed a veritable industry trading on representations of offenders and law enforcement, has sprung forth and spread [migrating] from the state to the commercial media and the political field … Everywhere the law-and-order guignol has become a core civic theatre.[73]

The word 'guignol' originates in French puppetry, and is used as an adjective to describe forms of popular entertainment which feature repugnant characters. Indeed, entire media genres, notably reality television, are today dedicated to the staging of public shaming rituals – in this twenty-first-century televisual guignol it is most often working-class women who are publicly puppeteered as figures for derision.[74]

While shaming sanctions have long been employed in authoritarian regimes around the world, the enthusiastic re-endorsement of 'humiliation sanctions' in the judicial systems of Western liberal democracies is indicative of the new illiberal state order being forged by world leaders like Orbán, Modi, Trump, Putin and others. What these political actors have in common is that they seek to reassert older caste, racial and gendered hierarchies of person value as a means of garnering political capital, and in service of profit-seeking projects of capitalist exploitation.

Tipping back into authoritarianism

Across the twentieth century, 'state racism' was the primary source of social conflict from which national sovereignty generated its legitimacy. Racism is the primary mechanism through which capitalist elites assuage discontent about social and economic inequalities 'at home': crafting racism to generate divisions within the working class, to garner political capital and legitimate exceptional measures. However, I want to argue that in the current conjuncture there is a more profound rupture taking place. In the last interview he gave before he died, Stuart Hall stated that the multiple crises which characterise the state we are in is not 'just a swing of the intellectual pendulum, not just the usual ins and outs of politics' but represents a profound shift in the machinations of racial capitalism.[75] As Hall suggested, if 'authoritarian populism' is the way in which 'the current crisis of capitalism is resolved', then we face the most significant global crisis since the Second World War.

Certainly, the reactivation of historical forms of stigma power – tried, tested and reworked strategies 'of domination, dispossession, expropriation, exploitation, and violence' – is a signal that the political organisation of capitalism is tipping ever further from the egalitarian promise of democracy towards repressive and oppressive forms of authoritarian rule.[76] As Hall writes, unlike 'classical fascism', this authoritarianism 'has retained most (though not all) of the formal representative institutions' and 'has been able to construct around itself an active popular consent'.[77] It is the argument of this book that stigma power is a key mechanism through which popular consent is forged. We are now seeing the emergence of a new kind of fascism, which Alain Badiou terms 'democratic fascism' (because we are voting for it).[78] The response of European governments to the refugee crisis marked a tipping point in this broader fascistic return, and I will now return to these events.

'A gigantic wave of racist state propaganda'

In 2015, Hungary had considerably more applications for asylum than Czechia, around 174,000, yet as part of the proposed EU quota scheme it was only asked to accept 1,294 asylum seekers. Despite the small scale of this request, on 2 October 2016 the Hungarian government held a nationwide referendum on the proposed European Union quota system. As the Hungarian philosopher Gáspár Tamás noted, what was most significant about this referendum was the 'gigantic wave of racist state propaganda' that preceded it. This ranged 'from giant billboards to new elementary school textbooks, from the internet to hundreds of thousands of personal phone calls civil servants were forced to make to mobilize for the "no" vote'.[79] Across Hungarian cities and major transport routes, and in public squares, parks and thoroughfares, giant billboards appeared with messages that included: 'Did you know that since the beginning of the immigration crisis more than 300 people have died as a result of terror attacks in Europe?'; 'Did you know that Brussels wants to settle a whole city's worth of illegal immigrants in Hungary?'; 'Did you know that since the beginning of the immigration crisis the harassment of women has risen sharply in Europe?'; 'If you come to Hungary don't take the jobs of Hungarians!'; 'If you come to Hungary, you have to keep our laws'. As Lydia Gall has detailed, this propaganda campaign 'cost Hungarian taxpayers the equivalent of over $18 million' – approximately $13,500 per asylum seeker that Hungary had been asked to grant refuge to.[80] This print propaganda was amplified by television stations which 'used newsbreaks during the European Football Championship, in June and the Olympic Games in August, to devote frequent airtime to "anti-migrant news items", depicting asylum seekers and refugees as criminals, terrorists and people who come to mooch on Western welfare systems'.[81] This was an exercise in state-funded racism on a scale and with an intensity not witnessed in Europe since the Nazi propaganda against Jewish citizens in the 1930s and 1940s – and it went viral.

Fascism online: transnational racist responses to Břeclav

The British right-wing tabloid newspaper the *Daily Mail* hosts the most visited news website in the world, the MailOnline, which attracts an international readership of 12 million people a day. On 2 September 2015, the MailOnline featured Zehl's photograph of the child being inked by the Czech police in a news story titled 'Fury as Czech police write numbers on arms of migrants "like concentration camp prisoners"'. This story attracted 4,000 readers' comments, extending over twenty-three pages, with posts from readers in the UK, Ireland, USA, Australia, New Zealand, Canada, Spain and Singapore. Some readers responded – as invited by the use of scare quotes around 'concentration camp' in the title – with outrage at the suggestion of any analogy between the inking of refugees' hands and concentration camp regimes, insisting, for example, that, 'it's no different than having your hand stamped as you enter a night club'. Many more suggested that more permanent and graphic forms of penal stigmatisation should be used to manage refugees at Europe's borders:

> They should write the id numbers on the forehead instead!

> You could inject them with an RFID tag, at least you could track them!

> Rubber stamp their foreheads instead!

> They should be made to wear a yellow badge so that members of the public know who they are and know to stay well away from them.

With the numbers involved and the desperate deceit used by many of these people tattoos would be a more effective option. If they behave well give them a yellow star to wear too. Pigs ears are clipped and tagged #justsaying

Just because the J E W S don't like it we must comply!

Dig pits and machine gun the lot of them – Cheaper to use gas.

Well done Czech police ... I'd brand them like cattle with a massive M on their foreheads!

Good idea – tattoo everyone with a barcode – easier to track

They should all be fingerprinted, DNA samples taken and photographed before tattooing i11eg@1 on their fore head [sic]

While it is easy to dismiss or disregard these kinds of discussion threads, they are important archives of everyday stigmacraft in contemporary media cultures. Our task, as Les Back suggests, is to 'develop a radical attentiveness' to racist speech, to understand the 'resonance and reach' of racist sentiments and conversations.[82] The imagined anonymity of internet forums, and devices such as the use of fabricated user names, offer users a licence to break social taboos on racist speech, and an opportunity to craft racism in extreme and virulent ways. Reading this discussion thread, it is evident there is enjoyment in provoking outrage, an intense pleasure in being racist with others in a community setting and by evading the censorship of forum moderators by, for example, placing spaces between letters in words like 'JEWS'. While some of the readers responded negatively to racist comments, for the majority the opportunity to be racist motivated their participation. As Kimberlé Crenshaw notes, 'racism helps to create an illusion of unity through the oppositional force of a symbolic "other". The establishment of an Other creates a bond, a burgeoning common identity of all nonstigma-tized parties'.[83]

The refugees arriving in Europe in the summer of 2015 are difficult to characterise in terms of a single religion, nationality or through racial colour lines. Perhaps to account for the difficulty in fixing a singular 'badge of race', the racism against refugees in the MailOnline thread conjures multiple figures and names: Muslims, Jews, Niggers, Arabs and terrorists morph into one another. Most notably, Nazi-era anti-Semitic practices are repurposed as anti-Muslim racism: 'I'd brand them like cattle with a massive M on their foreheads.' The graphic character of this online racism is striking, with many posts imagining different ways of stigma-tising refugees. Signs and words are imagined impressed, branded, tattooed upon migrant bodies, stressing the relationship between racism, writing and wounding uncovered in the genealogy of penal stigma. Also striking are the many calls for the segregation and confinement of these 'waste populations' in concentration camps: 'No one invited them to the Czech Republic!'; 'Like roach infes-tation'; 'Let the Germans set up some of their "special" camps in Poland for them'.

Scene two: Bělá-Jezová immigration detention centre, Czechia, 31 August 2015

Because Czechia receives so few refugees, there are only three immigration detention centres in the country. Coincidentally, on 31 August 2015, the very day that the refugees began the train journeys that ended at Břeclav, Anna Šabatová, the Czech govern-ment's Public Defender of Rights, made an unannounced visit to the Bělá-Jezová detention centre, a former Soviet army barracks. Šabatová's subsequent report offers insights into the abject condi-tions that would be faced by those refugees bussed from Břeclav to camps. Indeed, the situation she describes at Bělá-Jezová is so disturbing that it triggered a response from Zeid Ra'ad Al Hussein, the United Nations High Commissioner for Human Rights.

When she arrived at Bělá-Jezová, the chief of the Czech Alien Police at the centre tried to refuse Šabatová, and the four lawyers and two interpreters accompanying her, access, and attempted to remove the cameras they had brought to document conditions, even though the unannounced inspection of prisons and detention centres is a regular part of the role of Public Defender of Rights.[84]

Šabatová began her inspection by noting that Bělá-Jezová had increased its capacity from 270 to 700 beds in a period of six months. During her visit on 31 August, 659 people, including 147 children, were being detained. Šabatová described how a constant 'demonstration of force' was maintained throughout the centre by the 'presence of uniformed private security guards, police officers, riot police unit and police dogs'.

The refugees relayed their feelings 'of utter humiliation'. They told Šabatová that some of the police officers 'handled them roughly, or spit in front of them', and that private security guards called them terrorists.

Šabatová noted that people were frequently handcuffed and that others, including children, had insufficient clothing and shoes to keep warm and clean. Detainees described being given mattresses that were filthy and infested with lice. Some of those she spoke to had no hot meals, but were surviving on rations of bread and cheese. Some had no direct access to toilets or running water, and had to rouse guards to be released from the rooms in which they were locked each time they needed the bathroom. People also told her of humiliating strip and body cavity searches in front of families and children, ostensibly to make sure they were not hiding valuables; mobile phones, watches, shoelaces, belts and money were confiscated on their arrival.

The anxiety of being detained in these abject conditions was intensified by the fact that they are unable to contact their relatives. Many have no way to contact loved ones back home to tell them they are alive, or the means of finding family and friends from whom they were separated on their journey, or deliberately segregated from in detention.[85] People didn't know when they would be released and some didn't even know which country they were in.

Despite the claims of police at Břeclav that people were being inked as a means of keeping families together, Šabatová discovered that family members were frequently separated and placed in different detention centres.[86] Amidst this litany of details, she paused to note in her report: 'Simple description of the situation cannot fully convey the conditions in which these [people] were held, nor their psychological condition. ... They often come to believe they have been deprived of their humanity and treated as a "herd of animals"'. In a shocking passage, Šabatová details her discovery of an annex in a forest behind the main detention centre:

Out of sight of the main complex of buildings, additional housing is provided in housing containers in a forest accessible via a police-guarded pavement. [...] The container units are arranged in a rectangular, completely closed-off area. The area closed off by the containers is caged off and covered with welded iron mesh. The Facility management failed to explicitly inform me of the accommodation spaces outside the main area of the Facility. The container units in the forest were 'discovered' only at the very end of the inspection visit.

She says that when they forced access to this area of the detention camp, the people imprisoned began shouting out and raising signs and banners: 'We are refugees, not prisoners!' and 'Help us, please!' These people, she said, were caged liked animals.[87] 'I am appalled', Šabatová wrote, 'by the degree of dehumanisation present in the system of detention of foreign nationals in the Czech Republic, as well as the degrading treatment which the Facility's management tolerates and the living conditions in which children are held in the Facility.'[88]

To add to their humiliation, detainees were charged for their stay: ordinarily imprisoned for ninety days at a cost of €10 per person, per day. These charges were 'levied' from their confiscated cash and valuables. Many were left without any money in their possession and were presented with a bill for their outstanding debts to the Czech state. This is a 'final deterrent' as it is illegal to claim asylum in Czechia if you are financially indebted to the government.

The refugees were frequently released without prior warning, without even a map, directions or transport to the nearest train station. Left 'destitute in front of the gate of the camp, in the middle of the forest', they relied on assistance from the Czech migrant activist community to continue on their journeys to safety.[89] Perhaps, as one Czech activist wryly notes, on the very same train 'from which police dragged them two months ago in Břeclav'.[90]

Spectres of fascism

With regard to Czechia in 2015, the United Nations concluded that its violations of the human rights of migrants were neither isolated nor coincidental, but systematic: an integral part of a policy package designed to deter migrants and refugees from entering the country or staying there.[91] As Daniel Trilling writes, for migrants arriving in Europe today, racist violence takes many forms on the ground, from 'the violence carried out by uniformed police or prison guards, the violence of indifference in the face of a refugee crisis, or the violence of neglect as people waste years of their lives waiting for the European bureaucracy to answer their pleas'.[92]

This chapter has sought to demonstrate the role of a multi-faceted 'stigma machine of racism' in enabling this violence, examining the ways in which practices of stigmatisation dehumanise people to the point that it becomes possible to keep children caged in shipping containers in a Czech forest. The penal practices of stigma I have described are also a reminder that it is impossible to imagine or think about race and crisis in contemporary Europe without recourse to history. The tattooing of refugees, their removal from trains at night, the fearful and racist responses of local communities, the comments of MailOnline readers, with their calls for yellow stars, tattoos and gas chambers, the humiliating practices of strip-searching refugees, confiscating all their valuables and goods, and the abject and hidden conditions in which they are held, evoke ghosts of Europe's recent fascist past.

One argument of this chapter is that contemporary political struggles over borders in Europe pivot on 'the seething presence' of ghostly processions of twentieth-century refugees – whether in calls from the far right to detain the Břeclav refugees in Theresienstadt, or in claims that migrants are enacting 'white genocide', or in more liberal forms of memorialisation that seek to freeze 'real racism' in the past – or in 'the East'.[93] As Avery Gordon argues, the thing about haunting is that it is an 'animated state' that 'alters the way we normally separate and sequence the past, the present and the future', allowing a 'repressed or unresolved social violence' to make itself known.[94] The processions of people arriving at the borders today are entrapped at the same railway stations, waiting rooms, platforms and train tracks, and are even detained in some of the same camps and prisons where refugees were concentrated in the 1930s and 1940s.

Undertaking the research for this chapter, tracing the genealogy of penal stigma and border struggles in Europe, has involved being haunted by histories of violence. Racism is haunting. Yet reckoning with these ghosts is important because they have something valuable to tell us about the high stakes of Europe's current racist crisis. Indeed, the ways in which we confront these spectres is a matter of life and death. While the political conditions for the industrial-scale genocide of the 1940s do not currently exist in Europe, we are returning to a violent, divided and illiberal past – a past in which many millions were murdered, and many fought hard and were killed.

As noted in the introduction to this chapter, we are seeing the proliferation of walls, cages and camps around the world, from the concentration of an estimated 1 million Uyghur Muslims in China (which to date has seen little in the terms of an international response, from the United Nations or other transnational bodies), and the much publicised caging of thousands of migrants at the US–Mexico border, including the segregation of children from their parents. The enclosure, detention and imprisonment of people is not a new phenomenon, but the *mass* concentration of people on the basis of citizenship status, religious, ethnic or racial difference in ways which openly flout international laws and human rights protections established after the Second World War is an alarming trend.

In Europe in 2015 photographs and television footage of migrant arrivals, of rescues at sea, of overloaded boats, discarded life-jackets, lost objects and dead children on Mediterranean beaches became commonplace horrors; more than half a million people desperately paddled towards the shore on overloaded dinghies that year, while tourists sunbathed amongst the flotsam of failed crossings. At least 3,770 drowned making the crossing: 'They were murdered. Actually, they were massacred. The policy stipulated they should be left to die. So they died.'[95] As a Lampedusa fisherman told a BBC journalist in 2015, 'We often pull up skulls and bones in our nets'.[96] When people are stigmatised to the extent that they are no longer seen as human, it seems we can't comprehend the violence, we no longer see it, or we simply don't care.

'Fuck the refugees', a teacher makes a passing remark to the Czech writer and film-maker Andre Vltchek on a train from Prague. 'Those niggers should stay where they are.'[97]

Scene three: Břeclav train station, 11 March 1938

At midnight on 11 March 1938, a train carrying refugees was halted at Břeclav station. Drawing on eyewitness accounts, the British journalist George Gedye described how events unfolded that night. Earlier that evening, Austrian Chancellor Kurt von Schuschnigg had resigned, surrendering Austria to annexation by the Nazi German government. Jews, communists, Catholics, anti-fascists, artists and intellectuals scrambled to get on the last train from Vienna to Prague in order to escape before the German army entered the city. The train was supposed to leave at 11.15pm, but by 8pm 'thousands of people were pushing each other, squeezing themselves into the train while demanding to depart immediately'.[98] Before it was able to pull out of the station, Nazi Stormtroopers boarded, 'running through the carriages, armed with dog whips', looting and terrorising passengers. Finally, the train departed. Then, twenty minutes into its journey, it was stopped in the middle of the countryside by the SS, who proceeded to 'go through the train with a fine-toothed comb'. Men, women and children were dragged out and herded into vans. Gedye describes how: 'Those who remained were plundered quite openly of everything in their possession – money, jewellery, watches and furs.'[99]

After some hours, 'the trembling survivors found themselves moving off towards Břeclav and safety', every moment 'an agony for those who feared to be held up again'. Finally, they could see the lights of Břeclav; they had reached the safety of Czechoslovakian territory. The Czech police boarded and announced that all passengers with Austrian passports were to leave the train. The refugees were moved to a guarded waiting room, where they saw from a window that the train they had arrived on was departing for Prague without them. After some hours, Břeclav's Chief of Police came into the waiting room and announced that all Austrian nationals were to be returned to Vienna. As Gedye notes, 'one of those who was there and managed by a ruse to escape told me later in Prague that the scenes that followed this announcement were too painful for him to recall'.[100]

Some of those forcibly returned to Vienna that evening escaped by departing at Austrian towns en route, taking off on foot into surrounding forests. The rest arrived back in Vienna, where they were locked in a waiting room at the train station for twelve hours, and were subject to interrogations by the SS. Some were later released, others went 'straight to Dachau'.[101] In August 1938, the Anschluss was complete, and the Eternal Jew Exhibition was installed within Vienna Railway Station. By the autumn of 1938, Břeclav was annexed to Nazi Germany. Renamed Lundenburg, its local Jewish population was soon expelled. Its railway station became a node on the transnational train network used to deport Jews to Theresienstadt and extermination camps in Eastern Europe. Over the next few years, refugees halted at Břeclav on 11 March 1938 would return to this border town on special transports – this time their trains travelled straight on through to their final destinations.

Chapter 4

The stigma machine
of austerity

Stigma teaches children that accepting charity is a disgrace.
Stigma makes people ask whether the help is really that
essential. Stigma discourages dependence.

Charles Murray, political scientist, 2009

Austerity was a political choice. Cutting services instead of
raising taxes was a choice. To make it stick, they used stigma
as a weapon.

Paul Mason, writer and journalist, 2017

Friday 6 July 2018. I am at the public launch event for the
Morecambe Bay Poverty Truth Commission at Lancaster Town Hall.
It's one of thirteen such commissions running across the UK, which
are attempting to find local solutions to poverty in the wake of a
decade of 'austerity' – 'the deepest and most precipitate cuts ever
made in social provision' in the history of the British state.[1] Around
150 people have gathered inside the fading grandeur of Lancaster's
town hall for the launch of our local commission: an assortment of
local businesspeople, charities, food bank and citizen's advice volunteers, homelessness workers, religious leaders, members of refugee

and migrant organisations, police officers, firefighters, addiction and mental health workers, GPs, teachers and teaching assistants, local city councillors, food bank managers, community workers, church leaders, a number of medical practitioners and public health professionals, city counsellors and one of our two local Members of Parliament. We have been invited into this civic space, a seat of local government and decision making for over a century, to listen to the testimonies of a dozen local people about the poverty, hunger, home-lessness, mental distress and physical ill-health which have followed in the wake of a decade of cuts to state and local welfare provisions. It has taken six months of intensive support by community workers to enable these testifiers to find the courage to talk in public about personal experiences which involve extreme suffering and distress.

It is the turn of David, a young man in his early twenties, to speak. David makes his way tentatively to the centre of the large stage, supported by Jane, a community worker. He is visibly nervous and Jane places her hand in the small of his back, reassuring him, whispering words of support we cannot hear. This is an extract from his testimony:[2]

I was one of nine kids – my mum felt forced to drug deal, it was the only way she could feed us. The stress on her not knowing where the next meal was coming from – it all rubbed off on us kids. Kids absorb things like that, it's really hard living like that. The only thing that held us together was the community – the people on our estate. Everyone would chip in to buy food for a month for people like us who didn't have enough.

Nana was the heart of the estate, she took all the kids out, taking us on minibuses for days out. Out of her own pocket at first. So we had something to do cos we had nothing. And parents could have one day without worrying about feeding kids. Then she started running the community centre. The place was heaving with kids all the time. It was a tiny hut in the car park of our school. Everything happened there – it was all we had, all anyone had. We had parties there as kids; it was amazing, magical, a place of no worries. There was meals there too that was so important. If it wasn't for my nan and all she did for me and all the other kids, I would have killed myself.

Ten years ago the youth workers from the council came and did a project – a massive music gig with all the lads and girls from the local council estates. It was amazing – all us kids from same background, all in poverty, and without that project we'd just have ended up scrapping and gang wars cos it was the only way we had of releasing all the anger we had. The project brought everyone together. It stopped all the fighting, and gang crimes. It was the best thing I've ever done ever – it was amazing – everyone said that. Then the funding was taken away from us, and we were left with nothing.

Our school was good – I had no bullying there. Many of the kids had serious difficulties – ADHD, Asperger's – you weren't judged, they treated you like family, they got to know your parents, they went to appointments with you. You felt accepted there. They've ... you've ... shut that now too.

Then when you have nowhere to go and nothing to do, you get bullied – kids aged 13, 15 whatever, young kids, the main drug dealers get you to sell heroine and crack – you're so afraid of what will happen to you if you don't do it – and there's nothing else. If all the youth stuff hadn't been taken away we wouldn't have been pulled away to the streets ... to these men. A few of me mates had to hide guns for them. They pay you – and when you have younger brothers and sisters needing to be fed its stressful trying to make the right decision. I thought my mum never knew where we was getting the money from, I had a paper round, and pretended it was that I gave her.

I hold the councillors who made these decisions responsible for what happened to me. They don't understand what they destroyed by taking those activities away. It was the only freedom we had, and it was taken away. We were just a number to them.

Then everything goes from worse to worse, my family gets evicted, we are moved to another area where we don't know no one. Then when your property needs work doing to it and the landlord won't do it, it's condemned and you're moved on again — same thing happened again, condemned, moved on. It didn't matter if my mum had to live in her mate's one bed flat and sleep on the floor with my brothers and sisters. Nobody cares.

When you're in poverty you end up with nothing cos it's all taken away and nobody cares. I became homeless – but they said I was not a priority need as I was 24. Street homeless, the council tells me I am not a priority need. The council don't help you if you're homeless and young – it's all the charities and the churches. The council just tell you if you're sleeping at a charity shelter you're not sleeping rough. You have no hope. It feels like the government are trying to make a superior race – the rich get richer and the poor get poorer. That causes the poor to do crimes like robbing to feed their kids. How can this be fair?

The government believes in money more than human beings. All they do is take, take, take. They worship money instead of heart.

They give me a number – when you speak my name that means you want to talk to me. I am David John Roberts. When you give me a number – my national insurance number, my NHS number, my tax code – you just want to talk money. My name is David John Roberts. If I had one thing to say to the government, it would be treat me as you want to be treated. See me as a person, not a number. See me as living. I am flesh and blood.

The impact of David's testimony is palpable on those congregated in Lancaster Town Hall. All around me people are sobbing as he speaks. Passing tissues to each other to wipe away tears as they listen to his account of dispossession and dehumanisation. In the space of a decade, David saw the strangulation of all the vital lifelines, the support mechanisms and collective practices of care that made his childhood on a deprived social housing estate in this small Northern English city liveable: the closure of the 'magical' local community centre set up by his Nana; the evisceration of youth and other outreach services; the shutting down of the kind, caring and inclusive local school; the eviction of his family from their home and community.[3] The snuffing out of all these lifelines made David increasingly vulnerable to exploitation: the drug-dealing he felt compelled to undertake to feed himself and his siblings, the manipulation, violence and abuse he suffered at the hands of predatory criminal men, his own eventual addiction and street homelessness.

David's testimony offers a damning critique of material consequences of the radical contraction of the welfare state. His biography tracks a decade of decision making by local civil servants and politicians as they search for savings, butchering social provisions, redistributing resources, wealth, opportunities and value upwards – and away from working-class children and young people like him. He forces us to consider the ways in which austerity becomes embedded within communities, corroding social bonds, enclosing and closing off common goods and resources: 'All they do is take, take, take.'

If public finance is a form of politics which is ordinarily 'hidden in accounting columns',[4] David's story opens a window through which we can glimpse some of the effects of the erosion of the post-war welfare state in Britain, and the terrible price paid by children and young people for decisions taken by 'people with power' in buildings like Lancaster Town Hall.

David is also a theorist of stigma power. He details the relationship between the attrition of his own life chances and the mechanisms through which austerity was implemented, describing some of the stigmatising practices through which he found his 'flesh and blood' life reduced to numbers on a spreadsheet of cuts: the fact that his age, twenty-four, is the number which determines that he is not a 'priority need' for shelter when he becomes street homeless; the eight months he was 'sanctioned' by a Department of Work and Pensions job coach for missing an appointment not long after he gave his testimony: eight months without recourse to any public funds; and the reason he missed his meeting at the job centre was because he had picked up a few days' work. David experiences these governmental practices of numbering as violent, humiliating and dehumanising forms of objectification – forms of badging which exemplify the incremental subordination of his life to the logic of financial capitalism, a logic in which lives like his are deemed to be of little value. It is a market-driven society from which he has found himself progressively shut out, eventually abandoned to the streets. Austerity is lived by David as an endless fracking of security, opportunity, resources and hope.[5]

In bearing witness, David asks those gathered in the town hall to really look at him, to recognise through him – with him – the profound cruelty effected by this regime of 'fiscal discipline'. He asks us to acknowledge the ways in which austerity is *embodied* as he is badged as undeserving, devalued, made to feel like human waste, an object, a thing. David's testimony is also an accusation, for he is directly addressing those 'with power' seated in front of him, asking them/us to take responsibility for his dispossession and despair: 'I hold the councillors who made these decisions responsible for what happened to me.' You did this to me.

After David has finished speaking, there is a brief moment of silence. Then the congregation in Lancaster Town Hall start to stand up one by one. Soon the whole room is standing, and people start to clap. What I experience in this spontaneous response is a community witnessing David's social abjection.[6] An admission of the shameful truth which David has described, and a collective recognition of him as a person 'with heart'. It was an extraordinary enactment of what Sylvia Wynter describes as 'being human as praxis'.[7]

'I am David John Roberts.'

The austerity state

In November 2018, Philip Alston, the United Nations Special Rapporteur on extreme poverty and human rights, visited Britain on a fact-finding mission to ascertain the impact of a decade of austerity. In his interim (2018) and final reports (2019), which draw on a substantial body of independent evidence, Alston describes that what he witnessed was nothing less than the 'disappearance of the post-war British welfare state'. As he writes, 'although the United Kingdom is the world's fifth largest economy, one fifth of its population (14 million people) live in poverty, and 1.5 million of them experienced destitution in 2017'.[8] Alston draws particular attention to the disproportionate impacts of this 'disappearance' of the welfare state on those already on the losing end of the British class society: working-class children and young people, low-paid women, especially working-class women of colour, disabled people, and those living at the margins of Britain's increasingly punitive citizenship and residency regimes, including precarious migrant workers and asylum seekers.

The effects of the evisceration of state welfare has been well evidenced by academics, journalists and charitable organisations. As my friend and colleague Chris Grover summarises, the 'cuts and changes to social provision' made by the British government in the wake of the 2008 global financial crisis 'have contributed to increased poverty rates; falling living standards; the expansion of precarious wage; deepening disabilised, gendered and racialised inequalities; a colossal increase in homelessness and rough sleeping, and food and fuel poverty'.[9] In short, the austerity state is characterised by the inability of increasingly large swathes of people to access the basic resources of shelter, food, heating and healthcare which they require to adequately sustain the lives of themselves, their children, and disabled and elderly relatives. What this state-crafted, government-planned and -managed programme of 'disaster capitalism' has left in its wake is an immense crisis of social reproduction.[10] I use the word 'disaster' advisedly here, for what this nearly decade-long government programme of reform has effected is levels of precarity and vulnerability so dire that some poorer communities face circumstances of deprivation that resemble those found in the aftermath of wars and natural disasters.

The violent outcomes of this 'decisive break with the postwar consensus' and the 'profound reshaping of social life' it has set in motion are not hidden.[11] Nobody living in Britain in the last decade can have failed to notice the profound social changes effected by austerity. As Alston concludes, the social catastrophe precipitated by austerity 'is obvious to anyone who opens their eyes'.[12] Indeed, it is difficult *not* to see the effects of this programme of reform. For example, the growing numbers of people begging and sleeping rough on the streets of British towns and cities, in parks and playing fields. Rough sleeping, the smallest but most visible tip of the homelessness crisis, has risen by 165 per cent in England since 2010. Many local authorities have attempted to erase traces of rough sleeping and begging in public and commercial settings: by criminalising homeless people; through the forced movement of people from town and city centres; by introducing punitive bylaws, fines and sanctions, and in London and Liverpool through collusion with homelessness charities and the central government

Home Office to deport non-national homeless people from the state itself.[13] Despite these efforts, the scale of the homelessness crisis is impossible to hide.

Other symptoms of austerity, such as hunger and mental distress, are less acutely visible, and here both quantitative evidence and qualitative data is essential in enabling us to build a picture of what this 'disappearance' of the welfare state means. For example, we know that austerity reforms of the benefits system targeted working-age adults, and that this has had a particularly pronounced impact on levels of child poverty. Britain's leading independent microeconomic research institute, the Institute for Fiscal Studies, has detailed how austerity has wiped out the legacy of all previous attempts and political promises to eradicate child poverty. Indeed, child poverty, whether assessed via relative or absolute measures, has been increasing unremittingly since 2011. For example, it is estimated that 'by 2023 to 2024 the proportion of children living in relative poverty (after housing costs) is on course to hit 37%'.[14] As Alison Garnham, chief executive of the Child Poverty Action Group, states: 'It's increasingly evident, particularly to people working with children, that we're in a child poverty crisis. And it is primarily to do with the massive cuts to benefits.'[15]

A 2019 survey conducted by the National Education Union (NEU) among 8,600 school leaders, teachers and support staff, revealed that 97 per cent of staff in state-funded schools had seen a dramatic increase in poverty in schools, and were regularly required to feed and clothe children in their care. When asked to describe the impacts of this planned impoverishment, 'three out of four respondents said they saw children suffering from fatigue (78%), poor concentration (76%) or poor behaviour (75%); more than half said their students had experienced hunger (57%) or ill-health (50%)'.[16] Further, more than a third of those surveyed said children in the schools in which they worked had experienced stigmatised bullying as a consequence of poverty. Austerity is creating a hostile environment for children living in poverty in British schools.

While austerity cuts have been implemented with haste, many biosocial symptoms of austerity are slower to reveal themselves. Deprivation accumulates in bodies over lifetimes. Nevertheless, health professionals have already documented 'growing evidence of conditions not only exacerbated by poverty, but caused by it'.[17] For example, national-level data reveals rates of malnutrition amongst people admitted to hospital have doubled in the last decade, and there is an evidenced rise in diseases associated with poverty.[18] This striking phenomenon has been dubbed, by both medical practitioners and journalists, as marking the return of 'Victorian Diseases'. For example, there has been a rise in reported cases of tuberculosis (an especially acute disease amongst homeless populations), scarlet fever, whooping cough, gout and Vitamin D deficiency (linked to anecdotal reports from multiple health professionals of a rise in cases of childhood rickets, and osteomalacia – the adult form of the disease).[19]

That austerity is making people physically ill is underscored by the fact that life expectancy rates are declining amongst some population groups. In 2018, the National Office for Statistics published data that revealed that the predicted lifespan of deprived women in Britain had fallen for the first time since the 1920s, and that 'the gap in life expectancy between the poorest and most advantaged' women in England had reached a record high 'now standing at seven years and five months'.[20] Several subsequent studies have also suggested correlations between austerity cuts to adult social and elder care and rising excess mortality rates. In short, all the scientific evidence suggests that the 'disappearance of the post-war British welfare state' is foreshortening working-class lives, and the lives of others, the elderly, the disabled, without the necessary accumulated reserves of wealth to defend themselves or their loved ones against the grinding effects of the erosion of the social state.

In his interim and final report, Alston draws our attention to the now familiar economic origin story of austerity, noting how these 'far-reaching changes to the role of government' were 'sold' to the British electorate as 'being part of an unavoidable program of fiscal "austerity", needed to save the country from bankruptcy'.[21] However, as Alston concludes, 'the driving force' behind austerity was not economics; rather austerity is a political project underpinned by an ideological 'commitment to achieving radical social re-engineering'.[22] Alston notes that 'the experience of the United Kingdom … underscores the conclusion that poverty is a political choice': 'Austerity could easily have spared the poor, if the political will had existed to do so. Resources were available [which] could have transformed the situation of millions of people living in poverty, but the political choice was made to fund tax cuts for the wealthy instead.'[23]

If the economic rationale for austerity as a necessary debt reduction programme is fantastical, there was nevertheless considerable capital to be made through its implementation. In the case of austerity, the shock of the 2008 global banking crisis was seized upon as an opportunity not only to turn off the redistributive tap, but to frack the social state for profit by privatising public assets and services. In this regard, austerity, like previous historical rounds of capitalist enclosure, is a political ruse which has protected existing 'concentrations of elite wealth and power'.[24] Austerity has witnessed the wholesale harnessing of financial and legal mechanisms of deregulation, extracting as much value as possible from Britain's 'social estate', redistributing wealth, resources and land upwards.[25] The winners under austerity have been the financial and corporate elites, who have not only emerged with 'fortunes intact' but 'holding a larger than ever slice of the cake'.[26] This has led to the conclusion that 'austerity' is a proxy term for 'class war': a war of breathtaking cruelty waged against the poorest, the most disadvantaged and vulnerable members of British society.[27]

Austerity as enclosure

Austerity is a twenty-first-century enclosure movement. By this, I mean that it is a political programme that involves the fracking of public goods by those in the service of capital, in ways which are designed to upend the customary forms of social provision cemented in the mid-twentieth century. The programme of austerity which began in 2010 was characterised by the rapid closure of local hospitals and clinics, public libraries, local museums, post offices, children's nurseries, community and youth centres, day-centres and residential care homes for disabled people and pensioners, and the enclosure of common land, including parks and playing fields. The amount of services, facilities, buildings and land once held in common by local communities, now sold by cash-strapped local authorities to developers, or simply abandoned to decay, is staggering. The speed with which this expropriation has been undertaken has been shocking to witness. To take just one small example, in 2019 West Sussex county council, a relatively wealthy area of South East England, announced that it was cutting the budget 'it spends on housing support services for rough sleepers, victims of domestic abuse, care leavers, and frail older people in the county' from £6.3 million to £2.3 million. Implementing this budget cut entailed dismantling 'an entire social infrastructure of hostels, drop-in centres, and floating support teams built up over years'.[28]

What we are witnessing in austerity Britain is the enclosure of local 'welfare commons', namely those public goods and services established by local communities through long histories of philanthropy, charitable and worker contributions (e.g. local taxation) and grassroots agitation. Entire material infrastructures, buildings, services and land – including those hospitals and schools that local communities campaigned for, and often paraded through the streets for in the nineteenth century – are disappearing.

The local patchworks of welfare institutions and services built up over centuries were first absorbed into the British welfare state in the 1940s and 1950s. For the majority of citizens, the mid-twentieth-century 'statification' of welfare provisions brought significant improvements in terms of fairness of access, greater equality of treatment, and the national pooling of expertise and resources. Through privatisation, the British state is now expropriating these communal assets from the communities that originally fought for and financed them. Seen from the perspective of this longer history of welfare, austerity is nothing less than a government-orchestrated programme of theft.

It is not just buildings, essential services and material resources which have been enclosed in this process, but generations of public sector knowledge and expertise. Indeed, austerity has seen a million workers in the public sector lose their jobs.[29] Some statutory services have been contracted out to for-profit private sector organisations, where employment contracts are more precarious, work lower paid and conditions of work less protected. Swelling numbers of unpaid voluntary workers have attempted to keep services going, but after a decade of cuts many volunteers are burning out.

As social safety nets are cut away, people are falling through the gaps in the emergent uneven, fragmented patchwork of state and charitable provisions. The enclosure of the 'welfare commons' has accelerated what charities have described as an epidemic of social isolation and loneliness. Elderly people and disabled people have been enclosed in their homes. Children with special and complex needs can't get the support they require in school settings, and increasing numbers of children are now outside of formal education altogether. Young people like David are sleeping on the streets. Women are forced to remain with abusive partners as domestic violence shelters have been closed down. As Sisters Uncut, a collective 'fighting against budget cuts to domestic and sexual violence organisations and services in Britain' put it: 'They cut, we bleed.'[30]

'The political violence of the state is becoming normalised'

It is estimated that 10 per cent of the British population is now 'food insecure', a situation defined as 'experiencing hunger, inability to secure enough food of sufficient quality and quantity to enable good health and participation in society, and cutting down on food due to financial necessity'.[31] Food banks and other mass forms of charitable emergency food provision were almost unknown in Britain between 1950 and 2010. Now every city and town in Britain has a food bank, and some have several. In every deprived neighbourhood, networks of food clubs, food banks and other emergency feeding centres have sprung up. Every supermarket in every British town and city has an emergency food donation point near the checkouts. Special signs have been designed and printed for use on supermarket shelves, which direct shoppers to the non-perishable food and provisions most useful and/or urgently required by local foodbanks. Staff at the university where I work are now encouraged to donate monthly to our local food bank through a 'salary sacrifice' scheme. Students regularly hold collections for the local food bank.

I could go on – examples of the ways in which austerity has seeped its way into new forms of charitable giving is endless. My point is that the emergence of these new social and cultural infra-structures of alms-giving are inescapable in the everyday lives of all citizens, and in this respect the depth and scale of the poverty inaugurated by austerity is quite literally on public view. Yet, as Vicki Cooper and David Whyte suggest, after a decade of cuts we seem to have become so 'accustomed to the ease with which people are evicted and made homeless', the food banks, the street begging, and the mental health epidemic, 'that we do not make the most obvious of observations; that the age that we live in is one in which the political violence of the state is becoming normalised'.[32]

Unseeing austerity

One effect of the normalisation of austerity is that the depth and scale of the impoverishment it has effected is both hyper-visible, on every street corner and at every supermarket exit, and unseen or perhaps *unseeable*. Indeed, despite mountains of social scientific and statistical evidence of every form, kind and shape, the devastating effects of austerity are repeatedly denied by the politicians who implemented this programme of reform, by some, not all, of the journalists who report on it, and by 'ordinary' members of the public; for example, readers of a 2019 *Daily Mail* newspaper story on child hunger in Britain typically responded in online comments:

There is not one single kid in poverty in this country. Not a single one. Having a 360 instead of an Xbox One isn't poverty.

Parents are given benefits and they do not spend it on their children. Parents have the latest phones, large TVs, smoke, do drugs whilst children go hungry.

This poverty delusion is just unreal problems fabricated by the left wing media. What I see is virtually full employment, anybody that really wants a job has one. Lots of well-fed if not fat people not looking very hungry.[33]

The disavowal was underscored by the response of government ministers to the Alston report. While I was writing this chapter, the Chancellor of the Exchequer, Philip Hammond, was interviewed on *Newsnight*, the BBC's flagship television news programme, and summarily dismissed Alston's report as 'nonsense': 'I don't accept the UN rapporteur's report at all', he stated. 'Look around you, that's not what we see in this country.'[34] Certainly, Hammond's claim that the Alston report is untruthful because he cannot 'see' the effects of austerity is both disingenuous and chilling. Indeed, we might recall here Arundhati Roy's description of the erasure of the lived realities of caste discrimination in contemporary India as a 'Project of Unseeing'.

For neoliberal dogmatists like multimillionaire Hammond, who, as he puts it 'believe that a market economy is the way to deliver a prosperous future for Britain', austerity isn't the problem. There is nothing wrong, he says, with 'the theory of how a market economy is supposed to work, in generating and distributing wealth', because this is 'the way that the text books tell us it will work'. Rather, the problem is that people are currently not 'experiencing' this economic doctrine in the right way. What Hammond seems to be suggesting is that international experts on poverty such as Philip Alston need to be tutored in perceiving the effects of austerity differently, they need to *unsee* poverty – or perhaps to perceive the deepening pockets of poverty, illness, homelessness, hunger and avoidable deaths effected by austerity as a necessary *stage* in the implementation of market-based solutions to 'the problem' of state welfare itself.

Philip Alston notes that when he read about this 'total denial of a set of uncontested facts' in the British government responses to his report, he thought he might be reading 'a spoof'.[35] I know what he means, because the responses reminded me of Jonathan Swift's satirical 'A Modest Proposal' (1729), in which Swift famously suggested that if we retrain our gaze we might see the rising tide of beggarly Irish infants not as a problem, but as an opportunity; indeed, a source of revenue if fattened up as meat for the tables of the rich. The economist and statistician Howard Freidman draws on 'A Modest Proposal' in a satirical take on US advocates of extreme 'fiscal discipline', writing that 'the incessant whining of the poor for food, shelter, education, and other such extravagances has raised the decibel level so high that it's scarcely possible to enjoy a polo match or savor a glass of Château Lafite in peace'.[36]

The serious point is that in a political context where expert evidence about the effects of austerity, including evidence collated by the government's own official accounting bodies, can be so swiftly denied as 'nonsense', how might those concerned with rising levels of poverty in contemporary Britain articulate the evidence? This dilemma is exacerbated by the fact that poverty is often experienced as deeply shameful. People frequently go to great lengths to conceal the scale of the difficulties they are facing from others, including from their own families and friends. As Stephanie, whose story opened this book, notes:

> I was always taught that everything stays within 'these four walls'. The more debt I had, the more I had to isolate myself from everybody, because I couldn't go out with the same people or even share conversations with the same people. My life experience started to radically diverge from that of former friends ... we weren't going out anymore, going on holidays, buying things. We were living off food bank parcels and struggling to keep a roof over our heads. There was nobody I would have discussed my situation with. I desperately tried to hide it. The shame was overwhelming.

Seeing austerity

Poverty Truth is a grassroots social movement grounded in the following principles: that those with lived experiences of poverty need to have voice and agency in social and political decision making; that people in poverty are not the problem; that poverty is everybody's problem; and that effecting change begins with attitudinal change. At the core of the Poverty Truth movement is an understanding that stigmatising public beliefs about the causes of poverty are a block to social change, and that the sharing of lived experience is the first step in devising collective solutions. Poverty Truth is an anti-stigma movement.

The Morecambe Bay Poverty Truth Commission (currently) covers a geographical area in North West England that includes the small city of Lancaster, the neighbouring seaside town of Morecambe and surrounding rural villages. The Morecambe Bay Poverty Truth Commission is composed of around a dozen people who have experienced or who are experiencing poverty (those who have borne the brunt of the grinding effects of a decade of cuts), and a similar number of civic decision makers. Amongst the "experts of experience" on the Commission is David, whose testimony opened this chapter, and Stephanie, whose words opened this book. There is also Ian, an ex-soldier, a man in his late fifties who suffers from post-traumatic stress and physical disabilities which mean that he is unable to work. Ian has previously been street homeless and with help from a charity he has now found a home, but has to choose between heating his home and feeding himself because the state benefits he is entitled to fall below the income required to be both warm and adequately nourished.

Then there is Jack, a dad to four children, who is in full-time but low-paid work. Like 4 million workers in the austerity state, Jack is caught in 'in-work' poverty, meaning his income (wages and 'top-up' benefits) do not meet the basic needs of his family. Jack tells me how, at the end of each summer, he is reduced to 'begging and borrowing' from family and friends to pay for his children's school uniforms and school shoes.[37]

There is also Mark, an ex-addict who has turned his life around, and now works helping others in a local addiction treatment centre; Tiffany, who has long-standing physical disabilities and has struggled with negotiating changes to the disability welfare system;

Saskia, who is in long-term treatment for severe and enduring mental health problems; and Patricia, from our local Irish Traveller community, who is concerned her family and community will be evicted from their homes, as the local authority plans to sell their Traveller site as part of austerity cuts.

There is also Isla, a child poverty commissioner in her teens. In her testimony at the launch event in July 2018 at Lancaster Town Hall, Isla described how she felt ashamed at not being able to afford the £1 donation to charity on non-school uniform days, and how she suffered a breakdown when she and her mum faced eviction from her home – 'thinking what was the point in living anymore if I couldn't even look after my own mum. I kept sinking and sinking. Until I couldn't physically move with the weight of these feelings'.

Alongside people living in poverty, the Morecambe Bay Poverty Truth Commission includes many frontline workers, health professionals and charitable volunteers, who are working tirelessly to forge new networks of support to catch those now free-falling through the gaping holes left by the erosion of previously tax-funded structures of social provision and care. For example, a local firefighter describes to us the intensification of psychological distress in his team, a consequence of the fact that they are now so frequently called out to attempted suicides, and a police officer relates how people in our local area commit petty crimes in the hope of getting arrested, as being held in custody is their best hope of accessing mental and physical health services – a snapshot of desperation supported by nationwide evidence from police forces across the UK (see Conclusion). A senior GP shares his concerns about colleagues 'burning out' from the stress of trying to treat patients with physical and mental health conditions caused by deprivation – problems with causes they can't treat or solve. A youth worker relates how the teenagers he works with regularly admit that they are forced to steal from shops to feed and clothe themselves. A head teacher from a local primary school describes how children routinely arrive at her school hungry and have been found rifling through rubbish bins for food between lessons, eating discarded fruit cores. She tells us about an episode in which a parent passed out in her school hall 'through doing without meals' and describes the cumulative impact on staff of having to comfort ashamed and tearful mums at the school gates; mums who have no means of adequately feeding their children, of washing their clothes, of heating homes.

Working on the poverty commission has allowed me to forge new relationships with a wide range of people who have been impacted by the evisceration of the welfare state. It was through listening to the stories from the poverty commission that I fully came to appreciate the depth of despair and suffering which austerity has augmented within my local community. Community commissioners, and others with lived experiences of austerity cuts to welfare, health and social care, have taught me a vast amount about the fear, the shame and gnawing anxiety that accompany a hand-to-mouth existence in a society without secure safety nets. I have learnt also about the ripple effects of 'austerity trauma' on public sector workers and charitable volunteers.

The accounts of these different experts of experience are of critical importance in deepening our understanding of what the disappearance of the post-war British welfare state means in practice in people's everyday lives. Together they provide a documentary picture of the current crisis of basic social provisions of health, education and housing affecting so many within the British state. More than this, their experiences grant them the 'difficult double vision' that comes with living through a period of rapid social change.[38] What I mean by this is that in their various roles as 'service users', professionals, welfare workers and volunteers, they have had a front seat in the unfolding of this dramatic decade of social change. They have witnessed, and in many cases participated in, the practices through which the transition from functioning welfare systems to a denuded austerity state has been enacted.

Austerity in my own life

I know the geographical area covered by my local Poverty Truth Commission well, intimately in fact. This is the region in which I was born, grew up and was educated. I have lived in Lancaster for twenty-four years, almost all of my adult life. I work at Lancaster University as a sociologist, teaching and supervising students, and increasingly undertaking senior management and administrative work. I have brought up two children in this small city, one of whom still lives at home and attends the same local school as Isla. I am also the adult daughter of ageing, sick and disabled working-class parents and step-parents who live nearby. Like many adult children of sick or ageing parents, I am drawn continuously into engagements with health and social care providers as my family navigates depleted, complex and increasingly punitive systems of welfare, health and social care. Indeed, while I was writing *Stigma*, I spent a lot of time trying to access help and support for my parents, and experienced first-hand how austerity is accumulating in bodies, in families, in communities.

In May 2018, my step-dad Mohamed had a profoundly disabling stroke, which left him paralysed and wheelchair-bound at the age of sixty-three. Until his stroke, Mohamed had worked full-time on the minimum wage for a local furniture recycling charity. Navigating the welfare system to find appropriate care and support for him has been a challenge of Kafkaesque proportions. When we turned to a charity for advice on stroke rehabilitation and adult social care, we were told 'there is no adult social care or community stroke support in this area anymore'. Mohamed suffers from post-stroke psychosis, and we needed advice about how to interact with him in ways which wouldn't exacerbate his distress. We were told that there were no longer any clinical psychiatrists employed in our local area due to NHS cuts. In desperation, I used social media to find a psychiatrist who I could ask for guidance on how we should manage his psychotic symptoms. Mohamed now lives in a care home, and we are still struggling to access the support and rehabilitation services he requires. For example, we are currently trying to raise funds for an electric wheelchair to enable him to have a modicum of independent mobility; while he has been assessed as qualifying for an NHS wheelchair, we have been told there is three-year waiting list. As my mum reflects: 'It feels like they are just putting people like Mo in the dustbin, like human waste.'

Half a mile away from the care home in which Mo now lives, my dad John lives in a small privately rented house with his disabled wife, Liz. They don't live in poverty. They describe themselves as 'just about managing', with a household income made up of state old-age pensions, my dad's small fire brigade pension, and a disability allowance (for Liz, who is severely crippled with rheumatoid arthritis). They have no savings and own no property. My dad has just turned seventy. He began his working life at fourteen on a turkey farm, and later spent ten years as a fire-fighter, then working as painter and decorator and builder's labourer before he was forced by ill-health to stop work.

My dad had a massive heart attack in his early sixties, and now has inoperable heart failure. He also has osteoarthritis so severe he is in permanent chronic pain with highly restricted mobility. His heart is too weak to undergo the knee and hip replacement operations that would have eased his suffering. He struggles to get up out of a chair. Once he is standing, he can walk gingerly with the support of sticks, but he can no longer manage to climb the stairs in his home. Every evening he takes strong painkillers before he shuffles on his bottom up the stairs to get to his bedroom.

The only bathroom in his home is upstairs, so during the day he resorts to weeing in a bucket downstairs. He is on a social housing waiting list for a bungalow as he urgently needs a downstairs bedroom and bathroom, hand rails and a walk-in shower. In the context of the social housing crisis, it is likely to be a long wait – he is currently classified as being on the lowest band in terms of need. I helped my dad fill in the online application for adapted social housing. One of the questions asked what difference adapted housing would make to his life. When I asked him what to write, he said, 'Just tell them I would like a little dignity'. While I was writing this chapter my dad suffered a series of strokes and is currently, as he puts it with a smile, 'just about alive'.

As I shuttle back and forth, doing what I can to ease the lives of my disabled parents, I recall the 'dispirited and exhausted' words of the British sociologist Beverley Skeggs, who in a devastating account of her attempt to find adequate healthcare, social care and housing for her dying parents, concluded that this is a 'destroyed system with so little humanity, only profit'.[39]

Actively disabling people

Alongside forced movements of people, through evictions, displacement and homelessness, austerity immobilises people, as they find themselves progressively shut in, shut out and 'left behind'. The immobilising effects of austerity enclosures are vividly illustrated through the impact of austerity measures upon disabled people who are living through the most severe cuts to state-funded services of provision of *any group at any time in the history of the modern welfare state*.[40] To take just one example, the closure of a government fund called the Independent Living Fund (ILF) in 2015 saw the axing of care packages which supported '18,000 of the most severely disabled people in the country' to live independently.[41] Set up in 1988, the ILF was a crowning achievement of the disability rights movement in Britain, allowing people with severe impairments, on low incomes, to access care at home so that they could live outside residential settings – it was a direct outcome of the activism of people like Paul Hunt (Chapter 2). The government scrapped this £320 million fund completely, and devolved responsibility for care to local authorities, a process which has seen severe cuts in the care packages and allowances which enable people to live independent and dignified lives.

As Mo Stewart has detailed, austerity was explicitly designed to *contract* disability as an administrative category, in order to reduce the 'fiscal burden' of disabled people.[42] From 2010 onwards, a punitive welfare machinery was erected which sought to reclassify disabled people as able (to fend for themselves). The process of reassessing disabled people's ability to work involved the introduction of a testing regime called Work Capability Assessments – which was subcontracted to private multinational companies. Among many other consequences, this new testing regime has seen the removal of 75,000 adapted cars, powered wheelchairs and scooters from disabled people, leaving many quite literally enclosed within their homes.[43]

My step-mum Liz has rheumatoid arthritis in her hands and feet so severe that she requires a specially adapted car to drive. Liz had previously qualified for a welfare benefit called the Disability Living Allowance (DLA) through which she was able to lease a specially adapted car through a government-backed charitable scheme called Motability. While I was writing this chapter Liz was reassessed for disability support under the new austerity points-based system called Personal Independence Payments (PIP). Liz rang in tears to tell me that her adapted car was being taken away because she had missed the new criteria for 'enhanced mobility support' by two points. She considered an appeal, but an appeal meant losing a one-off bridging payment which would be essential in enabling them to afford to buy a second-hand adapted car.[44]

Just as emergency food provision has become normalised over the last decade, public outrage over the violent expropriation of resources from disabled people quickly dissipated, and those humiliated and imprisoned through these cuts and changes were left to seek charitable aid -- many now crowdsource for adapted vehicles and wheelchairs online.[45]

The retrenchment of state support to disabled people not only signals a fundamental shift in governmental attitudes to 'equal rights', but also a deeper shift in the political economy of dis/ability. For these cuts are not only adversely impacting on people with existing disabilities, but are actively disabling people, as those 'struggling under the financial strain', and the stress of proving their 'deservedness' within punitive systems of relief, become 'ill, physically and emotionally'.[46] For example, a 2014 National Health Service report revealed that 50 per cent of disabled benefit claimants have attempted suicide since the introduction of the work capability assessments.[47] A 2016 academic study revealed that 'each additional 10,000 people reassessed (using the WCA) in each area was associated with an additional 6 suicides, 2700 cases of reported mental health problems, and the prescribing of an additional 7020 antidepressant items'.[48]

In 2016, the United Nations Committee on the Rights of Persons with Disabilities visited Britain in response to information they had received from 2010 onwards from disability charities and civil rights organisations. This committee, which interviewed over 200 individuals, and collected 3,000 pages of evidence, concluded 'that there is reliable evidence that the threshold of grave or systematic violations of the rights of persons with disabilities has been crossed'.[49] Further, that the government 'expressly foresaw' the 'adverse impact' of austerity measures 'on persons with disabilities'. The dismissal of these reports by the British government is an abject lesson in the fact that human rights, civil rights, legal rights and political rights have little traction in the absence of basic economic rights, namely the right to access the resources required for a liveable life.

The uneven geography of austerity

Local perspectives on the impacts of austerity are particularly important because, as Alston notes, it is the local authorities 'which perform vital roles in providing a real social safety net' that have been most dramatically 'gutted' by cuts.[50] The services provided by local authorities include education, housing, transport and leisure and statutory responsibilities for providing services to vulnerable groups, including social care for the elderly, disabled adults and children. As recorded by the British government's Public Accounts Committee, the scale of cuts to local authorities is truly staggering. Central government grants to local authorities, which used to be the primary mechanism for redistributing national taxation to local areas, have seen on average 'a 49.1% real-terms funding reduction since 2010', with an additional 77 per cent reduction being implemented at the time of writing.[51] As Mia Gray and Anna Barford have detailed, 'the politics of austerity "dumped" the fiscal crisis onto the local state', effectively 'devolving austerity to the local level'.[52] What national-level accounts of the impact of austerity invariably conceal are correlations between the depth of cuts and areas of already existing high rates of poverty and deprivation; for example, 'within England, cities and local governments in the very north of the country saw the most severe cuts'.[53] In short, the effects of austerity are radically geographically uneven, with disproportionate impacts in poorer regions, such as the North of England where my family and I live.[54]

This is partly a consequence of a fundamental shift in the redistributive model through which local authorities are funded.

Government grants to local authorities are being incrementally 'devolved', and local governments are now increasingly required to raise much of their own income through local taxation (council tax and business rates) and the introduction of charges for services. This shift from a more universalist to a devolved funding model disadvantages poorer regions outside of the wealthier South East of England. In an attempt to manage this transition, local authorities are drawing on reserves; however, in poorer regions 'lower local property values mean there is less potential for local government to profit from renting or selling council assets, which could be used to buffer shrinking grants'.[55] In the context of the UK's London-centric journalism and media coverage, these differences in the spatial geographies of austerity matter profoundly in terms of our ability to *see* the differential impacts of the disappearance of the welfare state.

In 2018, a Midlands local authority, Northamptonshire County Council, declared itself bankrupt and central government-appointed commissioners assumed control over its budget: a process that saw 'radical service cuts and halted all new expenditures except for statutory services and the safeguarding of vulnerable people, and even these services have experienced cuts'.[56] The National Audit Office (NAO) has revealed that one in ten county councils could run out of reserves by 2021. If austerity continues (as currently planned), other local authorities will declare bankruptcy, as reserve funds are eroded and all existing assets sold off. The prospect of multiple bankruptcies in the public sector – which includes the bankruptcy of hospital and health trusts and schools, as well as local authorities – marks uncharted territory in the history of the modern British state.

My own local authority, Lancashire County Council, is amongst those facing bankruptcy. On 14 February 2019, in its latest attempt to balance the books, Lancashire County Council passed a £77 million package of cuts to services for vulnerable adults and children, and committed to finding an additional £135m of savings in the four years leading up to 2021–2022. As the council's Labour opposition leader Azhar Ali stated, if implemented these cuts will 'sink communities' and 'lead to the loss of lives'.[57] Protestors outside County Hall in Preston, the building in which elected local politicians gathered to vote on the latest proposed budget cuts, held up signs which said 'Valentine's Day Massacre'.

My intention here isn't to blame local authorities for cuts in budgets determined by national government. Nevertheless, it is important to draw attention to local fiscal responses to austerity, and to examine the ways in which the logic of neoliberal capitalism has become embedded within the structures of local government. As the housing and planning campaigner and scholar Michael Edwards argues, for some time local authorities have been encouraged, indeed compelled, to reimagine local resources and infrastructures (services, buildings, land) as financial assets, rather than as community resources whose value lies in their use.[58] It is important to register also how state actors have increasingly, if sometimes unwillingly, become participants in the implementation of neoliberal projects of 'accumulation through dispossession'. Further, implementing these changes takes significant time and labour, and over the last decade cutting budgets, demolishing services and enclosing local welfare commons has become the dispiriting day job of many civil servants and local politicians.

The devolution of austerity means in effect that people are unable to shape local decision making through elections, as the stripping bare of budgets means local politicians are effectively denuded of meaningful powers to change the situation faced by their constituents. At the same time, the outsourcing and privatisation of services and public goods have seen other structures of accountability fatally eroded – who do you hold to account if a for-profit service provider fails to provide safe or adequate care? For many, legal redress is no longer possible, as legal aid has also been closed off, as implemented in the 2012 Legal Aid, Sentencing and Punishment of Offenders Act. Unless you are wealthy enough to pay for legal representation, it is incredibly difficult to challenge decision making around housing, family law, immigration, employment or welfare. It is no coincidence that legal aid was diminished at the same time as the government's welfare revolution began.[59] In short, the democratic tools through which individuals and communities might in the past have held local decision makers to account have been severely blunted.

'We are completely beaten down by being dehumanised'

If you work as a sociologist on issues of poverty and welfare in the austerity state, you will encounter stigma everywhere. The word 'stigma' trips continually off tongues in everyday conversations about the experiences of those at the sharp end of the dismantling of the provisions, structures and institutions of the British welfare state. Indeed, stigma was the red thread that connected all the stories told by people with experiences of poverty on the Morecambe Bay Poverty Truth Commission. At the heart of every single account of living in poverty I have listened to were profoundly distressing experiences of being stigmatised, and the debilitating impact of the cumulative effects of stigma upon individuals' mental and physical health. As one commissioner describes it, 'We are completely beaten down by being dehumanised'.

The experiences of people on my local Poverty Commission track a decade of an ongoing attempt by the British government 'to permanently disable the protection state'[60] – a programme of reforms which the former Work and Pensions Secretary Iain Duncan Smith described in 2015 as 'nothing short of a revolution':

'the most ambitious programme of welfare reform for over a generation', 'a complete shift in the welfare culture in this country: no longer just pouring money in as Labour did, maintaining people in dependency'.[61] Austerity sought, in the parlance of politicians, to 'change people's behaviour', to make them more 'resilient' and 'less dependent'. This 'welfare revolution' rapidly saw the apparatus of the welfare state plunged into chaos; the privatisation of some services; a movement to online-only application processes; cuts to benefit payments; the introduction of workfare regimes; the use of psychometric testing regimes to assess applicants' 'attitude' and willingness to work; and a regime of punitive sanctions which saw benefits withdrawn for the slightest perceived infraction. Within a few short years, the government systematically redesigned the delivery of welfare provisions in ways that sought to humiliate people, a system of degradation rituals which sought to deter people from making a claim on the state for support. Stigma was used as a 'deterrent' ostensibly to force people off benefits and into work – an anathema in a social context of near full employment and where, for many, waged work is increasingly precarious and often no longer pays enough to meet basic needs.

People on the Poverty Commission also describe the cumulative impact of living in a society where stigma frames political and media coverage and debate around welfare issues, and the ways in which this all-pervasive 'welfare stigma' shapes people's attitudes towards them as scroungers, as fraudulent, as scum. Indeed, one of the things which working on the Poverty Commission has taught me is that it is imperative for us to theorise stigma on different scales and across multiple sites. If stigma is relational, it is a relation which not only exists between people in the immediacy of social interactions; stigma is a power relation which is exercised across the network of relations between people, society, media culture and the state. In order to counter stigma, it is imperative to track the relations between people's experiences of stigma in everyday contexts, and the governmental production of stigma. When we theorise stigma as embedded within political economies – as the lubricant of neoliberal capitalism – we can begin to understand how stigma functions to devalue entire groups of people, with the purpose of fortifying existing social hierarchies, reproducing inequalities and creating new opportunities for capital.

Welfare stigma as a rationing device

Governing welfare through stigma production is not a new phenomenon.[62] The cultivation of stigma has always played a pivotal role in the rationing of welfare, and in winning consent for periodic attacks on social provision. As Robert Walker argues, 'governments have over many centuries sought to employ stigma as a means of rationing benefits and encouraging personal independence', for 'reasons of ideology, opportunistic reactions to discriminatory public opinion, or pragmatic operational concerns'.[63] In short, stigma is 'a key mechanism in perpetuating the structures of self-interest that support the unequal distribution of resources in society'.[64]

In 1970 the sociologist Robert Pinker set out to classify different 'welfare systems' according to 'their stigmatising propensities'.[65] Pinker was working in a liberal tradition of social policy scholarship, which approaches the question of social provision and wealth redistribution as a compromise between 'the ethics of mutual aid' and 'the liberties of the free market'.[66] He suggests that twentieth-century welfare settlements – in liberal democracies such as Britain – operate on a sliding scale between socialist principles of mutual aid and reciprocity, and free-market principles of capitalist enterprise, and combine both 'therapeutic and stigmatising functions'.[67] Stigma, Pinker argues, is 'an administrative technique for rationing scarce resources'.[68]

States cultivate stigma through the deployment of particular cultural figures, such as the moral figure of the hard-working taxpayer and the abject figure of the welfare scrounger. This stigma production (from above) is employed to teach people to feel revulsion 'for stigmatising dependency', to habituate them 'to a place of lowly social esteem', to encourage them to accept feelings of inferiority, and through this process to become adapted to poverty (as a 'natural condition' of their position in class society).[69]

As I have highlighted throughout this book, stigma is a site of social and political struggle over value. Welfare stigma is not passively accepted by those it is impressed upon. It is a form of power characterised by coercion and resistance, and gives rise to intensive class struggles as people seek to defend themselves against shaming judgements. Pinker suggests that the 'level and intensity' of the class conflicts that follow in the wake of the periodic intensification of welfare stigma are 'determined by the ways in which people learn' or acquiesce to 'their welfare roles' and 'the extent to which the needful believe they have the right to demand from the privileged'.[70] In what follows, I will consider why stigma power proved so effective in winning consent for austerity reforms.

Neoliberal welfare stigma

Social policy scholars have argued that the rise of neoliberalism has been characterised by the deliberate restitution of stigma as a policy mechanism for reducing welfare costs and entitlements. This is not a trend confined to Britain; for example, a research project titled 'Shame, Social Exclusion and the Effectiveness of Anti-Poverty Programmes: A Study of Seven Countries' (2010–2012), led by Robert Walker at Oxford University, suggested that the heightened stigmatisation of redistributive programmes of state welfare is a global phenomenon.[71]

In *Good Times, Bad Times: The Welfare Myth of Them and Us* (2015), John Hills draws on social attitudes data to examine links between the growing stigmatisation of working-age people in receipt of benefits and implementation of cuts to state welfare.[72] Hills argues that during previous economic recessions, public support for welfare provisions has increased as poverty and hardship become visible in people's everyday lives. In contrast, in austerity Britain there has been a demonstrable hardening of public attitudes towards welfare claimants, particularly working-age benefits claimants. This is striking in a period of stagnating wages and insecure work, when welfare benefits have been diminishing, and poverty amongst groups historically seen as 'deserving', such as children and disabled people, has been rapidly increasing.[73] To explain this hardening of public attitudes, Hills examines the 'welfare myths' that underpin public support for austerity-era welfare retrenchment. He suggests that successive governments have deliberately *contracted* the meaning of 'welfare' – that is, what 'the welfare state' includes, means, denotes – and that welfare has been reimagined as an unaffordable system of cash benefits doled out to 'economically inactive' people, rather than the mass services, such as health and education, on which the vast majority of citizens depend. As Hill observes, a central challenge is how to contest the hegemony of this anti-welfare common sense.[74] It is the argument of this chapter that challenging welfare myths requires a deeper understanding of how welfare stigma operates as a form of power.

Social policy research offers ample evidence for changes in public opinions about welfare. However, there has been less consideration of precisely how (and by whom) public opinion is formed.[75] Attention to the precise mechanisms of welfare stigma, how it is produced and disseminated, is critical for understanding how the political project of austerity has been so effective. This involves examining how welfare stigma is produced, by whom, how it is represented and circulated. It means scrutinising the 'stimulation of stigma' around specific policies, and the impacts of this intensification of stigma on people's perceptions of themselves and others. It also, as I have detailed in previous chapters, involves a deeper historical analysis of the ways in which eruptions of stigma draw their energy from sedimented forms of classed, gendered, disablist and racist othering and oppression.

The implementation of austerity involved a concerted effort by different agencies of the state, notably politicians and those working in media industries, to re-story the 2008 financial crisis in the banking sector: first as a crisis of national debt, then as a crisis of the unaffordability of state welfare, and finally as a moral crisis which only a slash-and-burn approach to the social state could purge. In short, the political economy of austerity was lubricated by a moral economy of undeservedness, and was fuelled by stigma power.

'Bring back the welfare stigma'

There is nothing hidden about the state production of welfare stigma as a governmental strategy. In the context of the global rise of neoliberal economic orthodoxy, right-wing commentators have openly called for the intensification of welfare stigma as a means of slashing the social state. For example, in 2009 the American eugenicist political scientist Charles Murray argued that stigma has been an essential component of the government of welfare in the US. Murray contrasts 'the American Model', in which stigma is employed 'to discourage dependence', with a 'European model' that 'says that people should look upon assistance as a right'. According to Murray, 'stigma is the way out', the tool, the device, the machine required to break 'a cradle-to-grave system of government-decided support'.[76] In 2014, US Republican blogger and journalist Daniel Payne published a think-piece titled 'Bring Back the Welfare Stigma', in which he similarly stated: 'look to Europe, where many countries have *de-stigmatized* their way into astronomical debt levels and widespread, chronic citizen helplessness. Keeping welfare firmly in the stigmatized realm is not merely a conservative crusade; it's good policy, too'.[77] Murray's 1997 book, *What It Means to Be a Libertarian*, proposed that all social security be abolished, that government be reduced to the barest essentials (defence, law and order and environmental protections) and that state welfare provisions should be replaced by forms of 'localism', by which he meant charitable and voluntary sector support. This manifesto is in effect a blueprint for the denuded British austerity state, and stigma, as Murray encouraged, was the mechanism used to implement this project.

The war on welfare

In 2011, the then British prime minister, David Cameron, declared a 'war on welfare culture': 'The benefit system has created a benefit culture. It doesn't just allow people to act irresponsibly, but often actively encourages them to do so.'[78] The architects of austerity knew that effective *stigmacraft* would be critical to winning public consent for welfare reform. In short, in order to implement a project on the scale of austerity, you have to be able to make the public feel that those in receipt of 'welfare' – now reimagined as cash benefits rather than *all* public services – are not deserving. This involved a collective effort by politicians, policy makers and journalists to portray working-age people in receipt of benefits as 'an illegitimate burden on society'.[79] From 2010 onwards, and peaking in 2014/2015 when the main legislative plank of austerity, the Welfare Reform Act 2014, was being enshrined in law, an orchestrated alliance of political, civil society and media actors combined forces to craft a moral panic about welfare dependency.

This war on welfare culture took the form of a massive propaganda exercise in which an alliance of political and media forces combined in the production of a welfare stigma machine. This stigma machine churned out an abject cast of figures of dependency, who functioned as character props in the political storying of a welfare crisis. The three figures who organised this representational field were the hardworking taxpayer, the profligate scrounger and the conniving migrant. These figures were repeatedly weaponised in political speeches, reality television programmes and newspaper headlines, to manufacture grievances about the social and economic injustice of 'welfare dependency culture'.[80] 'This is a fight. We are really going to go after the welfare cheats', the austerity chancellor George Osborne declared in 2010. 'A welfare cheat is no different from someone who comes up and robs you in the street.'[81]

This project was extraordinary for its scale, the diversity of mediums and instruments it orchestrated, and its consistency in political messaging. Key themes about the need to root out the evils of benefit dependency were reproduced in every conceivable media and cultural form. For several years, the menace of welfare-dependent people was maintained as rolling news by politicians, government officials, think tanks, media executives, journalists and television producers. Most notably, there was 'an explosion' in British reality television programmes that centred on the everyday lives of people claiming benefits, a new genre that was dubbed 'poverty porn'.[82] Reality television producers churned out hundreds of hours of prime-time television programmes about 'real life' feckless, immoral, undeserving and deficient welfare claimants. A stigma feedback loop emerged in which the characters these television programmes makers constructed, and the storylines they scripted, would circulate across the public sphere, to be captured as 'evidence' for the necessity of austerity reforms. Consider, for example, the following parliamentary debate in the House of Commons on 13 January 2014:

Philip Davies (Conservative MP): Has the Secretary of State managed to watch programmes such as *Benefits Street* and *On Benefits & Proud*? If so, has he, like me, been struck by the number of people on them who manage to combine complaining about welfare reform with being able to afford to buy copious amounts of cigarettes, have lots of tattoos, and watch Sky TV on the obligatory widescreen television? Does he understand the concerns and irritation of many people who go to work every day and pay their taxes but cannot afford those kinds of luxuries?

Iain Duncan Smith (Secretary of State for Work and Pensions): My hon. Friend is right, many people are shocked by what they see. That is why the public back our welfare reform package, which will get more people back to work and end these abuses. All these abuses date back to the last Government, who had massive spending and trapped people in benefit dependency.[83]

Benefits broods

In '"Benefits Broods": The Cultural and Political Crafting of Anti-Welfare Commonsense' (2015) Tracey Jensen and I tracked the passage of the Welfare Reform Act (2012) through Parliament.[84] One of the most controversial elements of this legislation was 'the household benefits cap', which sought to restrict the total income a family could receive from state benefits. What we noted is that the passage of this act was accompanied by the intensive stigmatisation of what politicians termed 'welfare dependent families' and newspapers called 'Benefits Broods', namely poor families that included an above-average number of children.[85] Across multiple genres of media production – reality television, tabloid and broadsheet newspapers, social media, political speeches and policy publications

– the public were tutored to feel revulsion towards large families in receipt of state welfare benefits. Indeed, we mapped a *stigma relay* in which politicians would cite highly selective and often fictionalised media stories about families on benefits as empirical evidence in support of cuts to benefits. The crafting of representations of highly salacious, scandalous stories about 'Benefits Broods' operated as a moral device through which broader 'anti-welfare sentiments' could be fomented.

What this case study revealed is the central role that the media crafting of welfare stigma played as a mechanism of consent for austerity – particularly when austerity cuts targeted those traditionally considered deserving groups, such as children. As Pinker suggested, the 'imposition of a stigma by the privileged' is a mechanism through which the public is incited to condemn the so-called excessive 'demands of the poor' in ways which allow them to preserve 'their own sense of moral rectitude'.[86]

The role of governmental stigmacraft in winning legitimacy for a state-led initiative of enclosure, destruction and dispossession on the scale witnessed in austerity Britain cannot be understated. The production of welfare stigma was the mechanism through which public acquiescence to austerity was won.

'To you we're just human waste'

This welfare stigma machine churned through wider society, settling in institutional forms, embedding in the design of social policies, and infecting the culture, practices and attitudes of welfare workers. It changed the ways in which the public made evaluative judgements about inequality, welfare, poverty and need. It tutored the public to believe that people living in poverty were lazy or feckless, and that the forms of distress which followed in the wake of austerity were deserved – a consequence of people's own poor behaviours, bad choices and indiscipline. Indeed, it incited calls for harsher punishments.

These ideologies 'matter profoundly' because, as Antonio Gramsci argues, they become 'organic' to the life of society; they acquire 'a validity which is psychological; they organize human masses and create the terrain' within which we move and act, and through which we 'acquire consciousness' of our position.[87] As the Leeds Poverty Commission put it in their 'HuManifesto':

> When you're experiencing poverty, what really *grinds you down* is the way other people perceive you. The media often portray low-income families in unsympathetic and sometimes insulting terms. Feckless. Scroungers. Skivers. And this leads the public to think that the hard-up have only themselves to blame, and they treat them with disdain.[88]

The all-pervasive stigma-optics of austerity transformed ways of seeing poverty, hardening people's feelings to the suffering of those around them: those queuing outside the food banks springing up in every town and city, those bodies accumulating on every street corner and doorway. This changed how people related to each other, eroding structures of care, corroding compassion. 'People don't care about each other anymore', Stephanie says. As another member of my local Poverty Commission said to me, his face flushing with anger and shame: 'To you we're just human waste.'

'One constant cycle of judgement'

This welfare stigma machine also changed how people thought about themselves. I opened *Stigma* with Stephanie's story, which highlighted the ways in which welfare stigma saturates and permeates everyday encounters in the austerity state. Stephanie recounted a decade of stigmatising encounters with corporate agencies, banks and debt companies, and agencies of the state, job centre officials, the private sector medical professionals employed to assess her ability to undertake paid work. As she moves through the increasingly punitive landscape of austerity, Stephanie finds herself needled with stigma at every turn. It is inescapable, seeping incessantly into her world, through the discussions on the radio as she drives her car, the television programmes she watches with her daughter. Caught within the vice-like grip of the welfare stigma machine, she is increasingly unable to fend off the weight of stigma pressing down on her. She comes to anticipate stigma. She is enclosed by stigma:

> You only have to watch any programme and there is evidence there that your kind are hated. These people are stealing your taxes and you're thinking 'that is me they are talking about'. It is yet another channel into you. Trapped in this cycle of being hated by everybody. It keeps coming, it keeps on coming. It's relentless. Never ending. One constant cycle of judgement. Until you are ashamed to do anything.

While official statistical data provides evidence of austerity's effects, it doesn't fully capture how austerity *gets under the skin*. As China Mills argues, 'austerity is lived and felt as affective force and atmospheric fear, a pervasive psychological and bodily anxiety, shame, and anger, differing in intensity at different times, and fatiguing the body – physically and psychologically wearing it out'.[89] The violence of austerity is written on the skin, it digs itself into the flesh – an *epidermalization* of stigma which reverberates with the much longer penal history of stigma power. The stigma machine of austerity leaves permanent marks 'on the bodies of those condemned by the logic of the market never to prosper'.[90]

Stephanie carves welfare stigma into her skin. A practice of self-stigmatisation which, as she explains it, is an attempt to articulate and express the shame she feels – has been made to feel. By cutting the stigma which has been pressed upon her into her skin, Stephanie turns herself into a stigma object, as though if she can become *the thing* which the stigma machine has made her, if she can express the depth of her own self-loathing, she can say 'enough already' and break the cycle of stigma and shame.

There are many austerity stories like Stephanie's; there is nothing unusual about it, apart from how succinctly it compresses the links between crushing experiences of being stigmatised and the incessant force of mechanised top-down stigma production from above. Stephanie's austerity story is an indictment of those who crafted the welfare stigma machine. Her body is a witness statement. The scars and psychological wounds she bears testify to how stigma emerges within wider degrading systems of social classification.

The welfare stigma machine, which was crafted and designed to implement the political project of austerity, destroys people's mental health. Alongside the 'slow deaths' which can be attributed to austerity, Mills draws our attention to 'austerity suicides'. As she writes, in 2013 suicides reached a thirteen-year high in the UK, 'with population-level data linking this increase to austerity policies'.[91] Mills documents the entangled relationship between this marked increase in mental distress and the 'economy of the anxiety caused by punitive welfare retrenchment'; the internalisation of a market logic that assigns value through 'productivity'. As she writes:

> It is not a coincidence that some people deemed a 'burden' by neoliberal market logic would end their lives. People are killing themselves because they feel exactly the way the government is telling them they should feel – a burden. Put another way, people are killing themselves because austerity is killing them.

Austerity suicides may be read as the ultimate outcome of the internalisation of eugenic and market logic underlying welfare reform driven by austerity. Such deaths make visible the slow death endemic to austerity.[92]

As Mills cogently argues, attention to the psychic life of austerity is critical for understanding the threads of connection between the cumulative effects of stigma as lived experience and the governmental exercise of stigma – the relation which is at the heart of the reconceptualisation of stigma as power in this book.

Steve Tombs argues that 'austerity is a story about social inequality and avoidable business-generated, state-facilitated violence: that is, social murder'.[93] As Chris Grover reflects, Friedrich Engels' term 'social murder' is appropriate in the context of austerity because the 'detrimental consequences' of this programme are 'both known and avoidable'.[94] This diagnosis of 'social murder' echoes Ruth Gilmore's definition of racism as 'state sanctioned and/or extralegal production and exploitation of group differentiated vulnerabilities to premature death'.[95] Certainly, austerity seems designed to enact 'the unequal distribution of life and death'.[96] Indeed, in the austerity state any form of life that cannot 'produce values according to market logics' is 'ferreted out and strangled'.[97]

Welfare disinheritance

In *Regulating the Poor: The Functions of Public Welfare* (1971), Frances Fox Piven and Richard Cloward caution us against romantic and nostalgia accounts of the welfare state(s).[98] As they argue, the longer history of state welfare 'belies the popular supposition that government social policies, including relief policies, are becoming progressively more responsible, humane, and generous'.[99] As they note, 'the historical pattern is clearly not one of progressive liberalization; it is rather a record of periodically expanding and contracting relief rolls as the system performs its two main functions: maintaining civil order and enforcing work'.[100] While national governments have frequently been forced to intervene to ameliorate the impact of the 'untrammelled forces of the market-place', and while 'social welfare programmes' have periodically benefited 'those at the bottom of the economic order', impetus to action around poverty is as much guided by labour requirements as by charitable or moral imperatives, or indeed rights-based or social justice claims. Further, the British welfare state is not 'a thing', but a site of contradictory and contested institutional practices and policy formations. Welfare is a settlement between labour and capital which has always been compromised by gendered, classed and racialised inequalities. We might usefully recall Jeremy Bentham's plans for a carceral workfare welfare state at this juncture. We need also to remember the frequently obscured fact that Britain's welfare state was bankrolled by colonial enterprise, and the various systems of indentured and exploited labour this involved in places far from the geographical space of the British Isles.

Nevertheless, writing in the wake of a decade of austerity, where the most progressive aspects of the programmes of reform instituted by the post-war British welfare state are now in reverse gear; when the 'assumption that the state should play a redistributive role in ameliorating the consequences of capitalism' has been upturned; when the political architects of austerity have consigned democratic welfare dreams to the rubbish dump of history; when so much of the state infrastructure of social provision and care has been laid to waste; when those who seek access to state benefits and entitlements are, once more, deeply stigmatised, it is imperative to recall the powerful social effects of (partly) de-stigmatised welfare provisions.[101]

Welfare settlements represent a 'distinctive site of connection between people, politics and policies, constructing relationships, practices and identities of "citizenship"'.[102] Beveridge's welfare state provided not only a safety net, but was a structure of care and a site of imaginary investments which transformed the lives of people in post-war Britain.

The social historian Carolyn Steedman was a working-class child in the 1950s, a period when 'the state was practically engaged in making children healthy and literate'.[103] For Steedman, growing up during that first utopian blush of the post-war welfare settlement involved concrete material benefits. As she writes, 'It was a considerable achievement for a society to pour so much milk and so much orange juice, so many vitamins, down the throats of its children, and for the height and weight of those children to outstrip the measurements of only a decade before'.[104] What the broadly egalitarian welfare state era also bestowed was a new value system; as Steedman describes: 'My inheritance from those years is the belief (maintained always with some difficulty) that I do have a right to the earth.' She notes: 'I had a right to exist, was worth something.'[105]

The welfare inheritance so movingly described by Steedman has been stolen. The compromise between labour and capital which the twentieth-century welfare state represented in Britain no longer holds. Indeed, we are currently living through a period of disinheritance. If twentieth-century welfare capitalism transformed class relations in Britain, austerity is upending class society once more. Steedman's belief that she 'had a right to exist' and 'was worth something' has become David's cry of despair and rage: 'You have no hope. It feels like the government are trying to make a superior race – the rich get richer and the poor get poorer.'

It is not only that the current neoliberal assault on the welfare state has led to 'deepening inequalities of income, health and life chances' on 'a scale not seen since before the Second World War', but that those very groups who gained most from the British post-war settlement – women, children, disabled people and the multi-ethic working class – are now those most impacted by the deepening inequalities unfolding from its dismantlement.[106] Indeed, the historical inequalities and stigmatising classifications latent within systems of social provision are the stigma fault lines which have been fracked by the enclosure architects of austerity, and mined as a source of discontent through which to generate social divisions.[107] To obscure the political origins of the welfare crisis, the stigma machine of austerity purposefully generates class factions – the irony being that the undoing of the welfare settlement impacts (unevenly) on everybody, from cradle to grave.

The unsettling of the welfare settlement

Austerity is an anti-social and an anti-democratic movement which signals a deeper unravelling of the social contract between citizens and the state. That is, if British citizens are no longer collectively willing to meet the basic needs of children, disabled people, the elderly and other vulnerable citizens – for shelter, care and education through state-organised systems of wealth redistribution (taxation) – then what kind of state we are in? Can a state with only skeletal social provisions, a state in which the provisions which exist are so unequally distributed by geography, be called democratic? What kind of state is a state without a functioning welfare state?

In place of the 'big state' envisioned by architects of the British welfare state in the mid-twentieth century, what is emerging is an uneven patchwork of social provision. A pared down, stretched and stressed health and public sector pegged together by armies of unpaid charity volunteers, combined with the emergence of new private for-profit health, social care and educational provisions for those who can afford to pay. Indeed, in terms of widening economic, social and health inequalities, the austerity welfare state increasingly resembles that of the first decades of the twentieth century, when much welfare was dependent on philanthropists.[108] Many of Britain's poorest citizens are already reliant on the charity of the individuals and corporations whose predatory capitalism (and tax avoidance) contributed to the crisis we are in.

There are more than echoes of early historical periods of social provision in the austerity state, and it is with historical warnings about the abdication of the state, the erosion of democracy and the return of charity in mind that I want to conclude this chapter by returning to a final time to Lancaster Town Hall, and to a period before the post-war welfare state.

Ashton Hall, Lancaster Town Hall 1909

The public launch event for the Morecambe Bay Poverty Truth Commission on Friday 6 July 2018 was held in Ashton Hall, the largest room within the town hall. Lancaster Town Hall was opened in 1909, and was privately financed by a local industrialist, 'Lino King' James Williamson (1842–1930). Bestowed the title Lord Ashton in 1895, Williamson employed an estimated 25 per cent of Lancaster's working-age population, men and women and teenagers, in his Linoleum (oil cloth) factories, cotton mills and quarries.[109] Lancaster's principal industry in the nineteenth and early twentieth centuries was linoleum manufacture, a commodity which consisted of coating cotton to produce table cloths, floor-coverings, tiles and wall-coverings. The linoleum industry involved largely unskilled and semi-skilled manual labour, and was completely dominated by two employers, Williamson (Lord Ashton) and the Storey family. Williamson's Lune Mills factory complex was so vast that in 1894 it boasted that it was 'the largest manufactory of its class in the world': 'we may say, without any fear of contradiction, that the mammoth works on the banks of the Lune, at Lancaster, are the most extensive in the universe, that are owned and controlled solely by one individual'.[110] By the time he died, James Williamson, was one of the richest men in Europe. He was also a ruthless capitalist, an autocrat and a tyrant.

The sociologist Alan Warde argues that two features made Lancaster distinctive during its industrial heyday: its predominately unskilled and semi-skilled working-class population (the absence of either a large skilled working class or a significant middle class) and the striking 'quiescence of its working class'.[111] Indeed, this was a town notable for the absence of any significant recorded history of working-class struggle, its workforce remained largely un-unionised and neither of the Linoleum manufactures saw any significant strike in their histories, which spanned over a hundred years. Indeed, Williamson and the Storey family collaborated in their domination of the local labour market, refusing to employ workers who were sacked by the other, only recognising a very small number of unions (craft unions and no general unions), and secretly collaborating in setting local wage levels.[112] This left the vast majority of the town's workers without any political representation or bargaining power in the workplace. The domination of these firms over the local labour market continued into the 1970s.

In the 1970s, Elizabeth Roberts, a pioneer of oral history who studied and worked at Lancaster University, captured the views of many working-class people in Lancaster about Williamson's reign of terror over the town. For 'up to sixty years ... up to 1930 we lived in fear', one local man told her. 'You daren't open your mouth in Lancaster to criticise Lord Ashton.'[113] A former cotton mill worker, who began working for Williamson as a child of fourteen – while the town hall was being built – recalled a labour practice which subcontracted the work of unskilled trainees to skilled weavers, which made the weaver responsible for paying wages. In practice this meant that some weeks she didn't get paid at all: 'You see, after all was said and done it was slave labour. The manufactures got an awful lot of work for nothing. No wonder they got rich', she said.[114] Another former employee describes how Williamson treated his workers 'like dogs', recalling how the stonemasons employed in his quarry regularly died from silicosis: 'their life expectancy was 35 to 40, then they were finished'.[115]

Lancaster's working class simmered with resentment towards the 'philanthropy' bestowed on them by Williamson. It angered them that Williamson used the profits from their labour to fund the lavish town hall, parks and monuments, yet failed to do anything to address the low wages and slum conditions in which many of his workers lived. One of Roberts' interviewees, a local government worker, said: 'As an employer of labour and living in Skerton and knowing of a lot of the slums in Skerton, if he'd had the interest of the town at heart [think] how many houses he could have built'.[116] The interviewee goes on to explain how it would have been 'a flea bite to him', and 'he could have got his money back in rent in years and that would have been something for the town'. Indeed, entering some of the districts in Lancaster in the first decades of the twentieth century was, as his wife described it, 'like going into the depths of despair' – houses with 'no back way out, lack of fresh air ventilation, flue ventilation, small windows, even the window panes would be small squares and you could almost smell the atmosphere'.[117] These interviewees are at pains to stress that those living in these slum conditions were often 'very, very respectable' people; working families who had inadequate water supplies (sharing communal taps and outdoor toilets).[118] The lack of proper sanitation and the forced use of shared rubbish tips (middens) led to regular outbreaks of food poisoning, disease and high levels of child mortality. As a local doctor interviewed by Roberts recalls: 'The children were thin and skinny and very often anaemic. The parents had very poor wages. They go together, poverty and disease. Lack of hygiene, lack of opportunity.'[119]

Williamson was 'reputed to use a telescope at home to watch workers arriving at work in the mornings' and kept 'a black book' to record 'miscreant behaviour among his workforce'.[120] He also operated a sophisticated local surveillance network of informants who reported on the activities of local trades union activists and socialists: 'He used to have his spies out in the pubs.'[121] Through his networks, Williamson also extended complete control over local and national-level political representation, controlling local municipal elections and determining who would be the local MP; as one of Robert's interviewees put it: 'You had to be very careful who you talked to about who you voted for.'[122] During the period that Lancaster Town Hall was being constructed. Williamson was incensed by reports from his spies that local socialists and members of the Independent Labour Party (formed in 1893) were blaming him for high levels of in-work poverty. Williamson categorically denied that he paid poverty wages and furiously complained about socialist activists, who, as he wrote in a letter to a supporter, 'describe me as a thief and a robber'.[123]

The political struggle between Williamson and the working-class residents of Lancaster came to a head during local elections in 1911 in Skerton, a slum district where many of Williamson's workers lived, and close to where Williamson lived in a large Georgian stately home called Ryelands House. Williamson was incensed when the Liberal Party candidate (fielded by Williamson) only managed to hang on to his Skerton seat against the Independent Labour Party candidate by a single vote (which was the casting vote of the returning officer). The punishment Williamson meted out on his workers for this political betrayal made international news headlines.

On 11 November 1911, the *New York Times*, under the headline 'Ashton Warns Workers: Tells Employees He Will Close Shop Rather Than Raise Wages', reported on what it described as 'one of the most remarkable developments in the struggle between capital and labour' in modern times.[124] A short time after the local election Williamson posted a notice at Lune Mills, which stated there was to be an immediate cancellation of a previously agreed rise in wages. It said that 'we would rather close the whole works down tomorrow ... than allow for dissent', and that 'in the future' he would only employ those men 'who are loyal to their employer'. Williamson then proceeded to sack all those with a known association to the Labour Party.

He then turned his revenge on the wider town, making it clear he would also cease all future philanthropic investment in Lancaster. The mayor of Lancaster convened a special meeting in the new town hall, and a range of speakers were called upon to beg Williamson's forgiveness publicly – but to no avail. Williamson was then a particular kind of capitalist philanthropist, a man with a virtual monopoly over wage labour, who ploughed some of the profits, the surplus value created by working-class labourers, into the development of a town's civic and welfare estate. He expected absolute loyalty and gratitude in return for acquiescence to below subsistence-level wages.

'In 1909 when the town hall was opened', one man recounts how people sang, 'Linoleum, one pound and three, that is what I pay my men you see', in mocking reference to Williamson's poverty wages.[125] To celebrate the opening of the town hall, Williamson's wife, Lady Ashton, distributed special boxes of chocolates to the local schoolchildren. The children of Skerton 'returned' their chocolates, throwing them uneaten in their celebratory boxes over the wall into Williamson's Ryeland's estate.[126]

It is important to understand the current period of austerity in the context of local histories of struggles for living wages and decent housing – struggles against multimillionaires like James Williamson. It is a history engrained in the town hall in which I and another hundred people gathered in 2018 to listen to the testimonies of a dozen local people about the return of in-work poverty, hunger and homelessness. Lancaster is again a place in which too many people find their wages don't meet their living costs, who are reliant on tax credits, charitable and emergency food provisions. It is a place where medical practitioners document the return of diseases of poverty and want. These histories matter because we are returning to a state of unrestrained free-market capitalism, run by unrestrained free-market capitalists, who either cannot see or do not care about the austerity, suffering, pain and death by which they are surrounded. A state of charity. A state of fear.

Resisting the new enclosures

Understanding the history of austerity through the history of enclosures, and understanding the wounds of austerity as social and political injuries can assist in the forging of intersectional networks of care and solidarity, a praxis which Sita Balani describes as 'the kinship of the fucked over'.[127] As Silvia Federici notes, 'in a social system committed to the devaluation of our lives the only possibility of economic and psychological survival resides in our capacity to transform everyday practices into a collective terrain of struggle'.[128] Grassroots social movements like the Morecambe Bay Poverty Truth Commission are testimony to the ways in which communities are creating new systems of care and solidarity through which they can defend their families and communities against the stigma politics and pauperisation that the enclosure of the welfare commons has set in motion.

Whilst this chapter has focused on Britain and state welfare, the struggle for the future of welfare is necessarily an international one; a struggle for alternative economics, and for systems of redistribution which can also safeguard a planet which has been devastated by the history of colonial capitalism. As Federici argues, for resistance against the new enclosures to be sustainable, the real challenge is how we 'deprivatize our everyday lives and create cooperative forms of reproduction' not just here but everywhere.[129]

Chapter 5

Shame lives on the eyelids

the autobiographical example is not a personal story that folds onto itself ... it's about trying to look at one's own formation as a window onto social and historical processes ... to tell a story capable of engaging and countering the violence of abstraction.

Saidiya Hartman, scholar of African-American literature and history[1]

Kevin told me they weren't zoo exhibits or museum relics for people to come and gawp at. He wasn't having me going around telling tales about him and his mates for ten more offcomer wankers to laugh at and come and see.

Nigel Rapport, British Anthropologist[2]

'Why are you so interested in stigma?' a friend asked when I was beginning the research that became this book. I didn't answer. At least not then. In the years which followed, that question came to press heavily upon this project, upon me. I confess that at times it returned me to 'regions of my past' so painful that it threatened to unravel me completely.[3] To be sure, in terms of its intended contribution to knowledge, I felt clear about the purpose of this book. Namely, to enrich existing understandings of stigma by directing attention to histories of stigma power, and sites of stigma production, with a focus on how stigma is crafted and deployed 'to produce and reproduce social inequalities'.[4] However, researching stigma and talking about experiences of stigma with others, particularly through my work with the Morecambe Bay Poverty Truth Commission, has involved examining stigma scars of my own. Indeed, my friend's invitation to be attentive to stigma's particular hold over me led me to reflect on the more personal motivations behind this project, to dwell on my own history and the stigma injuries I have accrued in my own journey from a rebellious teenage girl who began her working life as a cleaner in an English village pub to the highly privileged position of a middle-aged Professor of Sociology at an English university, the authorial voice adopted in this book.

While I worked on *Stigma* proper, I began to write about my 'personal troubles' with stigma. This shadow stigma project initially comprised autobiographical fragments, but subsequently expanded in several directions, including a full-blown ancestral research project, and a local history project which I have drawn on throughout this book in returning repeatedly to Lancaster and the North West of England, the region I am from. Over time, this other stigma project became an increasingly important component of the research process, promoting new lines of inquiry and providing new perspectives on the materials on poverty, class and welfare stigma, on slavery and colonial histories, which I was gathering for the book. Slowly, I came to understand that this closet stigma project was at the heart of *Stigma*. That is, I began to understand my personal experiences of stigma as deeply entangled with my scholarly interest in stigma power and with the broader contribution *Stigma* seeks to make to intersectional forms of social analysis.

Sociological and social scientific writing on 'the stigmatised' often, despite its best intentions, reproduces the stigma it ostensibly seeks to document, analyse or give an account of. This is evident, for example, in Goffman's writing on stigma, which occludes the struggles of black citizens against the humiliations and violence of racial stigma and actively silences the testimonies and voices of the stigmatised. In order to trouble the power of stigma, we need to take great care in how we draw on the voices and experiences of others in our work.[5] This is not least because many of the methods available to us for undertaking research are inherited from European modernity; and, as we saw in the case of eugenicist roots of criminology (see Lombroso, Chapter 1), these methods were forged in racist, classist, misogynistic and disablist belief systems. In short, many social scientific methods emerge out of stigmatising systems of knowledge production. Which is why, as Christina Sharpe writes: 'Despite knowing otherwise we are often disciplined into thinking through and along lines that reinscribe our own annihilation, reinforcing and reproducing what Sylvia Wynter has called our "narratively condemned status".'[6] More than this, Sharpe adds, 'The methods most readily available to use sometimes, oftentimes, force us into positions that run counter to what we know'.[7]

This chapter reflects on how we might draw on our own *stigma injuries* and *stigma struggles* to research and write about stigma in ways which don't reproduce or naturalise existing stigmatising social hierarchies. The personal troubles with stigma I have chosen to share here are ordinary experiences, banal even in the context of British class society, but they are nevertheless experiences of the kind which we are expected to subdue, swallow or jettison in assuming what the sociologist Pierre Bourdieu termed 'the scholastic doxa' of 'those whose profession it is to think and/or speak about the world'.[8]

Mob cap and pinny

I was thirteen years old when I got my first regular paid job cleaning the toilets and bar of a pub (let's call this pub The Eagle) in the small, remote village in the Yorkshire Dales in England where I lived with my family (let's call this village Wanet). Early on Saturdays and Sunday mornings I would pitch up at the back door of the pub and collect the mop and bucket from the stone steps. Once inside I would pick up the cleaning caddy of bleach, polish and rags, pull my tabard off its peg and put on a pair of yellow rubber gloves. My work began in the toilets, picking cigarette butts out of the urinal, wiping piss from walls, scrubbing shit from toilet bowls, emptying sanitary bins and mopping tiled floors. I then moved into the bar area and the gloves came off. I collected discarded glasses, emptied ashtrays, wiped and polished the tables, before turning to the long wooden bar counter, where I removed damp towel beer mats and discarded any stained, picked at and doodled on cardboard beer mats, before wiping down and finally polishing the long beer-sticky wooden surface. Making the bar shine was my favourite part of the morning. I would then hoover the pub carpet, carefully arrange clean beer towels and mats on the bar and tables, before spraying the entire pub with an aerosol air freshener, a celebratory signal that all was clean and ready for lunchtime opening.

Before the front door of the pub was ceremoniously unlocked, other staff would appear from their various tasks in different parts of the building to gather in the bar for a morning brew: sweet milky tea, instant coffee and biscuits from the corner shop. There would be chat about the day's work to come and gossip about any 'goings on' the night before. I enjoyed this work, it was satisfying and I was good at it.

In time, I picked up an additional weekend and vacation job at a craft centre a mile or so outside the village, and for while I would begin my weekends scrubbing urinals, spend the middle of the day serving tea and cakes in the craft centre cafe, before heading back to the pub for an evening's work as a glass collector in the bar and washer upper in the kitchen. During school holidays, I worked continuously between pub and craft centre, earning enough money to pay my mum towards 'my upkeep'. By the time I was sixteen, I had saved enough to buy a second-hand motorbike which meant I could avoid the time lag of having to hitchhike my way between pub and craft centre.

The craft centre was in a refurbished eighteenth-century hay barn, and sold hand-crafted goods carefully chosen to curate a particular version of rural life: knitted jumpers with sheep on; landscape paintings; photographic books depicting dales life; rustic pottery which celebrated the rough contours and colours of the dales landscape; key rings made of old wooden printing blocks; egg timers made out of recycled bobbins from Lancashire mills – the waste products of a former industrial heyday.

The owners of the craft centre asked me to wear a uniform, a white lace pinafore and matching mob cap that signalled something between milkmaid and Victorian domestic servant. I suspected that this costume had been purchased specifically with me in mind. I don't remember anybody else being required to wear it. It was an attempt, I imagined, to make me respectable by taming my teenage appearance, then somewhere between a rocker and a mod, with shaved hair, jeans and motorbike boots. It was an effort to better satisfy the imagined 'tourist gaze' of the urban weekend walkers and holidaymakers who strayed into this remote dale, by making me fit in amongst the crafts, a historical drag act in which I played the part of 'authentic local wench'.[9] I resisted the deferent servitude this uniform implied by applying thicker eyeliner, brighter lipstick and wearing larger earrings – and engaged in 'foot-dragging' practices which included extended toilet breaks to smoke ciga-rettes.[10] Shameless defiance.

Don't get me wrong, I largely enjoyed my teenage jobs: I exercised choice and I didn't consider the work I undertook to be demeaning. Nevertheless, I was reminded of my hatred of this mob cap when I was undertaking historical research for this book. The historian Selina Todd describes how in the early decades of the twentieth century 'caps and aprons' became 'deeply unpopular signs of servants' difference from most other waged workers, and a mark of an employer's control over their employee's body, as well as their time'.[11] While domestic service was still the largest category of female employment in the inter-war years in Britain, being 'in service' was an increasingly stigmatised form of work, 'associated with poverty, lack of liberty and the broken promises of the Great War'.[12] In particular, working-class women from areas that had had high levels of skilled or semi-skilled female employment, such as Lancashire and Yorkshire mill towns, considered going into domestic service to be a demeaning step down. As the historian Lucy Lethbridge writes, 'Factory girls did not have to endure the daily petty humiliations of being at the beck and call of a condescending mistress; of having no set hours to call their own, of having pitifully few opportunities to meet men (or even other women)'.[13] While conditions of domestic employment varied greatly, increasing numbers of young women resented what Margaret Powell, in *Below Stairs*, her memoir about being a domestic servant, described as 'the feeling of being owned', and the 'enormous inferiority complex' this inculcated.[14]

Upper- and middle-class politicians, writers and newspaper columnists became preoccupied with the 'servant problem', and with the wider implications of this increasing resistance to domestic service for the future of British class society.[15] Todd points us to a 1919 government pamphlet, authored by Lady Ellen Askwith, which stated that 'domestic service must be reinvigorated in order to secure the future of the British race'.[16] The eugenicist understanding of class differences which underpinned this literature implied that the future of the better classes was dependent on the labour of working-class women (as nannies, care workers, domestic servants). It also points to a deeper fear, namely that the freedom of young working-class women posed a degenerative threat to 'the English stock'. That is, without the moral discipline and often severe social restrictions which constrained the lives of working-class women who spent their lives caring for others while living under the roof and beady eyes of their middle- and upper-class employers, working-class women would be more likely to marry young and have more children of their own.

For many amongst the upper and middle classes, working-class servitude was imagined as a moral good which bound together British class society in 'co-dependent harmony'.[17] Indeed, the most evangelical advocates for the preservation of class and gendered hierarchies in this period understood domestic service to be akin to a form of salvation which rescued young working-class women from the vices and squalor of working-class urban life. The bucolic social order of the traditional English village was central to this conservative social imaginary of service and servitude. As Lucy Lethbridge documents, social campaigners and philanthropists in the late nineteenth and early twentieth century, such as Harriet Barnard and Dr Barnardo, created residential village communities into which they interned working-class girls to train them for lives in domestic service.

Amidst the heightening tensions and the growing demands of the wider labour movement (which led to a general strike in 1926), 'defiance below stairs' grew and young women increasingly 'refused to adopt the subservience demanded of them'.[18] Confined in private households, domestic servants lacked the organisational and bargaining power of unionised workers, and Selina Todd describes how their revolt often took the form of small refusals; Powell describes how, when she graduated from housemaid to cook, her employer 'wanted me to wear a cap, but I wouldn't. It always struck me as a badge of servitude'.[19] Resistance also took the form of vicarious pleasures such as dressing up in their mistresses' clothes and jewellery and 'taking tea in the parlour' when their employers were out.[20]

By the 1920s the British government had begun designing penal workfare policies in an attempt to *press* working-class women into service, setting up government-funded institutions to train girls to acquire both the skills and subservient demeanours necessary for domestic work, and withholding dole (unemployment relief) from young women who refused to enter these new industry houses.[21] These workfare programmes were widely supported by the British press, which 'lamented the abuse of the dole' by women 'for whom domestic service is obviously a suitable employment'.[22]

The facade of the English pastoral

I grew up in a large working-class family in the 1970s and 1980s, decades dominated by the radical social changes and upheavals ushered in by Margaret Thatcher's Conservative government (1979–1990). Many others have written about Thatcherism and the ways in which it inaugurated the neoliberal programme of reforms which led us to the current British austerity state. Thatcher's capitalist crusade was underpinned by an authoritarian turn in law and order, and by the pitting of what she termed 'Victorian Values' against the social and sexual permissiveness 1960s and 1970s.[23] As Stuart Hall argued, what was novel about Thatcherism were the ways in which it tethered the values of free-market liberalism – 'individual responsibility, self-reliance, enterprise, competition, choice' – to conservative themes of 'family and nation, respectability, patriarchalism and order'; Hall termed this conjuncture 'authoritarian populism'.[24]

In the 1980s, the English village with its residual stratified agrarian order of local aristocratic landowners, middle-class vicars, shopkeepers, retired professionals, well-to-do farmers, working-class labourers and domestic servants became a key imaginary resource for Thatcherite nationalism.[25] Indeed, in an interview for the Walt Disney corporation in 1989, Thatcher revealed that her favourite film was *Mrs Miniver* (1942), an American-financed and Hollywood-made romantic drama which depicts the stoic suffering of a well-to-do middle-class housewife (who has a live-in housemaid and cook) in an English village during the Second World War. *Mrs Miniver* centres on the ways in which shared suffering forges a cross-class solidarity between local aristocrats, the middle classes and the working poor. This romance of resilience epitomised what Thatcher described as 'the spirit of the village'.[26]

During the Thatcher years, heritage industries flourished.[27] As Lucienne Loh argues, the social and cultural reconstruction of the English pastoral and its bucolic social order in the 1980s was fuelled both by economic policies aimed at regeneration and wider ideological efforts 'to revive imperial pride through a return to popular perceptions of the "local past" as a means to recreate a populist English nationalism'.[28] As Loh details, 'the countryside, along with its architectural icons – churches, abbeys, villages, cottages and manor homes', was imagined as 'a tangible record of past greatness inherently coded through white and imperial ideologies'.[29] This embrace of heritage culture saw the English countryside marketed to tourists as spaces of 'reprieve from the turmoil' of Britain's multi-ethnic cities (punctuated by riots throughout this period), white spaces from which long histories of migration and migrant labour were erased from view.[30] At the same time, those who lived in English rural communities were encouraged to imagine themselves and their culture as uniquely indigenous, a status 'underpinned by a shared allegiance to whiteness'.[31]

The social effects of Thatcher-era heritage culture, which formed one strand of a wider racist nationalism, were palpable growing up in a rural community in the 1980s. Shane Meadows' film *This Is England* (2006), set in an unidentified suburban town in the English Midlands in the 1980s, examines the ways in which English nationalism infiltrated working-class youth culture. Like Meadows, who is the same age and from a similar background to me, I experienced first-hand the ways in which local skinhead and mod youth cultures (of which I was a part) were penetrated by racist politics of the far right. Teenage friends and schoolmates flirted with far-right fascist groups such as the British National Party and the National Front, re-lacing their Dr Marten boots with red laces to show their affiliation with white supremacist politics, and furtively listening to the neo-Nazi Lancashire band Skrewdriver in their bedrooms.[32] As unemployment, precarity and poverty grew in the 1980s, 'the class which was called upon to bear the brunt of a deepening economic crisis' was increasingly 'divided and segmented – along racial lines'.[33]

While Thatcher romanticised the highly stratified class society of the English village, by the late 1980s rural communities in the North of England had suffered from a decade of the Conservative Party's devastating policies: the destruction of mining communities, rising unemployment, the decline of manufacturing jobs, the erosion of the welfare state, the closure of local schools, the end of subsidised bus routes, the selling off of council houses and a steep increase in second-home ownership in rural areas (which saw working-class people priced out of local housing markets). In these straitened economic circumstances, tourism had become an increasingly vital economic lifeline. There were keen incentives to satisfy the voyeuristic desire of urban visitors for nostalgic experiences of the English pastoral, an *olde worlde* rural idyll in which, it was imagined, the certainties of older classed, gendered and racialised hierarchies persisted. In the village where I lived and worked in my mob cap and pinny, everybody who depended on tourism for their livelihood participated in elements of the staged performance of class distinction and rural authenticity.

Are you really from here? Do you really live here? What is it like?, visitors would regularly ask us local kids – as though we didn't also live in the 1980s, listen to the same music on the same radio stations, watch the same television programmes, shop at the same super-markets as them; as though the village and those of us who lived in it were mummified in the imaginary historical time of *Mrs Miniver*.

Growing up under the weight of this kind of tourist gaze resonates with Edouard Glissant's description of the ossifying effects of the ethnographic gaze which fixes 'the object of scrutiny in static time'.[34] While compelled to labour for the tourist gaze, the community in Wanet employed a 'small arsenal' of strategies to defend against 'the scorn of outsiders and the stigma of being seen as old-fashioned'.[35] Despite the indignities labouring for tourists could involve, and the real class conflicts it masked, there was a shared understanding of the urban tourist as a gullible figure; we poked fun at visitors, calling them 'swivel heads' because of their habit of peering through our cottage windows and enquiring into our lives.

Moving away

When I was eighteen I left my village to do a degree at a Higher Education college in a large Northern post-industrial town a few hours' drive away. Higher education was then still free in England, and was in a period of mass expansion which prefigured the full marketisation of the sector. There were no fees to borrow at extortionate interest rates and the remnants of a maintenance grant system meant young people from working-class families could access financial support. The grant I received wasn't enough to cover basic living costs, so I worked in pubs in the evenings and at weekends, further developing the defined right-sided arm muscles, keen observational and conversational skills, and advanced arts of sexual self-defence required to work in the night-time economy. Sexual harassment, as I had learnt working in the village pub, was an unrelenting feature of bar work, and my skills at breaking up bar fights and speedily emptying a bar at closing time led to a lucrative stint as a bouncer.

My degree course in English Literature and Philosophy was taught in both day and evening classes on the site of a slightly dilapidated teacher training college. The college had begun life as a Mechanics Institute in 1824, and by the late 1980s was a sprawling amalgam of an art college, a technical college and a teacher training college, expanding over 150 years to meet the practical training needs and the intellectual and artistic aspirations of Northern mill workers. The majority of my fellow students were middle-aged working-class women, who, having brought up families and worked all their lives in modest part-time jobs, had sought out evening access courses to 'better themselves', a path which had led them onto part-time degree courses. Amongst these women were a sprinkling of unemployed men, and numbers were made up by a small group of mainly working-class teenagers like myself, misfits whose poor school grades meant they hadn't been able to gain places at the grander elite red-brick universities in nearby cities.

I was comfortable in this milieu, with no tiered lecture theatres, just small flat school-like classrooms with plastic chairs. Short lectures about philosophy and literature were followed by animated class discussions which sometimes continued late into the night in a nearby working men's club. It was in this easy college environment with familiar, bright and kind people around me that I discovered a deep craving for ideas, for learning, for reading. I didn't want to stop, to go back to the village, get an ordinary job and 'settle down'. I wanted to learn more. It felt unquenchable, this thirst for reading, for books, for knowledge.

People like you

Armed with enthusiastic references from my college lecturers, I applied for funding from a government research council to do a master's degree and made an application to a university several hours further south. I got an interview and scraped together money for the train fare. In retrospect, I don't know how I plucked up the courage to go. I can remember trembling with fear as I navigated my way to and around the grand buildings of the university campus. I knocked on the office door where I had been instructed to present myself. 'Enter', said a voice behind the door. The professor who led the MA programme had her eyes lowered on my application on the desk in front of her. Eventually she looked up, appraised me and said: 'We don't get many people like you here.'

At the time of my interview I didn't fully comprehend what this phrase 'people like you' meant. I understood that I was an unusual applicant, a young woman educated at a remote rural secondary modern school and without 'a proper' university degree, but I hadn't fully grasped the class politics of the highly stratified British university system. It was only after a term spent in the same professor's class, in which she shamed my contributions to discussions by insisting on correcting my pronunciation; it was only when I received the feedback on my first essay on which she scrawled a single comment, 'illiterate, please seek assistance at the writing support centre', that I began to understand that the remark 'people like you' was a value judgement about the way that *somebody like me* appeared to *somebody like her* – a Cambridge-educated Professor of English Literature.

People like you. It took a long time for me to understand that 'people like you' was a way of 'signalling class through euphemism'.[36] That 'people like you' was spoken in 'the historical-representational moralizing, pathologizing, disgust-producing register attached to working-class women'.[37] That 'people like you' was a value judgement about the ways in which working-classness was etched into my clothes, my body, my then thick Northern accent, my colloquial speech, my grammatical mistakes, my direct manner, my naivety, earnestness and shameless yearning. I was undisciplined. I was out of place. I was being shamed into place. Mob cap and pinny.

People like you. A phrase that would follow me around as I later attempted to carve out an academic career. Words still tattooed into my skin. Encounters which left scars. Welts which still itch and burn. 'People like you are the reason women shouldn't get PhD funding': the words used by a professor, a PhD supervisor, when I told him I was pregnant as I sat weeping with shame before them. 'You do know that somebody like you will never get a job at a university like this one': the advice of a friend, a middle-class academic, who discouraged me from applying for a post at the university where she worked. 'You do know that people like you are only here to do the teaching in this department': the Head of Department who stalled on signing off my first application for a research grant. I could go on.

There is nothing exceptional about the gendered and classed stigma I am relating here. These are ordinary humiliations which structure the lives of people from working-class backgrounds in their encounters with middle-class professionals, and in this case with elite British universities. Stories of these kinds have been related in autobiographical sociological writing for generations, and are increasingly the subject of sociological research – and even some largely half-hearted policy initiatives around the inclusion of working-class students in 'top' universities.

What I learnt from these experiences is that there are 'people everywhere waiting for you to slip up, to show signs of dirtiness and stupidity, so that they can send you back to where you belong'.[38] But what being stigmatised also gifted was a class consciousness that grew into a hard knot of shameless defiance.

Shameless defiance

In her searing memoir *Landscape for a Good Woman: A Story of Two Lives* (1987), the British historian Carolyn Steedman writes about the hidden injuries, 'the sad and secret stories' of social class.[39] Her memoir is about 'two lives' in multiple senses. It is an account of Steedman's mother's life and her own life, the entangled relationship between them, and the significant inter-generational changes in class relations effected by the post-war welfare state in Britain. It is also an account of Steedman's own two lives, her adult life as a 'bourgeois' career academic, and the life of the working-class girl that she carries with her, within her: the girl who is engraved in her skin and whom she carries on her back.

Landscape for a Good Woman opens with an account of a deeply stigmatising exchange between her working-class mother and a middle-class health visitor, who deems their barely furnished home as a place unfit for rearing a child. Witnessing her mother being shamed by the health visitor is a formative moment in Steedman's life. As she reflects:

> I will do everything and anything until the end of my days to stop anyone ever talking to me like that woman talked to my mother. It is in this place, this bare, curtainless bedroom, that lies my secret and shameful defiance. I read a woman's book, meet such a woman at a party (a woman now, like me) and think quite deliberately as we talk: we are divided: a hundred years ago I'd have been cleaning your shoes. I know this and you don't.[40]

Experiences of stigma can provoke a doubling of consciousness in which you see yourself through the eyes of others. In this respect, working-class consciousness is an awareness of your involuntary placement within a social hierarchy which is contingent on economic and social injustice and exploitation; a sense of placement which emerges when people 'put you in your place', experiences through which you suddenly inhabit a place from where you can perceive your 'person value'. As Steedman reflects: 'I think now of all the stories, all the reading, all the dreams that help us to see ourselves in the landscape, and see ourselves watching as well.'[41]

As Beverley Skeggs argues, 'conditions for personhood come into effect through regimes of value'.[42] However, the dominant values that a given society, organisation or ideology seeks to press upon you don't always have purchase; in fact, imposed values are often refused, reworked and returned. Skeggs emphasises the ways in which the working classes frequently fail to feel or embody the shame which (middle-class) social and cultural practices of class stigmatisation seek to inculcate. Stigma gives rise to resistance as people defend themselves against the shame which stigmatisation seeks to instil. Which is why the working classes, and especially working-class women, are so often decried for being *shameless*.

Class shame

Landscape for a Good Woman, like all truly insightful writing on social class in Britain, is sensitive to historical and generational twists and turns of class making. Steedman is critical of the tendency towards romantic accounts of working-class authenticity, which obfuscate understandings of class as historically contingent and relational forms of social classification. She describes the stories told by 'a whole generation of social escapees' in the 1930s who entered professional positions that allow them 'to speak of their working-class origins with authority'.[43] She argues that for men in this inter-war generation class was often worn as a badge of honour, and class mobility imagined as a heroic 'kind of accomplishment' – memories of their former working-class lives are frozen in the past, 'ossified', like insects in amber or coal in the mine. What is often obscured in these kinds of stories about social mobility is that 'class is a relationship, and not a thing'.[44]

Steedman argues that there is also a gendered dimension to these classed 'escape stories'.[45] As she writes, 'the attribution of psychological sameness to the figure in the working-class landscape has been made by men, for whom the transitions of class are at once more ritualized than they are for women, and much harder to make'.[46] By way of contrast, Steedman's account of her working-class childhood is framed not by 'the monolithic story of wage-labour and capital', nor is it told in that genre in which ordinary lives are transformed into soap operas, 'with each the picaresque heroine of her own hard times'.[47] Rather, Steedman focuses her account of growing up as a working-class girl in the 1950s on familial relationships and on the home – a workplace of unpaid labour which is for women often a site of intensive class conflict and struggle.

I am from the generation after Steedman, not a post-war scholarship boy or girl, or part of that post-war grammar school generation schooled in the arts of class passing. I was schooled at secondary moderns and comprehensives. I didn't experience poverty growing up, but sometimes we struggled to get by – my family income meant that I was entitled to free school dinners, school uniform vouchers, and when I went to college I qualified for what remained of a full government maintenance grant.

My parents came from different class backgrounds. My dad was from a large working-class family; he was brought up on a council estate; his mum worked in a fish and chip shop, and his dad worked in a hardware shop. My mum was the only child of middle-class professionals (schoolteachers who later had careers as a librarian and a college lecturer), and she was brought up in a large house on the better side of town. My mum got pregnant as a teenager and my parents had a shotgun wedding in the late 1960s.

My middle-class grandparents were a significant presence in my childhood, furnishing my siblings and me with books, occasionally taking us on trips to visit stately homes and to see plays and concerts. When we were children we were tutored to be on our best behaviour when they visited. They were a loving but sometimes disapproving presence. When I was growing up, I thought of my grandparents as 'posh', but they had been working-class scholarship kids who, very much like Steedman, had gone to grammar schools and became schoolteachers after the war. They styled themselves as educated and middle-class professionals – and worked hard to cloak their working-class roots through the acquisition of cultural capital.

My 'posh' grandma had begun her life as the illegitimate child of a domestic servant, later a hairdresser in a Yorkshire seaside town. She changed her name from working-class Ivy to middle-class Elizabeth when she left her childhood home in the 1920s to do a degree course (an extraordinary class transition for a woman from her background at this time). She never spoke about her childhood, and my sense is that her illegitimacy and modest roots were an enduring source of shame. Before she died, she burnt all the diaries and letters which she had assiduously written over her lifetime.

In his memoir *Returning to Reims*, the French sociologist Didier Eribon describes 'the discomfort that results from belonging to two different worlds, worlds so far separated from each other that they seem irreconcilable, and yet which coexist in everything that you are'.[48] As he writes, 'whatever you have uprooted yourself from or been uprooted from still endures as an integral part of who or what you are ... the traces of what you were as a child, the manner in which you were socialized, persist, even when the conditions in which you live as an adult have changed'.[49] When I read *Returning to Reims*, what resonated was Eribon's description of the 'intense experiences of shame related to class shame':[50] the melancholia which accompanies a 'spilt habitus', the feelings of sadness which often accompany a dislocating sense of lost roots and belonging.[51]

Being the anthropological object

By the time I finished my master's degree and returned North, my parents had divorced and had set up new homes with new partners, which eventually saw them move away from the village. Homeless and unemployed, I headed to Manchester, where my younger brother had started a furniture-making course and he and his girlfriend let me sleep on their sofa for a while. The rest of that year was one spent hanging onto the periphery of the academic margins by my grubby fingernails. Alongside work in bars, I managed to pick up odd bits of teaching on university access courses. One evening I was invited to a dinner by an academic who wanted me to meet his friend, an anthropology PhD student, who had just returned from a year's fieldwork in Papua New Guinea. It is important to note that at this juncture I had no idea what anthropology was, or what fieldwork might entail. Being invited to dinner at an anthropologist's was both a terrifying and exotic prospect.

The evening began with a slideshow. We sat in the dark drinking wine while our host projected photographic slides from a carousel slide projector onto the wall of her apartment. Images of the people she had studied and lived with for a year began to appear before us, sound-tracked by the whine of the projector fan and clicks as each new slide slotted into place. Sometimes the anthropologist appeared with the people she had lived with, scenes straight out of a colonial scrapbook.[52] When the evening drew to a close, the host tried to include me in the conversation by asking me where I was from. When I told her the name of my village, she gasped and gazed at me open-mouthed, before exclaiming, 'I don't believe it, my PhD supervisor did his fieldwork there!'

That night I dreamt about the images projected onto the anthropologist's wall, the whirr of the fan, the carousel rotating, the moment of darkness before the click which announced a new image

– and suddenly there projected on the wall is the farmer who threatened to shoot our straying dogs, click, the ladies who ran the post office, click, the drunken pub landlord, click, the guy who grew weed up the valley, click, the local bikers gathered for their Sunday ride, click, the school friend who concealed her pregnancy, click, the back seat of the school bus, click, weekend walkers in boots and anoraks, click, fights at the village disco, click, the fell run at the summer fete, click, flooded fields, click, teenagers drinking cider in the graveyard, click, kids swimming in the river, click, bringing sheep down from the fells for lambing, click, my friends beating pheasants for the local aristocrats, click, my dad painting a cottage, click, my brother skinning a rabbit for the pot, click, my mum riddling the stove; and there I am, a gangly teenager at the edge of one of images, punk hair, heavy eyeliner, smudged mascara, click, there I am being dragged by my hair to the headteacher's office at school for misbehaviour, click, there I am again scrubbing the urinals, click, evading groping hands in the pub, click, smoking cigarettes with my friends, click, serving cafe tables in mob cap and pinny.

The dinner guests don't recognise that I am in the images. They talk about the culture of the rural community; they share comments, offer analysis, make judgements. It is impossible for them to imagine that the object of the fieldwork might be right there with them in the room and on the wall at the same time, in the same space and historical time. Served up on the wall to be consumed at an academic dinner party. I shrink into the chair. I make myself as small as possible. I want to disappear. I feel I should confess that I am one of the natives on the wall. That I am the ethnographic object. But my mouth is full of wool. There is no position from which to speak – the figures in the slideshow are silent; they are artefacts to be gazed at, spoken for and about. I am caught in 'the spy-glass of anthropology'.[53] I am overwhelmed with shame. I radiate shame.

The sociologist Helen Merrell Lynd argues that shame is most acutely felt when it is unanticipated, when we are taken by surprise, 'caught off guard'.[54] Lynd describes this as the 'astonishment of seeing different parts of ourselves, conscious and unconscious, suddenly coming together, and coming together with aspects of the world we had not recognised'.[55] The shock of finding myself caught in the gaze of another, of being captured in shame, was particularly heightened in this, my first encounter with the ethnographic gaze. It is a scene of shame which remains burnt into my eyelids.[56]

When my friend asked me why I was interested in stigma, I was immediately transported back to the scene in the anthropologist's living room and to this dream, in which the colonial theatre of anthropology was transposed into the class theatre of my childhood.

Telling practices

A few years later I tracked down a copy of a book by the anthropologist's supervisor, Nigel Rapport. It was called *Diverse World-Views in an English Village* (1993) and I discovered that Rapport had undertaken an ethnographic study of the village in which I had lived, a village he names *Wanet*. *Diverse World-Views*, as I might introduce it now to my students, is a micro-social analysis of social interactions and kinship relations in a remote rural village in the North of England between 1980 and 1981. It is often cited as one of the foundational texts of a subfield of anthropology called 'the anthropology of Britain', and it has been praised by sociologists of rural Britain for its 'acute sensitivity' to the diversity of the ordinary lives it depicts.[57]

As an ethnography employing classic observer-participant methods, *Diverse World-Views in an English Village* is reminiscent of Erving Goffman's PhD thesis *Communication Conduct in an Island Community*, an ethnography undertaken in Unst in the

Shetland Islands between 1949 and 1951. That study became the basis for Goffman's first and most famous book, *The Presentation of Self in Everyday Life* (1956), for which he received the American Sociological Association's MacIver award in 1961. The most striking similarity between these studies is that both Goffman and Rapport undertook their research surreptitiously, employing covert methods and adopting a feigned persona to study local people.

In a rare reflection on ethnographic methods – a talk which was, ironically, furtively recorded against his wishes and published after his death – Goffman shared his 'rules of the trade about getting into a place' to conduct (undercover) ethnographic research. As he explained:

> You have to anticipate being questioned by the people whom you study so you engage in providing a story that will hold up should the facts be brought to their attention. So you engage in what are sometimes called 'telling' practices. ... I like a story such that if they find out what you are doing, the story you presented could not be an absolute lie.[58]

Goffman told the residents of Unst that he was studying the local economy and Rapport told the villagers in Wanet that he was studying local history.

In *Diverse World-Views* Rapport reveals (to his reader) the 'telling practices' he employed to explain to local people what he was doing in Wanet: 'having used the term "anthropology" once or twice ... and being received with a polite but alarmed silence, I realised that history ... was a more acceptable subject'.[59] Rapport reveals that this deception was counselled by his doctoral supervisor, who advised him to be 'extremely careful' in 'how he explained himself', 'to be discreet and cautious', to 'give little away', to avoid 'the accoutrement of formal sociological research: camera, notebooks, tape-recorder for these smacked of the outsider' and to dissociate himself from 'the tourist, the visitor, the second-home owner'.[60] Under the guise of a history student looking for casual work, Rapport describes his attempts to 'penetrate' the community in Wanet by taking on jobs, first in a cafe, then as a farm labourer, all the while making regular field trips to a village pub, which he calls The Eagle.

In a chapter titled 'The Ethics of the Research', Rapport considers his decision to choose a remote Northern rural village as the field site for his research and the 'natives of Cumbria' as his 'informants'.[61] He offers an account of himself in his early twenties as a naive young man, eager to embark on his PhD fieldwork. He reflects also on his limited vantage point as a public school boy, a Cambridge graduate, from a privileged middle-class background. 'I had had a comfortable upbringing and had looked out over a large back lawn onto the cramped housing estates beyond but I espoused a deep empathy with the have-nots who had to achieve by struggling and did not inherit with grace.'[62] Thus, it was constrained by what he terms 'the archetypal idioms of the middle-class Anglo-Saxon academic' that Rapport arrived in Wanet with 'a vision of ethnography as both scientifically demanding and heroic'.[63]

I was a scientist about to gain 'his' people, his fund of private data with which to address academic debate. Mine ... would be a British empire: an ethnographical fortress in England not in some remote and backward area of Africa or South East Asia. Studying the natives of Cumbria, I felt, was not the perpetuation of a harmful act so much as a pilgrimage; or, at least a chance for me to partake in a joint celebration of our Britishness ... It was true I was going to Cumbria to gather information on them but my feelings were of friendship, modesty, respect, even longing.[64]

This was the first ethnography I had ever read and, despite the opening claim that 'my informants and their valley homes appear in this book in disguised forms', I could immediately identify all of the people in it. They appeared before me as cardboard cut-outs of the flesh-and-blood people I had grown up with, figures through which the reader is invited to voyeuristically peer into village life, 'close-up but always from the outside looking in' and 'through a glass darkly'.[65]

Jack Katz notes that 'Much of the market for ethnography is built on a sense of a radical difference, distance between the "them" about whom the ethnographer writes and the "us" to whom ethnographic texts are directed'.[66] Clearly I wasn't the intended reader of *Diverse World-Views in an English Village*. Indeed, when I first read this book in my early twenties, I read it from a reading position which wasn't invited or available within the text itself. I read it as one of those he 'gathered information on'; one of the natives whom Rapport had sought to collect as 'his fund of private data'. I read this book as the anthropological object.

As I read, I searched for traces of my former life. I went to school with the children of his informers, friends and classmates, old boyfriends. I ate meals with the family he lived with and whose conversations he secretly memorised, transcribed, edited; private intimate conversations, words spoken in confidence. I waited tables in the cafes he frequented. I cleaned the toilets he pissed in, polished the brass and worked behind the bar of the pub in which he drank. As I read, I watched the anthropologist watching us. 'Brian and I were leaning on the bar, sharing a pint and eyeing up the bevies of tourist women who frequently seemed to fill the pub on holiday weekend.'[67] As I read I pictured him in The Eagle, busy, as he puts it, 'chatting up everything on two legs in a skirt – and, no doubt through short-sightedness, a few *things* that were not'.[68] I felt his gaze on my back as I wiped down the tables in the craft centre cafe, and cheerily served customers in my mob cap and pinny. I pictured myself in these scenes, a vulnerable young working-class woman, waiting on tables, pulling pints, and evading the unwanted sexual advances of older men. I felt, I feel, ashamed.

As the historian Ruth Leys notes, 'shame is an emotion that is routed through the eyes' and 'the logic of shame is a scene of exposure (this is true even if the scene is only an imagined one and the observer is not an external spectator but an internalized other)'.[69] Shame is a feeling of being exposed to a gaze which produces a view of yourself which you cannot control. More than this, shame 'is held to concern not your actions but who you are; that is, your deficiencies and inadequacies as a person as these are revealed to the shaming gaze of the other'.[70]

Rapport didn't reveal that the reason he was in Wanet was to study us. He didn't tell us that he was memorising our conversations, 'secreting notes' about his person and 'writing up my journal at night'.[71] Planning the thesis he would write about us, dreaming of publishing that thesis as a book, a book that he seemingly never contemplated *people like them, people like us, people like me* would read. He promised, however, to reveal insights into *the native point of view*. Rapport writes, 'What I was up to felt rather like snooping'.[72] But he 'banishes' these thoughts, consoles himself that his research was 'for the advance of understanding and the betterment of science', and justifies his unease in not explaining 'my project in its own terms' by the labour he provides in local cafes and farms.[73]

> I was aware of the basic inequality inherent in the whole exercise – I had not asked to study them and they had not invited me – but by accepting their aggression, granting them daily superordination, and adopting uncomplainingly whatever lowly statuses they chose to accord me, I tried to salve the sore of my writing them up later.[74]

As Karen Jacobs notes, 'the dirty little secret of the participant-observer method is the masking or denial of the complexity of the intersubjective encounter between fieldworker and native, as well as the power relations that result from this encounter'.[75]

Speaking back

In 1979, the anthropologist Nancy Scheper-Hughes published an ethnography of a remote rural village in Ireland titled *Saints, Scholars and Schizophrenics: Mental Illness in Rural Ireland*. When the book was reviewed in the Irish press, journalists were quickly able to identify the village she had undertaken her research in, and the local community she had studied soon bought and read her book. As a consequence, Scheper-Hughes found herself embroiled in a public controversy about the ethics of her research. In the preface to the 2001 paperback edition of the book, Hughes describes making a return visit in 1981 to the community and being met with hostility. As she reflects, within 'the traditional fieldwork paradigm our once colonized subjects remain disempowered and mute', now she has to face 'the native reader' – they are hurt and they are angry.[76] The villagers confront her and question the ethics of her research. They tell her that 'There is quite a difference between whispering something beside a fire or across a counter and seeing it printed for the world to see'. 'It becomes a public shame.'[77] In response to her insistence that she had carefully anonymised their words, they reply:

> You think we didn't, each of us, sit down poring over every page until we had recognised the bits and pieces of ourselves strewn about here and there. You turned us into amputees with hooks for fingers and some other blackguard's heart beating inside our own chest. How do you think I felt reading my words come out of some Tom-O or Pat-O or some publican's mouth?[78]

While Rapport concealed his real purpose for being in Wanet, he reveals that some local people didn't believe the reasons he gave for being there. I suspect they never did, attuned as they are, and as I was, to living under the weight of the tourist gaze. Rapport makes several references to the ways in which he was challenged in the field: 'Sid cornered me behind a table in The Eagle, and told me he had made phone calls about me and saw through my lies … "aren't you gonna go and write about your experiences here? Aren't you studying something like sociology?"'[79] Rapport writes:

> Just before I left the field, I remember phoning a good friend in Cardiff and telling her how fed up I was with the fieldworking and the roles I had adopted in Wanet. 'Look on the bright side', she said, 'Soon you'll be leaving those country bumpkins behind, and what they think won't matter anymore'.[80]

While *Diverse World-Views in an English Village* promises the reader 'diversity' in 'world views', the central difference which comes into view is that between the anthropologist, his imagined reader (liberal, educated, academic) and those 'country bumpkins' whose voices he steals, ventriloquises and picks through: *what they think won't matter anymore.*

'I question, in hindsight', Rapport writes, 'the ethics of my behaviour in adopting the persona of observing-participant' but 'I feel that my constructions of the people they were and the relations they shared one year quite a while ago *do not harm them now*'.[81] What is the measure of harm?

When I read *Diverse World-Views* today, now reading it as a middle-aged sociology professor with significant cultural capital, it still provokes a painful and shameful sense of splitting – as I encounter myself and my childhood community as *written for* and *written about*.[82] I don't know whether my old school friends, work colleagues and neighbours would care about what is written in this book, whether they would feel angry, exploited or ashamed if they read the intimate and private conversations Rapport transcribed;

his views about their parent's marriages, the publication of gossip about love affairs, details of family disputes, ill-feelings about business dealings, the presentation of them as xenophobic, illiberal and narrow-minded. I felt when I first read this book – and still feel – that this ethnography is an unkind picture of the small, isolated rural community in which I grew up in the 1980s. A series of 'brutal ... sketches of other people's lives ... assimilated to the perspective of the participant-observer'.[83]

Alongside the problematic ethics of covert ethnography, what also struck me when I reread *Diverse World Views* is its lack of sociological imagination. What I mean by this is the absence of any sustained attempt to link the personal troubles of the people it studies to broader structures of government. Instead, they, we, are imagined as existing in an 'interactional microcosm severed from its institutional moorings and seemingly devoid of material determinism and power vectors'.[84]

Sociological imagination

In *The Sociological Imagination* (1959), the American sociologist Charles Wright Mills famously stated that 'no social study that does not come back to the problem of biography, of history and their intersections within a society has completed its intellectual journey'.[85] Indeed, the promise of sociology is the critical sensibility which it cultivates when we tease out 'the public issue or problem contained in the private trouble'.[86] This forging of connections between the personal and the political, between individual biographies and the histories that shape them, is particularly urgent today. As the sociologists Nicholas Gane and Les Back argue, 'in a neoliberal world which seeks to tear asunder private troubles from public issues, and thereby turn social uncertainty into a personal failure that is divorced from any collective cause or remedy, the linking of biography and history is a vital part of a sociology that is both politically and publicly engaged'.[87]

C. Wright Mill's understanding of sociology as an imaginative practice which ties individual biographies to history has its roots in the extraordinary body of work produced by the sociologist W.E.B. Du Bois (1868–1963).[88] For Du Bois, being a black man in America 'at the dawning of the Twentieth Century' bestowed him with a 'double-consciousness', which he describes as being 'gifted with second-sight of seeing yourself'.[89] It is 'a peculiar sensation', he writes, 'this sense of always looking at one's self through the eyes of others, of measuring one's soul by the tape of a world that looks on in amused contempt and pity'.[90] In *The Souls of Black Folk*, a collection of essays published in 1903, Du Bois puts this gift of double-consciousness to work as a sociological method, deftly weaving together autobiographical experiences, the 'Sorrow Songs' of black spirituals, social history, and economic and statistical data into a shattering account of the 'studied humiliations' of anti-black racism.[91]

Stigma is a distinctly psychosocial concept. What I mean by this is that it is a concept which describes the traffic between the individual and the social world, between personal troubles and social, political and economic forces. Stigma power is an analytic that allows us to examine the relay between practices which impress stigma upon people, and how these impressions affect the ways in which people perceive themselves and others. It is important to pay attention to stigma precisely because it captures the movement between external and internal processes of de/valuation. Stigma is a productive force that marks out and classifies people as a means of subjugating them. Stigma is a disciplinary form of power that seeks to transform people, to change attitudes, behaviour, and how we make value judgements about others. Stigma is also a dehumanising force of power that infiltrates, pierces and deflates your sense of yourself. Stigma functions through subjection; it makes people abject.[92]

Yet, as Du Bois suggests, being stigmatised can provoke a consciousness of the ways in which we are 'figured against the backdrop of history'.[93] The doubling of consciousness effected by social stigma – between experiences of being devalued or dehumanised by others and an awareness of oneself as human and valuable nonetheless – makes us wakeful. Resisting stigma generates what the poet Dionne Brand describes as a 'shimmering alertness' to 'what things come together to make us up at a particular moment'.[94] It stirs an awareness of how power is written on our skin, awakening us to the relationship between our biographical lives and the stigmatised positionalities scripted for us by others. Indeed, I made the decision to include some autobiographical fragments from this *shadow* stigma project in this chapter, precisely because my experiences of being stigmatised, including the formative experience of discovering myself caught in the anthropological gaze, have been such important critical gift in my subsequent work as a sociologist, a teacher, a writer, a poverty commissioner, an activist.

One of the arguments of *Stigma* is that the double-consciousness which being stigmatised effects is a resource for resistance. That is, being aware of how we are 'figured against the backdrop of history' makes us question those systems of economic injustice, practices of political domination and stratified social hierarchies which we might otherwise simply absorb or passively accept as inevitable or deserved.[95] As Dionne Brand puts it, 'One enters a room and history follows; one enters a room and history precedes'. She goes on:

> History is already seated in the chair in the empty room when one arrives. Where one stands in a society seems always related to this historical experience. Where one can be observed is relative to that history. ... How do I know this? Only by self-observation, only by looking. Only by feeling. Only by being a part, sitting in the room with history.[96]

Chapter 6

Conclusion

Rage against the stigma machines

Stigma (noun): Ineffaceable stains of blood, supposed to remain on the floor of a room where a murder has been committed.

Oxford English Dictionary

In spring 2016 three members of the British Royal Family, Prince William and his wife Catherine (the Duke and Duchess of Cambridge) and Prince Harry, launched Heads Together, 'a new campaign to end stigma around mental health'.[1] Heads Together is an umbrella organisation for eight existing UK-based mental health charities that together have 'decades of experience in tackling stigma, raising awareness, and providing vital help for people with mental health challenges'.[2] Bringing these charities together under one organisational 'brand', Heads Together seeks to harness the significant media power of the popular younger members of the Royal Family.

The publicity for this campaign states that while there has been progress 'in recent decades', stigma remains a 'key issue' in preventing people with 'mental health challenges' accessing the help and support they need. As Prince William puts it, 'people can't and won't seek help because they are ashamed about what people might think'.[3] To this end, Heads Together is focused on eradicating stigma as a barrier to seeking help, through initiatives that centre on encouraging individual disclosures of mental distress. As they describe it, 'shattering stigma on mental health starts with simple conversations. When you realise that mental health problems affect your friends, neighbours, children and spouses, the walls of judgement and prejudice around these issues begin to fall'.[4]

To facilitate these conversations, Heads Together has mobilised an array of communications technologies, developing a website, harnessing social media platforms (Facebook, Twitter and Instagram), and devising hashtags, such as #oktosay and #thereforme, under which people can share their experiences. To illustrate the stigma-shattering potential of disclosure, the Heads Together website has also published a series of short films, featuring celebrities and public figures in conversation with family and colleagues: these include the American pop star Lady Gaga discussing her mental health with Prince William (over Skype), the ex-footballer Rio Ferdinand talking with his agent about bereavement, and the ex-New Labour Communications Director, Alastair Campbell, discussing his cyclical depressions with his partner, the journalist Fiona Miller. Alongside these well-known pubic figures, there are films featuring 'ordinary' members of the public, such as ambulance drivers talking about experiences of mental distress in the aftermath of stressful events at work. Through this accumulation and dissemination of individual conversations, Heads Together aims 'to help change the national conversation on mental health', effecting a transformation in British public attitudes.

Since the publication fifty years ago of Erving's Goffman's *Stigma: Notes on the Management of a Spoiled Identity* (1963), there has been 'an explosive growth' of research and social action around stigma.[5] Stigma has become a way of seeing, describing and understanding a vast array of discriminatory social attitudes and practices. We have become accustomed to thinking about stigma as a problem of restrictive or oppressive social norms that can be alleviated through what Goffman termed 'benevolent social action'.[6] Indeed, much stigma research is motivated by a concern with changing attitudes and behaviours; through, for example, increasing people's 'tolerance' for particular stigmatised conditions, or devising strategies that assist the stigmatised in managing the responses of others. This research has had a significant impact on health and social policy, in the form of proposals, models, strategies and professional training programmes for stigma management. Indeed, anti-stigma initiatives have become central to charitable and public health campaigns aimed at 'raising awareness' and 'combatting stigma' in a vast range of social and institutional settings.[7] Heads Together emerged from this paradigm of stigma thinking.

There is much to be admired about the values and ambitions of Heads Together, including the candour of Princes Harry and William about their own struggles with mental distress following the death of their mother, Diana. As William Davies writes: 'Harry's admission that he had ignored his own emotional distress for several years before eventually having counselling was a valuable contribution, from a figure more commonly associated with laddish machismo. William's focus on male suicide statistics was also a good use of his celebrity.'[8]

Further, all the existing evidence supports the claims of Heads Together that 'unresolved mental health problems lie at the heart of some of our greatest social challenges'.[9] Indeed, the stigma that shrouds mental health problems is not only damaging and discriminatory but often exacerbates mental distress. As clinical psychologist John Read and his colleagues argue: 'Negative attitudes ... lead to discrimination in many domains, including the workplace and housing, and to rejection by family and friends. They can also lead, via anticipated and actual discrimination and internalized stigma, to decreased life satisfaction and self-esteem, and to increased alcohol use, depression and suicidality.'[10]

However, while Prince William states that '[it's time] to feel normal about mental health, it's the same as physical health', psychologists like Read have begun to question the effectiveness of the 'mental illness is an illness like any other' approach advocated by anti-stigma programmes.[11] Indeed, research suggests that the embracing of biogenetic rather than social explanations of mental distress risks amplifying the very stigmatising attitudes and discriminations which these campaigns ostensibly seek to eliminate. So while, as Davies argues, the 'idea that one is simply "unwell"' might provide comfort 'to people wrestling with their own depression or anxiety', it simultaneously veils over 'a whole host of more fundamental cultural, political and economic questions regarding the distribution of distress in our society – the sorts of questions that the Duke of Cambridge would be less likely to grapple with'.[12]

'Hands off our stories'

There is also concern amongst mental health survivors and activists about the impact that anti-stigma campaigns that solicit, share and publicise personal stories of mental distress might have on individuals, given the facts of discrimination against people with diagnosed mental health conditions. For example, in terms of potential consequences, there are substantive differences between a prince or a pop star sharing their struggles with mental distress in carefully curated publicity, and a precarious worker disclosing to an employer, or a young person sharing online. Indeed, the recent and significant increase in the sharing of mental distress in online spaces encouraged by these kinds of anti-stigma campaigns obscures an entire host of potentially negative impacts, likely to be highly determined by a person's relative social position and status.

In 2012, a group of Canadian scholar-activists affiliated with 'Mad Studies' published an account of a community event, 'Recovering Our Stories: A Small Act of Resistance', which sought to trouble the 'appropriation' of personal experiences of psychiatric distress by mental health organisations and charities.[13] As they detail, while the sharing of testimonies has long been a central strategy of grassroots mental health activism, particularly in struggles against psychiatric authority, what concerns them is the ways in which these strategies have increasingly been adopted (co-opted) by charitable and governmental bodies.[14] In particular, they are apprehensive about the commodification of personal stories of psychiatric distress and recovery in 'wellbeing marketplaces' that are increasingly dominated by powerful corporate actors.[15] As they argue, this market is often aligned with the interests of those organisations (state, commercial or third sector), rather than those of 'mad people themselves'. In this context, personal stories of mental health, they write, 'function to garner support from authority figures such as politicians and philanthropists, to build the organizational "brand" regardless of program quality, and to raise operating funds during times of economic constraint'.[16] Further, they argue, there is a marked shift away 'from the history of psychiatric survivor storytelling' as means to question critically social norms and provisions, towards forms of storying that 'solidify hegemonic accounts of mental illness'.[17] This critique of mainstream anti-stigma campaigns draws attention to how 'mad stories' risk being 'sanitised' in ways that 'do little to change the way that agencies function or to address broader issues such as poverty, unemployment and discrimination'.[18] In short, in focusing on individual stories of disclosure and recovery, questions about the causes of stigma and mental distress are frequently airbrushed out of picture.

In order to alert 'the community to the dangers of storytelling', the Canadian scholars and activists devised a project entitled 'Hands off Our Stories', which included the production of information cards and a humorous button badge 'displaying the words *patient porn* stroked out by a red diagonal line'.[19] Designed to warn people of the risks of freely giving their personal stories to mental health organisations, these information cards had the following 'tips' printed on them:

- Participation is voluntary. You can always say no.
- Ask yourself, who profits from you telling your story?
- What purpose does personal story sharing serve?
- How do large organizations use stories to make material change?
- Story telling as an exercise of labour/work. Do you get paid?
- The internet lasts forever. Because of the technology available today, your interview or story will likely be accessible to the public for a very long time. That includes future employers and landlords.[20]

The 'Hands Off Our Stories' project is a salient reminder that stigmatisation arises in contexts that are shaped by unequal relations of power, and that stigma *and* anti-stigma initiatives are the site of intensive social struggles. Attempts to ameliorate social stigma (of any kind) are limited from the outset, if they fail to take account of 'the political economy of stigmatization and its links to social exclusion'.[21]

The political economy of stigma

In January 2017, the Heads Together campaign was lent political support of the highest order when the then British Prime Minister Theresa May stated in a speech to the Charity Commission that: 'For too long mental illness has been something of a hidden injustice in our country, shrouded in a completely unacceptable stigma and dangerously disregarded as a secondary issue to physical health'.[22] Alongside tackling stigma, May made a specific commitment to address 'shortfalls in mental health services', which she described as 'plans to tackle the burning injustice of mental illness'.[23] However, the promise that mental health funding would be a key priority of her premiership, her assurances of additional resources for mental health services, and her promise to create parity between state funding for mental and physical health conditions were met with incredulity by many British health professionals – and failed to materialise.

Mental health services in the UK are so 'notoriously underfunded' that they are 'often referred to as a "Cinderella service"'.[24] As Mary O'Hara details, mental health provision was also 'hit hard and early by austerity measures and this pattern has continued'.[25] Cuts to services have taken place in a context of rapidly increasing need. For example, in 2017 several regional NHS trusts reported a 60 per cent increase in the previous twelve-month period in referrals to mental health crisis teams (a crisis referral is made in urgent cases when, for example an individual is in extreme distress and felt to be at risk of self-harm which may endanger their life or those of others). This surge in crisis referrals was likely, in part, due to people being unable to access first-tier services, such as counselling, at earlier stages of need: One in ten people currently wait two weeks to get an appointment with a general practitioner; many thousands have to wait six months or more for a mental health assessment or counselling appointment.

One consequence of the combination of a marked increase in levels of mental distress and a correlative decrease in availability of support is that the police (and the fire service) are becoming a de facto frontline mental health service. As Vikram Dodd notes: 'The number of calls handled by the Metropolitan police [London's regional police force] in which someone was concerned about a person's mental health hit a record 115,000 in the last year: on average 315 a day, or about 13 an hour. Volumes have grown by nearly a third since 2011–12.'[26] Dodd, a journalist, reports cases in which 'ill people struggling to find help commit crimes to obtain treatment', noting how one woman 'on crutches walked a mile to smash a shop window in Hereford, then called the police herself, believing that was the best way to get access to mental health services'.[27] I have heard similar anecdotal evidence through my own work with the Poverty Commission.

If one of the aims of Heads Together is to eradicate stigma in order that people are willing and able to access services, the timing of this campaign inevitably begs the question what kinds and what quality of services actually exist for those in need, both now and, if the current programmes of austerity cuts continue, in the future. Furthermore, it is important to note that while the charities supported by Heads Together lead important programmes of mental health support, the form these take is largely the provision of information, helplines and online forums and not the kinds of intensive counselling and/or acute psychiatric health services that many people in Britain (those without private sources of funding, or in private health care schemes) are currently having difficulties accessing. Indeed, it is imperative that we understand the erosion of mental health services in the context of the wider political economy of NHS reform.[28] All of this isn't to say that talking about mental distress with friends and families can't lessen social stigma, but rather that anti-stigma initiatives which want to remove barriers to seeking help but that don't simultaneously address *either* the erosion of public service provision *or* the deeper social causes of increased levels of mental distress will likely be limited in their impact.

Neoliberalism makes you sick

Let's unpack this a little further. In the UK, it is not only that mental health services have been historically underfunded, but that cuts to services are taking place in a period in which there has been a significant and sustained increase in anxiety, depression and suicides.[29] In *Politics Make You Sick: Neoliberal Epidemics*, Ted Schrecker and Clare Bambra detail the ways in which state adoption of neoliberal economic policies characterised by 'reductions in workplace rights, job security, pay levels and welfare rights' has 'led to large increases in chronic stress across large parts of the population of many countries'.[30] This governmental production of chronic stress is (unequally) distributed across the population and 'gets under the skin' through multiple and 'well understood' psychosocial mechanisms,[31] a fact to which people like Stephanie affected by changes to the state benefits system, and wider social and public attitudes to welfare claimants, so powerfully testify (see Introduction and Chapter 4).

This neoliberal epidemic of insecurity has been exacerbated in Britain and elsewhere by political responses to the 2008 global financial crisis. As detailed in *Stigma*, the British coalition government (2010–2015) and the subsequent Conservative government (2015–present) responded to this crisis in the banking sector by implementing austerity, 'an attempt to permanently disassemble the protection state'.[32] It is not only that austerity-driven reforms have intensified an existing neoliberal epidemic of chronic stress, but, as detailed, this programme of cuts to social provision has been enacted and legitimated through strategies of (state-sanctioned) welfare stigma production.

As I have argued throughout *Stigma*, we require *more thorough historical and political* understandings of stigma if we are to address the multiple crises we are in. This necessitates supplementing approaches focused primarily on ameliorating the effects of stigma towards a consideration of the social causes and political function of particular modalities of stigma production, to ascertain not only where and by whom stigma is crafted, but who profits from stigma power.

Following the stigma money

Alongside the eight charitable partners who are the major beneficiaries of funds raised by Heads Together, the campaign has four corporate partners. These include the retail bank Virgin Money, Dixons Carphone – 'Europe's leading specialist electrical and telecommunications retailer and services company' – the global corporate giant Unilever, and BlackRock – 'a global leader in investment management, risk management and advisory services for institutional and retail clients'.[33] In short, Heads Together is bankrolled by some of the very corporate and financial organisations that are the beneficiaries of neoliberal economic policies (and the austerity reforms) that are eroding state welfare and social care, and in doing so are exacerbating mental distress amongst the poorest and most vulnerable members of our society.

To take just one example from among the list of Heads Together's corporate partners: Virgin Money (UK) began life as a personal finance company which primarily sold debt, through credit card services. In 2008, the British bank Northern Rock collapsed in the wake of the US sub-prime mortgage crisis, and the British government took the bank into national ownership. It then split the bank into two parts, Northern Rock plc and Northern Rock Asset Management, with the bad debt (approx. £21bn) parcelled into the latter. The government later sold Northern Rock plc to Virgin Money at a loss to the taxpayer estimated to be between £400m and £650m. The figures continue to be disputed, but what we can say with certainty is that British taxpayers not only subsidised Virgin Money in its acquisition of the salvageable part of this bank, but also absorbed a massive amount of private financial sector debt – money which could have been used to fund mental health services.

Virgin Money is one part of Virgin Group Ltd, a multinational venture capital conglomerate. In 2010, Virgin set up a new arm, called Virgin Care, with which it sought to expand its interests into the private UK health services market, thus capitalising on the government's programme to privatise state health services, a process rapidly accelerated under the guise of austerity-driven reforms. Gill Plimmer notes that 'the provision of community services and mental healthcare is one of the biggest growth areas for healthcare companies and accounts for about half of all NHS outsourcing deals put out to tender'. As she writes, 'according to LaingBuisson, the industry analysts, the market for out-of-hospital services could be worth £10bn–£20bn a year'.[34] At the time of writing, Virgin Care had acquired NHS contracts amounting to over £2 billion. Services run by Virgin Care include Primary Care (GP services and hospitals), Adult Social Care (including social workers), Community Health, Prison Healthcare and Child Mental Health Services.

Several whistle-blowers, among them the Labour MP for Dewsbury, Paula Sherriff, have spoken out about unethical practices and misconduct within some of the health services Virgin now runs in place of the state, and multiple failures in service have been tracked and documented by campaign groups such as NHS for Sale.[35] In short, Virgin Group has been a key beneficiary of government programmes of austerity-driven welfare reforms since 2010, profiting from the privatisation of social provision. Given this, we might want at least to question the claim of this predatory for-profit private healthcare provider that it shares the mission of Heads Together 'of ending stigma, changing the conversation on mental health and giving people the tools they need to help themselves and each other with their mental health'.[36]

It was in the immediate context of austerity, the mass and overtly politicised stigma production from above which accompanied this political project of the privatisation (enclosure) of public goods and services, and the distress and suffering this created, that I grew frustrated with understandings of stigma which are decoupled from power, history, economics and politics.[37] When I began the research for this book, I started by immersing myself in the social scientific literature on stigma, seeking research that spoke to my concern with stigma as a form of power. I found that social and political questions, such as 'how stigma is used by individuals, communities and the state to produce and reproduce social inequality', was either missing from or mutated within much of the literature.[38]

Stigma is not alone in noticing this gap; there is now a growing body of research that evidences how stigma impacts on particular groups and populations cumulatively over time, through, for example, the design of discriminatory social policy and laws, and the embedding of stigma in institutional practices.[39] An inter-disciplinary consensus is emerging on the ways in which 'stigma feeds upon, strengthens and reproduces existing inequalities'.[40] What *Stigma* has sought to contribute to this research is a much more historical and political understanding of stigma as a form of classificatory power, and in particular to supplement the focus on individual experience with a consideration of stigma from the point of view of its production.

In *Stigma*, this shift in perspective has been vertical (looking upwards to sites of stigma production) and temporal (taking long views on histories of stigma practices), while focusing throughout on developing a new understanding of stigma as a violent practice of exploitation and social control. In order to track the history of stigma as *a history of practices*, I researched the etymology of stigma, read classics scholarship, histories of slavery, imperialism and colonialism, and the history of capitalist enclosures. Then I read Franz Kafka's short story 'In the Penal Colony' (1919) and I began to think about stigma as a machine.

Penal stigma in the colony

'In the Penal Colony' recounts the visit of a European gentleman scholar-explorer to a French colony in the tropics. The commandant of the colony has invited the explorer to witness the execution of a native soldier. The story is set at the scene of the execution in a desolate sandy valley on the outskirts of the colonial settlement, where the condemned man has been led shackled in thick chains which bind him from collared neck, to wrists and ankles. The narrative centres on the demonstration of a gruesome machine, used to torture residents of the colony to death by repetitively tattooing a sentence into their flesh: 'whatever commandment the prisoner has disobeyed is written upon the body'.[41]

The sentence to be inscribed on the bodies of the condemned is programmed into the machine by the officer, the penal colony's sole judge and executioner. As this particular prisoner has been condemned to death for disobedience and insulting behaviour to a superior, the officer is calibrating the machine to kill him with the words 'honour thy superiors'. As the officer readies the machine, he explains to the explorer that this 'ingenious device' was invented by the deceased former Commandant of the penal colony, and that this 'procedure and method of execution' has since fallen out of favour. Indeed, the officer is the only person left in the colony who can operate the machine. The officer describes to the explorer how these macabre public executions used to attract 'hundreds of spectators', but neither the new Commandant of the colony nor any of the residents of the colony now feel compelled to attend. Indeed, the officer suspects that the Commandant is deliberately withholding the resources required to repair the increasingly dilapidated machine in order that he might introduce a more enlightened penal system to the colony. Hoping to convince the explorer of the value of this barbaric method of execution, so he might later testify to the Commandant on its behalf, the officer details the workings of the machine in elaborate detail and 'with great zeal'.[42]

The machine is made up of three parts: the Bed, a coffin-like wooden cot in which the naked prisoner is strapped, with a felt gag in his mouth 'to prevent him screaming and biting his tongue to pieces'; the Designer, which hangs above the bed and contains the cogs and mechanisms that drive the machine; and the Harrow, a glass armature studded with needles which shuttles between the Bed and the Designer on a steel ribbon tattooing the body of the condemned man. As the body is tattooed by the Harrow it is slowly turned over in the Bed to make 'fresh space for writing'.[43] The officer explains that those gathered at the execution are able to 'watch the inscription taking form', the needles 'writing deeper and deeper' into the flesh until 'the Harrow has pierced him quite through'.[44]

We discover that within the judicial system of this colony, those condemned to die in the machine are not informed in advance of their pending execution or even what crime they are alleged to have committed; there is no hearing, and no opportunity to mount a defence. Rather, the officer explains that the 'guiding principle' of justice in the colony is 'Guilt is never to be doubted'.[45] As he describes, the prisoner only becomes 'enlightened' to the nature of their infraction as the sentence is slowly etched into their flesh over a period of twelve hours. As they bleed to death the condemned begin 'to understand the inscription', deciphering it through their 'wounds'. The execution ends when the corpse is ejected from the machine into a pit in the ground.[46]

'In the Penal Colony' has inspired many artists and thinkers, and has been widely deployed as a metaphor for the 'machinery' and 'mechanics of power'.[47] It condenses several of the themes central to the reconceptualisation of stigma developed over the course of this book: stigma as penal tattoo, stigma as a technology of discipline and punishment, stigma as the machinery of racism, and stigma as a mechanism for the operations of colonial capitalism. Indeed, from the 'colony' of the title onwards, this is a story 'marked and saturated' with 'colonial motifs'.[48]

This work of civilisation is an enormous and continual butchery

Franz Kafka, a Czech-born German-speaking Jew, grew up in a social and cultural context structured by European colonial domination of the globe. Indeed, 'In the Penal Colony' was drafted in 1914, at the apex of the 'Scramble for Africa' (1881–1914), three decades during which European states (initially through subsidiary companies and third-party franchises) colonialised 90 per cent of the African continent (10 million square miles or territory, and 110 million people), a theft of land and resources which saw mass indentured labour, enslavement, torture and killings.[49] Atrocities committed by German colonists, who lynched and enslaved people, raped women and girls, and starved entire peoples to death in concentration camps, was widely documented, publicised and debated in German-speaking public life while Kafka was writing.

When Kafka penned 'In the Penal Colony', a debate was raging in the European press about different colonial methods, which ranged between criticism of *civilising* approaches 'which treated the natives with too much leniency' and criticism of policies which centred on repression, forced labour, torture and 'extermination'.[50] Indeed, Kafka would have been familiar with figures such as the celebrity explorer and colonialist Carl Peters, an apostle of *Rücklosigkeit* (ruthless imperialism) and advocate of 'machine-gun diplomacy' who bragged to readers of journals such as *The Society for German Colonisation* about his employment of barbaric methods to subjugate colonised peoples.[51] Radical German nationalists (the precursors of Nazi fascism) and bellicose racist colonialists like Peters argued that 'the colonies were fundamentally different moral realms' where it would be disastrous to apply 'European' standards of morality and justice.[52]

We know from the detailed research of Kafka scholars that he was intimately familiar with these debates. Indeed, one of Kafka's favourite uncles, Joseph Löwy, worked from 1891 to 1902 in the Congo as chief of commercial sections on a railway built by forced labour.[53] The colonisation of the Congo, initially an entirely corporate affair led by the Belgian King Leopold, has been described as 'perhaps the most convulsive episode ever to take place in African colonial history, and certainly one of the most devastating interventions against a human population on the historic record'.[54]

There was a highly organised international campaign against King Leopold's genocidal activities in 'the Congo Free State' (1885–1908) in the first years of the twentieth century, leading eventually to a change of government, with the Belgian state finally taking formal control from Leopold (as 'the Belgian Congo'). This scenario of regime change echoes that which frames Kafka's story, namely from a colonial administration unrestrained in its barbaric use of punishments, to a regime which promises to be more 'enlightened'. Contemporary reports about Leopold's Congo, compiled by missionaries and activists, describe it as 'a state of terrorism', a 'death-trap', a place of 'bloody barbarities', killings and mutilations.[55] Congo, wrote Mark Twain, is a 'land of graves, the Congo free graveyard'.[56] A speaker in a debate on Congo in the Belgian Parliament in July 1903 concluded that 'this work of civilisation is an enormous and continual butchery', involving 'vampire groups of financial associations' who wring their profits 'from the blood and misery of natives'.[57]

It was in the midst of colonial propaganda, native uprisings and growing political unease within Europe about bloody methods of torture and oppression in Africa that Kafka condensed colonial violence into the metaphor of his tortuous stigma machine; yet he was not the first to do so. Machine technology was, as Edward Baptist notes, a popular metaphor for colonial capitalism, which depicted 'changes as unending progress, change in which machines extracted power from nature and yielded it to human beings'.[58]

In his letters, Kafka describes being enthralled by two fiction-alised memoirs written by former German army officer and colonial explorer Oskar Weber, *Letters of a Coffee Planter: Two Decades of German Labour in Central America* (1913) and *The Sugar Baron: South American Adventures of a Former German Officer* (1914). In these colonial adventure stories, Weber describes the ingenious inventions that lubricated colonial extraction in the Americas, including the mechanical workings of sugar presses designed to twist and turn pieces of sugar cane until they expelled their syrup, and a machine that shelled coffee beans by vibrating them inside a metal drum lined with cotton wool.[59]

Alongside these new machines devised to process cash crops from colonial plantations, Weber also details some of the *penal machines* innovated to *press* labour from enslaved and/or inden-tured workers, including stockades and whipping machines.[60] Notably, in 'In the Penal Colony', the officer explains that the native man condemned to die in the machine was initially punished by being whipped across the face by his captain for sleeping on duty. The officer explains that it was the man's insolent response to being lashed – 'Throw that whip away or I'll eat you alive' – which has led to his execution.

In the *Half Has Never Been Told: Slavery and the Making of American Capitalism*, Edward Baptist examines the myth that inno-vations in machine technology (such as the cotton gin) increased productivity in Southern US cotton plantations in the nineteenth century. (Between 1801 and 1862, the amount of cotton picked daily by enslaved people increased 400 per cent). Through a detailed examination of the changing management techniques employed on cotton plantations, Baptist evidences that this increase in cotton production was in fact an outcome of more efficient systems for the exploitation and torture of enslaved pickers. In short, it wasn't ingenious new machines that were responsible for the spectacular increase in cotton production; rather a dramatic increase in physical violence, combined with meticulous systems of record keeping, transformed cotton pickers *into machines*. As Baptist notes: 'For many southwestern whites, whipping was a gateway form of violence ... in the sources that document the expansion of cotton production, you will find ... every instrument of torture used at one time or another: sexual humiliation, mutilation, electric shocks, solitary confinement in "stress positions", burning, even waterboarding.'[61] As Baptist concludes, we don't ordinarily see torture 'as a factor of production', but 'systematised torture was central to the industrial revolution, and thus to the birth of the modern world'.[62] In the late nineteenth and early twentieth century, the tortuous management techniques developed to monetise plantation labour in the American South were imported into Africa by European colonialists as they attempted to turn colonised people into profit-making machines.

In his research on contemporary sources of 'In the Penal Colony', Paul Peters draws our attention to a series of cartoons by Thomas Heine in a 1904 edition of the popular German satirical magazine *Simplicissimus*.[63] Titled 'Colonial Powers', these four illustrations depict the differing techniques employed by European powers in the scramble for Africa. The second illustration in this series, titled 'That's how the Englishman colonizes', depicts an English colonialist, dressed in tweed, force-feeding an African man whisky. The man is held in a giant vice, operated by a soldier, which squeezes gold out of him, while a missionary enlightens him by reading from a Bible. This was Heine's take on the English colonial mantra of 'Commerce, Christianity and Civilisation'.

Figure 6.1 'That's how the Englishman colonises' (So kolonisiert der Engländer). Cartoon from a series of four on 'Colonial Power' by Thomas Theodor Heine published in the German satirical magazine *Simplicissimus*, 3 May 1904.

If, like the contraption in this cartoon, Kafka's stigma machine can be read as a metaphor for how power is inscribed in bodies, the power in question is *colonial power*, and the body is the condemned body of the colonised subject. Indeed, Kafka's machine might be read as a condensed metaphor for the entire machinery of colonialisation: a terrifying, extraneous mechanical force that throttles and strangles those caught in its grasp.[64] As Silvia Federici notes, it was 'the human body and not the steam engine, and not even the clock, [that] was the first machine developed by capitalism'.[65] It is stigma machines which are set to work to accomplish the transformation of people into non-human work machines, wringing profits from blood and misery.

Stigma machines

Stigma has examined some of the orchestrated alliances of social forces, mediums and technologies through which stigma power is crafted and activated to govern populations. It has sought to illustrate some of the ways in which stigma power exerts itself, what forms it takes, and how it seeds itself across different scales of social life. In recalibrating our understanding of stigma as a form of power that is entangled with long histories of colonial capitalism, this book seeks to make stigma a more useful analytic tool, a device for thinking more deeply about how power etches itself on people as a means of dehumanising and devaluing them.

The concept of 'stigma machines' is intended to open up new ways of thinking about stigma as a punitive apparatus, to allow for richer historical understandings of the meaning of stigma as marks of disgrace or infamy, signs of severe censure or condemnation, which are impressed upon a person. As I imagine them, stigma machines are the mechanisms through which power penetrates bodies; machines of inscription set in motion through concerted efforts in order to immobilise, wound, humiliate and/or dehumanise those caught within their grasp. The stigma machine is a conceptual device which seeks to direct attention 'upwards' and onto processes of stigma production. That is, thinking about stigma as a machine, or rather as a series of machines, forces us to focus on the mechanisms of stigma production, and the instruments through which stigma is impressed upon bodies in order to subjugate them, as stigma is cranked into operation in support of extractive capitalist political economies.

In thinking about stigma as a machinery of inequality, this book has sought to trouble individualistic understandings of stigma by developing a more structural understanding of stigma as a classificatory form of power. Of course, stigma machines take different forms, depending on the governmental and media systems through which they are composed and the specific political and economic requirements of those who assemble and operate them. Sites of stigma production that coalesce in the formation of these machines today include: the institutional forms of stigma politics exercised by states, particularly by politicians, spin-doctors and think tanks; the stigmacraft engaged in by media and cultural industries, including public relations, journalism, news media, advertising, film, television and digital corporations, digital technologies and platforms; as well as everyday stigma interactions, including racist, disablist and misogynistic hate speech in face-to-face and online settings.

In 2018, the graphic artist Tom Morris and I collaborated to visualise the concept of the stigma machine. Drawing on Kafka and Thomas Heine's colonial machines, we designed a stigma machine in the form of an animated Gif (see Figure 6.2). Our stigma machine invokes histories of colonial capitalism, but connects these histories to the current global authoritarian (re)turn by highlighting the pivotal role played by digital technologies in the contemporary production of stigma in service of extractive systems of capitalism.

Machine breaking

As the explorer in Kafka's 'In the Penal Colony' watches the condemned man being strapped into the stigma machine, he admits he is perturbed by 'the injustice of the procedure and the inhumanity of the execution', but he is reluctant to intervene in the abject spectacle unfolding before him. He explains that he 'travelled only as an observer, with no intention at all of altering other people's methods of administering justice'.[66] He reminds the reader that this is after all a colony 'where extraordinary measures' were undoubtedly needed to keep discipline.[67] Further, he sees the condemned man, 'a complete stranger, not a fellow countryman', as not fully human, but as 'a stupid-looking wide-mouthed creature with bewildered hair and face', 'a submissive dog' with 'blubber lips'.[68] However, when pushed by the officer for his views on this barbaric system of justice, the explorer states that he cannot

Figure 6.2 'Stigma machine', still from an animated
Gif made by Tom Morris, 2018.

support it. In resignation that this marks the end of the road for his stigma machine, the officer frees the condemned man, strips naked and climbs inside it himself. However, rather than gradually tattoo its final judgement ('Be Just') into the officer's body, the machine breaks down and jolts out of control, unceremoniously stabbing the officer to death, leaving his head gouged by a spike hanging over the pit.

The gruesome end of Kafka's story, this image of the machine breaking down and 'vomiting up its own mechanical innards', reminded me of the long history of machine breaking in England (and wider Europe);[69] a history that Karl Marx described as 'the strife between workman and machine' which from the seventeenth century onwards saw people rise up to destroy shearing machines, threshing machines, power looms and more, as they sought to resist the pauperism effected by land enclosures and the factory system.[70] What people were protesting at when they destroyed machines was the destruction of their lives, livelihoods and health by machine work. The inhuman effects of such work in England were recorded by men like Fredrick Eden in *The State of the Poor* (1797) and Friedrich Engels in *The Condition of the Working Class in England* (1845), who both detail the crippling disabilities caused by factory work in Lancashire mills. Machine-breaking revolts protested at the conversion of humans into work-machines, or what Silvia Federici describes as 'the mechanization of the proletarian body' itself.[71] People broke machines in protest at their pauperisation and dehumanisation by the capitalist machine.

As historian Peter Linebaugh reminds us, all instances of capitalist enclosure – from 'the open fields of England enclosed by Acts of Parliament' to 'the customs of the sikep villagers of Java' – have been 'accomplished by terrifying machines': the man-of-war, the steam engine, the cotton gin, threshing machines, plantation whipping machines and machine guns.[72] For those caught in the maul of these machines, they are experienced not as technologies of improvement or progress 'but as hell itself'.[73]

The emergence of capitalism as a world system has seen hundreds of years of revolts by people against the machine systems which have sought to dehumanise and enclose their lives. From the seizing and scuttling of slave ships, to continual acts of resistance to the dehumanisation and tortures of plantation labour, enslaved people led machine-breaking struggles for freedom and equality. Most pivotal amongst these freedom struggles, but often still untaught in European history lessons, was the Haitian Revolution (1791–1804). This two-decade revolt saw the enslaved rise up and destroy hundreds of sugar, coffee and indigo plantations, declare freedom from colonial rule, and create a free black state. As Michel-Rolph Trouillot has argued, the Haitian Revolution was 'unthinkable' because it so decisively broke with the renaissance world view upon which the stratified hierarchies of human life that underpin the global capitalist world order were built. As Trouillot puts it, it was a revolution by those who had been designated positions at 'the bottom of the human world' against 'Man (with a capital M)'.[74] This revolution overthrew European colonial capitalism, and the stigma machines assembled to reproduce it. In doing so, it fundamentally and irrevocably challenged 'the ontological order of the West and the global order of colonialism'.[75] This revolution indelibly shaped the freedom movements of the twentieth century.[76]

Freedom movements

In the mid-twentieth century, a dizzying array of grassroots struggles for equality and justice exploded across the world. As Virdee puts it: 'By the late 1960s, large parts of humanity across the world were in collective motion in pursuit of that most basic of human aspirations, to make life more liveable.'[77] Anti-colonial movements, civil rights and black power movements, indigenous rights movements, Dalit and Adivasi rights movements, Labour movements, feminist and LGBT movements, disabled people's movements, and more, drew on experiential knowledge of dehumanisation, oppression and subjugation as a means of radically questioning the systems of human stratification that subtend capitalist and colonial societies.

Alongside concrete demands for equality and justice, what these diverse emancipatory movements held in common is that they emerged out of people's collective demands to be recognised as equal, that is as equally human. As Stokely Carmichael put it in 1966: 'I am black. I know that. I also know that while I am black I am a human being.'[78] At their most radical, these movements for equality were abolitionist movements, in that they sought to overthrow Eurocentric colonial, patriarchal, white supremacist, heteronormative, classist and disablist templates of 'the human' grounded in what Katherine McKittrick terms the manufacture of profitable and brutal hierarchies of human difference.[79]

Many of these freedom movements were 'informed by socialism', 'a socialism stretched and refashioned to articulate with race, anti-colonialism, gender as well as class'.[80] That is, these were freedom movements against colonial capitalism, concerned with the redistribution of resources – of land, wealth, rights and, crucially, 'person value'.[81] Indeed all of these movements were, broadly speaking, movements against the capitalist enclosure of communal resources and social relations.[82] These were movements for humanity against the dehumanising violence of the colonial capitalist machine.

Satnam Virdee argues that neoliberalism should be understood as 'a capitalist counter-revolution' against the freedom movements of the twentieth century;[83] a capitalist revolution that seeks to extract the remaining vestiges of the social, political and economic gains won through freedom struggles over the course of the previous century of struggle. The capitalist counter-revolution of neoliberalism is manifest in the re-emergence of authoritarian politics across the world today – in the mainstreaming of ethno-nationalism, in the ascendance of far-right white (and Hindu) supremacist politicians, parties and policies, in the cultivation of nostalgia for Empire, in calls for a return to 'traditional' patri-archal and heteronormative social structures, in the erosion of democracy, and access to systems of legal justice and redress, in the deepening of surveillance and police powers, in expanding prison populations, and in the marked rise in racist, disablist and misog-ynistic forms of hate speech in public life. Indeed, stigma politics is a *leitmotif* of the current conjuncture tangible in the intensifica-tion of everyday racisms and racial violence, in malicious forms of welfare stigma and disability hate crimes, and in an upsurge in malevolent misogyny and sexual violence. It is insufficient to call this a 'backlash' against progressive values and/or liberal demo-cratic norms (as we saw in Chapter 2, liberal norms inherited from European Enlightenment traditions are often precisely mechanisms of oppression). What we are witnessing is a much more system-atic ideological war against the radical humanising anti-capitalist anti-colonial politics that underpinned mid-twentieth-century social movements for justice and equality.

The new machine politics

Stigma was written as a response to *the state of emergency* in which it was conceived and during which it was written, a period of heightened colonial capitalist extraction and enclosure, of displace-ment and dispossession. Indeed, the violence of colonial capitalism is alive and kicking in everything we are and do – in the T-shirts we wear made by sweated labour in distant factories, in the books we read packed by precarious machine workers in Amazon ware-houses, in wars for oil, in the continued pollution and plunder of the Earth's natural resources. As Silvia Federici notes, 'Though Marx was acutely aware of the murderous character of capitalist development ... he viewed it as a necessary step in the process of human liberation' that would create 'the material conditions for the liberation of humanity from scarcity and necessity'.[84] She goes on to say that Marx also assumed 'that the violence that had presided over the earliest phases of capitalist expansion would recede with the maturing of capitalist relations, when the exploitation and disciplining of labor would be accomplished mostly through the workings of economic laws. In this, he was deeply mistaken'.[85]

Stigma politics is playing a pivotal role in winning democratic consent for the widening social decomposition, inequalities and injustices that we see all around us. Stigma politics functions 'by dividing, on a continuously renewed basis' those it seeks to govern.[86] In the process, it foments electoral and popular consent for deepening inequalities. Indeed, stigma is an 'indispensable weapon in the armoury of the state elites', amplifying social divisions through devaluation, in ways designed to soften the way for further rounds of capitalist enclosure and accumulation.[87] In short, global corporate capital, which is and has always been colonial capitalism, feeds vampire-like on the divisions that stigma politics inculcates.

Understanding stigma as a mechanism of rule through division allows for new insights into how the current authoritarian return has proved effective in securing political power. What I mean by this is that stigma power is a governmental strategy which functions through the amplification of stigmatising forms of difference. Stigma is used to pit people against each other in struggles over resources and value. In this way, social solidarities are fractured, and opposition to the anti-social, anti-human movement of capital is neutered and neutralised. Stigma politics is a reign of terror that is designed to disarm resistance.

I wrote *Stigma* during the 2016 US election, the 2016 UK Brexit campaign and the 2019 Indian election. What is clear from these events is the extent to which the current rise of authoritarian neoliberalism is characterised by 'machine politics' facilitated by for-profit digital technologies (often termed 'platform capitalism').[88] *Stigma* has touched a little upon the role of digital stigma power within this new 'machine politics', from algorithmic engines of oppression,[89] digital surveillance technologies, 'digital poor houses'[90] and the troll factories of propaganda production. These digital stigma machines buttress the current global authoritarian re/turn and pose a fundamental challenge to human freedom. These epistemological forms of warfare are pitted against liberal democratic forms, seeking to win consent for authoritarian rule.

However, as I have sought to demonstrate throughout this book, it is a mistake to focus exclusively on the novelty of contemporary forms of stigma production and dissemination in political propaganda and the manipulation of public opinion. As the historian Timothy Snyder reminds us, in the 1930s European fascists harnessed the 'new media' of radio and cinema, 'to create a drumbeat of propaganda'.[91] While the mediums and machines through which stigma power reverberates to generate divisions within the body politic are subject to constant innovation, much of what we label as 'new' – including the content and forms that stigmatising propaganda takes – has deep historical roots.

Governmental orchestrations of stigma aren't a new phenomenon. On the contrary, the increased velocity of stigma has affective purchase because it draws upon engrained histories of practice, and established cannons of knowledge. For example, while US presidents may not have used Twitter before, the repetition of untruths and the use of rallies to mass a base of supporters into frenzied mob violence are tried and tested tactics of fascistic forms of stigma politics. Similarly, 'excoriating the behaviour of the poor' through 'rituals of public degradation' has always been central to the government of welfare, even while forms and methods of *badging the poor* have changed (see Chapter 4).[92]

The insistence upon the new often serves to obscure earlier atrocities and limits our capacity to learn from the past. In *Stigma*, paying attention to the history of stigma, its figures and cultural imaginaries, reminds us of the extent to which the contemporary 'dynamics of naming and valuation' are embedded within much longer practices of discipline and control.[93] There is little which is novel about neoliberalism, and there is little which is new about stigma power.

Common humanity

Stigma has focused on continuities and connections in stigma practices across time and place. It has detailed the long penal history of stigma *as a means of producing* a rich, thick account of the social and political function of stigmatisation as a constituent mechanism of colonial capitalism. Employing genealogical methods and tracing several lines or infrastructures of stigma power, it has argued that stigma is designed, crafted and activated to govern populations on multiple scales and in diverse sites and, crucially, that stigma production *from above* accelerates in periods of political and economic turmoil, often in response to particular demands of capital (and capitalists).

It is the argument of *Stigma* that the knowledge garnered through histories of penal stigmatisation is critical for understanding how inequalities are produced and, further, that histories of anti-stigma struggles might inform resistance to the authoritarian turn that characterises the political present.

We can track the violence of stigma through particular strands and call it by different names – such as racism, classism, disabilism and misogyny – but by focusing on 'stigma power', I have attempted to forge an intersectional concept that might allow for a tracking of historical continuities, connections and commonalities between manifold forms and practices of classificatory violence which discipline 'humanity into full humans, not-quite-humans, and nonhumans'.[94] To adopt a phrase from Yasmin Gunaratnam, stigma 'can help us to understand the bodily toll of interlocking injustices, while intersectionality can provide a means to think about the social complexity of an individual's suffering'.[95] In short, it was in search of *common ground* that I decided to work with stigma, or rather rework it. That is, my intention has been to re-conceptualise stigma in ways that explicate its function as a dehumanising praxis of subjugation which through the dehumanisation and devaluation of people enables the capitalist enclosure of land, resources and social life.

In February, 1982, the American writer and civil rights activist Audre Lorde gave a lecture titled 'Learning from the 60s' as part of an event to celebrate the life and work of Malcolm X. She said:

> Within each one of us there is some piece of humanness that knows we are not being served by the machine which orchestrates crisis after crisis and is grinding all our futures into dust. If we are to keep the enormity of the forces aligned against us from establishing a false hierarchy of oppression, we must school ourselves to recognize that any attack against Blacks, any attack against women, is an attack against all of us who recognize that our interests are not being served by the systems we support. Each one of us here is a link in the connection between anti-poor legislation, gay shootings, the burning of synagogues, street harassment, attacks against women, and resurgent violence against Black people.[96]

Resistance against the stigma machines which characterise the contemporary world has seen new tactics and strategies of machine breaking emerge: the environmental protestors who lock themselves into vehicles and buildings to resist environmental degradation and to protest against the climate emergency; the global movement of disability rights protestors who use their wheelchairs as weapons to block government buildings in 'die in' protests against draconian changes in medical, health and social care that have seen a global roll-back in disabled people's rights; the hackers who expose the innards of the machine politics that is seeding white supremacist ideologies across the world.

The challenge is how we draw together these 'intertwined vectors of struggle for freedom' against practices of power which operate through the cultivation of stigmatising differences; forging solidarities with which to break the machines that are grinding our futures into dust.[97] There are political risks in focusing on commonalities rather than differences; however the humanity-annihilating capacity of stigma power can only be resisted through solidarity practices, precisely because the capitalist counter-revolution we are living through operates by exploiting differences, by crafting hierarchies of person value and exacerbating class, gendered and racialised divisions.[98] Indeed, speaking, reading and thinking about connected histories of stigma power is part of a decolonising process of reparative justice that supports the building of solidarity movements; critical practices which Paul Gilroy describes as the 'ongoing collective work of salvage'.[99] This work is essential if we are to resist the divisive forces of identitarian politics, 'salvage humanity' and rise in rage together against the stigma machines.[100]

Notes

This book is the culmination of several years of research, and I have attempted to capture as much source material as possible in these notes within the limited space available. The citations are intended to indicate both quoted material, signal debts to the research of others and point to further reading. Any errors and omissions are my own.

Introduction

1 Where appropriate I have used pseudonyms to protect the identities of people whose testimonies I have drawn on in this book, but I use their words with their consent.

2 George Osborne, 'There Is a Dependency Culture', 28 February 2008, https://conservative-speeches.sayit.mysociety.org/speech/599696

3 Workfare is the term used to describe welfare programmes in which you are required to undertake unpaid work in order to receive state benefit payments, ordinarily unemployment benefits. The introduction of austerity in 2010 saw a dramatic shift in policies, with workfare and other conditions designed into the benefits system. For a good account of this shift see Anne Daguerre and David Etherington, 'Workfare in 21st Century Britain: The Erosion of Rights to Social Assistance' (Middlesex University, November 2014), http://workfare.org.uk/images/uploads/docs/Workfare_in_21st_century_Britain-Final.pdf, and also the research undertaken by anti-workfare activist groups such as Boycott Workfare, http://www.boycottworkfare.org/

4 Mary O'Hara, 'As a Jobcentre Adviser, I Got "Brownie Points" for Cruelty', *The Guardian*, 4 February 2015, https://www.theguardian.com/society/2015/feb/04/jobcentre-adviser-play-benefit-sanctions-angela-neville

5 Ibid.

6 Child Tax Credit was a benefit available to low-income households to assist with the costs of raising a child, it has now been replaced with Universal Credit. In Stephanie's case the tax authorities stated that she had erroneously claimed an additional element of this benefit relating to childcare costs for a few weeks one summer; in actuality she was entitled to this supplement, but the enquiry to ascertain this took a further two years, during this period all her Child Tax Credit income was frozen.

7 Salil Shetty, 'Foreword, Amnesty International Report 2016/17: State of Human Rights', 2017, 12, https://www.amnesty.org/download/Documents/POL1048002017ENGLISH.PDF

8 Ibid., 12.

9   Ian Hacking, *Historical Ontology* (Cambridge, MA: Harvard University Press, 2004), 12.

10 William Howard, *My Diary, North and South* (Boston: T.O.H.P. Burnham, 1863). In *My Diary North and South* Howard is using the stigmata on the bodies of the enslaved to illustrate 'the misery and cruelty' of North American plantation slavery, a system of exploitation and dehumanisation he describes as grounded in 'radical evils'. Ibid., 170, 332.

11 The *Barbados Slave Code* was reprinted in David McCord, *The Statutes at Large of South Carolina: Acts Relating to Charleston, Courts, Slaves, and Rivers*, vol. 7 (Columbia, SC: A.S. Johnston, 1840). This book includes several legal statues for the branding and torture of enslaved people. The note which prefaces this collection reminds the reader that as many of these bloody laws are 'British, not American Laws', 'the free people of South Carolina have no cause to blush' at the legalised torture of unfree black lives.

12 Catherine Hall, 'Gendering Property, Racing Capital', in *History after Hobsbawm: Writing the Past for the Twenty-First Century* (Oxford: Oxford University Press, 2018), 17–34. As Catherine Hall notes, while 'law was not the original basis for slavery ... the slave codes of the British Caribbean were essential for its continuance'. Ibid., 23.

13 Du Bois in Marcus Rediker, *The Slave Ship: A Human History* (New York: Viking, 2008), 4.

14 Ibid., 268.

15 The Kongo Kingdom covered a large area of west-central Africa; it was an independent state from around the fourteenth century until 1857, when it became a vassal state of the Portuguese empire.

16 In Adam Hochschild, *King Leopold's Ghost: A Story of Greed, Terror and Heroism in Colonial Africa* (London: Pan, 2012), 13.

17 Edward Baptist, *The Half Has Never Been Told: Slavery and the Making of American Capitalism* (New York: Basic Books, 2014), xvii, 354, 142.

18 The Captain Fowler referred to in this runaway advertisement might be John Fowler, who worked as a slave trader and as an agent for a Bristol slave trader in this period. If it is the same Fowler, he later settled in Jamaica as a plantation owner, and his will lists the 167 enslaved people that he owned. See 'Legacies of British Slave-Ownership', https://www.ucl.ac.uk/lbs/person/view/2146650237

19 The abolitionist Granville Sharp estimated that there were 20,000 black people living in London in the mid-eighteenth century. See Gretchen Gerzina, *Black England: Life before Emancipation* (London: John Murray, 1995), 5.

The social position of black Georgians, and their place and treatment within society, varied. The available evidence suggests that those who were settled in Britain, as distinguished from those who had escaped ships at ports, mostly worked in roles such as indentured apprentices, domestic servants, or as sailors or dock workers. William Hogarth depicted black servants in London living 'very much part of the community of the poor'. David Dabydeen, 'The Black

Figure in 18th-Century Art', BBC History, 2011, https://www.bbc.co.uk/ history/british/abolition/africans_in_art_gallery_01.shtml

The database Runaway Slaves in Britain project (begun in 2018) is further developing our understanding of black life in Georgian Britain. Many of these adverts are for slaves who had run away from ships; in some cases they appear to be waged sailors. Others are children who had run away from apprenticeships or domestic service.

20 Historical practices of black surveillance (and counter-practices of black sousveillance) are tracked by Simone Browne in *Dark Matters: On the Surveillance of Blackness* (Durham, NC: Duke University Press, 2015).

21 Baptist, *The Half Has Never Been Told*, 141. The US-based Freedom on the Move database is the first major digital database of fugitive slave ads, from North America, it was begun in 2018 and is online at https://freedomonthemove.org

22 In Anon, *Oxford English Dictionary (Online)* (Oxford: Oxford University Press, n.d.).

23 Sukhdev Sandhu, 'The First Black Britons', BBC History, 2011, http://www. bbc.co.uk/history/british/empire_seapower/black_britons_01.shtml

24 Browne, *Dark Matters*, 26.

25 Catherine Hall, 'Gendering Property, Racing Capital', *History Workshop Journal* 78, no. 1 (2014): 23.

26 Karl Marx, *Capital: A Critique of Political Economy*, 1st English edition (Moscow: Progress Publishers, 1887), 181, https://www.marxists.org/archive/marx/works/ download/pdf/Capital-Volume-I.pdf. Throughout this book I am drawing on the editions of Marx's writing which are freely available at marxists.org.

27 Melinda Elder, 'The Liverpool Slave Trade, Lancaster and Its Environs', in *Liverpool and Transatlantic Slavery*, ed. David Richardson, Suzanne Schwarz and Anthony Tibbles (Liverpool: Liverpool University Press, 2007), 121. See also Melinda Elder, *The Slave Trade and the Economic Development of 18th Century Lancaster* (Edinburgh: Edinburgh University Press, 1992); Bruce Mouser, 'Iles de Los as Bulking Center in the Slave Trade, 1750–1800', *Outre-Mers: Revue d'histoire* 313 (1996): 77–91.

28 Eric Williams, *Capitalism and Slavery* (Chapel Hill, NC: University of North Carolina Press, 1944), 95.

29 Ibid., 95.

30 James Baldwin in Zora Neale Hurston, *Barracoon: The Story of the Last Slave* (London: Harper Collins, 2018), 136.

31 Baptist, *The Half Has Never Been Told*, 146.

32 Robert Pinker, 'Stigma and Social Welfare', *Social Work* 27, no. 4 (1970): 13–17.

33 Michel Foucault, *Discipline & Punish: The Birth of the Prison*, trans. Alan Sheridan (New York: Vintage, 1995), 25.

34 Ibid., 34.

35 Christina Sharpe, *In the Wake: On Blackness and Being* (Durham, NC: Duke University Press, 2016), 25.

36   Marx, *Capital: A Critique of Political Economy*, 508.

37   Pinker, 'Stigma and Social Welfare', 17.

38   Stuart Hall in Beverley Skeggs, 'The Dirty History of Feminism and Sociology: Or the War of Conceptual Attrition', *The Sociological Review* 56, no. 4 (2008): 682.

39   Bruce G. Link and Jo Phelan, 'Stigma Power', *Social Science & Medicine*, Structural Stigma and Population Health, 103 (2014): 30.

40   Oliver Bonnington and Diana Rose, 'Exploring Stigmatisation among People Diagnosed with Either Bipolar Disorder or Borderline Personality Disorder: A Critical Realist Analysis', *Social Science & Medicine* 123 (2014): 7.

41   Ibid., 24.

42   Richard Parker and Peter Aggleton, 'HIV and AIDS-Related Stigma and Discrimination: A Conceptual Framework and Implications for Action', *Social Science & Medicine* 57, no. 1 (July 2003): 17, 13.

43   On authoritarian neoliberalism see Ian Bruff and Cemal Burak Tansel, 'Authoritarian Neoliberalism: Trajectories of Knowledge Production and Praxis', *Globalizations* 16, no. 3 (16 April 2019): 233–44; Cemal Burak Tansel, ed., *States of Discipline: Authoritarian Neoliberalism and the Contested Reproduction of Capitalist Order*. Transforming Capitalism (Lanham, MD: Rowman & Littlefield International, 2017).

44   David Garland in John Pratt et al., eds., *The New Punitiveness: Trends, Theories, Perspectives* (Portland, OR: Willan Pub, 2005), xiii.

45   Mona Lynch, 'Supermax Meets Death Row: Legal Struggles Around the New Pun', in *The New Punitiveness: Trends, Theories, Perspectives*, ed. John Pratt et al. (Cullompton, Devon: Willan Pub, 2005), 79.

46   Zygmunt Bauman, 'The Crisis of the Human Waste Disposal Industry', *Tikkun* 17, no. 5 (2002): 41–47.

47   Graham Scambler, 'Heaping Blame on Shame: "Weaponising Stigma" for Neoliberal Times', *The Sociological Review* 66, no. 4 (2018): 766–82; Kirsteen Paton, 'Beyond Legacy: Backstage Stigmatisation and "Trickle-up" Politics of Urban Regeneration', *The Sociological Review* 66, no. 4 (2018): 919–34.

48   Michel-Rolph Trouillot, *Silencing the Past: Power and the Production of History* (Boston: Beacon Press, 1995), 25.

49   Michel Foucault, 'Nietzsche, Genealogy, History', in *The Foucault Reader: An Introduction to Foucault's Thought*, ed. Paul Rabinow (London: Penguin, 1991), 83.

50   Donna Haraway, *Donna Haraway Reads the National Geographics of Primates*, 1987, https://www.youtube.com/watch?v=eLN2ToEIlwM

51   Donna Haraway, *The Haraway Reader* (New York: Routledge, 2004), 338.

52   William Walters, *Governmentality: Critical Encounters* (London: Routledge, 2012), 116.

53   David Owen in ibid., 115.

54   Jenna Loyd and Anne Bonds, 'Where Do Black Lives Matter? Race, Stigma,

and Place in Milwaukee, Wisconsin', *The Sociological Review* 66, no. 4 (2018): 898–918; Joe Feagin and Zinobia Bennefield, 'Systemic Racism and U.S. Health Care', *Social Science & Medicine* 103 (2014): 7–14.

The concept of racial capitalism emerges out of the work of Cedric Robinson, and in short designates an understanding of the economic history of capitalism as inextricably intertwined with histories of colonial exploitation, and capitalist forms of government as operating through the inculcation of race, class, caste (and gendered divisions). For theories and debates about racial capitalism I recommend: Cedric J. Robinson, *Black Marxism: The Making of the Black Radical Tradition* (Chapel Hill, NC: University North Carolina Press, 2000); Robin Kelley, 'Cedric J. Robinson: The Making of a Black Radical Intellectual', *Counterpunch* (blog), 17 June 2016, https://www.counterpunch.org/2016/06/17/cedric-j-robinson-the-making-of-a-black-radical-intellectual/; Robin D.G. Kelley, *What Is Racial Capitalism and Why Does It Matter?* (University of Washington, 2017), https://www.youtube.com/watch?v=--gim7W_jQQ; Satnam Virdee, 'Racialized Capitalism: An Account of Its Contested Origins and Consolidation', *The Sociological Review* 67, no. 1 (2019): 3–27; Silvia Federici, *Caliban and the Witch: Women, The Body and Primitive Accumulation* (Brooklyn, NY: Autonomedia, 2004); Gargi Bhattacharyya, *Rethinking Racial Capitalism: Questions of Reproduction and Survival* (Lanham, MD: Rowman & Littlefield Publishers, 2018).

55 Erving Goffman, *Asylums: Essays on the Social Situation of Mental Patients and Other Inmates* (Chicago: Aldine, 1961); Erving Goffman, *The Presentation of Self in Everyday Life* (Edinburgh: Social Science Research Centre, University of Edinburgh, 1956; New York: Doubleday, 1959).

56 Erving Goffman, *Stigma: Notes on the Management of a Spoiled Identity* (New York: Simon & Schuster, 1986), 2.

57 Robinson, *Black Marxism*, 318.

58 Gurminder K. Bhambra, 'A Sociological Dilemma: Race, Segregation and US Sociology', *Current Sociology* 62, no. 4 (2014): 472.

59 Virdee, *The Sociological Review*, 4.

60 Ibid.

61 Gurminder K. Bhambra, *Connected Sociologies* (London: Bloomsbury, 2014), 1.

62 Cornel West, *Race and Social Theory: Towards a Genealogical Materialist Analysis* (blog), 2016, http://www.versobooks.com/blogs/2568-race-and-social-theory-towards-a-genealogical-materialist-analysis

As Gurminder K. Bhambra, Dalia Gebrial and Kerem Nişancıoğlu define it, decolonising 'First, is a way of thinking about the world which takes colonialism, empire and racism as its empirical and discursive objects of study; it re-situates these phenomena as key shaping forces of the contemporary world, in a context where their role has been systematically effaced from view. Second, it purports to offer alternative ways of thinking about the world and alternative forms of political praxis.' Gurminder K. Bhambra, Dalia Gebrial and Kerem Nişancıoğlu, 'Introduction: Decolonising the University?', in *Decolonising the University*, ed. Gurminder K. Bhambra, Dalia Gebrial and Kerem Nişancıoğlu (Chicago: Pluto Press, 2018), 2.

63 Ethno-nationalist ideologies draw on mythic ideas of the nation as bounded by common ethnic heritage and shared ancestry, and are often evoked through metaphors of blood and soil. A classic example of which is the Nazi *Volksgemeinschaft* ideology – see Chapter 3.

64 Karen Fields and Barbara J. Fields, *Racecraft: The Soul of Inequality in American Life* (London: Verso, 2012).

65 Bauman, 'The Crisis of the Human Waste Disposal Industry'.

66 Federici, *Caliban and the Witch*, 12–13.

67 David Harvey in Jessica Perera, 'The London Clearances: Race, Housing and Policing' (Institute of Race Relations, 20 February 2019), http://www.irr.org.uk/news/the-london-clearances-a-background-paper-on-race-housing-and-policing/

68 Ibid., 9.

69 David Harvey in ibid., 15.

70 Jamie Longazel, 'Moral Panic as Racial Degradation Ceremony: Racial Stratification and the Local-Level Backlash against Latino/a Immigrants', *Punishment and Society* 15, no. 1 (2013): 97.

71 Harold Garfinkel, 'Conditions of Successful Degradation Ceremonies', *American Journal of Sociology* 61, no. 5 (1956): 420–24.

72 On the practice of shorting in stock markets, see the film *The Big Short*, Dir. Adam McKay, 2015.

73 Marx, *Capital: A Critique of Political Economy*, 534.

74 I am paraphrasing and drawing from an analysis offered by Tansel here in his excellent introduction to the edited collection, *States of Discipline*.

75 Federici, *Caliban and the Witch*, 17.

76 Judith Butler, *Giving an Account of Oneself* (New York: Fordham University Press, 2005), 106.

77 'Fighting Shame', Leeds Poverty Commission, the Joseph Rowntree Foundation & The Guardian. Online at: https://www.youtube.com/watch?v=Bhx3jKEwbFA

78 Virdee, *The Sociological Review*, 3.

Chapter 1

1 Michel De Certeau, *The Practice of Everyday Life*, trans. Steven Rendall (Berkeley: University of California Press, 1984), 140.

2 Aman Sood, '"Jeb Katri" Tattoo Gone, but Scarred for Life', *The Tribune*, 10 October 2016, https://www.tribuneindia.com/news/punjab/community/-jeb-katri-tattoo-gone-but-scarred-for-life/307407.html

3 I have woven together these events from several different news, legal and academic sources and my account is necessarily partial.

4 Sood, '"Jeb Katri" Tattoo Gone, but Scarred for Life'. Shoe garlanding is an antiquated form of caste humiliation in India, widely practised against Dalits

by privileged caste Hindus. In *Jai Bhim Comrade* (2012), the documentary filmmaker Anand Patwardhan examines events which involved the desecration of statue of Ambedkar with a garland of shoes in a Dalit community in Mumbai in 1997, and led to street demonstrations and the murder of ten protestors by police. Patwardhan's film tells the story of Vilas Ghogre, a left-wing poet and Dalit activist, who hung himself in protest and despair in the aftermath of this violence.

5   Kanchan Vasdev, 'For 5 Women Branded on Their Foreheads, Verdict Too Little after 23 Years of Humiliation', *The Indian Express*, 16 October 2016, https://indianexpress.com/article/india/india-news-india/amritsar-punjab-tattoo-women-forehead-humiliation-police-theft-jeb-katri-3090699/

6   Sood, '"Jeb Katri" Tattoo Gone, but Scarred for Life'.

7   Baljit Balli, 'How Jebkatri Tattooing Case Became Headlines in 1993 … ?', Babushahi, 10 October 2016, http://www.babushahi.com/tirchhinazar. php?oid=985

8   Arun Ray, *National Human Rights Commission of India: Formation, Functioning and Future Prospects*, Vol. 1 (New Delhi: Khama, 2004), 158–59.

9   Vasdev, 'For 5 Women Branded on Their Foreheads, Verdict Too Little after 23 Years of Humiliation'.

10   Vipin Puppy, 'Brand of Shame', *India Legal*, 9 November 2016, http://www. indialegallive.com/special-story/brand-of-shame-15551. See also Anon, 'CBI Court Punishes Punjab Police 23 Years after They Tattooed "PICKPOCKET" on the Forehead of Four Women', *Mail Online India*, 9 October 2016, https://www.dailymail.co.uk/indiahome/indianews/article-3828738/ CBI-court-punishes-Punjab-police-23-years-tattooed-PICKPOCKET-forehead-four-women.html

11   Vishal Rambani and Avtar Singh, '"Assume I Am a Thief, a Jeb Katri; Why Tattoo It on My Forehead?"', 9 October 2016, http://www.hindustantimes. com/punjab/assume-i-am-a-thief-a-jeb-katri-why-tattoo-it-on-my-forehead/ story-z3uWxeuVAzfeQB6S4QxvUN.html

12   Sangrur Baghrian, 'Three Cops Get 3 Years Jail for "Jeb Katri" Tattoo on Forehead – Times of India', *The Times of India*, 9 October 2016, http:// timesofindia.indiatimes.com/city/chandigarh/Three-cops-get-3-years-jail-for-jeb-katri-tattoo-on-forehead/articleshow/54758895.cms

13   Clare Anderson, 'Godna: Inscribing Indian Convicts in the Nineteenth Century', in *Written on the Body: The Tattoo in European and American History* (London: Reaktion, 2000), 108.

14   Rambani and Singh, '"Assume I Am a Thief, a Jeb Katri"'.

15   De Certeau, *The Practice of Everyday Life*, 141.

16   Christopher Jones, 'Tattooing and Branding in Graeco-Roman Antiquity', *Journal of Roman Studies* 77 (1987): 142.

17   Jane Caplan, 'Introduction', in *Written on the Body: The Tattoo in European and American History*, ed. Jane Caplan (London: Reaktion, 2000), xvi. In this quotation Caplan is drawing on Jones' research.

18   In Page duBois, *Slaves and Other Objects* (University of Chicago Press, 2008), 108.

19   Mark Gustafson, 'The Tattoo in the Later Roman Empire and Beyond', in *Written on the Body: The Tattoo in European and American History*, ed. Jane Caplan (London: Reaktion, 2000), 25.

20   Ibid.

21   Ibid., 23.

22   Ibid., 25. As Gustafson writes (ibid., 25):
      The face is, without a doubt, the worst place to receive a tattoo against one's wishes. Not only does it defy most attempts at concealment, but the face is also commonly viewed as the reflection of one's person, of the self, the soul. ... The gaze of the onlooker is virtually inescapable; there is little defence against it. The ancient Mediterranean city was a face-to-face society, and the discipline of physiognomics – that is, the attempt to detect one's character, disposition, or destiny from external, especially facial, features – was more than an idle pastime.

23   Ibid.

24   Christopher Jones, 'Stigma and Tattoo', in *Written on the Body: The Tattoo in European and American History*, ed. Jane Caplan (London: Reaktion, 2000), 9.

25   Jones, 'Tattooing and Branding in Graeco-Roman Antiquity', 149.

26   Valerius Maximus in ibid., 153.

27   Page duBois, *Torture and Truth* (New York: Routledge, 1991), 24.

28   Ibid., 73.

29   Delphic maxims are 147 proverbs inscribed in stone at the temple of Apollo in Delphi, an ancient sanctuary which the Greeks considered to be the geographic centre of the world. On this example of the penal tattoo 'know thyself' from Herondas, see Steven Connor, *The Book of Skin* (Ithaca, NY: Cornell University Press, 2004); duBois, *Torture and Truth*.

30   Gustafson, 'The Tattoo in the Later Roman Empire and Beyond', 22.

31   Connor, *The Book of Skin*, 74.

32   Gustafson, 'The Tattoo in the Later Roman Empire and Beyond', 24.

33   Ibid., 22.

34   Thrace was roughly speaking a dominion which stretched across modern-day Turkey, Bulgaria and north-eastern Greece.

35   The Greek essayist Plutarch suggests that the Maenads (mad women), followers of the god Dionysus, had been tattooed by their husbands as a punishment for killing Orpheus.

36   See Caplan, 'Introduction', xvi.

37   Jones, 'Tattooing and Branding in Graeco-Roman Antiquity', 148.

38   In Jones, 'Stigma and Tattoo', 14–15.

39   Gustafson, 'The Tattoo in the Later Roman Empire and Beyond', 23.

40   Jones, 'Tattooing and Branding in Graeco-Roman Antiquity', 142. To illustrate the importance of tattooing in capturing a labour force, Jones draws

our attention to how the Roman Emperor Caligula (AD 12–41) even 'had many people of the better sort' marked with tattoos (stigmatum notis) before condemning them 'to the mines and the paving of roads'. ibid., 151.

41   Gustafson, 'The Tattoo in the Later Roman Empire and Beyond', 22.

42   Jones, 'Stigma and Tattoo', 12.

43   Apuleius, *Metamorphoses (The Golden Ass)*, ed. and trans. J. Arthur Hanson, vol. 2 (Cambridge, MA: Harvard University Press, 1996), 148–49.

44   Walter Scheidel, 'The Comparative Economics of Slavery in the Greco-Roman World', Princeton/Stanford Working Papers in Classics, 2005, https://papers. ssrn.com/sol3/papers.cfm?abstract_id=1096417

45   DuBois, *Torture and Truth*, 4.

46   Ibid., 62.

47   Jennifer Trimble, 'The Zoninus Collar and the Archaeology of Roman Slavery', *American Journal of Archaeology* 120, no. 3 (2016): 447.

48   Ibid., 457.

49   Ibid., 447.

50   David Olusoga, *Black and British: A Forgotten History* (London: Macmillan, 2016), 94.

51   We don't know what happened to the runaway Ann. Her story is imagined in the graphic novel *Freedom Bound* which draws on the 'Runaway Slaves in Britain' archive. Warren Pleece, *Freedom Bound: Escaping Slavery in Scotland* (Glasgow: BHP Comics, 2018). See also the short film *1745 – An Untold Story of Slavery* (2017) inspired by the runaway advertisements archive, which tells the story of two sisters torn from their home in Nigeria and sold into slavery who try to retake their freedom in the Scottish Highlands.

     A little of the life of Dr Gustavus Brown is recorded. He migrated permanently to Virginia, and his will listed a number of enslaved people as his property, but not an Ann. His son of the same name was also a physician and attended George Washington on his deathbed. Washington, the first President of the United States (1789 to 1797), owned 317 enslaved people when he died.

52   Trimble, 'The Zoninus Collar and the Archaeology of Roman Slavery', 462.

53   Olusoga, *Black and British: A Forgotten History*, 94.

54   Benjamin Isaac, *The Invention of Racism in Classical Antiquity* (Princeton, NJ: Princeton University Press, 2004), 3.

55   Robinson, *Black Marxism*, xiii.

56   Ibid., 11. On the persistence of slavery within Europe see also Federici, *Caliban and the Witch*.

57   Mark Gustafson, 'Tattooing', in *The Historical Encyclopedia of World Slavery*, ed. Junius Rodriguez, vol. 1 (Santa Barbara, CA: ABC-CLIO, 1997), 629.

58   Mary Beard, *Women & Power: A Manifesto* (London: Profile, 2017), 17.

59   Trimble, 'The Zoninus Collar and the Archaeology of Roman Slavery', 463.

60   Beard, *Women & Power: A Manifesto*, 16. Beard attributes this quote to a second-century AD writer, but it is usually sourced to Plutarch (142 AD).

See Kate Wilkinson, *Women and Modesty in Late Antiquity* (Cambridge: Cambridge University Press, 2015), 93–94.

61 DuBois, *Torture and Truth*, 70.

62 Beard, *Women & Power: A Manifesto*, 20.

63 Ibid., 6.

64 Ibid., 6.

65 Ibid., 8.

66 Sandy Bardsley, *Venomous Tongues: Speech and Gender in Late Medieval England* (Philadelphia: University of Pennsylvania Press, 2006).

67 In *England's Grievance Discovered* (London: R. Ibbitson, 1655), 111, Ralph Gardiner writes: 'John Wilis of Ipswich upon his Oath said, that he … was in Newcastle six months ago, and there he saw one Ann Biulestone [Bidlestone] drove through the streets by an Officer of the same Corporation, holding a rope in his hand, the other end fastned to an Engine called the Branks, which is like a Crown, it being of Iron, which was musled over the head and face, with a great gap or tongue of Iron forced into her mouth, which forced the blood out. And that is the punishment which the Magistrates do inflict upon chiding, and scoulding women, and that he hath often seen the like done to others'.

68 Jenny Paull, 'The Scold's Bridle', Lancaster Castle (blog), n.d., http://www.lancastercastle.com/history-heritage/further-articles/the-scolds-bridle/

69 Anon, *Oxford English Dictionary (Online)*.

70 Patricia McDaniel, *Shrinking Violets and Caspar Milquetoasts: Shyness, Power, and Intimacy in the United States, 1950–1995* (New York: New York University Press, 2003), 26.

71 Edward Palmer Thompson, 'Rough Music Reconsidered', *Folklore* 103, no. 1 (1992): 3.

72 Lynda Boose, 'Scolding Brides and Bridling Scolds: Taming the Woman's Unruly Member', *Shakespeare Quarterly* 42, no. 2 (1991): 207.

73 I have taken this extract of Dorothy Waugh's testimony from David Booy, ed., *Personal Disclosures: An Anthology of Self-Writings from the Seventeenth Century*. Early Modern Englishwoman, 1500–1750 (Aldershot: Ashgate, 2002), 349–50. The original text can be found in *The Lambs Defence against Lyes* (London: Giles Calvert, 1659), 29–30.

74 Federici, *Caliban and the Witch*, 101.

75 Ibid., 186.

76 Ibid., 101.

77 Ibid., 101.

78 Ibid., 186.

79 For a good overview of online stigma and misogyny see Emma A. Jane, *Misogyny Online: A Short (and Brutish) History*. Sage Swifts (Thousand Oaks, CA: Sage, 2016).

80 See also the phenomena of 'revenge porn' in which men – and it is almost always men – post naked or otherwise intimate pictures or footage of ex-partners on public websites as a shaming punishment.

81 Nicola Henry and Anastasia Powell, 'Technology-Facilitated Sexual Violence: A Literature Review of Empirical Research', *Trauma, Violence, & Abuse* 19, no. 2 (April 2018): 195–208.

82 For some historical source materials on slave masks see, for example, J.F. Johnson, *Proceedings of the General Anti-Slavery Convention, Called by the Committee of the British and Foreign Anti-Slavery Society* (London: John Snow, 1843); George James Bruce, *Brazil and the Brazilians, Portrayed in Historical and Descriptive Sketches* (London: Methuen, 1915); Thomas Ewbank, 'Cruelty to Slaves', in *The Brazil Reader: History, Culture, Politics*, ed. Thomas Levine and John Crocitti (Durham, NC: Duke University Press, 1999), 138–42.

83 Grada Kilomba, *Plantation Memories: Episodes of Everyday Racism* (Munster: UNRAST-Verlag, 2008), 16.

84 On the history and significance of Escrava Anastácia see John Burdick, *Blessed Anastácia: Women, Race, and Popular Christianity in Brazil* (New York: Routledge, 1998).

85 Caplan, 'Introduction', xi.

86 James Cook, *Captain Cook's Journal during the First Voyage around the World* (London: Elliot Stock, 1893).

87 Jane Caplan, *Speaking Scars – The Tattoo* (Museum of London, 2014), https://www.gresham.ac.uk/lectures-and-events/speaking-scars-the-tattoo

88 Ibid.

89 Andrew Gentes, *Exile, Murder and Madness in Siberia, 1823–61* (London: Palgrave Macmillan, 2010).

90 A *katorshniki* (public slave) had a different social status to a serf who was indentured to a private landowner. See also Orlando Patterson, *Slavery and Social Death: A Comparative Study* (Cambridge, MA: Harvard University Press, 1982).

91 On the history of Lancaster Castle see https://www.lancastercastle.com/history-heritage/a-dark-history/crime-punishment/. The Lancaster Assizes was known colloquially as 'the hanging court' for its propensity for capital punishment.

92 You can explore this database online at www.slavevoyages.org

93 James Walvin, *Slavery in Small Things: Slavery and Modern Cultural Habits* (Chichester: Wiley Blackwell, 2017), 87.

94 See David Olusoga's *Black and British: A Forgotten History* for the euphemistic use of the phrases 'West Indies Trade' and 'West Indies Trader' in British heritage culture and social history, and the ways these terms conceal the involvement of wealthy and successful elites in slavery.

95 Caplan, 'Introduction', xv.

96 Sharpe, *In the Wake*, 142.

97 Patricia Saunders, 'Fugitive Dreams of Diaspora: Conversations with Saidiya Hartman', *Anthurium: A Caribbean Studies Journal* 6, no. 1 (2008): 3.

The artist Lubaina Himid has worked extensively on the Georgian history of Lancaster, and wider black histories in Britain. For example, in her art installation 'Naming the Money' (2004), Himid intervenes in the nameless and speechless histories of black lives in Britain. As she describes it, 'Naming the Money is made up of 100 life-size painted cut-out figures. This is the story of the slave/servant but also of the emigre and the asylum seeker. Each cut-out has a real name, each one is able to say who they actually are but each one lives with their new name and their new unpaid occupation attempting somehow to reconcile the two. Every person in the installation is trying to tell you something, each has a voice that can be heard via the soundtrack playing in the gallery space or as text on an invoice collaged to his/her back.' See http:// lubainahimid.uk/portfolio/naming-the-money/

98   Hundreds of Jacobite rebels were held in Lancaster Castle after the failed rebellions of 1715 and 1745. Many were transported as indentured labour to the West Indies and Virginia, some on slave trading ships from Liverpool (travelling not as slaves but as prisoners to serve sentences as indentured labour). Some later returned to Britain, others remained and became plantation and slave-owners. This history is just beginning to be explored, see Tom Devine, ed., *Recovering Scotland's Slavery Past: The Caribbean Connection* (Edinburgh: Edinburgh University Press, 2015). At the time of writing, new research on the links between the Jacobites and slavery was being undertaken by Catriona McIntosh, head of education at the Culloden Battlefield Visitor Centre, which is run by the National Trust for Scotland.

99   Mai's tattoos were an object of intense public curiosity and gave rise to a brief fashion in tattooing amongst aristocratic elites.

100 See Katherine McKittrick, 'Yours in the Intellectual Struggle: Sylvia Wynter and the Realization of the Living', in *Sylvia Wynter: On Being Human as Praxis*, ed. Katherine McKittrick (Durham, NC: Duke University Press, 2015).

101 Beverley Skeggs, 'The Forces That Shape Us: The Entangled Vine of Gender, Race and Class', *The Sociological Review* 67, no. 1 (2019): 28–35.

102 Edward Palmer Thompson, *The Making of the English Working Class* (New York: Vintage, 1963).

103 Robinson, *Black Marxism*, 31.

104 Robert Allen, *Enclosure and the Yeoman* (Oxford: Clarendon, 1992).

105 Jim Crace, Harvest (London, Picador, 2013).

106 Peter Linebaugh, *The Magna Carta Manifesto: Liberties and Commons for All* (Berkeley: University of California Press, 2009), 57.

107 Ibid., 57.

108 Thompson, *The Making of the English Working Class.*

109 Ibid., 217.

110 Ibid., 219.

111 Ibid., 217.

112 Ibid., 219.

113 Ibid., 220.

114 Paul Spicker, *Stigma and Social Welfare* (Creative Commons, 2011), 11, http:// openair.rgu.ac.uk

115 Karl Polanyi, *The Great Transformation: The Political and Economic Origins of Our Time* (Boston, MA: Beacon Press, 2001), 37.

116 Thompson, *The Making of the English Working Class*, 63.

117 Marx, *Capital: A Critique of Political Economy*, 523.

118 Ibid., 523.

119 Ibid., 523.

120 Ibid., 507.

121 Anon, *Oxford English Dictionary (Online)*.

122 William Cobbett, *Cobbett's Political Register*, vol. 30 (London: Cox and Baylis, 1816), 691.

123 Vivienne Richmond, *Clothing the Poor in Nineteenth-Century England* (Cambridge: Cambridge University Press, 2013), 189.

124 Robbie Shilliam, *Race and the Undeserving Poor: From Abolition to Brexit* (Newcastle: Agenda Publishing, 2018), 13.

125 Henry Mayhew, *London Labour and the London Poor* (Oxford: Oxford University Press, 2012), 346. Mayhew's ethnographic study of London's poor grew out of a journalistic assignment to investigate a severe outbreak of cholera in Bermondsey in 1849. London was so geographically segregated by extremes of wealth and poverty in this period that Mayhew described himself as a 'traveller in the undiscovered country of the poor' who was bringing back stories about people 'of whom the public has less knowledge than of the 'most distant tribes of the earth'. Ibid., 3.

126 Richmond, *Clothing the Poor in Nineteenth-Century England*, 289.

127 Polanyi, *The Great Transformation*, 105.

128 Karl Marx, *Grundrisse: Foundations of the Critique of Political Economy*, trans. Martin Nicolaus (London: Penguin, 1973), 526, https://www.marxists.org/archive/marx/works/1857/grundrisse

129 Edward Wakefield, *England and America: A Comparison of the Social and Political State of Both Nations*, vol. 1 (London: Richard Bentley, 1883), 47.

130 Ibid., 47.

131 In Bentham we have an example of what today we might call a neoliberal state interventionist. A policy guru, government advisor and enclosure propagandist who argued for massive state intervention in order to set the market free.

132 Charles Bahmueller, *The National Charity Company: Jeremy Bentham's Silent Revolution.* (Berkeley: University of California Press, 1981), 104. See also Gertrude Himmelfarb, 'Bentham's Utopia: The National Charity Company', *Journal of British Studies* 10, no. 1 (1970): 80–125. Bentham's writings on the poor laws have been collected and edited in a number of different places, the most comprehensive collections are Jeremy Bentham, 'Tracts on Poor Laws and Pauper Management', in *The Works of Jeremy Bentham, Volume 8*, ed. John Bowring (Edinburgh: William Tait, 1841); Jeremy Bentham, *The Collected Works of Jeremy Bentham: Writings on the Poor Laws, Vol. 1*, ed. Michael Quinn (Oxford: Oxford University Press, 2001).

133 Bentham, 'Tracts on Poor Laws and Pauper Management', 367.

134 The Speenhamland system was a system for topping up wages to subsistence levels – pegged to the price of bread. It was developed in 1795 to alleviate the distress caused by high grain prices. The introduction of this system to supplement wages was in part an attempt to contain uprisings and resistance in what were famine conditions, an insurance measure against a revolutionary threat during a period which saw the French Revolution and the American Revolution. See Polanyi, *The Great Transformation*. Speenhamland was adopted in modified forms across many counties in England in the late eighteenth and early nineteenth century. It was highly controversial as it allowed employers to keep wages artificially deflated. It was at the time, and remains today, at the centre of political and economic debates about poverty, welfare and taxation – as it effectively is a measure through which taxpayers subsidise employers for below-subsistence wages. This system continues in modified forms in benefit systems such as tax credits (now universal credit) in the UK today.

135 Bentham, 'Tracts on Poor Laws and Pauper Management', 369.

136 Ibid., 369.

137 Himmelfarb, 'Bentham's Utopia', 88.

138 Reminiscent of the ways in which the British Prime Minister Margaret Thatcher sought to enrol the middle classes to neoliberal projects of privatisation through the selling of shares in formally public goods and assets some 150 years later.

139 Bentham, 'Tracts on Poor Laws and Pauper Management', 392.

140 Ibid., 374.

141 Ibid., 370. Bentham's incarcerated pauper labourers would have had little or no recourse to the law, and would have been stripped of any residual sense of themselves as subjects with rights (citizens). Indeed, the company's coercive powers to apprehend and detain people would be unlimited. The pauper would be defined 'by his own action in applying for relief' and it was the company alone that would determine 'whether he had any property, honest means of livelihood, or prospect of honest education, and therefore whether he should be confined to an industry-house'. Himmelfarb, 'Bentham's Utopia', 89.

142 On the relationship between Bentham and Hanway and their panoptical industry houses see Alessandro Stanziani, 'The Traveling Panopticon: Labor Institutions and Labor Practices in Russia and Britain in the Eighteenth and Nineteenth Centuries', *Comparative Studies in Society and History* 51, no. 4 (2009): 53.

143 Bentham in Bahmueller, *The National Charity Company*, 122.

144 Himmelfarb, 'Bentham's Utopia', 124.

145 Ibid., 120.

146 See ibid., 83.

147 Bentham in ibid., 83–84.

148 Bentham in ibid., 123.

149 In his 'View of the Hard Labour Bill', Bentham had proposed that chemical washes be applied to the face of every prisoner spelling out the name and sentence of those incarcerated. See Jeremy Bentham, *View of the Hard Labour*

Bill: Draft of a Bill, to Punish by Imprisonment and Hard-Labour, Certain Offenders; and to Establish Proper Places for Their Reception (London: T. Payne and Son, 1778). Bentham returns to the theme of identity washing in his plans for his national charity company, proposing the establishment of a universal register of names (a national census). He also, in scribbled footnotes in one version of his pauper manuscripts, suggests that a system of permanently tattooing people was the most utilitarian solution. Caplan argues that he was unwilling to publish this tattooing proposal because his previous ideas about identity-washing criminals and tattooing everybody at birth had caused outrage. On Bentham's proposals for a 'universal tattoo' and how this informed modern systems of identification such as passports, identity cards, and digital forms of identification see Jane Caplan and John Torpey, eds., *Documenting Individual Identity: The Development of State Practices in the Modern World* (Princeton, NJ: Princeton University Press, 2001), 65; Sophie Coulombeau, 'Jeremy Bentham's Universal Tattoo' radio podcast https://www.bbc.co.uk/programmes/p020v6gb

150 For a detailed account of the innovation of management and accountancy techniques on American cotton plantations, which were exported back into Europe, see Baptist, *The Half Has Never Been Told*.

151 Samuel Bentham was a naval engineer and entrepreneur who was employed by Prince Grigori Potemkin to manage the estate of Krichev in the Mogilev province of White Russia (modern-day Belarus), which had been partitioned from Poland in 1772 during a period of Russian imperial expansion under Catherine the Great. In return for managing this colonial estate, Samuel Bentham was granted a house, servants and a large bonded serf labour force (unfree labour). For Samuel, assuming the position of overseer of this colony meant assuming a role akin to an oligarch. Letters from this period reveal that he was, initially at least, struggling to manage an unruly multi-ethnic immigrant workforce, composed of bonded Russian serfs, local peasants, Polish Jews and British workers – the latter group had been enticed to migrate from England by the Bentham family to work as foreman, craftspeople and household servants. Samuel negotiated a business arrangement with the Prince which made him a major shareholder in the industrial works on the estate. He set about industrialising the colony, introducing steam-powered engines, tools and machines imported from England. Alongside these technological innovations, he developed new managerial systems of workplace supervision and discipline. For example, Samuel designed a new circular factory building in which workers (serfs) could be supervised by means of an inspector's lodge at the centre of the building, the lodge was to be punctured by peepholes, which meant the workers wouldn't know when and if they were being watched. It was from these unrealised architectural plans that Jeremy Bentham designed his famous panoptical prison plan, which in turn formed the basis for his pauper industry houses scheme. What I want to underscore here is that it is significant that the idea of the panopticon, which, as many theorists from Foucault onwards

have argued, had a significant role in the emergence of modern 'surveillance societies', originated in the context of the management of unfree labour on a Russian colony. Additionally, the history of European serfdom and the 'second serfdom' in Eastern Europe from the fifteenth century is too often occluded from our understanding of the history of modernity, capital, capitalism, colonialism and the modern state. For more on the Bentham brothers time in Russia see Ian Christie, 'Samuel Bentham and the Western Colony at Krichev', *The Slavonic and East European Review* 48, no. 111 (1970): 232–47; Simon Werrett, 'Potemkin and the Panopticon: Samuel Bentham and the Architecture of Absolutism in Eighteenth Century Russia', *Journal of Bentham Studies* 2 (1999): 1–25; Stanziani, 'The Traveling Panopticon ; Philip Steadman, 'Samuel Bentham's Panopticon', *Journal of Bentham Studies*, 1 January 2012. On serfdom as a class and gendered relation, and anti-feudal struggles against enserfment see Federici, *Caliban and the Witch*. On the second serfdom see Immanuel Maurice Wallerstein, *Capitalist Agriculture and the Origins of the European World-Economy in the Sixteenth Century: With a New Prologue* (Berkeley: University of California Press, 2011).

152 Bentham, 'Tracts on Poor Laws and Pauper Management', 382.

153 Himmelfarb, 'Bentham's Utopia'.

154 Ibid., 123.

155 Thompson, *The Making of the English Working Class*, 267.

156 Virginia Eubank, *Automating Inequality: How High-Tech Tools Profile, Police, and Punish the Poor* (London: Picador, 2019).

157 Mitchell Dean, *The Constitution of Poverty: Toward a Genealogy of Liberal Governance*. Routledge Revivals (London: Routledge, 2012), 3.

158 Robinson, *Black Marxism*, 81.

159 Gurminder K. Bhambra and John Holmwood, 'Colonialism, Postcolonialism and the Liberal Welfare State', *New Political Economy* 23, no. 5 (2018): 578.

160 Williams, *Capitalism and Slavery*, 52.

161 See Elder, *The Slave Trade and the Economic Development of 18th Century Lancaster*.

162 Marx, *Capital: A Critique of Political Economy*, 573.

163 In ibid., 537–38.

164 The colonies of Demerara, Essequibo and Berbice on the Caribbean coast of South America became British Guiana in 1831. After independence in 1966, this territory became the Co-operative Republic of Guyana.

165 The Slavery Abolition Act of 1833 'formally freed 800,000 Africans who were then the legal property of Britain's slave owners'. Many people, including John Bond, became millionaires overnight, when the British government legislated that taxpayers would compensate this already wealthy group of aristocrats, landowners and middle-class inheritors 'for the loss of their "property"'. Details of the huge windfall (approximately £2 million pounds) received by John Bond as part of a £17 billion package of compensation paid to former slave owners, can be tracked in the British Legacies of Slave-Ownership

archive. British taxpayers only finishing paying off the debt incurred by this compensation package in 2015. David Olusoga, 'The History of British Slave Ownership Has Been Buried: Now Its Scale Can Be Revealed', *The Guardian*, 15 July 2015, https://www.theguardian.com/world/2015/jul/12/british-history-slavery-buried-scale-revealed

166 George Pinckard, *Notes on the West Indies: Written During the Expedition Under the Command of the Late General Sir Ralph Abercromby*, vol. 3 (London: Hurst, Rees and Orme, 1806), 73.

167 Ibid., 74.

168 Ibid., 67.

169 Ibid., 66.

170 Katy Kellaway, 'Lubaina Himid: The Turner Prize Nominee Making Black Lives Visible', *The Guardian*, 24 September 2017, https://www.theguardian.com/artanddesign/2017/sep/24/lubaina-himid-turner-prize-2017-interview

171 On the shoddy trade see http://www.bbc.co.uk/bradford/content/articles/2007/02/26/slavery_west_yorkshire_feature.shtml

172 Alan Rice, 'The Cotton That Connects, the Cloth That Binds', *Atlantic Studies* 4, no. 2 (2007): 292. Rice is an important Lancashire-based historian of the Black Atlantic who works collaboratively with Lubaina Himid. He was central to a 2005 Slave Trade Arts Memorial Project in Lancaster which saw the first quayside monument to victims of the slave trade in Britain. Rice also regularly undertakes history walks in Lancaster which I have been fortunate enough to participate in and have learnt much from.

173 See Rice, 'The Cotton That Connects, the Cloth That Binds'. For the history of the cotton famine see also Olusoga, *Black and British: A Forgotten History*.

174 Marx, *Capital: A Critique of Political Economy*, 195.

175 Walter Johnson, 'The Pedestal and the Veil: Rethinking the Capitalism/Slavery Question', *Journal of the Early Republic* 24, no. 2 (2004): 306.

176 In *Race and the Undeserving Poor: From Abolition to Brexit* (2018), Robbie Shilliam details how the British welfare state emerged out of distinctions between the deserving and undeserving poor, and how these distinctions were grounded in and produced through stigmatising analogies to the black slave.

177 Ibid., 178, 180.

178 Cesare Lombroso, *Criminal Man* (New York: G.P. Putnam's & Sons, 1911), xii.

179 Ibid., 45.

180 Caplan, *Speaking Scars – The Tattoo*.

181 Jimena Canales and Andrew Herscher, 'Criminal Skins: Tattoos and Modern Architecture in the Work of Adolf Loos', *Architectural History* 48 (2005): 238. The tattoo became central in this period to aesthetic writing on taste and beauty. See for example 'The Lamp of Beauty' (1849), in which John Ruskin illustrates ugly forms of architectural ornamentation by pointing to practices of tattooing amongst 'primitive' people, a practice he terms 'monstrification'.

182 Caplan, *Speaking Scars – The Tattoo*.

183 Canales and Herscher, 'Criminal Skins', 238. While savages and criminals could be identified by their propensity to ornament their skin with tattoos, women's concern with ornamentation in clothing revealed how they also 'had fallen behind in their development'. As Loos concluded, in a vicious critique of the rise of the fashion industry 'women's ornament goes back to the savage'.

184 Loos in ibid., 239.

185 On the concept of 'territorial stigma' see, for example, Loïc Wacquant, Tom Slater and Virgílio Borges Pereira, 'Territorial Stigmatization in Action', *Environment and Planning A: Economy and Space* 46, no. 6 (June 2014): 1270–80; Loyd and Bonds, 'Where Do Black Lives Matter?'

186 Canales and Herscher, 'Criminal Skins', 239.

187 The artist Renzo Martens examines the occluded colonial capitalist history of art markets through his controversial work which connects the political aesthetics of 'the white cube' to the history of the colonial plantation, and the continuing exploitation of Congolese plantation workers today. See his film *Episode III – Enjoy Poverty* (2008), and his lecture on this project here: https://www.youtube.com/watch?v=rsZbO0vxSWw

188 William Dalrymple, 'The East India Company: The Original Corporate Raiders', *The Guardian*, 4 March 2015, https://www.theguardian.com/world/2015/mar/04/east-india-company-original-corporate-raiders

189 Thomas Paine, 'Reflections on the Life and Death of Lord Clive', *Pennsylvania Magazine*, 1775, http://thomaspaine.org/questionable-authorship/reflections-on-the-life-and-death-of-lord-clive.html

190 Ibid.

191 In ibid.

192 Amartya Sen, 'Imperial Illusions', *The New Republic*, 31 December 2007, https://newrepublic.com/article/61784/imperial-illusions

193 Bentham's views on slavery, forced labour and colonialism shifted and changed during his lifetime. He had a friendship with ardent utilitarian imperialist and company employee James Mill – author of the highly influential racist tract *The History of British India* (1817). Both Bentham and Mill are often described as anti-colonialist thinkers – an assessment with which I profoundly disagree. What Bentham saw in the East India Company was the multiple advantages of a privately owned company subsidised by, but at arms length from, government. A private–public partnership which allowed the company to circumnavigate legal and other systems of accountability – while also having recourse to public funds (including the support of the British army and navy). Today, this kind of state–corporate partnership is often described or imagined as new, novel or neoliberal but was actually the model through which the modern liberal British state was founded. In short, the history of the English democratic state, the history of 'the mother of all parliaments', is a corporate history of empire and colonialism.

194 Arundhati Roy, 'The Doctor and the Saint', in *Annihilation of Caste: The Annotated Critical Edition*, ebook (London: Verso, 2014), 107.

195 Anderson, 'Godna', 108. See also Clare Anderson, *Legible Bodies. Race, Criminality and Colonialism in South Asia* (Oxford: Berg, 2004).

196 Anderson, 'Godna', 108.

197 The mass movement of labour intensified after the formal end of slavery in the Americas and West Indies, with more than a million Indians transported as bonded labour to plantations in places such as British Guiana. On this see, for example, Gaiutra Bahadur, *Coolie Woman: The Odyssey of Indenture* (London: Hurst & Company, 2016).

198 See Anderson, 'Godna'.

199 Ibid., 115–16.

200 Ibid., 113.

201 Roy, 'The Doctor and the Saint', 91.

202 In contemporary India, the words Dalit and Adivasi are the collective terms most often used for those who reside on the bottom rung of Indian social hierarchies.

Adivasi translates as indigenous, and refers to traditionally nomadic peoples. There are at least 100 million Adivasi people in India. Adivasi populations have been displaced over centuries, by the enclosure of land inaugurated during colonialism, and the continuing enclosures and forced evictions from land which have been a signal feature of the Indian capitalist state. See, for example Alf Gunvald Nilsen's important work on Adivasis and the state, including Alf Gunvald Nilsen, *Adivasis and the State: Subalternity and Citizenship in India's Bhil Heartland*. South Asia in the Social Sciences 7 (Cambridge: Cambridge University Press, 2018).

Dalits account for circa 200 million of India's 1.3 billion people. The word 'Dalit' is a literal translation of a Marathi word meaning broken people. Dalit signifies 'those who have been broken, ground down by those above them in a deliberate and active way. There is in the word itself an inherent denial of pollution, karma, and justified caste' (Zelliot in Hugo Gorringe, 'Subaltern Politics and Dalit Studies', *The Journal of Imperial and Commonwealth History* 37, no. 1 (2009): 152. It is used to describe those previously classified as 'untouchables' in the Hindu caste system. The capitalised use of the term 'Dalit' emerged out of Ambedkaian anti-caste politics, social movements such as the Dalit Panthers (1972-1980s) and more recent movements such as #dalitlivesmatter.

203 Anderson, 'Godna', 105. The Criminal Tribes Act had its roots in a 1830s campaign by an East Indian Company administrator William Sleeman against 'the Thugee' – believed to be professional gang of murderers and robbers. By 1840 Sleeman's war against the Thugs had largely dissipated, with those imagined as belonging to this group either hung or transported to other British colonies as convict labour. Those who were transported often had the words 'Convicted Thug' tattooed on their forehead.

204 In 1902 Risley wrote from India to the anthropologist T.S. Sinclair describing tattooing amongst 'Gypsy-like classes' in Bengal. In 1901 Risley was appointed Director of Ethnography for India. In 1910, when he was based back in England,

he became President of the Royal Anthropological Institute of Great Britain and Ireland. His career is a case study in the colonial histories of social science disciplines and methods. For some background on Risley's publications see C.J. Fuller, 'Ethnographic Inquiry in Colonial India: Herbert Risley, William Crooke, and the Study of Tribes and Castes: Ethnographic Inquiry in Colonial India', *Journal of the Royal Anthropological Institute* 23, no. 3 (2017): 603–21.

205 Anderson, 'Godna', 105. Anderson draws our attention to a 1915 directive issued to the police in Punjab which instructs them to recognise one particular criminal tribe through specific tattoo marks on the hands and face. She adds that 'such groups resisted this stigmatization, enlarging or changing their tattoos in order to counter the marks of identification recorded by the police'.

206 See Preeti Nijhar, *Law and Imperialism: Criminality and Constitution in Colonial India and Victorian England* (London: Routledge, 2009). As Nijhar argues, there are many similarities in this period between government through caste in colonial India, and the government of the poor within Europe.

207 Andrew Major, 'State and Criminal Tribes in Colonial Punjab: Surveillance, Control and Reclamation of the Dangerous Classes', *Modern Asian Studies* 33, no. 3 (1999): 657–88. See also Nijhar, *Law and Imperialism*.

208 Gopal Guru, 'The Language of Dalit-Bahujan Political Discourse', in *Dalit Identity and Politics: Cultural Subordination and the Dalit Challenge*, ed. Ghanshyam Shah (New Delhi: Sage, 2001), 97. See also Guru's important book on caste stigma and politics, *Humiliation: Claims and Context* (New Delhi: Oxford University Press. 2011).

209 Varsha Torgalkar, '69 Years After Independence, There Are Still Tribes That Are Considered "Born Criminal"', *Youth Ki Awaaz* (blog), 2016, https://www.youthkiawaaz.com/2016/08/denotified-tribes-discrimination-and-violence/

210 Hugo Gorringe, 'Subaltern Politics and Dalit Studies', *Journal of Imperial and Commonwealth History* 37, no. 1 (1 March 2009): 151–55.

211 Sambaiah Gundimeda, *Dalit Politics in Contemporary India* (New York: Routledge, 2016), 7.

212 See Dalit Panthers, 'Dalit Panthers Manifesto' (Bombay, 1973), http://democracyandclasstruggle.blogspot.com/2016/01/india-dalit-panthers-manifesto-bombay.html. On the history of the Dalit Panthers see Ja Vi Pavāra, *Dalit Panthers: An Authoritative History*, trans. Rakshit Sonawane (New Delhi: Forward Press, 2017).

213 Sarah Gandee, 'August 2017 Marks More than One Independence Day in India', *History Workshop* (blog), 8 August 2017, http://www.historyworkshop.org.uk/august-2017-marks-more-than-one-independence-day-in-india/

214 Ibid.

215 Ibid.

216 Torgalkar, '69 Years after Independence'.

217 C.R. Bijoy, 'Adivasis of India: A History of Discrimination, Conflict and Resistance', in *This Is Our Homeland: A Collection of Essays on the Betrayal of Adivasi Rights in India* (Bangalore: Equations, 2007), 22.

218 Friederycke Haijer, 'Human Rights and Dignity of Dalit Women' (Netherlands: Report of the Conference in The Hague, 2006), http://www.indianet.nl/pdf/humanrightsdalitwomen.pdf

219 Ruth Manorama of the National Federation of Dalit Women in Laura Brueck, *Writing Resistance: The Rhetorical Imagination of Hindi Dalit Literature* (New York: Columbia University Press, 2014), 56.

220 On Dalit women's accounts of the use of sexual violence and rape as a mechanism to terrorise communities see, for example, Brueck, *Writing Resistance*.

221 Roy, 'The Doctor and the Saint', 33.

222 Ibid., 33.

223 Ibid., 24.

224 Ibid., 35.

225 Ibid., 35.

226 Ibid., 36.

227 Ibid., 35.

228 Ibid., 183.

229 Ibid., 35, 85.

230 On the history of criminal tribes see Anand Yang, 'Dangerous Castes and Tribes: The Criminal Tribes Act and the Magahiya Doms of Northeast India', in *Crime and Criminality in British India*, ed. Anand Yang (Tucson: University of Arizona Press, 1986), 108–27; Sanjay Nigam, 'Disciplining and Policing the "Criminals By Birth", Part 1: The Making of a Colonial Stereotype – The Criminal Tribes and Castes of North India', *Indian Economic & Social History Review* 27, no. 2 (1990): 131–64.

231 Utkarash Anand, 'Police Brutality: SC Asks Punjab, Bihar to Explain', *The Indian Express* (blog), 7 March 2013, http://indianexpress.com/article/news-archive/web/police-brutality-sc-asks-punjab-bihar-to-explain/

232 Roy, 'The Doctor and the Saint', 29.

233 Ibid., 29. It is notable that the policemen convicted of forcibly tattooing the women were not convicted under the Scheduled Caste and Scheduled Tribe (Prevention of Atrocities) Act (1989) which is ostensibly intended to protect people against caste-based violence. In what they describe as a hidden apartheid against Adivasi and Dalit people, a 2007 Human Rights Watch report states that Indian police 'detain, torture, and extort money from Dalits without fear of punishment', detailing the extent to which 'the custodial torture and killing of Dalits, rape and sexual assault of Dalit women, and looting of Dalit property by the police 'are condoned, or at best ignored'. Human Rights Watch, 'Hidden Apartheid: Caste Discrimination against India's "Untouchables"' (Human Rights Watch, 12 February 2007), https://www.hrw.org/report/2007/02/12/hidden-apartheid-caste-discrimination-against-indias-untouchables#_ftn38

234 See ibid.

235 Rambani and Singh, '"Assume I Am a Thief, a Jeb Katri"'. Devi's stubborn articulation of her rights denies the reduction of Adivasi women to passive victimhood. Indeed, the persistence of Devi and the other surviving women

in their fight for justice is a testament to ways in which a century of anti-caste struggles have led to a new political understanding of caste stigma and violence as political injustices and a human rights issue.

236 Gundimeda, *Dalit Politics in Contemporary India*, 203.

237 Roy, 'The Doctor and the Saint', 33.

238 Ibid., 34.

239 BBC News, 'Indian Groups Raise Caste Question', BBC News Website, 6 September 2001, http://news.bbc.co.uk/1/hi/world/south_asia/1528181.stm

240 Roy, 'The Doctor and the Saint', 34.

241 Nathuram Godse, the man who assassinated Gandhi in 1948, was a member of the RSS.

242 Priyamvada Gopal, 'Narendra Modi: Britain Can't Simply Shrug off This Hindu Extremist', *The Guardian*, 14 April 2014, https://www.theguardian.com/commentisfree/2014/apr/14/narendra-modi-extremism-india

243 Ibid.

244 An organisation called Factchecker.in tracks hate crimes in India and began collating a database in 2008.

245 See Raheel Dhattiwala and Michael Biggs, 'The Political Logic of Ethnic Violence: The Anti-Muslim Pogrom in Gujarat 2002', *Politics and Society* 40, no. 4 (2012): 483–516.

246 Arundhati Roy, 'The Silence Is the Loudest Sound', *New York Times*, 15 August 2019, https://www.nytimes.com/2019/08/15/opinion/sunday/kashmir-siege-modi.html

247 Bentham is keen to stress the reformist and humane qualities of his scheme, which, in place of corporeal punishments (such as whipping and flogging), would employ softer psycho-social methods of coercion and surveillance to extract labour and profit. Bentham's proposals for the mass incarceration of criminals and the poor converged with penal reform in the colonies in the same period, which saw the building of prisons, workhouses and houses of correction. In the wake of the emancipation of slaves, and the labour crisis it provoked, the criminalisation of the black poor and systems such as convict leasing intensified. See Paton on this in Jamaica, and Bentham's influence therein: Diana Paton, *No Bond but the Law: Punishment, Race, and Gender in Jamaican State Formation, 1780–1870*. Next Wave (Durham, NC: Duke University Press, 2004).

248 Alexander Weheliye, *Habeas Viscus: Racializing Assemblages, Biopolitics, and Black Feminist Theories of the Human* (Durham, NC: Duke University Press, 2014), 3.

249 Stuart Hall, 'Race, The Floating Signifier', 1997, https://www.mediaed.org/transcripts/Stuart-Hall-Race-the-Floating-Signifier-Transcript.pdf

250 Epidermalization is a term developed by Fanon to describe the ways in which (anti-black) racism is inscribed in and on the body. He uses this term as an alternative to internalisation as a way of emphasising how blackness is produced in encounters with white others and white culture in colonial and

post-colonial societies. In short, for Fanon epidermalization describes the ways in which racial stigma is inscribed on skin, reinforcing what Du Bois described as 'the color line'. See Frantz Fanon, *Black Skin, White Masks* (London: Pluto Press, 1986). In the terms set out in this book, epidermalization is understood more expansively as a form of penal stigmatisation, that is, as an outcome of governmental systems of stigma power, which alongside racism might include the ways in which other stigmatising differences are impressed upon people in order to subjugate them.

Chapter 2

1   From Thompson's 'Exhortation', a poem published in 1933 in *Liberator*, the newspaper of the communist-led League for Negro Rights, cited in Robin D.G. Kelley, *Race Rebels: Culture, Politics, and the Black Working Class* (New York: Free Press, 1996), 103.

2   In Stokely Carmichael, *Black Power* (University of Berkeley, 1966), https://www.youtube.com/watch?v=dFFWTsUqEaY. I have chosen to use Stokely Carmichael's birth name, rather than his later chosen name Kwame Ture, to reflect the name he used during the period of activism and writing referenced in this chapter.

3   North Carolina A&T State University was then a segregated black university, established on 9 March 1891 as the Agricultural and Mechanical College for the Colored Race. In 1969 a confrontation between the National Guard and student activists on this campus culminated in what Martha Biondi described as 'the most massive armed assault ever made against an American university', when the army was drafted in to raid a male dormitory, which saw hundreds of students taken into police custody. See Martha Biondi, *The Black Revolution on Campus* (Berkeley: University of California Press, 2014), 158.

4   Rebecca Cerese and Steven Channing, *February One: The Story of the Greensboro Four*, Documentary (Independent Lens, 2003), http://www.pbs.org/independentlens/

5   For Goffman's understanding of the interaction order, see Erving Goffman, 'The Interaction Order: American Sociological Association, 1982 Presidential Address', *American Sociological Review* 48, no. 1 (1983).

6   Angela Davis, 'Political Prisoners, Prisons, and Black Revolution', in *Voices of a People's History of the United States* (New York: Seven Stories Press, 2010), 496.

7   Bhambra, 'A Sociological Dilemma', 480.

8   Ibid., 480.

9   I am using Jibreel Khazan's chosen name here, as it is the name he uses in most of the interview material drawn on in this chapter, but he was known in 1960 by his birth name Ezell Blair.

10   Sit-ins against anti-black racism and segregation can be traced back to 1943 when Congress of Racial Equality (CORE) activists occupied a Chicago

restaurant that refused service to Black customers. See August Meier and Elliott M. Rudwick, *CORE: A Study in the Civil Rights Movement, 1942–1968* (New York: Oxford University Press, 1973); Kenneth T. Andrews and Michael Biggs, 'The Dynamics of Protest Diffusion: Movement Organizations, Social Networks, and News Media in the 1960 Sit-Ins', *American Sociological Review* 71, no. 5 (2006): 752–77.

11   Emily Langer, 'Franklin McCain, Who Helped Inspire Sit-Ins for Civil Rights as Part of Greensboro Four, Dies', *The Washington Post*, 13 June 2014, https://www.washingtonpost.com/national/franklin-mccain-who-helped-inspire-sit-ins-for-civil-rights-as-part-of-greensboro-four-dies/2014/01/13/8c39840e-7c6e-11e3-9556-4a4bf7bcbd84_story.html

12   Cerese and Channing, *February One: The Story of the Greensboro Four.*

13   Crystal M. Fleming and Aldon Morris, 'Theorizing Ethnic and Racial Movements in the Global Age: Lessons from the Civil Rights Movement', *Sociology of Race and Ethnicity* 1, no. 1 (2015): 113. Some television news footage of the sit-in movement from 1963, including some clips from Greensboro, can be viewed on the NBC online news archive here: http://www.nbcnews.com/video/today-in-history/22886961#22886961

14   Peniel E. Joseph, *Stokely: A Life* (New York: Basic Civitas, 2014), 19.

15   Anne Moody, *Coming of Age in Mississippi* (New York: Dial Press, 1968), 238.

16   Harry Haywood, *Negro Liberation* (New York: International Publishers, 1948), 138.

17   W.E.B. Du Bois, *The Souls of Black Folk* (New Haven, CT: Pennsylvania State University Electronic Classics, 2006), 153.

18   Dorie Ladner, Joyce Ladner and Joseph Mosnier, *Dorie Ann Ladner and Joyce Ladner Oral History Interview Conducted by Joseph Mosnier*, 2011, https://www.loc.gov/item/afc2010039_crhp0054/

19   Kelley, *Race Rebels*, 79.

20   Paul Gilroy, *There Ain't No Black in the Union Jack: The Cultural Politics of Race and Nation* (London: Routledge, 2002), xiii; Malcom X, 'Malcom X in Cairo Urges African Aid to U.S. Negroes', *The Militant*, 1964, 2.

21   Herb Boyd, *We Shall Overcome With 2 Audio CDs: The History of the Civil Rights Movement as It Happened* (Naperville, IL: Sourcebooks MediaFusion, 2004).

22   Cerese and Channing, *February One: The Story of the Greensboro Four.*

23   Jibreel Khazan, *Interview with Jibreel Khazan* (International Civil Rights Center & Museum, Greensboro, undated), http://www.sitinmovement.org/

24   Gary Younge, '1963: The Defining Year of the Civil Rights Movement', *The Guardian*, 7 May 2013, http://www.theguardian.com/world/2013/may/07/1963-defining-year-civil-rights

25   Erving Goffman, 'The Interaction Order: American Sociological Association, 1982 Presidential Address', *American Sociological Review* 48, no. 1 (1983): 2.

26   Ibid., 4.

27   Ibid., 4. For Goffman's understanding of social world as a theatre see Erving
      Goffman, *The Presentation of Self in Everyday Life*, Repr. (London: Penguin,
      1990).

28   Goffman, 'The Interaction Order', 5.

29   Ibid., 6.

30   Ibid., 6.

31   Patricia Hill Collins, 'Pushing the Boundaries or Business as Usual? Race,
      Class, and Gender Studies and Sociological Inquiry', in *Sociology in America:
      A History*, ed. Craig Calhoun (Chicago: Chicago University Press, 2007), 585.
          The Free Speech Movement burst onto the UC Berkeley campus in 1964,
      inspired first by the civil rights movement, and later student-led opposition to
      the Vietnam War, see Jo Freeman, *At Berkeley in the Sixties: The Education of
      an Activist, 1961–1965* (Bloomington: Indiana University Press, 2004).

32   Cedric J. Robinson, *Black Movements in America* (New York: Routledge,
      2013), 145.

33   Keeanga-Yamahtta Taylor, *From #BlackLivesMatter to Black Liberation*
      (Chicago: Haymarket Books, 2016), 37.

34   See Freeman, *At Berkeley in the Sixties*.

35   Gary Marx, 'Role Models and Role Distance: A Remembrance of Erving
      Goffman', *Theory and Society* 13, no. 5 (1984): 657.

36   This black student would have been in an extremely small minority at Berkeley
      in 1961. It is estimated that there were only 100 Black students enrolled at
      the university in 1960, out of a student population of 20,000. Accounts of
      Berkeley from this period describe disaffection and alienation amongst black
      students, both in terms of their minority status on campus, and in terms of
      the whiteness and the conservatism of academic curriculums. See Donna Jean
      Murch, *Living for the City: Migration, Education, and the Rise of the Black
      Panther Party in Oakland, California* (Chapel Hill: University of North
      Carolina Press, 2010).

37   Khazan, *Interview with Jibreel Khazan*.

38   Goffman, *Stigma: Notes on the Management of a Spoiled Identity*, Preface, 2.

39   George Crabb, *English Synonyms Explained, in Alphabetical Order* (London:
      Baldwin, Cradock, and Joy and T. Boosey, 1816).

40   Goffman, *Stigma: Notes on the Management of a Spoiled Identity*, 6.

41   Ibid., 32.

42   Ibid., 2.

43   Ibid., 138–39.

44   Ibid., 1.

45   Fredric Jameson, 'On Goffman's Frame Analysis', *Theory and Society* 3, no. 1
      (1976): 129.

46   Erving Goffman, *Asylums: Essays on the Social Situation of Mental Patients
      and Other Inmates* (Chicago: Aldine, 1962); Erving Goffman, *Presentation of
      Self in Everyday Life* (1956) *The Presentation of Self in Everyday Life* (London,
      Allen Lane, 1969; Repr. London: Penguin, 1990).

47   Heather Love, 'Close Reading and Thin Description', *Public Culture* 25, no. 371 (2013): 419.

48   Goffman, *Stigma: Notes on the Management of a Spoiled Identity*, Preface.

49   Love, 'Close Reading and Thin Description', 420.

50   Steven J. Taylor, Robert Bogdan and Marjorie DeVault, *Introduction to Qualitative Research Methods: A Guidebook and Resource* (New York: John Wiley, 2015), 176.

51   Love, 'Close Reading and Thin Description', 423.

52   Goffman, *Stigma: Notes on the Management of a Spoiled Identity*, Preface.

53   Love, 'Close Reading and Thin Description'. Love argues that Goffman's 'primary method of abstract synthesis is supplemented, perhaps even challenged, by the trace of the embodied, affective experience of social others, both fictional and real, archived in his footnotes', Heather Love, 'Feeling Bad in 1963', in *Political Emotions*, ed. Janet Staiger, Ann Cvetkovich and Ann Reynolds (London: Routledge, 2010), 118. In some ways this chapter seeks to realise that challenge by forcing Goffman into dialogue with those he reduces to footnotes.

54   Susan Schweik, 'Stigma Management', *Disability Studies Quarterly* 34, no. 1 (2014), http://dsq-sds.org/article/view/4014/3539. Schweik also argues, and I concur that within disability studies it is Paul Hunt's and not Goffman's *Stigma* which we should 'claim and honor'.

55   Goffman, *Stigma: Notes on the Management of a Spoiled Identity*, 25.

56   Kristie Dotson, 'Tracking Epistemic Violence, Tracking Practices of Silencing', *Hypatia* 26, no. 2 (2011): 243.

57   Goffman, *Stigma: Notes on the Management of a Spoiled Identity*, 112.

58   Ibid., 112, n.18.

59   W.E.B. Du Bois, 'The Looking Glass', *The Crisis: A Record of the Darker Races* (December 1916), 86.

60   Paul Hunt, 'A Critical Condition', in *Stigma: The Experience of Disability*, ed. Paul Hunt (London: Geoffrey Chapman, 1966), 159.

61   Ibid., 145.

62   Ibid., 153.

63   James Baldwin, *The Fire Next Time* (London: Penguin, 2017), 80. *The Fire Next Time* is composed of two non-fiction essays. The first is written in the form of a letter to his fourteen-year-old nephew on the occasion of the hundredth anniversary of emancipation (from slavery), and focuses on themes of race and racism in American history. Baldwin writes to his nephew: 'Please try to remember that what they believe, as well as what they do and cause you to endure does not testify to your inferiority but to their inhumanity'. In the second essay, Baldwin writes of 'being worn down to a cutting edge by the incessant and gratuitous humiliation and danger one encountered every working day, all day long. ... I was thirteen and was crossing Fifth Avenue on my way to the Forty-second street library, and the cop in the middle of the street muttered as I passed him, Why don't you niggers stay uptown where you belong?' Ibid., 16, 26. Baldwin was a theorist of stigma power.

64 Hunt, 'A Critical Condition', 49.

65 For critical reflections on Goffman and Hunt's different contributions to thinking disability stigma see Jeffrey Brune et al., 'Forum Introduction: Reflections on the Fiftieth Anniversary of Erving Goffman's Stigma', *Disability Studies Quarterly* 34, no. 1 (2 January 2014), http://dsq-sds.org/article/view/4014

66 Du Bois, 'The Looking Glass', 86.

67 Goffman, *Stigma: Notes on the Management of a Spoiled Identity*, 127–28.

68 Ibid., 81.

69 Ibid., 7, n.10.

70 Ibid., 128.

71 Ibid., 129.

72 Ibid., 4.

73 Ibid., 4.

74 Ibid., 44, 46, 95.

75 Ibid., 9, 14.

76 Ibid., 146.

77 W.E.B. Du Bois, *Dusk of Dawn: An Essay Toward an Autobiography of a Race Concept* (Oxford: Oxford University Press, 2007), 59, 126.

78 Davis, 'Political Prisoners, Prisons, and Black Revolution', 496.

79 Killian and Grigg in Stokely Carmichael and Charles Hamilton, *Black Power: The Politics of Liberation in America* (New York: Vintage, 1992), 31.

80 Goffman, *Stigma: Notes on the Management of a Spoiled Identity*, 46.

81 Ibid., 46.

82 Patricia Williams, 'Metro Broadcasting, Inc. v. FCC: Regrouping in Singular Times', *Harvard Law Review* 104, no. 2 (1990): 542–43.

83 Lewis Gordon, 'Is the Human a Teleological Suspension of Man? Phenomenological Exploration of Sylvia Wynter's Fanonian and Biodicean Reflections', in *After Man, Towards the Human: Critical Essays on the Thought of Sylvia Wynter*, ed. Anthony Bogues (Kingston, Jamaica: Ian Randle, 2006), 255.

84 Lewis Gordon, *What Fanon Said: A Philosophical Introduction to His Life and Thought* (London: Hurst & Company, 2015), 22.

85 Goffman, *Stigma: Notes on the Management of a Spoiled Identity*, 108.

86 Goffman, 'The Interaction Order', 6.

87 Goffman, *Stigma: Notes on the Management of a Spoiled Identity*, 116.

88 Ibid., 135, 130, 121.

89 Ibid., 116.

90 Ibid., 110.

91 Ibid., 110.

92 Williams, 'Metro Broadcasting, Inc. v. FCC', 543.

93 Roderick A. Ferguson, *Aberrations in Black: Towards a Queer of Color Critique* (Minneapolis: University of Minnesota Press, 2003), 55.

94 Stephen Steinberg, *Race Relations: A Critique* (Stanford, CA: Stanford University Press, 2007), 42.

95   Ibid., 42.

96   Ladner et al., *Dorie Ann Ladner and Joyce Ladner Oral History Interview*.

97   In 2017 Carolyn Bryant admitted that the testimony she gave in court, namely that Till had sexually harassed her, was untrue. See Rory Carroll, 'Woman at Center of Emmett Till Case Tells Author She Fabricated Testimony', *The Guardian*, 27 January 2017, https://www.theguardian.com/us-news/2017/jan/27/emmett-till-book-carolyn-bryant-confession

98   Anne Rubin, 'Reflections on the Death of Emmett Till', *Southern Cultures* 2, no. 1 (1995): 45.

99   Christopher Benson and Mamie Till-Mobley, *Death of Innocence: The Story of the Hate Crime That Changed America* (New York: Ballantine, 2003), 151.

100 Audre Lorde, *The Collected Poems of Audre Lorde* (New York: W.W. Norton, 2002), 340.

101 Gary Younge, *No Place like Home: A Black Briton's Journey through the American South* (London: Picador, 1999), 108.

102 Cerese and Channing, *February One: The Story of the Greensboro Four*.

103 Ladner et al., *Dorie Ann Ladner and Joyce Ladner Oral History Interview*.

104 Joyce Ladner, *The Death of White Sociology* (New York: Random House, 1973).

105 Jodi Melamed, *Represent and Destroy: Rationalizing Violence in the New Racial Capitalism* (Minneapolis: University of Minnesota Press, 2011).

106 Manning Marable, *How Capitalism Underdeveloped Black America: Problems in Race, Political Economy, and Society* (London: Pluto Press, 2000), 106.

107 Hortense Spillers, *Black, White, and in Color: Essays on American Literature and Culture* (Chicago: University of Chicago Press, 2003), 21.

108 Fields and Fields, *Racecraft: The Soul of Inequality in American Life*, 25–26.

109 Paul Gilroy, 'Race and Racism in "the Age of Obama"' (The Tenth Annual Eccles Centre for American Studies Plenary Lecture given at the British Association for American Studies Annual Conference, London: British Library, 2013), 7.

110 Carmichael, *Black Power*.

111 Davis, 'Political Prisoners, Prisons, and Black Revolution', 496.

112 James Boggs, *Pages from a Black Radical's Notebook: A James Boggs Reader*, ed. Stephen M. Ward (Detroit: Wayne State University Press, 2011), 135.

113 W.E.B. Du Bois, 'On Being Ashamed of Oneself: An Essay on Race Pride', *The Crisis: A Record of the Darker Races*, 1933, 199.

114 Gordon Parks, 'Whip of Black Power', *Life Magazine*, 19 May 1967, 80.

115 Abdelmalek Sayad, *L'Immigration Ou Les Paradoxes de l'altérité: L'illusion Du Provisoire* (Paris: Raisons d'agir, 2006), 173.

116 Charles Euchner, 'Roy Wilkins's Reluctant Tribute to W.E.B. Du Bois', *Beacon Broadside* (blog), 2010, https://www.beaconbroadside.com/broadside/2010/08/excerpt-roy-wilkinss-reluctant-tribute-to-web-du-bois.html

117 Ibid.

118 Du Bois, *The Souls of Black Folk*, 5, 13.

119 Les Back and Maggie Tate, 'For a Sociological Reconstruction: W.E.B. Du Bois, Stuart Hall and Segregated Sociology', *Sociological Research Online* 20, no. 3 (2015): 15, http://www.socresonline.org.uk/20/3/15.html

120 Kelley, 'Cedric J. Robinson'.

121 Carmichael and Hamilton, *Black Power*, ix, viii.

122 Michelle Alexander, *The New Jim Crow: Mass Incarceration in the Age of Colorblindness* (New York: The New Press, 2010).

123 There are some signs of a new interest in the relationship between racism, stigma and power. For some recent scholarship on racism and/as stigma, see, for example: Glenn Loury, *The Anatomy of Racial Inequality* (Cambridge, MA: Harvard University Press, 2013). Michèle Lamont et al., *Getting Respect: Responding to Stigma and Discrimination in the United States, Brazil, and Israel* (Princeton, NJ: Princeton University Press, 2018); J. Lorand Matory, *Stigma and Culture: Last-Place Anxiety in Black America* (Chicago: University of Chicago Press, 2015); Caroline Howarth, 'Race as Stigma: Positioning the Stigmatized as Agents, Not Objects', *Journal of Community and Applied Social Psychology* 16, no. 6 (2006): 442–45.

Chapter 3

1 Fields and Fields, *Racecraft*, 102.

2 Infomobile, 'Greek Authorities Mark Arms of in Crete Stranded Syrian Refugees with Registration Numbers', *Infomobile: Information with, about and for Refugees in Greece* (blog), 15 May 2015, http://infomobile.w2eu. net/2015/05/15/greek-authorities-mark-arms-of-in-crete-stranded-syrian-refugees-with-registration-numbers/

3 Phillip Connor, 'Number of Refugees to Europe Surges to Record 1.3 Million in 2015' (Pew Research Centre, 2016), https://www.pewresearch.org/ global/2016/08/02number-of-refugees-to-europe-surges-to-record-1-3-million-in-2015/

4 The 1990 Dublin Convention updated by the 2003 Dublin II regulation, and the 2013 Dublin III regulation, stipulates that asylum applications should ordinarily be processed in the first country of arrival.

5 Peter Foster, 'One Year Ago, Angela Merkel Dared to Stand up for Refugees in Europe: Who Else Even Tried?', *The Telegraph*, 24 August 2016, http:// www.telegraph.co.uk/news/2016/08/24/one-year-ago-angela-merkel-dared-to-stand-up-for-refugees-in-eur/

6 Jan Flemr, 'Czech Police Spark Uproar by Tagging Refugees with Numbers', *Times of Israel*, 2 September 2015, http://www.timesofisrael.com/czech-police-spark-uproar-by-tagging-refugees-with-numbers/

7 Ruth Dureghello in Anon, 'Marking Numbers on Refugees' Arms Recalls Holocaust, Italian Jewish Leaders Say,' *Jewish Telegraphic Agency*, 3 September 2015, https://www.jta.org/2015/09/03/global/marking-numbers-on-refugees-arms-recalls-holocaust-italian-jewish-leaders-say

8 Anon, 'Czech Extremist Adam Bartoš: Put the Refugees in a Former Nazi Concentration Camp', Britskelisty, 2015, http://blisty.cz/art/78865.html

9   Jan Čulík, 'Why Is the Czech Republic So Hostile to Muslims and Refugees?', *Europe Now*, 2017, http://www.europenowjournal.org/2017/02/09/why-is-the-czech-republic-so-hostile-to-muslims-and-refugees/#_edn34

10 Ibid.

11 'Czech President Miloš Zeman Says Refugees Are Like a "Tsunami That Will Kill Him"', *Huffington Post*, 1 September 2015, http://www.huffingtonpost.co.uk/2015/09/01/eu-migrant-crisis-refugees-tsunami-czech_n_8069350.html

12 Silja Schultheis, 'The Refugee Policy of the Visegrád Countries: "No One Invited You"', *Heinrich-Böll-Stiftung*, 15 September 2015, https://cz.boell.org/en/2015/09/15/refugee-policy-visegrad-countries-no-one-invited-you

13 Michal Hrabal, 'Kdy Si Ty Stany Odvezete? Ptala Se Žena Na Setkání s Lidmi z Ministerstva', *Breclavsky Denik.Cz*, September 2015, my translation, https://breclavsky.denik.cz/zpravy_region/kdy-si-ty-stany-odvezete-ptala-se-zena-na-setkani-s-lidmi-z-ministerstva-20150908.html

14 Ibid.

15 Amnesty International, 'USA: "You Don't Have Any Rights Here"', 2018, https://www.amnesty.org/en/latest/research/2018/10/usa-treatment-of-asylum-seekers-southern-border/

16 Hopkins in Sam Jones, 'UN Human Rights Chief Denounces Sun over Katie Hopkins "Cockroach" Column', *The Guardian*, 24 April 2015, https://www.theguardian.com/global-development/2015/apr/24/katie-hopkins-cockroach-migrants-denounced-united-nations-human-rights-commissioner. Hopkins, who is connected to several white supremacist groups and movements, has risen to international prominence during the Trump presidency, and is currently a regular political pundit on US television news networks.

17 Spillers, *Black, White, and in Color*, 210.

18 Ash Amin, 'The Remainders of Race', *Theory, Culture & Society* 27, no. 1 (2010): 3, 6.

19 Hall, 'Race, The Floating Signifier'.

20 Jacques Derrida, 'Racism's Last Word', *Critical Inquiry* 12, no. 1 (1985): 292.

21 Ibid., 292.

22 See Patrick Hamm, Lawrence King and David Stuckler, 'Mass Privatization, State Capacity, and Economic Growth in Postcommunist Countries', *American Sociological Review* 77, no. 2 (2012): 295–324.

23 Adam Blanden, 'Central and Eastern Europe as Playground of a Conservative Avant-Garde', *Open Democracy*, 3 October 2015, https://www.opendemocracy.net/en/can-europe-make-it/central-and-eastern-europe-as-playground-of-conservative-avant-garde/

24 Kurt Biray, 'Communist Nostalgia in Eastern Europe: Longing for the Past', *Open Democracy*, 10 November 2015, https://www.opendemocracy.net/en/can-europe-make-it/communist-nostalgia-in-eastern-europe-longing-for-past/

25 Jodi Dean, *The Communist Horizon* (London: Verso, 2012), 40.

26 Jeffrey Isaac, 'Is There Illiberal Democracy? A Problem with No Semantic Solution', *Eurozine*, 9 August 2017, https://www.eurozine.com/is-there-illiberal-democracy/

27 Amnesty, 'Fenced Out: Hungary's Violations of the Rights of Refugees and Migrants' (London: Amnesty International, 2015), https://www.amnesty.org/download/Documents/EUR2726142015ENGLISH.pdf

28 Anon, 'Former Czech President Václav Klaus: "Immigration Is Not a Human Right. Europe Is Committing a Suicide"', *Britskelisty*, 2 September 2015, https://blisty.cz/art/78735-former-czech-president-vaclav-klaus-immigration-is-not-a-human-right-europe-is-committing-a-suicide.html

29 In Čulík, 'Why Is the Czech Republic So Hostile to Muslims and Refugees?' Petr Hampl is a sociologist and well-known anti-Islamic and anti-immigrant activist. In 2017 he founded the Czech Society for Civilization Studies.

30 Mnislav Zelený-Atapana, 'Je Na Řadě Genocida Bělochů v Evropě?', *Lidové Noviny*, 18 July 2016, my translation, http://www.lidovky.cz/diskuse-je-na-rade-genocida-belochu-v-evrope-fe0-/nazory.aspx?c=A160718_135549_ln_nazory_mct

31 See for example 'European Islamophobia Report 2017' (Turkey: SETA: Foundation for Political, Economic and Social Research, 2018), https://www.islamophobiaeurope.com/wp-content/uploads/2018/04/EIR_2017.pdf

32 Anon, 'Minister Signals Possibility of Allowing Refugees to Cross Czech Territory to Germany', *Hello Czech Republic*, 2 September 2015, http://www.czech.cz/en/Vie-Travail/Minister-signals-possibility-of-allowing-refugees

33 Barbora Cernušáková, 'Trains to Nowhere – Hungary's Harsh Welcome for Refugees', Amnesty International (blog), 4 September 2015, https://www.amnesty.org/en/latest/news/2015/09/trains-to-nowhere-hungary-harsh-welcome-for-refugees/

34 William Turvill, 'Journalists "Pushed Away" from "Distressing Scenes" Involving Migrants at Hungarian Train Station', *Press Gazette UK*, 3 September 2015, https://www.pressgazette.co.uk/journalists-pushed-away-distressing-scenes-involving-migrants-hungarian-train-station/

35 Magdalena Nowicka, 'I Don't Mean to Sound Racist But...: Transforming Racism in Transnational Europe', *Ethnic and Racial Studies* 41, no. 5 (2018): 825.

36 Ibid., 827.

37 Zelený-Atapana, 'Je Na Řadě Genocida Bělochů v Evropě?', my translation.

38 Stefano Fella and Carlo Ruzza, 'Understanding European Anti-Racisms', in *Anti-Racist Movements in the EU: Between Europeanisation and National Trajectories* (Chippenham: Palgrave Macmillan, 2013), 212.

39 Nowicka, 'I Don't Mean to Sound Racist But...'.

40 Alana Lentin, 'Learning from Lisa Lowe', 2017, http://www.alanalentin.net/2017/03/03/learning-from-lisa-lowe/

41 Agnes Gagi et al., 'Beyond Moral Interpretations of the EU "Migration Crisis": Hungary and the Global Economic Division of Labor', *LeftEast*,

2016, http://www.criticatac.ro/lefteast/beyond-moral-interpretations-of-hu-eu-migration-crisis/

42   Ibid.

43   Ambalavaner Sivanandan, 'Foreword: Racial Violence and the Brexit State' (Institute for Race Relations, 2016), http://www.irr.org.uk/app/uploads/2016/11/Racial-violence-and-the-Brexit-state-final.pdf

44   Zygmunt Bauman, *Modernity and the Holocaust* (Ithaca, NY: Cornell University Press, 1989), 27.

45   Ibid., 78.

46   Ibid., 78.

47   Ibid., 78.

48   In Mohamed Adhikari, '"Streams of Blood and Streams of Money": New Perspectives on the Annihilation of the Herero and Nama Peoples of Namibia, 1904–1908', *Kronos* 34 (2008): 309. In this review essay Adhikari gives an overview of the key literature (up to 2008) on the relationship between Nazi-era fascism and the Herero and Nama genocides. See also the forthcoming Jürgen Zimmerer, *From Windhoek to Auschwitz: On the Relationship between Colonialism and the Holocaust* (London: Routledge, forthcoming 2021).

49   David Olusoga and Casper Erichsen, *The Kaiser's Holocaust: Germany's Forgotten Genocide and the Colonial Roots of Nazism* (London: Faber and Faber, 2010).

50   Jon Bridgman and Leslie Worley, 'Genocide of the Hereros', in *Century of Genocide: Critical Essays and Eyewitness Accounts*, ed. Samuel Totten, William Parsons and Israel Charny (New York: Routledge, 2004), 27.

51   Ibid., 30; Jeremy Sarkin-Hughes, *Germany's Genocide of the Herero: Kaiser Wilhelm II, His General, His Settlers, His Soldiers* (Cape Town: UCT Press, 2010).

52   Jason Burke and Philip Oltermann, 'Germany Moves to Atone for "Forgotten Genocide" in Namibia', *The Guardian*, 25 December 2016, https://www.theguardian.com/world/2016/dec/25/germany-moves-to-atone-for-forgotten-genocide-in-namibia

53   Véronique Chemla, 'Le Premier Génocide Du XXe Siècle: Herero et Nama Dans Le Sud-Ouest Africain Allemand, 1904–1908', *Véronique Chemla* (blog), 24 April 2019, http://www.informaction.info/iframe-le-premier-genocide-du-xxe-siecle

54   Spillers, *Black, White, and in Color*, 19–20.

55   Frantz Fanon, *The Wretched of the Earth* (London: Penguin Classics, 2001), 80.

56   Olusoga and Erichsen, *The Kaiser's Holocaust*, 7.

57   George Gedye, *Fallen Bastions: The Central European Tragedy* (London: Victor Gollancz, 1939), 503. The yellow star resurrected much older forms of Jewish badging in Europe, which can be traced back to the eighth century, underscoring the continuation (and periodic intensification) of penal forms of *marking out* race–class distinctions.

58   Ruth Elias, *Triumph of Hope: From Theresienstadt and Auschwitz to Israel*, trans. Margot Bettauer Dembo (New York: John Wiley & Sons, 1999), 109–10.

59 Primo Levi, *If This Is a Man*, ed. Stuart Woolf (New York: The Orion Press, 1959), 39.

60 Bauman, *Modernity and the Holocaust*, 227.

61 Primo Levi, 'Primo Levi's Heartbreaking, Heroic Answers to the Most Common Questions He Was Asked About "Survival in Auschwitz"', *New Republic*, 17 February 1986, https://newrepublic.com/article/119959/interview-primo-levi-survival-auschwitz

62 James Whitman, 'What Is Wrong with Inflicting Shame Sanctions', *Yale Law Journal* 107, no. 4 (1998): 1083.

63 German History in Documents and Images, 'The Eternal Jew [Der Ewige Jude] Film Poster 1940', German Historical Institute Washington (blog), n.d., http://ghdi.ghi-dc.org/sub_image.cfm?image_id=2331

64 Foucault, *Discipline & Punish*, 8.

65 Ibid., 8.

66 Ibid., 32.

67 Whitman, 'What Is Wrong with Inflicting Shame Sanctions', 1055.

68 In Dan Kahan, 'Shaming Punishments', in *Encyclopedia of Crime and Justice*, ed. Joshua Dressler (New York: Macmillan, 2002), https://www.encyclopedia.com/law/legal-and-political-magazines/shaming-punishments

69 Ibid.

70 David Skeel, 'Shaming in Corporate Law', *University of Pennsylvania Law Review* 149, no. 6 (2001): 1811.

71 Whitman, 'What Is Wrong with Inflicting Shame Sanctions', 1059.

72 Jennifer Jacquet, *Is Shame Necessary? New Uses for an Old Tool* (London: Penguin, 2016).

73 Loïc Wacquant, 'Crafting the Neoliberal State: Workfare, Prisonfare, and Social Insecurity', *Sociological Forum* 25, no. 2 (2010): 2016.

74 On reality television and the public shaming of women see, for example, Beverley Skeggs and Helen Wood, *Reacting to Reality Television: Performance, Audience and Value* (New York: Routledge, 2012).

75 Stuart Hall and Sut Jhally, 'The Last Interview: Stuart Hall on the Politics of Cultural Studies', *Media Education Foundation*, 2016, 4, https://www.mediaed.org/transcripts/The-Last-Interview-Transcript.pdf

76 Weheliye, *Habeas Viscus*, 1.

77 Stuart Hall, 'The Great Moving Right Show', in Stuart Hall, *Selected Political Writings: The Great Moving Right Show and Other Essays*, ed. Sally Davison, David Featherstone and Bill Schwarz (London: Lawrence and Wishart, 2017), 174.

78 Alain Badiou, 'Alain Badiou: Reflections on the Recent Election', 15 November 2016, https://www.versobooks.com/blogs/2940-alain-badiou-reflections-on-the-recent-election

79 G.M. Tamás, 'Anti-Immigration Referendum Sunday in Hungary', *Open Democracy*, 2 October 2016, https://www.opendemocracy.net/en/can-europe-make-it/anti-immigration-referendum-sunday-in-hungary/

80   Lydia Gall, 'Hungary's War on Refugees', 2016, https://www.hrw.org/news/2016/09/16/hungarys-war-refugees

81   Ibid.

82   Les Back, 'An Ordinary Virtue', *New Jewish Thought* (blog), 2008, http://research.gold.ac.uk/2326/

83   Kimberlé Williams Crenshaw, 'Race, Reform and Retrenchment', in *Theories of Race and Racism: A Reader*, ed. Les Back and Jon Solomos (London: Routledge, 2009), 550.

84   Anna Šabatová, 'Facility for Detention of Foreigners Bělá-Jezová: Evaluation of Systematic Visit. Public Defenders of Rights, Ombudsman' (Public Defender of Rights, 9 September 2015), 4, https://www.ochrance.cz/fileadmin/user_upload/ochrana_osob/ZARIZENI/Zarizeni_pro_cizince/Report_Bela-Jezova.pdf

85   See ibid., 7.

86   See also Martina Ahmed-Čermáková, 'Strach a Hnus v Bělé-Jezové', 2015, http://a2larm.cz/2015/09/strach-a-hnus-v-bele-jezove/

87   Šabatová, 'Facility for Detention of Foreigners Bělá-Jezová', 13.

88   Ibid., 13.

89   Ahmed-Čermáková, 'Strach a Hnus v Bělé-Jezové'.

90   Ibid.

91   United Nations, 'Zeid Urges Czech Republic to Stop Detention of Migrants and Refugees', 22 October 2015, http://www.ohchr.org/EN/NewsEvents/Pages/DisplayNews.aspx?NewsID=16632&LangID=E#sthash.t6NZThkl.dpuf

92   Daniel Trilling, 'What to Do with the People Who Do Make It Across?', 8 October 2015, https://www.lrb.co.uk/v37/n19/daniel-trilling/what-to-do-with-the-people-who-do-make-it-across

93   Avery Gordon, *Ghostly Matters: Haunting and the Sociological Imagination* (Minneapolis: University of Minnesota Press, 1997), 195.

94   Avery Gordon, 'Some Thoughts on Haunting and Futurity', *Borderlands* 10, no. 2 (2011), http://www.borderlands.net.au/vol10no2_2011/gordon_thoughts.pdf

95   Dan Hodges, 'The 900 Refugees Drowned in the Mediterranean Were Killed by British Government Policy', *The Telegraph*, 20 April 2015, https://www.telegraph.co.uk/news/general-election-2015/politics-blog/11549721/The-900-refugees-dead-in-the-Mediterranean-were-killed-by-British-government-policy.html

96   Reported by the BBC journalist Secunder Kermani on twitter, April 2015. See also Emma Jane Kirby, *The Optician of Lampedusa: A Tale of Rescue and the Awakening of Conscience* (London: Penguin, 2017), a semi-fictionalised account of the experience of people in Lampedusa in the wake of mass drownings at sea.

97   Andre Vltchek, 'In Prague You Get Beaten for Defending Refugees', *Counterpunch*, 30 October 2015, https://www.counterpunch.org/2015/10/30/in-prague-you-get-beaten-for-defending-refugees/

98   Gedye, *Fallen Bastions: The Central European Tragedy*, 301.

99   Ibid., 301.
100   Ibid., 301.
101   Ibid., 301.

Chapter 4

1   Peter Taylor-Gooby, *The Double Crisis of the Welfare State and What We Can Do about It* (Basingstoke: Palgrave Macmillan, 2013), viii.

2   Published here with David's permission but under a pseudonym.

3   At the time of this school's closure 6 per cent of pupils came from Gypsy, Roma and Traveller families, 40 per cent of pupils had special educational needs and 40 per cent were eligible for free school meals. In short, this school was meeting a range of diverse needs, and was well known for supporting children with behavioural and emotional problems, and children from disadvantaged backgrounds. It was closed because it was assessed as not performing well enough in academic league tables, and had falling numbers of pupils.

4   Mia Gray and Anna Barford, 'The Depths of the Cuts: The Uneven Geography of Local Government Austerity', *Cambridge Journal of Regions, Economy and Society* 11, no. 3 (2018): 541.

5   This is my own use of the term 'fracking', a word adopted and adapted from the controversial environment-destroying practice of hydraulic fracking (to recover gas and oil from shale rock under the earth). I employ fracking as a metaphor in this book for the ways in which the machinery of capitalism extracts value from people and common land and resources *at any cost*. Fracking is a descriptor for the depths to which capitalists will plunge in their search for new arenas of profit. Fracking was on my mind throughout the period I was researching and writing this book. In 2015 Lancashire Country Council (local government) turned down a commercial planning application (by Cuadrilla) to frack on the Fylde coast in North Lancashire near where I live, but this decision was soon overturned by the central Conservative government. In the years that followed anti-fracking campaigners worked tirelessly to resist the operations of this commercial fracking company. Hundreds of people were arrested during protests which saw activists lying in roads to stop trucks carrying drilling equipment, sometimes locking their bodies onto vehicles and buildings. When fracking eventually commenced in 2018, my local area was beset by earthquakes. At the time of writing, commercial fracking has been paused in England. My use of the term fracking is intended to draw attention to the ways in which neoliberalism, and the forms of austerity which characterise late neoliberalism, marks an intensification of capitalist enclosures which is destroying human welfare *and* degrading the natural environment.

6   See Imogen Tyler, *Revolting Subjects: Social Abjection and Resistance in Neoliberal Britain* (London: Zed, 2013).

7   McKittrick, 'Yours in the Intellectual Struggle', 7.

8   Philip Alston, 'Visit to the United Kingdom of Great Britain and Northern Ireland: Report of the Special Rapporteur on Extreme Poverty and Human

Rights' (Human Rights Council, United Nations, 2019), 1, https://undocs.org/A/HRC/41/39/Add.1

9   Chris Grover, 'Violent Proletarianisation: Social Murder, the Reserve Army of Labour and Social Security "Austerity" in Britain', *Critical Social Policy* 39, no. 3 (2019): 339.

10   See Naomi Klein, *The Shock Doctrine: The Rise of Disaster Capitalism* (London: Penguin Books, 2008). I use the term social reproduction here in the sense meant by feminist economists, namely as a term which describes the labour (most often the unpaid domestic and care work undertaken by women) required to sustain the life of oneself and dependent others. Welfare settlements such as the British welfare state partly socialised social reproduction, through the provision of services such as state-funded care for children and the elderly. The current crisis in social reproduction is particularly acute in respect of social and elder care, and care work has been progressively privatised and financialised.

11   Hall, 'The Great Moving Right Show', 2.

12   Alston, 'Visit to the United Kingdom of Great Britain and Northern Ireland'.

13   See Mark Townsend, 'Secret Plan to Use Charities to Help Deport Rough Sleepers', *The Guardian*, 6 July 2019, https://www.theguardian.com/politics/2019/jul/06/home-office-secret-plan-charities-deport-rough-sleepers; Imogen Tyler, 'Deportation Nation', *Journal for the Study of British Cultures* 25, no. 1 (2018): 25–41.

14   Sarah Marsh, 'British Children Living in Poverty "Could Hit Record High" – Report', *The Guardian*, 20 February 2019, https://www.theguardian.com/society/2019/feb/20/british-children-living-in-poverty-could-hit-record-high-report

15   Patrick Kingsley, 'Universal Credit Has Left Children so Undernourished Schools Are Offering Free Breakfasts', *The Independent*, 1 October 2018, https://www.independent.co.uk/news/long_reads/children-undernourished-universal-credit-austerity-welfare-reforms-poverty-hunger-food-bank-a8557276.html

16   Sally Weale, 'Tired, Hungry and Shamed: Pupil Poverty "Stops Learning"', *The Observer*, 14 April 2019, https://www.theguardian.com/education/2019/apr/14/tired-hungry-shamed-pupil-poverty-stops-learning

17   Michael Savage and Dulcie Lee, '"I Regularly See Rickets": Diseases of Victorian-Era Poverty Return to UK', *The Guardian*, 23 December 2017, https://www.theguardian.com/society/2017/dec/23/poorer-children-disproportionately-need-hospital-treatment

18   Source NHS digital data, https://digital.nhs.uk/data-and-information/find-data-and-publications/supplementary-information/2018-supplementary-information-files/hospital-admissions-for-scurvy-rickets-and-malnutrition

19   At the time of writing the British Paediatric Surveillance Unit team were due to report on research completed in 2017 on incidences of nutritional rickets amongst children and young people.

20   May Bulman, 'Life Expectancy of Poorest Girls in England Falls for First Time

on Record since 1920s, Figures Show', *The Independent*, 2018, https://www.independent.co.uk/news/uk/home-news/life-expectancy-poorest-girls-women-england-ons-a8235471.html

21   Philip Alston, 'Statement on Visit to the United Kingdom, by Professor Philip Alston, United Nations Special Rapporteur on Extreme Poverty and Human Rights' (United Nations, 16 November 2018), https://www.ohchr.org/EN/NewsEvents/Pages/DisplayNews.aspx?NewsID=23881&LangID=E

22   Ibid.

23   Ibid.

24   Vickie Cooper and David Whyte, 'Introduction: The Violence of Austerity', in *The Violence of Austerity* (London: Pluto Press, 2017), 11.

25   Ibid., 11.

26   Juliette Garside, 'Recession Rich: Britain's Wealthiest Double Net Worth since Crisis', *The Guardian*, 26 April 2015, https://www.theguardian.com/business/2015/apr/26/recession-rich-britains-wealthiest-double-net-worth-since-crisis. See also Andrew Sayer, *Why We Can't Afford the Rich* (Bristol: Policy Press, 2016).

27   See Cooper and Whyte, 'Introduction: The Violence of Austerity'.

28   Patrick Butler, 'Lives Will Be Lost If Plans to Slash Housing Support Services Go Ahead, Charities Warn', *The Guardian*, 20 February 2019, https://www.theguardian.com/society/2019/feb/20/lives-lost-housing-cuts-rough-sleepers-west-sussex-homeless

29   Anthony Barej, 'GMB Highlights 1 Million Public Sector Jobs Lost since 2010', *Public Finance: News and Insight for Public Finance Professionals*, 18 September 2017, https://www.publicfinance.co.uk/news/2017/09/gmb-highlights-1-million-public-sector-jobs-lost-2010

30   See Akwugo Emejulu and Leah Bassel, 'Women of Colour's Anti-Austerity Activism', in *The Violence of Austerity*, ed. Vickie Cooper and David Whyte (London: Pluto Press, 2017), 117–22.

31   Patrick Butler, 'More than 8 Million in UK Struggle to Put Food on Table, Survey Says', *The Guardian*, 6 May 2016, https://www.theguardian.com/society/2016/may/06/more-than-8-million-in-uk-struggle-to-put-food-on-table-survey-says

32   Cooper and Whyte, 'Introduction: The Violence of Austerity', 24.

33   These comments are typical of the almost 3,000 made in the thread under this story about child hunger. However, it is notable, given the right-wing framing of the story, which invites cynicism about levels of child poverty in Britain, that there is significant challenge and debate amongst the readers in the thread. It is also important to note in relation to the comment about 'fat people' that obesity can be sign of malnutrition, as cheap processed foods are often high in carbohydrate (sugar) and fat, but are nutritionally deficient. Obesity is now considered the major health crisis facing developed nations, and is a leading cause of premature deaths and cancer.

34   This interview with Philip Hammond is available to watch here: https://www.youtube.com/watch?v=7SLDiguOksw

35 Robert Booth, 'UN Poverty Expert Hits Back over UK Ministers' "Denial of Facts"', *The Guardian*, 24 May 2019, https://www.theguardian.com/society/2019/may/24/un-poverty-expert-hits-back-over-uk-ministers-denial-of-facts-philip-alston

36 Howard Friedman, 'America's Looming Demographic Challenge', *The Huffington Post* (blog), 2013, https://www.huffpost.com/entry/americas-looming-demograp_b_3422807?guccounter=1&guce_referrer=aHR0cHM6Ly-93d3cuZ29vZ2xlLmNvbS8&guce_referrer_sig=AQAAACCH0GFZbn8EbU-33LeqxpKpabxWlIJlPCClT7JhVqEgqrohkC7FkfJvJLmPYL52_iVhI6i-HL5VF0tV2_a0v6fw6bzC-C3_lTKKlT8mNpOApCsLvBux7YT0qgO325Gh-pN0AkTuM_1puAWFZTy9gGEJZN3yAiw8lkcwuaxKsUoj6a6

37 School uniform grants were once available to poorer families, including my own family in the 1980s. These grants have now been largely been abolished. Various charitable initiatives have sprung up in their place, including school uniform denotation points.

38 Carolyn Steedman, *Landscape for a Good Woman: A Story of Two Lives* (London: Virago, 1987), 123.

39 Beverley Skeggs, 'A Crisis in Humanity: What Everyone with Parents Is Likely to Face in the Future', *The Sociological Review* (blog), 2019, https://www.thesociologicalreview.com/a-crisis-in-humanity-what-everyone-with-parents-is-likely-to-face-in-the-future/

40 For an overview of changes to disability benefits see Mo Stewart, *Cash Not Care: The Planned Demolition of the UK Welfare State* (London: New Generation Publishing, 2016); Frances Ryan, *Crippled: Austerity and the Demonization of Disabled People* (London: Verso, 2019).

41 Ryan, *Crippled: Austerity and the Demonization of Disabled People*, 81.

42 Mo Stewart, 'State Crime by Proxy: Corporate Influence on State Sanctioned Social Harm', *Journal of Critical Psychology, Counselling and Psychotherapy* 18, no. 4 (2018), 217–27.

43 See the ongoing activism of Disabled People against the Cuts (2010–present) and Black Triangle (2010–present) who have campaigned against and researched the impacts of these cuts.

44 On the impact of PIP and loss of access to the Motability scheme on disabled people's independence see Ryan, *Crippled: Austerity and the Demonization of Disabled People*.

45 Anon, 'Disabled Patients "Relying on Crowdfunding" for Wheelchairs', *The Guardian*, 27 June 2017, https://www.theguardian.com/society/2017/jun/27/disabled-patients-relying-on-crowdfunding-for-wheelchairs. See also Ryan, *Crippled: Austerity and the Demonization of Disabled People*.

46 Cooper and Whyte, 'Introduction: The Violence of Austerity', 2.

47 In Stewart, 'State Crime by Proxy'.

48 B. Barr et al., '"First Do No Harm": Are Disability Assessments Associated with Adverse Trends in Mental Health? A Longitudinal Ecological Study', *Journal of Epidemiology & Community Health* 70, no. 4 (2016):

339–45. See also Ryan, *Crippled: Austerity and the Demonization of Disabled People*.

49   The United Nations Reports on the Rights of Persons with Disabilities can be accessed here: https://tbinternet.ohchr.org/_layouts/15/treatybodyexternal/ TBSearch.aspx?Lang=en&TreatyID=4&DocTypeCategoryID=7

50   Alston, 'Statement on Visit to the United Kingdom'.

51   See the 2017 Financial sustainability of local authorities inquiry, https:// www.parliament.uk/business/committees/committees-a-z/commons-select/ public-accounts-committee/inquiries/parliament-2017/financial-sustainability-local-authorities-17-19/

The structure of local government in Britain is complex, involving different kinds and tiers of government in different places. In short, there are four main types of local authority in England: 27 county councils (which devolve some services to 201 lower tier district councils – town and small city councils), 92 unitary authorities (including 'metropolitan districts', cities and some large towns) which manage all resources and services centrally, and 33 London boroughs. Amongst these different types of local authority, county councils have borne the most significant cuts, and receive substantially lower levels of funding for key services such as social care, county schools and children's services. In total, central government funding received by County Councils will have decreased by 93 per cent by 2020 – a shortfall which is supposed to be met through local taxation and enterprise.

52   Gray and Barford, 'The Depths of the Cuts', 558.

53   Ibid., 551.

54   Devolved national systems of welfare spending mean that Scotland, Wales and Northern Ireland have had slightly higher levels of protection from austerity cuts than English authorities.

55   Gray and Barford, 'The Depths of the Cuts', 553.

56   Ibid., 557.

57   Anon, 'Lancashire Councillors Approve £77m of Service Cuts', BBC News Website, 15 February 2017, https://www.bbc.co.uk/news/uk-england-lancashire-47250117

58   Michael Edwards, 'The Housing Crisis and London', *City* 20, no. 1 (2016): 222–37. See also David Madden and Peter Marcuse, *In Defence of Housing: The Politics of Crisis* (London: Verso, 2016).

59   Iain Duncan Smith, 'Iain Duncan Smith: Labour Only Stands for Welfare Dependency', *The Telegraph*, 15 February 2015, https://www.telegraph.co.uk/ news/politics/comment/11413813/Iain-Duncan-Smith-Labour-only-stands-for-welfare-dependency.html

60   Cooper and Whyte, 'Introduction: The Violence of Austerity', 1.

61   Duncan Smith, 'Iain Duncan Smith: Labour Only Stands for Welfare Dependency'.

62   Paul Spicker's 1984 thesis *Stigma and Social Welfare*, offers a long historical overview of the entangled relationship between stigma and relief in England from the medieval period onwards.

63   Robert Walker, *The Shame of Poverty* (Oxford: Oxford University Press, 2014), 65.

64   Ibid., 184.

65   Pinker, 'Stigma and Social Welfare', 13.

66   Ibid., 13.

67   Ibid., 13.

68   Ibid., 15.

69   Ibid., 14.

70   Ibid., 14.

71   see Walker, *The Shame of Poverty*; Robert Walker et al., 'Poverty in Global Perspective: Is Shame a Common Denominator?', *Journal of Social Policy* 42, no. 2 (2013): 215–33; Elaine Chase and Robert Walker, 'The Co-Construction of Shame in the Context of Poverty: Beyond a Threat to the Social Bond', *Sociology* 47, no. 4 (1 August 2013): 739–54.

72   John Hills, *Good Times, Bad Times: The Welfare Myth of Them and Us*. (Bristol: Policy Press, 2014).

73   See Elizabeth Dowler and Hannah Lambie-Mumford, 'Introduction: Hunger, Food and Social Policy in Austerity', *Social Policy and Society* 14, no. 3 (2015): 411–15.

74   For an account of how common sense is crafted and its social and political uses with respect to neoliberal policy regimes, see Stuart Hall and Alan O'Shea, 'Common-Sense Neoliberalism', *Soundings* 55, no. 55 (13 December 2013): 9–25.

75   The 2012 study, 'Benefits Stigma in Britain', a research project commissioned by the disability charity Turn2us, and undertaken by a team of policy experts coordinated by the University of Kent, sought to assess 'the impact of stigma and other social influences on applying for benefits'. 'Benefits Stigma in Britain' details the ways in which 'the language and coverage' around welfare benefits have become increasingly stigmatised since the late 1990s. While this research was undertaken at the beginning of austerity cuts to welfare, it evidences an intensification of negative media depictions since 2008, with an increasing emphasis on the deservedness of claimants.

76   Charles Murray, 'Stigma Makes Generosity Feasible', *AEIdeas: A Public Policy Blog from AEI* (blog), 30 November 2009, http://www.aei.org/publication/stigma-makes-generosity-feasible/

77   Daniel Payne, 'Bring Back the Welfare Stigma', *The Federalist*, 21 August 2014, http://thefederalist.com/2014/08/21/bring-back-the-welfare-stigma/

78   David Cameron, 'PM's Speech on Welfare Reform Bill' (17 February 2011), https://www.gov.uk/government/speeches/pms-speech-on-welfare-reform-bill

79   Daguerre and Etherington, 'Workfare in 21st Century Britain'. This report is part of an ESRC-funded study which examines the recent evolution of welfare reform in the US and the UK.

80   Duncan Smith, 'Iain Duncan Smith: Labour Only Stands for Welfare Dependency'.

81   Andrew Woodcock, 'Benefit Cheats Are "Mugging Taxpayers" Says Osborne',
     The Independent, 17 October 2010, https://www.independent.co.uk/news/uk/
     politics/benefit-cheats-are-mugging-taxpayers-says-osborne-2109134.html

82   See Tracey Jensen, 'Welfare Commonsense, Poverty Porn and Doxosophy',
     Sociological Research Online 19, no. 3 (2014): 3; Sara De Benedictis, Kim Allen
     and Tracey Jensen, 'Portraying Poverty: The Economics and Ethics of Factual
     Welfare Television', *Cultural Sociology* 11, no. 3 (September 2017): 337–58;
     Tracey Jensen, *Parenting the Crisis: The Cultural Politics of Neo-Liberal
     Parent-Blame* (Bristol: Policy Press, 2018).

83   Iain Duncan Smith and Philip Davies, 'House of Commons Hansard' (2014),
     https://hansard.parliament.uk/Commons/2014-01-13/debates/
     14011313000027/TopicalQuestions?highlight=%22benefits%20
     street%22#contribution-14011313000180

84   Tracey Jensen and Imogen Tyler, '"Benefits Broods": The Cultural and Political
     Crafting of Anti-Welfare Commonsense', *Critical Social Policy* 35, no. 4
     (November 2015): 470–91; Jensen, *Parenting the Crisis*.

85   Women have 1.9 children on average in Britain. In 2017 additional welfare
     reforms came into force which saw child and family benefit entitlements
     restricted to the first two children in each family – a policy many consider in
     breach of the United Nations Convention on the Rights of the Child – to which
     the UK government was a signatory in 1992.

86   Pinker, 'Stigma and Social Welfare', 14.

87   Antonio Gramsci, *Selections from the Prison Notebooks of Antonio Gramsci*,
     trans. Quintin Hoare and Geoffrey Nowell Smith (London: Lawrence &
     Wishart, 1971), 377.

88   Leeds Poverty Commission 'HuManifesto', http://www.leedspovertytruth.org.
     uk/humanifesto/

89   China Mills, '"Dead People Don't Claim": A Psychopolitical Autopsy of UK
     Austerity Suicides', *Critical Social Policy* 38, no. 2 (2018): 302–22.

90   Paul Mason in preface to Jim Mortram, *Small Town Inertia* (Liverpool:
     Bluecoat Press, 2017). Jim Mortram's photographic book is an important
     documentary account of the impact of austerity in Britain.

91   Mills, '"Dead People Don't Claim"', 303.

92   Ibid., 317.

93   Tombs in Grover, 'Violent Proletarianisation', 314.

94   Ibid., 350.

95   Ruth Wilson Gilmore, *Golden Gulag: Prisons, Surplus, Crisis, and Opposition
     in Globalizing California* (Berkeley: University of California Press, 2007), 28.

96   Elizabeth A. Povinelli, *Economies of Abandonment: Social Belonging and
     Endurance in Late Liberalism* (Durham, NC: Duke University Press, 2011), 3.

97   Ibid., 22.

98   Frances Fox Piven and Richard Cloward, *Regulating the Poor: The Functions
     of Public Welfare*, updated edition (New York: Vintage, 1993).

99   Ibid., xv.

100 Ibid., xvii.

101 Sandra Morgen and Jeff Maskovsky, 'The Anthropology of Welfare 'Reform': New Perspectives on U.S. Urban Poverty in the Post-Welfare Era', *Annual Review of Anthropology* 32 (2003): 327.

102 John Clarke, *Changing Welfare, Changing States* (London: Sage, 2004), 12.

103 Steedman, *Landscape for a Good Woman*, 122.

104 Ibid., 122.

105 Ibid., 122.

106 Stuart Hall, Doreen Massey and Michael Rustin in Jensen and Tyler, '"Benefits Broods"', 472.

107 In Britain, as elsewhere in the world, a person's right to welfare, by which I mean the ability to access the resources required for a liveable life (housing, work, education, healthcare etc.), has become increasingly determined by exclusionary, punitive and highly racialised regimes of citizenship. On this see, for example, Hannah Jones et al., *Go Home? The Politics of Immigration Controversies* (Manchester: Manchester University Press, 2017); Tyler, 'Deportation Nation'.

108 Iain Hay and Samantha Muller, 'Questioning Generosity in the Golden Age of Philanthropy: Towards Critical Geographies of Super-Philanthropy', *Progress in Human Geography* 38, no. 5 (October 2014): 635–53.

109 See Alan Warde, 'Conditions of Dependence: Working-Class Quiescence in Lancaster in the Twentieth Century', *International Review of Social History* 35, no. 1 (1990): 71–105.

110 Sue Ashworth, *The Lino King: The Life and Times of Lord Ashton* (Lancaster: Lancashire Museums, 1989).

111 Warde, 'Conditions of Dependence ', 42.

112 Ibid.; Nigel Todd, 'A History of Labour in Lancaster and Barrow-in-Furness c. 1890–1920' (Lancaster University, 1976).

113 Local Government Worker, Mr B.3.L (p.15), born 1890. Elizabeth Roberts Working Class Oral History Archive, Regional Heritage Centre, Lancaster University: https://www.regional-heritage-centre.org

114 Textile Worker, A.1.L (p.12), born 1908. Elizabeth Roberts Working Class Oral History Archive, Regional Heritage Centre, Lancaster University: https://www.regional-heritage-centre.org

115 Warehouseman, Mr V.1.L (p.8), born 1908. Elizabeth Roberts Working Class Oral History Archive, Regional Heritage Centre, Lancaster University: https://www.regional-heritage-centre.org

116 Local government worker, Mr B.3.L (p.42), born 1890. Elizabeth Roberts Working Class Oral History Archive, Regional Heritage Centre, Lancaster University: https://www.regional-heritage-centre.org

117 Housewife, Mrs B.3.L (p.19) born 1894. Elizabeth Roberts Working Class Oral History Archive, Regional Heritage Centre, Lancaster University: https://www.regional-heritage-centre.org

118 Local government worker, Mr B.3.L (p.19), born 1890. Elizabeth Roberts Working Class Oral History Archive, Regional Heritage Centre, Lancaster University: https://www.regional-heritage-centre.org

119 Medical Doctor K.1.P (p.8), born 1900. Elizabeth Roberts Working Class Oral History Archive, Regional Heritage Centre, Lancaster University: https://www. regional-heritage-centre.org

The evidence of this local doctor resonates with contemporary accounts of the relationship between growing poverty and ill-health in the region. In 2017 a local GP in the Lancaster district noted in a television interview that: 'We have seen things like rickets and other conditions that are associated with malnourishment. It was quite common back in Victorian times. We wouldn't expect to see this in a developing nation.' In response a local MP suggested that claims of growing child poverty in the district were exaggerated by left-wing activists, and demanded a retraction from the local health authority. The political fall-out made local, national and international headlines. See for example, Patrick Kingsley, 'In Britain, Even Children Are Feeling the Effects of Austerity', *New York Times*, 26 September 2018, https://www.nytimes. com/2018/09/26/world/europe/uk-austerity-child-poverty.html

120 Warde, 'Conditions of Dependence', 56.

121 Local government worker, Mr B.3.L (p.16) born 1890. Elizabeth Roberts Working Class Oral History Archive, Regional Heritage Centre, Lancaster University: https://www.regional-heritage-centre.org

122 Local government worker, Mr B.3.L (p.16), born 1890. Elizabeth Roberts Working Class Oral History Archive, Regional Heritage Centre, Lancaster University: https://www.regional-heritage-centre.org. Williamson served as a Liberal MP for the city (1886–95) and was controversially bestowed with a peerage, becoming the Lord Ashton in 1895.

123 See Todd, 'A History of Labour in Lancaster and Barrow-in-Furness'; Warde, 'Conditions of Dependence'.

124 Anon, 'Ashton Warns Workers: Tells Employees He Will Close Shops Forever Rather Than Raise Wages', *New York Times*, 10 November 1911.

125 Local government worker, Mr B.3.L (p.34), born 1890. Elizabeth Roberts Working Class Oral History Archive, Regional Heritage Centre, Lancaster University: https://www.regional-heritage-centre.org

126 Ashworth, *The Lino King*. There is some historical dispute about whether the children ate the chocolates before they threw the celebratory wrappings back over the wall. I hope they ate them before they made their protest.

127 Sita Balani, 'Apna: One of Our Own', *Discover Society* (blog), 3 April 2019, https://discoversociety.org/2019/04/03/viewpoint-apna-one-of-our-own/

128 Silvia Federici, *Re-Enchanting the World: Feminism and the Politics of the Commons* (Oakland, CA: PM Press / Kairos, 2019), 184.

129 Federici, *Re-Enchanting the World*, 184.

Chapter 5

1   Patricia Saunders, 'Fugitive Dreams of Diaspora: Conversations with Saidiya Hartman', *Anthurium: A Caribbean Studies Journal* 6, no. 1 (2008): 5.

2   Nigel Rapport, *Diverse World-Views in an English Village* (Edinburgh: Edinburgh University Press, 1993), 57.

3   Didier Eribon, *Returning to Reims* (London: Allen Lane, 2018), 218.

4   Parker and Aggleton, 'HIV and AIDS-Related Stigma and Discrimination', 17.

5   Du Bois, *The Souls of Black Folk.*

6   Sharpe, *In the Wake: On Blackness and Being*, 13.

7   Ibid., 12.

8   Pierre Bourdieu, *Practical Reason: On the Theory of Action* (Stanford, CA: Stanford University Press, 1998), 129.

9   John Urry, *The Tourist Gaze: Leisure and Travel in Contemporary Societies*, Theory, Culture & Society (London: Sage Publications, 1990).

10   See Scott on 'foot-dragging, dissimulation, false compliance, pilfering, feigned ignorance' as everyday forms of resistance. James C. Scott, *Weapons of the Weak: Everyday Forms of Peasant Resistance* (New Haven, CT: Yale University Press, 2000).

11   Selina Todd, *The People: The Rise and Fall of the Working Class* (London: John Murray, 2015), 25–26.

12   Ibid., 41.

13   Lucy Lethbridge, *Servants: A Downstairs View of Twentieth-Century Britain* (London: Bloomsbury, 2013), 94.

14   Margaret Powell, *Below Stairs* (New York: St. Martin's Press, 2012), 35, 190. Powell's best-selling memoir was first published in 1968.

15   As Todd argues, 'the servant problem' was partly about the difficulty of getting and retaining servants, but also expressed deeper fears about the dissenting working class and the erosion of class hierarchies. Todd, *The People*, 21. See also Lethbridge, *Servants.*

16   Todd, *The People*, 39.

17   Lethbridge, *Servants*, 87.

18   Todd, *The People*, 25.

19   Powell, *Below Stairs*, 130.

20   Todd, *The People*, 27.

21   These efforts to press girls into service were more fully nationalised after the Second World War, when the government sponsored centres to train girls for domestic work, as recorded in 1948 Pathe news reel footage from the period: https://www.britishpathe.com/video/domestic-school-1. This is an interesting example of the ways in which state welfare programmes often attempted to re-establish class-based social hierarchies.

22   Todd, *The People*, 38.

23   For this quotation and a wider analysis of Thatcher's innovation of Victorian Values see Raphael Samuel, 'Mrs. Thatcher's Return to Victorian Values', *Proceedings of the British Academy* 78 (1992): 9–29.

24 Stuart Hall, *The Hard Road to Renewal: Thatcherism and the Crisis of the Left* (London: Verso, 1988), 2.

25 While Thatcher didn't openly advocate for the return of live-in domestic servants, her particular brand of conservative feminism was clearly aimed at the advancement of that segment of middle-class women who could afford to buy in domestic help. As Thatcher reflected on her own experiences of combining motherhood and a professional career in a 1990 Pankhurst lecture: 'You have to seek reliable help – a relative or what my mother would have called "a treasure". Someone who brought not only her work but her affections to the family.' Margaret Thatcher, 'Pankhurst Lecture to the 300 Group' (18 July 1990), https://www.margaretthatcher.org/document/108156

The increase in precariously employed low-paid cleaners (and low paid child-minders) which characterises late twentieth and early twentieth-first century domestic work emerged in wake of Thatcher's policies which de-industrialised Britain, drove down working-class wages (partly through attacks on unions), and conversely opened up salaried work to increasing numbers of women. In short, the movement of women into the professional careers in the latter half of the twentieth century has been wholly dependent on the exploited labour of working-class women.

26 Margaret Thatcher, TV Interview for Walt Disney Corporation, 15 March 1989, https://www.margaretthatcher.org/document/107455

27 Lucienne Loh, 'Comparative Postcolonial Ruralities and English Heritage: Julian Barnes's *England, England* and Kiran Desai's *The Inheritance of Loss*', *The Journal of Commonwealth Literature* 51, no. 2 (June 2016): 96. Stuart Hall, reflecting on the whitewashing of English culture and society in this period, writes that 'the development of an indigenous British racism in the post-war period begins with the profound historical forgetfulness – what I want to call the loss of historical memory, a kind of historical amnesia, a decisive mental repression – which has overtaken the British people about race and empire'. Stuart Hall, 'Racism and Reaction', in *Stuart Hall, Selected Political Writings: The Great Moving Right Show and Other Essays*, ed. Sally Davison, David Featherstone and Bill Schwarz (London: Lawrence and Wishart, 2017), 145.

28 Loh, 'Comparative Postcolonial Ruralities and English Heritage', 307.

29 Lucienne Loh, 'Rural Heritage and Colonial Nostalgia in the Thatcher Years: V.S. Naipaul's *The Enigma of Arrival*', in *Thatcher & After*, ed. Louisa Hadley and Elizabeth Ho (London: Palgrave Macmillan UK, 2010), 96.

30 Ibid., 96. To understand some of the impacts, legacies and lived experience of this white-washing of the English countryside, see geographer Divya Tolia-Kelly's work on British-Asian experiences of the Lake District. Divya Tolia-Kelly, 'Fear in Paradise: The Affective Registers of the English Lake District Landscape Re-Visited', *The Senses and Society* 2, no. 3 (2007): 329–51.

31 Satnam Virdee, *Racism, Class and the Racialized Outsider* (Basingstoke: Palgrave Macmillan, 2014), 103.

32 This popular eruption of fascism gave rise to mass left-wing resistance, notably 'Rock Against Racism', on this movement see Dave Renton, *Never Again: Rock against Racism and the Anti-Nazi League 1976–1982*. Routledge Studies in Fascism and the Far Right (London: Routledge/Taylor & Francis Group, 2019).

33 Hall, *The Hard Road to Renewal*, 152.

34 Édouard Glissant, *Caribbean Discourse: Selected Essays*, trans. J. Michael Dash (Charlottesville: University Press of Virginia/CARAF Books, 1999).

35 Rapport, *Diverse World-Views in an English Village*, 37–38.

36 Bev Skeggs, 'The Making of Class and Gender through Visualizing Moral Subject Formation', *Sociology* 39, no. 5 (December 2005): 967.

37 Ibid., 967.

38 Steedman, *Landscape for a Good Woman*, 34.

39 Ibid., 2.

40 Ibid., 2.

41 Ibid., 24.

42 Beverley Skeggs, 'Imagining Personhood Differently: Person Value and Autonomist Working-Class Value Practices', *The Sociological Review* 59, no. 3 (1 August 2011): 496.

43 Steedman, *Landscape for a Good Woman*, 15.

44 Thompson, *The Making of the English Working Class*, 9.

45 Steedman, *Landscape for a Good Woman*, 15.

46 Ibid., 14.

47 Ibid., 113.

48 Eribon, *Returning to Reims*, 12.

49 Ibid., 11–12.

50 Over the years I have discussed some of these experiences with others, particularly with women from working-class backgrounds in academia, and most especially with young women whom I have supported, supervised or mentored. While I have never written about these experience of class stigma and shame before, in retrospect much of my scholarly interest in abjection, stigma and shame originates in what Didier Eribon describes as 'autobiography recast as historical and theoretical analysis that is grounded in personal experience'. Ibid., 20.

51 Ibid., 17.

52 Much later, in trying to make sense of that evening, I read about the resistance of Papua New Guineans to missionaries and visiting anthropologists, their struggles over photographic images captured without their permission, how they sought to defend themselves against the anthropological gaze by sabotaging fieldwork, and the historical role of anthropology with vis a vis colonial expropriation and domination. The writer and educator Paulias Matane, who served as Papua New Guinea's first ambassador to the US, allegedly stalked the funeral service of anthropologist Margaret Mead as he was enraged at superlative tributes about her work in New Guinea. Sean Dorney, *Papua New Guinea: People Politics and*

History since 1975 (Milsons Point, NSW: Random House Australia, 1990). I also began to understand how ethnographic objects are not found, but are made; that is, that they 'become ethnographic' through processes of telling and conventions of display which mask the power relations integral to their production. The Imperial gaze has been extensively written about in anthropology, a discipline which has been forced to confront its colonial past. Notably, this kind of critical reflection has been much more absent in sociology, which has used similar ethnographic methods to study working-class and racialised populations and groups within Europe, North America and elsewhere. One of the things I want to underscore in this chapter is precisely the ways in which decolonising the social sciences requires us to interrogate histories and methods of knowledge production (such as ethnography) across disciplines and places, including within former geographic centres of colonial power.

53 Karen Jacobs, 'From "Spy-Glass" to "Horizon": Tracking the Anthropological Gaze in Zora Neale Hurston', *NOVEL: A Forum on Fiction* 30, no. 3 (1997): 329.

54 Helen Merrell Lynd in Pamela Fox, *Class Fictions: Shame and Resistance in the British Working-Class Novel, 1890–1945*. Post-Contemporary Interventions (Durham, NC: Duke University Press, 1994), 13.

55 Ibid., 13.

56 'Shame Lives on the Eyelids' is a Greek Proverb, for reference see Anne Carson, 'Euripides to the Audience', *London Review of Books*, September 2002, https://www.lrb.co.uk/v24/n17/anne-carson/euripides-to-the-audience

57 Jonathan Murdoch and Andy Pratt, 'From the Power of Topography to the Topography of Power: A Discourse on Strange Ruralities', in *Contested Countryside Cultures: Otherness, Marginalisation, and Rurality*, ed. Paul J. Cloke and Jo Little (London: Routledge, 1997), 62.

58 Erving Goffman, 'On Fieldwork', *Journal of Contemporary Ethnography* 18, no. 2 (1989): 126–27. Goffman tells his audience – PhD students about to embark on fieldwork – that in order to really exploit a place, 'you've got to be with a range of people, be with the lowest people first. The higher people will "understand", later on, that you were "really" just studying them. But you can't start at the top and move down'.

59 Rapport, *Diverse World-Views in an English Village*, 56.

60 Ibid., 70.

61 Ibid., 69–70.

62 Ibid., 71.

63 James Clifford, 'On Ethnographic Authority', *Representations*, no. 2 (1983): 124.

64 Rapport, *Diverse World-Views in an English Village*, 69–70.

65 Nancy Scheper-Hughes, 'Ire in Ireland', *Ethnography* 1, no. 1 (7 January 2000): 128.

66 Jack Katz, 'Ethnography's Warrants', *Sociological Methods & Research* 25, no. 4 (May 1997): 393.

67 Rapport, *Diverse World-Views in an English Village*, 59.

68 Ibid., 59, my emphasis.

69 Ruth Leys, *From Guilt to Shame: Auschwitz and After* (Princeton, NJ: Princeton University Press, 2007), 126.

70 Ibid., 11.

71 Rapport, *Diverse World-Views in an English Village*, 73.

72 Ibid., 71.

73 Ibid., 1971.

74 Ibid., 73.

75 Jacobs, 'From "Spy-Glass" to "Horizon"', 332.

76 Nancy Scheper-Hughes, *Saints, Scholars and Schizophrenics: Mental Illness in Rural Ireland*, twentieth anniversary, updated and expanded edition (University of California Press, 2001), xv; see also Scheper-Hughes, 'Ire in Ireland'.

77 Scheper-Hughes, *Saints, Scholars and Schizophrenics*, xviii.

78 Ibid., xiv.

79 Rapport, *Diverse World-Views in an English Village*, 59–60.

80 Ibid., 74.

81 Ibid., 73.

82 Perhaps because of his famously cool, detached style of writing, I also experienced reading Goffman in this way, finding *Stigma: Notes on the Management of a Spoiled Identity* as 'filled with a violence that those at whom it is directed would not be able to avoid feeling were they ever to come across it'. Eribon, *Returning to Reims*, 95.

83 Clifford, 'On Ethnographic Authority', 127.

84 Loïc Wacquant, 'Scrutinizing the Street: Poverty, Morality, and the Pitfalls of Urban Ethnography', *American Journal of Sociology* 107, no. 6 (2002): 1480.

85 Charles Wright Mills, *The Sociological Imagination* (Harmondsworth: Penguin, 1959), 6.

86 Nicholas Gane and Les Back, 'C. Wright Mills 50 Years On: The Promise and Craft of Sociology Revisited', *Theory, Culture & Society* 29, no. 7–8 (2012): 405.

87 Ibid., 405.

88 See Aldon Morris, *The Scholar Denied: W.E.B. Du Bois and the Birth of Modern Sociology* (Oakland: University of California Press, 2015), for an account of the segregation of Du Bois' work and that of his Atlantic School from the sociological canon.

89 Du Bois, *The Souls of Black Folk*, 9.

90 Ibid., 9.

91 Ibid., 153.

92 For an account of what I term 'social abjection' see Tyler, *Revolting Subjects*.

93 Dionne Brand, *Convocation 2018: University of Toronto*, 2018, https://www.youtube.com/watch?v=zJKmp6eh6Ag

94 Ibid.

95 Ibid.

96 Dionne Brand, *A Map to the Door of No Return: Notes to Belonging* (Toronto: Vintage Canada, 2001), 25.

Conclusion

1   Quotations from 'Heads Together' are taken from their website https://www.headstogether.org.uk/

2   Charity partners include organisations such as the Campaign Against Living Miserably (CALM), a national charity dedicated to preventing male suicide, and YoungMinds, 'the UK's leading charity championing the wellbeing and mental health of children and young people'.

3   CALM, 'William and Harry in Their Own Words', *CALMzine*, 25 April 2017.

4   Heads Together, 2017.

5   Stephen Hinshaw, *The Mark of Shame: Stigma of Mental Illness and an Agenda for Change* (Oxford: Oxford University Press, 2009), 25.

6   Goffman, *Stigma: Notes on the Management of a Spoiled Identity*, 5.

7   7. For a recent review of the literature on stigma see Bernice A. Pescosolido and Jack K. Martin, 'The Stigma Complex', *Annual Review of Sociology* 41, no. 1 (14 August 2015): 87–116.

8   William Davies, 'On Mental Health, the Royal Family Is Doing More than Our Government', *The Guardian*, 20 April 2017, https://www.theguardian.com/commentisfree/2017/apr/20/mental-health-royal-family-government-children-illness; William Davies, *The Happiness Industry: How the Government and Big Business Sold Us Well-Being* (London: Verso, 2016).

9   Heads Together, 2017.

10   J. Read et al., 'Prejudice and Schizophrenia: A Review of the "Mental Illness Is an Illness like Any Other" Approach', *Acta Psychiatrica Scandinavica* 114, no. 5 (1 November 2006): 304.

11   See for example, Patrick W. Corrigan, 'How Clinical Diagnosis Might Exacerbate the Stigma of Mental Illness', *Social Work* 52, no. 1 (January 2007): 31–39; Lynn C. Holley, Layne K. Stromwall and Kathy E. Bashor, 'Reconceptualizing Stigma: Toward a Critical Anti-Oppression Paradigm', *Stigma Research and Action* 2, no. 2 (31 January 2012); Bonnington and Rose, 'Exploring Stigmatisation'; Brigit McWade, 'Recovery as Policy as a Form of Neoliberal State Making', *Intersectionalities: A Global Journal of Social Work Analysis, Research, Polity, and Practice* 5, no. 3 (2016): 62–81.

12   Davies, 'On Mental Health, the Royal Family Is Doing More than Our Government'; Davies, *The Happiness Industry*.

13   Lucy Costa et al., '"Recovering Our Stories": A Small Act of Resistance', *Studies in Social Justice* 6, no. 1 (16 October 2012): 85.For account of the emerging scholar-activist discipline of 'Mad Studies' see Brenda A. LeFrançois, Robert Menzies and Geoffrey Reaume, eds., *Mad Matters: A Critical Reader in Canadian Mad Studies* (Toronto: Canadian Scholars' Press Inc., 2013).

14   Costa et al., '"Recovering Our Stories"', 85.

15   Ibid., 89.

16   Ibid., 86.

17   Ibid., 87.

18   Ibid., 90; McWade, 'Recovery as Policy as a Form of Neoliberal State Making'.

19 Costa et al., '"Recovering Our Stories"', 96.

20 Ibid., 93.

21 Parker and Aggleton, 'HIV and AIDS-Related Stigma and Discrimination', 17.

22 Theresa May, 'Prime Minister Unveils Plans to Transform Mental Health Support', 2017, https://www.gov.uk/government/news/prime-minister-unveils-plans-to-transform-mental-health-support

23 Ibid.

24 Mary O'Hara, 'Mental Health and Suicide', in *The Violence of Austerity*, ed. Vickie Cooper and David Whyte (London: Pluto Press, 2017), 37.

25 Ibid., 37–38. To take one example, in 2017 an investigation by *Pulse*, a news forum for UK General Practitioners, found that 'increasing numbers of vulnerable children are being refused vital mental health treatment that is recommended by their GP. Figures obtained from 15 mental health trusts revealed that 60% of GP referrals to child and adolescent mental health services (CAMHS) lead to no treatment and a third are not even assessed'. Carolyn Wickware, 'CCGs Cutting Spending on Mental Health despite NHS Pledges', *Pulse*, 25 April 2017, http://www.pulsetoday.co.uk/clinical/mental-health/ccgs-cuttingspending- on-mental-health-despite-nhs-pledges/20034293.article

26 Vikram Dodd, 'Police "Picking up Pieces of Mental Health System", Says Watchdog', *The Guardian*, 27 November 2018, https://www.theguardian.com/society/2018/nov/27/police-mental-health-system-patients

27 Ibid.

28 For the NHS in England, these reforms took legal form in the Health & Social Care Act (2013). On this act and its consequences for the NHS in terms of the privatisation and the fragmentation of services, see Jacky Davis, John Lister and David Wrigley, *NHS for Sale: Myths, Lies & Deception* (London: The Merlin Press, 2015).

29 O'Hara, 'Mental Health and Suicide'; Cooper and Whyte, 'Introduction: The Violence of Austerity'; David Stuckler and Sanjay Basu, *The Body Economic: Why Austerity Kills: Recessions, Budget Battles, and the Politics of Life and Death* (New York: Basic Books, 2013).

30 Ted Schrecker and C. Bambra, *How Politics Makes Us Sick: Neoliberal Epidemics* (Houndmills, Basingstoke: Palgrave Macmillan, 2015), 42.

31 Ibid., 43.

32 Cooper and Whyte, 'Introduction: The Violence of Austerity', 1.

33 Gill Plimmer, 'Virgin Care Sues NHS after Losing Surrey Child Services Deal', *The Financial Times*, 2017, https://www.ft.com/content/297e7714-089f-11e7-97d1-5e720a26771b

34 Ibid.

35 See also Youssef El-Gingihy, *How to Dismantle the NHS in 10 Easy Steps* (Winchester: Zero Books, 2015), 3.

36 Heads Together, 2017.

37 Paul Gilroy, 'Never Again: Refusing Race and Salvaging the Human' (4 June 2019), https://www.holbergprisen.no/en/news/holberg-prize/2019-holberg-lecture-laureate-paul-gilroy

38 Parker and Aggleton, 'HIV and AIDS-Related Stigma and Discrimination', 17.

39 See for example, Mark L. Hatzenbuehler et al., 'Structural Stigma and All-Cause Mortality in Sexual Minority Populations', *Social Science & Medicine*, Structural Stigma and Population Health, 103 (February 2014): 33–41; Alicia Lukachko, Mark L. Hatzenbuehler and Katherine M. Keyes, 'Structural Racism and Myocardial Infarction in the United States', *Social Science & Medicine, Structural Stigma and Population Health*, 103 (February 2014): 42–50.

40 Parker and Aggleton, 'HIV and AIDS-Related Stigma and Discrimination', 14.

41 Franz Kafka, 'In the Penal Colony', in *Franz Kafka: The Complete Short Stories*, trans. Willa Muir (London: Vintage, 2005), 144.

42 Ibid., 140.

43 Ibid., 140.

44 Ibid., 150.

45 Ibid., 145.

46 Ibid., 150.

47 Foucault, *Discipline & Punish*, 138. To give just a few examples of art inspired by 'In the Penal Colony'; the track 'Colony' by post-punk band Joy Division (1980); an opera written by acclaimed US composer Philip Glass (2000); and Iranian film-maker Narges Kalhor's short film *Darkhish* (2009), in which Kafka's machine is reimagined as representing the barbarism of contemporary Iranian prison regimes.

48 Paul Peters, 'Witness to the Execution: Kafka and Colonialism', *Monatshefte* 93, no. 4 (2001): 403.

49 Thomas Pakenham, *The Scramble for Africa: 1876–1912* (London: Abacus, 1995).

50 Anon, 'The Rising in German South-West Africa', *The Times*, 14 November 1904.

51 See Lora Wildenthal, '"When Men Are Weak": The Imperial Feminism of Frieda von Bülow', *Gender & History* 10, no. 1 (April 1998): 53–77. Peters founded the Gesellschaft für deutsche Kolonisation (Society for German Colonisation) in 1884.

52 Lora Wildenthal, *German Women for Empire, 1884–1945*. Politics, History, and Culture (Durham, NC: Duke University Press, 2001), 73.

53 Löwy worked in colonial Panama before being employed in the Congo for a decade. He later worked in the German colony of Tsingtau (now Qingdao) in China. For more on Löwy and his influence on Kafka see Anthony Northey, *Kafka's Relatives: Their Lives and His Writing* (New Haven, CT: Yale University Press, 1991); John Zilcosky, *Kafka's Travels: Exoticism, Colonialism, and the Traffic of Writing* (New York: Palgrave, 2004).

54 Peters, 'Witness to the Execution: Kafka and Colonialism', 403.

55 Quoted in Mark Twain, *King Leopold's Soliloquy: A Defense of His Congo Rule* (Boston, MA: The P.R. Warren Co., 1905), 17. *King Leopold's Soliloquy* (1905) is a political satire written in the form of a fictional monologue in which Leopold speaks in defence of his actions; it quotes extensively from reports

compiled by the Congo Reform Association. European and American activists exposed atrocities in the Congo Free State to the public through the Congo Reform Association, and the work of writers and artists.

56 In ibid., 38.

57 In ibid., 41.

58 Baptist, *The Half Has Never Been Told*, 81.

59 See Zilcosky, *Kafka's Travels*; Peter Neumeyer, 'Franz Kafka, Sugar Baron', *Modern Fiction Studies* 17 (1971): 5–16.

60 See Zilcosky, *Kafka's Travels*; Neumeyer, 'Franz Kafka, Sugar Baron'.

61 Baptist, *The Half Has Never Been Told*, 142.

62 Ibid., 141.

63 Heine was the most important satirical German artist of the period, and co-editor of *Simplicissius*. The archive of this magazine is online here: http://www.simplicissimus.info/index.php?id=5

64 I am drawing here on Albert Memmi, *The Colonizer and the Colonized* (London: Earthscan, 2003).

65 Federici, *Caliban and the Witch*, 146.

66 Kafka, 'In the Penal Colony', 151.

67 Ibid., 146.

68 Ibid., 140.

69 Connor, *The Book of Skin*, 39.

70 Marx, *Capital: A Critique of Political Economy*, 287. On machine breaking see also Thompson, *The Making of the English Working Class*; Linebaugh, *The Magna Carta Manifesto*.

71 Federici, *Caliban and the Witch*, 12.

72 Linebaugh, *The Magna Carta Manifesto*, 106.

73 Ibid., 106.

74 Trouillot, *Silencing the Past*, 77, 76.

75 Ibid., 89.

76 Ibid., 81.

77 Satnam Virdee, 'The Racialized Outsider as the Conscience of Modernity' (British Sociological Association Conference Keynote Lecture, 2019).

78 Carmichael, *Black Power*.

79 McKittrick, 'Yours in the Intellectual Struggle', 3.

80 Virdee, 'The Racialized Outsider as the Conscience of Modernity'.

81 Skeggs, 'Imagining Personhood Differently'.

82 Federici, *Caliban and the Witch*, 9.

83 Virdee, 'The Racialized Outsider as the Conscience of Modernity'.

84 Federici, *Caliban and the Witch*, 12.

85 Ibid., 12.

86 Virdee, 'The Racialized Outsider as the Conscience of Modernity', 3.

87 Ibid., 3.

88 Fred Turner, 'Machine Politics: The Rise of the Internet and a New Age of Authoritarianism', *Harper's Magazine*, 2019, http://fredturner.stanford.edu/wp-content/uploads/Turner-Machine-Politics-Harpers-Magazine-2019-01.pdf

89 Safiya Noble, *Algorithms of Oppression: How Search Engines Reinforce Racism* (New York: New York University Press, 2018).

90 Eubank, *Automating Inequality*.

91 Timothy Snyder, *On Tyranny: Twenty Lessons from the Twentieth Century* (London: Bodley Head, 2017), 71.

92 Piven and Cloward, *Regulating the Poor*, 396.

93 Spillers, *Black, White, and in Color*, 198.

94 Weheliye, *Habeas Viscus*, 3.

95 Yasmin Gunaratnam, 'Intersectional Pain: What I've Learned from Hospices and Feminism of Colour', *Open Democracy*, 4 August 2015.

96 Audre Lorde, 'Learning from the 60s' (February 1982), https://www.blackpast.org/african-american-history/1982-audre-lorde-learning-60s/

97 Angela Davis, *The Meaning of Freedom* (San Francisco, CA: City Lights Books, 2012), 197.

98 See Gilroy, 'Never Again: Refusing Race and Salvaging the Human'.

99 Ibid.

100 Ibid.

Bibliography

Adhikari, Mohamed. '"Streams of Blood and Streams of Money": New Perspectives on the Annihilation of the Herero and Nama Peoples of Namibia, 1904–1908.' *Kronos* 34 (2008): 303–20.

Ahmed-Čermáková, Martina. 'Strach a Hnus v Bělé-Jezové', 2015. http://a2larm. cz/2015/09/strach-a-hnus-v-bele-jezove/

Alexander, Michelle. *The New Jim Crow: Mass Incarceration in the Age of Colorblindness*. New York: The New Press, 2010.

Allen, Robert. *Enclosure and the Yeoman*. Oxford: Clarendon, 1992.

Alston, Philip. 'Statement on Visit to the United Kingdom, by Professor Philip Alston, United Nations Special Rapporteur on Extreme Poverty and Human Rights.' United Nations, 16 November 2018. https://www.ohchr.org/EN/NewsEvents/ Pages/DisplayNews.aspx?NewsID=23881&LangID=E

Alston, Philip. 'Visit to the United Kingdom of Great Britain and Northern Ireland: Report of the Special Rapporteur on Extreme Poverty and Human Rights.' Human Rights Council, United Nations, 2019. https://undocs.org/A/ HRC/41/39/Add.1

Amin, Ash. 'The Remainders of Race.' *Theory, Culture & Society* 27, no. 1 (2010): 1–23.

Amnesty. 'Fenced Out: Hungary's Violations of the Rights of Refugees and Migrants.' London: Amnesty International, 2015. https://www.amnesty.org/ download/Documents/EUR2726142015ENGLISH.pdf

Amnesty International. 'USA: "You Don't Have Any Rights Here"', 2018. https:// www.amnesty.org/en/latest/research/2018/10/usa-treatment-of-asylum-seekers- southern-border/

Anand, Utkarash. 'Police Brutality: SC Asks Punjab, Bihar to Explain.' *The Indian Express* (blog), 7 March 2013. http://indianexpress.com/article/news-archive/ web/police-brutality-sc-asks-punjab-bihar-to-explain/

Anderson, Clare. 'Godna: Inscribing Indian Convicts in the Nineteenth Century.' In *Written on the Body: The Tattoo in European and American History*, 102–17. London: Reaktion, 2000.

Anderson, Clare. *Legible Bodies: Race, Criminality and Colonialism in South Asia*. Oxford: Berg, 2004.

Andrews, Kenneth T., and Michael Biggs. 'The Dynamics of Protest Diffusion: Movement Organizations, Social Networks, and News Media in the 1960 Sit-Ins.' *American Sociological Review* 71, no. 5 (2006): 752–77.

Anon. 'Ashton Warns Workers: Tells Employees He Will Close Shops Forever Rather Than Raise Wages.' *New York Times*, 10 November 1911.

Anon. 'CBI Court Punishes Punjab Police 23 Years after They Tattooed "PICKPOCKET" on the Forehead of Four Women.' *Mail Online India*, 9 October 2016. https://www.dailymail.co.uk/indiahome/indianews/article-3828738/CBI-court-punishes-Punjab-police-23-years-tattooed-PICKPOCKET-forehead-four-women.html

Anon. 'Czech Extremist Adam Bartoš: Put the Refugees in a Former Nazi Concentration Camp.' *Britskelisty*, 2015. http://blisty.cz/art/78865.html

Anon. 'Disabled Patients "Relying on Crowdfunding" for Wheelchairs.' *The Guardian*, 27 June 2017. https://www.theguardian.com/society/2017/jun/27/disabled-patients-relying-on-crowdfunding-for-wheelchairs

Anon. 'Former Czech President Václav Klaus: "Immigration Is Not a Human Right. Europe Is Committing a Suicide".' *Britskelisty*, 2 September 2015. https://blisty.cz/art/78735-former-czech-president-vaclav-klaus-immigration-is-not-a-human-right-europe-is-committing-a-suicide.html

Anon. 'Lancashire Councillors Approve £77m of Service Cuts.' BBC News Website, 15 February 2017. https://www.bbc.co.uk/news/uk-england-lancashire-47250117

Anon. 'Marking Numbers on Refugees' Arms Recalls Holocaust, Italian Jewish Leaders Say.' *Jewish Telegraphic Agency*, 3 September 2015. https://www.jta.org/2015/09/03/global/marking-numbers-on-refugees-arms-recalls-holocaust-italian-jewish-leaders-say

Anon. 'Minister Signals Possibility of Allowing Refugees to Cross Czech Territory to Germany.' *Hello Czech Republic*, 2 September 2015. http://www.czech.cz/en/Vie-Travail/Minister-signals-possibility-of-allowing-refugees

Anon. *Oxford English Dictionary (Online)*. Oxford: Oxford University Press, n.d.

Anon. 'The Rising in German South-West Africa.' *The Times*, 14 November 1904.

Apuleius. *Metamorphoses (The Golden Ass)*. Edited and translated by J. Arthur Hanson. Vol. 2. Cambridge, MA: Harvard University Press, 1996.

Ashworth, Sue. *The Lino King: The Life and Times of Lord Ashton*. Lancaster: Lancashire Museums, 1989.

Back, Les. 'An Ordinary Virtue.' *New Jewish Thought* (blog), 2008. http://research.gold.ac.uk/2326/

Back, Les, and Maggie Tate. 'For a Sociological Reconstruction: W.E.B. Du Bois, Stuart Hall and Segregated Sociology.' *Sociological Research Online* 20, no. 3 (2015): 15. http://www.socresonline.org.uk/20/3/15.html

Badiou, Alain. 'Alain Badiou: Reflections on the Recent Election,' 15 November 2016. https://www.versobooks.com/blogs/2940-alain-badiou-reflections-on-the-recent-election

Baghrian, Sangrur. 'Three Cops Get 3 Years Jail for "Jeb Katri" Tattoo on Forehead – Times of India.' *Times of India*, 9 October 2016. http://timesofindia.indiatimes.com/city/chandigarh/Three-cops-get-3-years-jail-for-jeb-katri-tattoo-on-forehead/articleshow/54758895.cms

Bahadur, Gaiutra. *Coolie Woman: The Odyssey of Indenture*. London: Hurst & Company, 2016.

Bahmueller, Charles. *The National Charity Company: Jeremy Bentham's Silent Revolution*. Berkeley: University of California Press, 1981.

Balani, Sita. 'Apna: One of Our Own.' *Discover Society* (blog), 3 April 2019. https://discoversociety.org/2019/04/03/viewpoint-apna-one-of-our-own/

Baldwin, James. *The Fire Next Time*. London: Penguin, 2017.

Balli, Baljit. 'How Jeb Katri Tattooing Case Became Headlines in 1993 …?' *Babushahi*, 10 October 2016. http://www.babushahi.com/tirchhinazar.php?oid=985

Baptist, Edward. *The Half Has Never Been Told: Slavery and the Making of American Capitalism*. New York: Basic Books, 2014.

Bardsley, Sandy. *Venomous Tongues: Speech and Gender in Late Medieval England*. Philadelphia: University of Pennsylvania Press, 2006.

Barej, Anthony. 'GMB Highlights 1 Million Public Sector Jobs Lost since 2010.' *Public Finance: News and Insight for Public Finance Professionals*, 18 September 2017. https://www.publicfinance.co.uk/news/2017/09/gmb-highlights-1-million-public-sector-jobs-lost-2010

Barr, B., D. Taylor-Robinson, R. Loopstra, A. Reeves, and M. Whitehead. '"First Do No Harm": Are Disability Assessments Associated with Adverse Trends in Mental Health? A Longitudinal Ecological Study.' *Journal of Epidemiology & Community Health* 70, no. 4 (2016): 339–45.

Bauman, Zygmunt. *Modernity and the Holocaust*. Ithaca, NY: Cornell University Press, 1989.

Bauman, Zygmunt. 'The Crisis of the Human Waste Disposal Industry.' *Tikkun* 17, no. 5 (2002): 41–47.

BBC News. 'Indian Groups Raise Caste Question.' *BBC News Website*, 6 September 2001. http://news.bbc.co.uk/1/hi/world/south_asia/1528181.stm

Beard, Mary. *Women & Power: A Manifesto*. London: Profile, 2017.

Benson, Christopher, and Mamie Till-Mobley. *Death of Innocence: The Story of the Hate Crime That Changed America*. New York: Ballantine, 2003.

Bentham, Jeremy. *The Collected Works of Jeremy Bentham: Writings on the Poor Laws, Vol. 1*. Edited by Michael Quinn. Oxford: Oxford University Press, 2001.

Bentham, Jeremy. 'Tracts on Poor Laws and Pauper Management.' In *The Works of Jeremy Bentham, Volume 8*, edited by John Bowring. Edinburgh: William Tait, 1841.

Bentham, Jeremy. *View of the Hard Labour Bill: Draft of a Bill, to Punish by Imprisonment and Hard-Labour, Certain Offenders; and to Establish Proper Places for Their Reception*. London: T. Payne and Son, 1778.

Bhambra, Gurminder K. 'A Sociological Dilemma: Race, Segregation and US Sociology.' *Current Sociology* 62, no. 4 (2014): 472–92.

Bhambra, Gurminder K. *Connected Sociologies*. London: Bloomsbury, 2014.

Bhambra, Gurminder K., and John Holmwood. 'Colonialism, Postcolonialism and the Liberal Welfare State.' *New Political Economy* 23, no. 5 (2018): 574–87.

Bhambra, Gurminder K., Dalia Gebrial, and Kerem Nişancıoğlu. 'Introduction: Decolonising the University?' In *Decolonising the University*, edited by Gurminder K. Bhambra, Dalia Gebrial, and Kerem Nişancıoğlu, 1–18. Chicago: Pluto Press, 2018.

Bhattacharyya, Gargi. *Rethinking Racial Capitalism: Questions of Reproduction and Survival*. Cultural Studies and Marxism. Lanham, MD: Rowman & Littlefield Publishers, 2018.

Bijoy, C.R. 'Adivasis of India: A History of Discrimination, Conflict and Resistance.' In *This Is Our Homeland: A Collection of Essays on the Betrayal of Adivasi Rights in India*, 16–28. Bangalore: Equations, 2007.

Biondi, Martha. *The Black Revolution on Campus*. Berkeley: University of California Press, 2014.

Biray, Kurt. 'Communist Nostalgia in Eastern Europe: Longing for the Past.' *Open Democracy*, 10 November 2015. https://www.opendemocracy.net/en/can-europe-make-it/communist-nostalgia-in-eastern-europe-longing-for-past/

Blanden, Adam. 'Central and Eastern Europe as Playground of a Conservative Avant-Garde.' *Open Democracy*, 3 October 2015. https://www.opendemocracy.net/en/can-europe-make-it/central-and-eastern-europe-as-playground-of-conservative-avant-garde/

Boggs, James. *Pages from a Black Radical's Notebook: A James Boggs Reader*. Edited by Stephen M. Ward. Detroit: Wayne State University Press, 2011.

Bonnington, Oliver, and Diana Rose. 'Exploring Stigmatisation among People Diagnosed with Either Bipolar Disorder or Borderline Personality Disorder: A Critical Realist Analysis.' *Social Science & Medicine* 123 (2014): 7–17.

Boose, Lynda. 'Scolding Brides and Bridling Scolds: Taming the Woman's Unruly Member.' *Shakespeare Quarterly* 42, no. 2 (1991): 179–213.

Booth, Robert. 'UN Poverty Expert Hits Back over UK Ministers' "Denial of Facts".' *The Guardian*, 24 May 2019. https://www.theguardian.com/society/2019/may/24/un-poverty-expert-hits-back-over-uk-ministers-denial-of-facts-philip-alston

Booy, David, ed. *Personal Disclosures: An Anthology of Self-Writings from the Seventeenth Century*. Early Modern Englishwoman, 1500–1750. Aldershot: Ashgate, 2002.

Bourdieu, Pierre. *Practical Reason: On the Theory of Action*. Stanford, CA: Stanford University Press, 1998.

Boyd, Herb. *We Shall Overcome with 2 Audio CDs: The History of the Civil Rights Movement as It Happened*. Naperville, IL: Sourcebooks MediaFusion, 2004.

Brand, Dionne. *A Map to the Door of No Return: Notes to Belonging*. Toronto: Vintage Canada, 2001.

Brand, Dionne. *Convocation 2018: University of Toronto*, 2018. https://www.youtube.com/watch?v=zJKmp6eh6Ag

Bridgman, Jon, and Leslie Worley. 'Genocide of the Hereros.' In *Century of Genocide: Critical Essays and Eyewitness Accounts*, edited by Samuel Totten, William Parsons, and Israel Charny, 15–50. New York: Routledge, 2004.

Browne, Simone. *Dark Matters: On the Surveillance of Blackness*. Durham, NC: Duke University Press, 2015.

Bruce, George James. *Brazil and the Brazilians, Portrayed in Historical and Descriptive Sketches*. London: Methuen, 1915.

Brueck, Laura. *Writing Resistance: The Rhetorical Imagination of Hindi Dalit Literature*. New York: Columbia University Press, 2014.

Bruff, Ian, and Cemal Burak Tansel. 'Authoritarian Neoliberalism: Trajectories of Knowledge Production and Praxis.' *Globalizations* 16, no. 3 (16 April 2019): 233–44.

Brune, Jeffrey, Rosemarie Garland-Thomson, Susan Schweik, Tanya Titchkosky, and Heather Love. 'Forum Introduction: Reflections on the Fiftieth Anniversary of Erving Goffman's Stigma.' *Disability Studies Quarterly* 34, no. 1 (2 January 2014). http://dsq-sds.org/article/view/4014

Bulman, May. 'Life Expectancy of Poorest Girls in England Falls for First Time on Record since 1920s, Figures Show.' *The Independent*, 2018. https://www.independent.co.uk/news/uk/home-news/life-expectancy-poorest-girls-women-england-ons-a8235471.html

Burdick, John. *Blessed Anastácia: Women, Race, and Popular Christianity in Brazil.* New York: Routledge, 1998.

Burke, Jason, and Philip Oltermann. 'Germany Moves to Atone for "Forgotten Genocide" in Namibia.' *The Guardian*, 25 December 2016. https://www.theguardian.com/world/2016/dec/25/germany-moves-to-atone-for-forgotten-genocide-in-namibia

Butler, Judith. *Giving an Account of Oneself.* New York: Fordham University Press, 2005.

Butler, Patrick. 'Lives Will Be Lost If Plans to Slash Housing Support Services Go Ahead, Charities Warn.' *The Guardian*, 20 February 2019. https://www.theguardian.com/society/2019/feb/20/lives-lost-housing-cuts-rough-sleepers-west-sussex-homeless

Butler, Patrick. 'More than 8 Million in UK Struggle to Put Food on Table, Survey Says.' *The Guardian*, 6 May 2016. https://www.theguardian.com/society/2016/may/06/more-than-8-million-in-uk-struggle-to-put-food-on-table-survey-says

CALM. 'William and Harry in Their Own Words.' *CALMzine*, 25 April 2017.

Cameron, David. 'PM's Speech on Welfare Reform Bill.' House of Commons, Westminster, 17 February 2011. https://www.gov.uk/government/speeches/pms-speech-on-welfare-reform-bill

Canales, Jimena, and Andrew Herscher. 'Criminal Skins: Tattoos and Modern Architecture in the Work of Adolf Loos.' *Architectural History* 48 (2005): 235–256.

Caplan, Jane. 'Introduction.' In *Written on the Body: The Tattoo in European and American History*, edited by Jane Caplan. London: Reaktion, 2000.

Caplan, Jane. *Speaking Scars – The Tattoo.* Museum of London, 2014. https://www.gresham.ac.uk/lectures-and-events/speaking-scars-the-tattoo

Caplan, Jane, and John Torpey, eds. *Documenting Individual Identity: The Development of State Practices in the Modern World.* Princeton, NJ: Princeton University Press, 2001.

Carmichael, Stokely. *Black Power.* University of Berkeley, 1966. https://www.youtube.com/watch?v=dFFWTsUqEaY

Carmichael, Stokely, and Charles Hamilton. *Black Power: The Politics of Liberation in America.* New York: Vintage, 1992.

Carroll, Rory. 'Woman at Center of Emmett Till Case Tells Author She Fabricated Testimony.' *The Guardian*, 27 January 2017. https://www.theguardian.com/us-news/2017/jan/27/emmett-till-book-carolyn-bryant-confession

Carson, Anne. 'Euripides to the Audience.' *London Review of Books*, September 2002. https://www.lrb.co.uk/v24/n17/anne-carson/euripides-to-the-audience

Cerese, Rebecca, and Steven Channing. *February One: The Story of the Greensboro Four*. Documentary. Independent Lens, 2003. http://www.pbs.org/independentlens/

Cernušáková, Barbora. 'Trains to Nowhere – Hungary's Harsh Welcome for Refugees.' *Amnesty International* (blog), 4 September 2015. https://www.amnesty.org/en/latest/news/2015/09/trains-to-nowhere-hungary-harsh-welcome-for-refugees/

Chase, Elaine, and Robert Walker. 'The Co-Construction of Shame in the Context of Poverty: Beyond a Threat to the Social Bond.' *Sociology* 47, no. 4 (1 August 2013): 739–54.

Chemla, Véronique. 'Le Premier Génocide Du XXe Siècle: Herero et Nama Dans Le Sud-Ouest Africain Allemand, 1904–1908.' *Véronique Chemla* (blog), 24 April 2019. http://www.informaction.info/iframe-le-premier-genocide-du-xxe-siecle

Christie, Ian. 'Samuel Bentham and the Western Colony at Krichev.' *The Slavonic and East European Review* 48, no. 111 (1970): 232–47.

Clarke, John. *Changing Welfare, Changing States*. London: Sage, 2004.

Clifford, James. 'On Ethnographic Authority.' *Representations*, no. 2 (1983): 118–46.

Cobbett, William. *Cobbett's Political Register*. Vol. 30. London: Cox and Baylis, 1816.

Collins, Patricia Hill. 'Pushing the Boundaries or Business as Usual? Race, Class, and Gender Studies and Sociological Inquiry.' In *Sociology in America: A History*, edited by Craig Calhoun, 572–604. Chicago: Chicago University Press, 2007.

Connor, Phillip. 'Number of Refugees to Europe Surges to Record 1.3 Million in 2015.' Pew Research Centre, 2016. https://www.pewresearch.org/global/2016/08/02/number-of-refugees-to-europe-surges-to-record-1-3-million-in-2015/

Connor, Steven. *The Book of Skin*. Ithaca, NY: Cornell University Press, 2004.

Cook, James. *Captain Cook's Journal during the First Voyage around the World*. London: Elliot Stock, 1893.

Cooper, Vickie, and David Whyte. 'Introduction: The Violence of Austerity.' In *The Violence of Austerity*, 1–31. London: Pluto Press, 2017.

Corrigan, Patrick W. 'How Clinical Diagnosis Might Exacerbate the Stigma of Mental Illness.' *Social Work* 52, no. 1 (January 2007): 31–39.

Costa, Lucy, Jijian Voronka, Danielle Landry, Jenna Reid, Becky Mcfarlane, David Reville, and Kathryn Church. '"Recovering Our Stories": A Small Act of Resistance.' *Studies in Social Justice* 6, no. 1 (16 October 2012): 85–101.

Coulombeau, Sophie. *Jeremy Bentham's Universal Tattoo*. New Generation Thinkers, 2014. https://www.bbc.co.uk/programmes/p020v6gb

Crabb, George. *English Synonyms Explained, in Alphabetical Order*. London: Baldwin, Cradock, and Joy and T. Boosey, 1816.

Crenshaw, Kimberlé Williams. 'Race, Reform and Retrenchment.' In *Theories of Race and Racism: A Reader*, edited by Les Back and Jon Solomos, 549–60. London: Routledge, 2009.

Čulík, Jan. 'Why Is the Czech Republic so Hostile to Muslims and Refugees?' *Europe Now*, 2017. http://www.europenowjournal.org/2017/02/09/why-is-the-czech-republic-so-hostile-to-muslims-and-refugees/#_edn34

'Czech President Miloš Zeman Says Refugees Are Like a "Tsunami That Will Kill Him".' *Huffington Post*, 1 September 2015. http://www.huffingtonpost.co.uk/2015/09/01/eu-migrant-crisis-refugees-tsunami-czech_n_8069350.html

Dabydeen, David. 'The Black Figure in 18th-Century Art.' BBC History, 2011. https://www.bbc.co.uk/history/british/abolition/africans_in_art_gallery_01.shtml

Daguerre, Anne, and David Etherington. 'Workfare in 21st Century Britain: The Erosion of Rights to Social Assistance.' Middlesex University, November 2014. http://workfare.org.uk/images/uploads/docs/Workfare_in_21st_century_Britain-Final.pdf

Dalit Panthers. 'Dalit Panthers Manifesto.' Bombay, 1973. http://democracyandclassstruggle.blogspot.com/2016/01/india-dalit-panthers-manifesto-bombay.html

Dalrymple, William. 'The East India Company: The Original Corporate Raiders.' *The Guardian*, 4 March 2015. https://www.theguardian.com/world/2015/mar/04/east-india-company-original-corporate-raiders

Davies, William. 'On Mental Health, the Royal Family Is Doing More than Our Government.' *The Guardian*, 20 April 2017. https://www.theguardian.com/commentisfree/2017/apr/20/mental-health-royal-family-government-children-illness

Davies, William. *The Happiness Industry: How the Government and Big Business Sold Us Well-Being*. London: Verso, 2016.

Davis, Angela. 'Political Prisoners, Prisons, and Black Revolution.' In *Voices of a People's History of the United States*, 494–98. New York: Seven Stories Press, 2010.

Davis, Angela. *The Meaning of Freedom*. San Francisco, CA: City Lights Books, 2012.

Davis, Jacky, John Lister, and David Wrigley. *NHS for Sale: Myths, Lies & Deception*. London: The Merlin Press, 2015.

De Benedictis, Sara, Kim Allen, and Tracey Jensen. 'Portraying Poverty: The Economics and Ethics of Factual Welfare Television.' *Cultural Sociology* 11, no. 3 (September 2017): 337–58.

De Certeau, Michel. *The Practice of Everyday Life*. Translated by Steven Rendall. Berkeley: University of California Press, 1984.

Dean, Jodi. *The Communist Horizon*. London: Verso, 2012.

Dean, Mitchell. *The Constitution of Poverty: Toward a Genealogy of Liberal Governance*. Repr. Routledge Revivals. London: Routledge, 2012.

Derrida, Jacques. 'Racism's Last Word.' *Critical Inquiry* 12, no. 1 (1985): 290–299.

Devine, Tom, ed. *Recovering Scotland's Slavery Past: The Caribbean Connection*. Edinburgh: Edinburgh University Press, 2015.

Dhattiwala, Raheel, and Michael Biggs. 'The Political Logic of Ethnic Violence: The Anti-Muslim Pogrom in Gujarat 2002.' *Politics and Society* 40, no. 4 (2012): 483–516.

Dodd, Vikram. 'Police "Picking up Pieces of Mental Health System", Says Watchdog.' *The Guardian*, 27 November 2018. https://www.theguardian.com/society/2018/nov/27/police-mental-health-system-patients

Dorney, Sean. *Papua New Guinea: People Politics and History since 1975*. Milsons Point, NSW: Random House Australia, 1990.

Dotson, Kristie. 'Tracking Epistemic Violence, Tracking Practices of Silencing.' *Hypatia* 26, no. 2 (2011): 236–257.

Dowler, Elizabeth, and Hannah Lambie-Mumford. 'Introduction: Hunger, Food and Social Policy in Austerity.' *Social Policy and Society* 14, no. 3 (2015): 411–15.

Du Bois, W.E.B. *Dusk of Dawn: An Essay Toward an Autobiography of a Race Concept*. Oxford: Oxford University Press, 2007.

Du Bois, W.E.B. 'On Being Ashamed of Oneself: An Essay on Race Pride.' *The Crisis: A Record of the Darker Races*. New York: Crisis Publishing Co., 1933.

Du Bois, W.E.B. *The Souls of Black Folk*. New Haven: The Pennsylvania State University Electronic Classics, 2006.

Du Bois, W.E.B. 'The Looking Glass.' *The Crisis: A Record of the Darker Races*. December 1916.

DuBois, Page. *Slaves and Other Objects*. Chicago: University of Chicago Press, 2008.

DuBois, Page. *Torture and Truth*. New York: Routledge, 1991.

Duncan Smith, Iain. 'Iain Duncan Smith: Labour Only Stands for Welfare Dependency.' *The Telegraph*, 15 February 2015. https://www.telegraph.co.uk/news/politics/comment/11413813/Iain-Duncan-Smith-Labour-only-stands-for-welfare-dependency.html

Duncan Smith, Iain, and Philip Davies. House of Commons Hansard (2014). https://hansard.parliament.uk/Commons/2014-01-13/debates/14011313000027/TopicalQuestions?highlight=%22benefits%20street%22#contribution-14011313000180

Edwards, Michael. 'The Housing Crisis and London.' *City* 20, no. 1 (2016): 222–37.

Elder, Melinda. 'The Liverpool Slave Trade, Lancaster and Its Environs.' In *Liverpool and Transatlantic Slavery*, edited by David Richardson, Suzanne Schwarz, and Anthony Tibbles, 118–37. Liverpool: Liverpool University Press, 2007.

Elder, Melinda. *The Slave Trade and the Economic Development of 18th Century Lancaster*. Edinburgh: Edinburgh University Press, 1992.

El-Gingihy, Youssef. *How to Dismantle the NHS in 10 Easy Steps*. Winchester: Zero Books, 2015.

Elias, Ruth. *Triumph of Hope: From Theresienstadt and Auschwitz to Israel*. Translated by Margot Bettauer Dembo. New York: John Wiley & Sons, 1999.

Emejulu, Akwugo, and Leah Bassel. 'Women of Colour's Anti-Austerity Activism.' In *The Violence of Austerity*, edited by Vickie Cooper and David Whyte, 117–22. London: Pluto Press, 2017.

Eribon, Didier. *Returning to Reims*. London: Allen Lane, 2018.

Eubank, Virginia. *Automating Inequality: How High-Tech Tools Profile, Police, and Punish the Poor*. London: Picador, 2019.

Euchner, Charles. 'Roy Wilkins's Reluctant Tribute to W.E.B. Du Bois.' *Beacon Broadside* (blog), 2010. https://www.beaconbroadside.com/broadside/2010/08/excerpt-roy-wilkinss-reluctant-tribute-to-web-du-bois.html

'European Islamophobia Report 2017.' Turkey: SETA: Foundation for Political, Economic and Social Research, 2018. https://www.islamophobiaeurope.com/wp-content/uploads/2018/04/EIR_2017.pdf

Ewbank, Thomas. 'Cruelty to Slaves.' In *The Brazil Reader: History, Culture, Politics*, edited by Thomas Levine and John Crocitti, 138–42. Durham, NC: Duke University Press, 1999.

Fanon, Frantz. *Black Skin, White Masks*. London: Pluto Press, 1986.

Fanon, Frantz. *The Wretched of the Earth*. London: Penguin Classics, 2001.

Feagin, Joe, and Zinobia Bennefield. 'Systemic Racism and U.S. Health Care.' *Social Science & Medicine* 103 (2014): 7–14.

Federici, Silvia. *Caliban and the Witch: Women, the Body and Primitive Accumulation*. Brooklyn, NY: Autonomedia, 2004.

Federici, Silvia. *Re-Enchanting the World: Feminism and the Politics of the Commons*. Kairos. Oakland, CA: PM, 2019.

Fella, Stefano, and Carlo Ruzza. 'Understanding European Anti-Racisms.' In *Anti-Racist Movements in the EU: Between Europeanisation and National Trajectories*, 209–40. Chippenham: Palgrave Macmillan, 2013.

Ferguson, Roderick A. *Aberrations in Black: Towards a Queer of Color Critique*. Minneapolis: University of Minnesota Press, 2003.

Fields, Karen, and Barbara J. Fields. *Racecraft: The Soul of Inequality in American Life*. London: Verso, 2012.

Fleming, Crystal M., and Aldon Morris. 'Theorizing Ethnic and Racial Movements in the Global Age: Lessons from the Civil Rights Movement.' *Sociology of Race and Ethnicity* 1, no. 1 (2015): 105–26.

Flemr, Jan. 'Czech Police Spark Uproar by Tagging Refugees with Numbers.' *Times of Israel*, 2 September 2015. http://www.timesofisrael.com/czech-police-spark-uproar-by-tagging-refugees-with-numbers/

Foster, Peter. 'One Year Ago, Angela Merkel Dared to Stand up for Refugees in Europe. Who Else Even Tried?' *The Telegraph*, 24 August 2016. http://www.telegraph.co.uk/news/2016/08/24/one-year-ago-angela-merkel-dared-to-stand-up-for-refugees-in-eur/

Foucault, Michel. *Discipline & Punish: The Birth of the Prison*. Translated by Alan Sheridan. New York: Vintage, 1995.

Foucault, Michel. 'Nietzsche, Genealogy, History.' In *The Foucault Reader: An Introduction to Foucault's Thought*, edited by Paul Rabinow, 76–100. London: Penguin, 1991.

Fox, Pamela. *Class Fictions: Shame and Resistance in the British Working-Class Novel, 1890–1945*. Post-Contemporary Interventions. Durham, NC: Duke University Press, 1994.

Freeman, Jo. *At Berkeley in the Sixties: The Education of an Activist, 1961–1965.* Bloomington: Indiana University Press, 2004.

Friedman, Howard. 'America's Looming Demographic Challenge.' *The Huffington Post* (blog), 2013. https://www.huffpost.com/entry/americas-looming-demograp_b_3422807?guccounter=1&guce_referrer=aHR0cHM6Ly93d3cuZ29vZ2xlLmNvbS88&guce_referrer_sig=AQAAACCH0GFZbn8EbU33LeqxpKpabxWlIJlPCClT7JhVqEgqrohkC7FkfJvJLmPYL52_iVhI6iHL5VF0tV2_a0v6fw6bzC-C3_lTKKlT8mNpOApCsLvBux7YT0qgO325GhpN0AkTuM_1puAWFZTy9gGEJZN3yAiw8lkcwuaxKsUoj6a6

Fuller, C.J. 'Ethnographic Inquiry in Colonial India: Herbert Risley, William Crooke, and the Study of Tribes and Castes: Ethnographic Inquiry in Colonial India.' *Journal of the Royal Anthropological Institute* 23, no. 3 (2017): 603–21.

Gagi, Agnes, Tamás Gerőcs, Linda Szabó, and Márton Szarvas. 'Beyond Moral Interpretations of the EU "Migration Crisis": Hungary and the Global Economic Division of Labor.' *LeftEast*, 2016. http://www.criticatac.ro/lefteast/beyond-moral-interpretations-of-hu-eu-migration-crisis/

Gall, Lydia. 'Hungary's War on Refugees,' 2016. https://www.hrw.org/news/2016/09/16/hungarys-war-refugees

Gandee, Sarah. 'August 2017 Marks More than One Independence Day in India.' *History Workshop* (blog), 8 August 2017. http://www.historyworkshop.org.uk/august-2017-marks-more-than-one-independence-day-in-india/

Gane, Nicholas, and Les Back. 'C. Wright Mills 50 Years On: The Promise and Craft of Sociology Revisited.' *Theory, Culture & Society* 29, no. 7–8 (2012): 399–421.

Gardiner, Ralph. *England's Grievance Discovered.* London: R. Ibbitson, 1655.

Garfinkel, Harold. 'Conditions of Successful Degradation Ceremonies.' *American Journal of Sociology* 61, no. 5 (1956): 420–24.

Garside, Juliette. 'Recession Rich: Britain's Wealthiest Double Net Worth since Crisis.' *The Guardian*, 26 April 2015. https://www.theguardian.com/business/2015/apr/26/recession-rich-britains-wealthiest-double-net-worth-since-crisis

Gedye, George. *Fallen Bastions: The Central European Tragedy.* London: Victor Gollancz, 1939.

Gentes, Andrew. *Exile, Murder and Madness in Siberia, 1823–61.* London: Palgrave Macmillan, 2010.

German History in Documents and Images. 'The Eternal Jew [Der Ewige Jude] Film Poster 1940.' *German Historical Institute Washington* (blog), n.d. http://ghdi.ghi-dc.org/sub_image.cfm?image_id=2331

Gerzina, Gretchen. *Black England: Life before Emancipation.* London: John Murray, 1995.

Gilmore, Ruth Wilson. *Golden Gulag: Prisons, Surplus, Crisis, and Opposition in Globalizing California.* Berkeley: University of California Press, 2007.

Gilroy, Paul. 'Never Again: Refusing Race and Salvaging the Human.' Paper presented at the 2019 Holberg Lecture, by Laureate Paul Gilroy, 4 June 2019. https://www.holbergprisen.no/en/news/holberg-prize/2019-holberg-lecture-laureate-paul-gilroy

Gilroy, Paul. 'Race and Racism in "the Age of Obama".' The Tenth Annual Eccles Centre for American Studies Plenary Lecture given at the British Association for American Studies Annual Conference. London: British Library, 2013.

Gilroy, Paul. *There Ain't No Black in the Union Jack: The Cultural Politics of Race and Nation.* London: Routledge, 2002.

Glissant, Edouard. *Caribbean Discourse: Selected Essays.* Translated by J. Michael Dash. CARAF Books. Charlottesville: University Press of Virginia, 1999.

Goffman, Érving. *Asylums: Essays on the Social Situation of Mental Patients and Other Inmates.* Chicago: Aldine, 1962.

Goffman, Erving. 'On Fieldwork.' *Journal of Contemporary Ethnography* 18, no. 2 (1989): 123–32.

Goffman, Erving. *Stigma: Notes on the Management of a Spoiled Identity.* New York: Simon & Schuster, 1986.

Goffman, Erving. 'The Interaction Order: American Sociological Association, 1982 Presidential Address.' *American Sociological Review* 48, no. 1 (1983): 1–17.

Goffman, Erving. *The Presentation of Self in Everyday Life.* Edinburgh: Social Science Research Centre, University of Edinburgh, 1956; New York: Doubleday, 1959; Repr. London: Penguin, 1990.

Gopal, Priyamvada. 'Narendra Modi: Britain Can't Simply Shrug off This Hindu Extremist.' *The Guardian*, 14 April 2014. https://www.theguardian.com/commentisfree/2014/apr/14/narendra-modi-extremism-india

Gordon, Avery. *Ghostly Matters: Haunting and the Sociological Imagination.* Minneapolis: University of Minnesota Press, 1997.

Gordon, Avery. 'Some Thoughts on Haunting and Futurity.' *Borderlands* 10, no. 2 (2011). http://www.borderlands.net.au/vol10no2_2011/gordon_thoughts.pdf

Gordon, Lewis. 'Is the Human a Teleological Suspension of Man? Phenomenological Exploration of Sylvia Wynter's Fanonian and Biodicean Reflections.' In *After Man, Towards the Human: Critical Essays on the Thought of Sylvia Wynter*, edited by Anthony Bogues, 237–57. Kingston, JA: Ian Randle, 2006.

Gordon, Lewis. *What Fanon Said: A Philosophical Introduction to His Life and Thought.* London: Hurst & Company, 2015.

Gorringe, Hugo. 'Subaltern Politics and Dalit Studies.' *The Journal of Imperial and Commonwealth History* 37, no. 1 (2009): 151–55.

Gramsci, Antonio. *Selections from the Prison Notebooks of Antonio Gramsci.* Translated by Quintin Hoare and Geoffrey Nowell Smith. London: Lawrence & Wishart, 1971.

Gray, Mia, and Anna Barford. 'The Depths of the Cuts: The Uneven Geography of Local Government Austerity.' *Cambridge Journal of Regions, Economy and Society* 11, no. 3 (2018): 541–63.

Grover, Chris. 'Violent Proletarianisation: Social Murder, the Reserve Army of Labour and Social Security "Austerity" in Britain.' *Critical Social Policy* 39, no. 3 (2019): 335–55.

Gunaratnam, Yasmin. 'Intersectional Pain: What I've Learned from Hospices and Feminism of Colour.' *Open Democracy*, 4 August 2015.

Gundimeda, Sambaiah. *Dalit Politics in Contemporary India*. New York: Routledge, 2016.

Guru, Gopal. *Humiliation: Claims and Context*. New Delhi: Oxford University Press, 2011.

Guru, Gopal. 'The Language of Dalit-Bahujan Political Discourse.' In *Dalit Identity and Politics: Cultural Subordination and the Dalit Challenge*, edited by Ghanshyam Shah, 97–107. New Delhi: Sage, 2001.

Gustafson, Mark. 'Tattooing.' In *The Historical Encyclopedia of World Slavery*, edited by Junius Rodriguez, 1:629. Santa Barbara, CA: ABC-CLIO, 1997.

Gustafson, Mark. 'The Tattoo in the Later Roman Empire and Beyond.' In *Written on the Body: The Tattoo in European and American History*, edited by Jane Caplan, 17–31. London: Reaktion, 2000.

Hacking, Ian. *Historical Ontology*. Cambridge, MA: Harvard University Press, 2004.

Haijer, Friederycke. 'Human Rights and Dignity of Dalit Women.' Netherlands: Report of the Conference in The Hague, 2006. http://www.indianet.nl/pdf/humanrightsdalitwomen.pdf

Hall, Catherine. 'Gendering Property, Racing Capital.' *History Workshop Journal* 78, no. 1 (2014): 22–38.

Hall, Catherine. 'Gendering Property, Racing Capital.' In *History after Hobsbawm: Writing the Past for the Twenty-First Century*, 17–34. Oxford: Oxford University Press, 2018.

Hall, Stuart. 'Race, the Floating Signifier.' 1997. https://www.mediaed.org/transcripts/Stuart-Hall-Race-the-Floating-Signifier-Transcript.pdf

Hall, Stuart. 'Racism and Reaction.' In *Stuart Hall, Selected Political Writings: The Great Moving Right Show and Other Essays*, edited by Sally Davison, David Featherstone, and Bill Schwarz, 142–57. London: Lawrence and Wishart, 2017.

Hall, Stuart. 'The Great Moving Right Show.' In *Stuart Hall, Selected Political Writings: The Great Moving Right Show and Other Essays*, edited by Sally Davison, David Featherstone, and Bill Schwarz, 172–86. London: Lawrence and Wishart, 2017.

Hall, Stuart. *The Hard Road to Renewal: Thatcherism and the Crisis of the Left*. London: Verso, 1988.

Hall, Stuart, and Sut Jhally. 'The Last Interview: Stuart Hall on the Politics of Cultural Studies.' *Media Education Foundation*, 2016. https://www.mediaed.org/transcripts/The-Last-Interview-Transcript.pdf

Hall, Stuart, and Alan O'Shea. 'Common-Sense Neoliberalism.' *Soundings* 55, no. 55 (13 December 2013): 9–25.

Hamm, Patrick, Lawrence King, and David Stuckler. 'Mass Privatization, State Capacity, and Economic Growth in Postcommunist Countries.' *American Sociological Review* 77, no. 2 (2012): 295–324.

Haraway, Donna. *Donna Haraway Reads The National Geographic on Primates*, 1987. https://www.youtube.com/watch?v=eLN2ToEIlwM

Haraway, Donna. *The Haraway Reader*. New York: Routledge, 2004.

Hatzenbuehler, Mark L., Anna Bellatorre, Yeonjin Lee, Brian K. Finch, Peter Muennig, and Kevin Fiscella. 'Structural Stigma and All-Cause Mortality in Sexual Minority Populations.' *Social Science & Medicine*, Structural Stigma and Population Health, 103 (February 2014): 33–41.

Hay, Iain, and Samantha Muller. 'Questioning Generosity in the Golden Age of Philanthropy: Towards Critical Geographies of Super-Philanthropy.' *Progress in Human Geography* 38, no. 5 (October 2014): 635–53.

Haywood, Harry. *Negro Liberation*. New York: International Publishers, 1948.

Henry, Nicola, and Anastasia Powell. 'Technology-Facilitated Sexual Violence: A Literature Review of Empirical Research.' *Trauma, Violence, & Abuse* 19, no. 2 (April 2018): 195–208.

Hills, John. *Good Times, Bad Times: The Welfare Myth of Them and Us*. Bristol: Policy Press, 2014.

Himmelfarb, Gertrude. 'Bentham's Utopia: The National Charity Company.' *Journal of British Studies* 10, no. 1 (1970): 80–125.

Hinshaw, Stephen. *The Mark of Shame: Stigma of Mental Illness and an Agenda for Change: Stigma of Mental Illness and an Agenda for Change*. Oxford: Oxford University Press, 2009.

Hochschild, Adam. *King Leopold's Ghost: A Story of Greed, Terror and Heroism in Colonial Africa*. London: Pan, 2012.

Hodges, Dan. 'The 900 Refugees Drowned in the Mediterranean Were Killed by British Government Policy.' *The Telegraph*, 20 April 2015. https://www. telegraph.co.uk/news/general-election-2015/politics-blog/11549721/The-900-refugees-dead-in-the-Mediterranean-were-killed-by-British-government-policy. html

Holley, Lynn C., Layne K. Stromwall, and Kathy E. Bashor. 'Reconceptualizing Stigma: Toward a Critical Anti-Oppression Paradigm.' *Stigma Research and Action* 2, no. 2 (31 January 2012).

Howard, William. *My Diary, North and South*. Boston: T.O.H.P. Burnham, 1863.

Howarth, Caroline. 'Race as Stigma: Positioning the Stigmatized as Agents, Not Objects.' *Journal of Community and Applied Social Psychology* 16, no. 6 (2006): 442–45.

Hrabal, Michal. 'Kdy Si Ty Stany Odvezete? Ptala Se Žena Na Setkání s Lidmi z Ministerstva.' *Breclavsky Denik.Cz*, September 2015. https://breclavsky.denik. cz/zpravy_region/kdy-si-ty-stany-odvezete-ptala-se-zena-na-setkani-s-lidmi-z-ministerstva-20150908.html

Human Rights Watch. 'Hidden Apartheid: Caste Discrimination against India's "Untouchables".' Human Rights Watch, 12 February 2007. https://www.hrw. org/report/2007/02/12/hidden-apartheid/caste-discrimination-against-indias-untouchables#_ftn38

Hunt, Paul. 'A Critical Condition.' In *Stigma: The Experience of Disability*, edited by Paul Hunt, 145–49. London: Geoffrey Chapman, 1966.

Hurston, Zora Neale. *Barracoon: The Story of the Last Slave*. London: Harper Collins, 2018.

Infomobile. 'Greek Authorities Mark Arms of in Crete Stranded Syrian Refugees with Registration Numbers.' *Infomobile: Information with, about and for Refugees in Greece* (blog), 15 May 2015. http://infomobile.w2eu.net/2015/05/15/greek-authorities-mark-arms-of-in-crete-stranded-syrian-refugees-with-registration-numbers/

Isaac, Benjamin. *The Invention of Racism in Classical Antiquity*. Princeton, NJ: Princeton University Press, 2004.

Isaac, Jeffrey. 'Is There Illiberal Democracy? A Problem with No Semantic Solution.' *Eurozine*, 9 August 2017. https://www.eurozine.com/is-there-illiberal-democracy/

Jacobs, Karen. 'From "Spy-Glass" to "Horizon": Tracking the Anthropological Gaze in Zora Neale Hurston.' *NOVEL: A Forum on Fiction* 30, no. 3 (1997): 329–60.

Jacquet, Jennifer. *Is Shame Necessary? New Uses for an Old Tool*. London: Penguin, 2016.

Jameson, Fredric. 'On Goffman's Frame Analysis.' *Theory and Society* 3, no. 1 (1976): 119–33.

Jane, Emma A. *Misogyny Online: A Short (and Brutish) History*. 1st edition. Sage Swifts. Thousand Oaks, CA: SAGE ltd, 2016.

Jensen, Tracey. *Parenting the Crisis: The Cultural Politics of Neo-Liberal Parent-Blame*. Bristol: Policy Press, 2018.

Jensen, Tracey. 'Welfare Commonsense, Poverty Porn and Doxosophy.' *Sociological Research Online* 19, no. 3 (2014): 3.

Jensen, Tracey, and Imogen Tyler. '"Benefits Broods": The Cultural and Political Crafting of Anti-Welfare Commonsense.' *Critical Social Policy* 35, no. 4 (November 2015): 470–91.

Johnson, J.F. *Proceedings of the General Anti-Slavery Convention, Called by the Committee of the British and Foreign Anti-Slavery Society*. London: John Snow, 1843.

Johnson, Walter. 'The Pedestal and the Veil: Rethinking the Capitalism/Slavery Question.' *Journal of the Early Republic* 24, no. 2 (2004): 299–308.

Jones, Christopher. 'Stigma and Tattoo.' In *Written on the Body: The Tattoo in European and American History*, edited by Jane Caplan, 1–16. London: Reaktion, 2000.

Jones, Christopher. 'Tattooing and Branding in Graeco-Roman Antiquity.' *Journal of Roman Studies* 77 (1987): 139–55.

Jones, C.P. 'Stigma and Tattoo.' In *Written on the Body: The Tattoo in European and American History*, edited by Jane Caplan, 1–16. London: Reaktion, 2000.

Jones, Hannah, Yasmin Gunaratnam, Gargi Bhattacharyaa, William Davies, Sukhwant Dhaliwal, Kirsten Forket, Emma Jackson, and Roiyah Saltus. *Go Home? The Politics of Immigration Controversies*. Manchester: Manchester University Press, 2017.

Jones, Sam. 'UN Human Rights Chief Denounces Sun over Katie Hopkins "Cockroach" Column.' *The Guardian*, 24 April 2015. https://www.theguardian.

com/global-development/2015/apr/24/katie-hopkins-cockroach-migrants-denounced-united-nations-human-rights-commissioner

Joseph, Peniel E. *Stokely: A Life*. New York: Basic Civitas, 2014.

Kafka, Franz. 'In the Penal Colony.' In *Franz Kafka: The Complete Short Stories*, translated by Willa Muir, 140–67. London: Vintage, 2005.

Kahan, Dan. 'Shaming Punishments.' In *Encyclopedia of Crime and Justice*, edited by Joshua Dressler. New York: Macmillan, 2002. https://www.encyclopedia.com/law/legal-and-political-magazines/shaming-punishments

Katz, Jack. 'Ethnography's Warrants.' *Sociological Methods & Research* 25, no. 4 (May 1997): 391–423.

Kellaway, Katy. 'Lubaina Himid: The Turner Prize Nominee Making Black Lives Visible.' *The Guardian*, 24 September 2017. https://www.theguardian.com/artanddesign/2017/sep/24/lubaina-himid-turner-prize-2017-interview

Kelley, Robin. 'Cedric J. Robinson: The Making of a Black Radical Intellectual.' *Counterpunch* (blog), 17 June 2016. https://www.counterpunch.org/2016/06/17/cedric-j-robinson-the-making-of-a-black-radical-intellectual/

Kelley, Robin D.G. *Race Rebels: Culture, Politics, and the Black Working Class*. New York: Free Press, 1996.

Kelley, Robin D.G. *What Is Racial Capitalism and Why Does It Matter?* University of Washington, 2017. https://www.youtube.com/watch?v=--gim7W_jQQ

Khazan, Jibreel. *Interview with Jibreel Khazan*. International Civil Rights Center & Museum, Greensboro, undated. http://www.sitinmovement.org/

Kilomba, Grada. *Plantation Memories: Episodes of Everyday Racism*. Munster: UNRAST-Verlag, 2008.

Kingsley, Patrick. 'In Britain, Even Children Are Feeling the Effects of Austerity.' *New York Times*, 26 September 2018. https://www.nytimes.com/2018/09/26/world/europe/uk-austerity-child-poverty.html

Kingsley, Patrick. 'Universal Credit Has Left Children so Undernourished Schools Are Offering Free Breakfasts.' *The Independent*, 1 October 2018. https://www.independent.co.uk/news/long_reads/children-undernourished-universal-credit-austerity-welfare-reforms-poverty-hunger-food-bank-a8557276.html

Kirby, Emma Jane. *The Optician of Lampedusa: A Tale of Rescue and the Awakening of Conscience*. London: Penguin, 2017.

Klein, Naomi. *The Shock Doctrine: The Rise of Disaster Capitalism*. London: Penguin Books, 2008.

Ladner, Dorie, Joyce Ladner, and Joseph Mosnier. *Dorie Ann Ladner and Joyce Ladner Oral History Interview Conducted by Joseph Mosnier*, 2011. https://www.loc.gov/item/afc2010039_crhp0054/

Ladner, Joyce. *The Death of White Sociology*. New York: Random House, 1973.

Lamont, Michèle, Graziella Moraes Silva, Hannah Herzog, Jessica Welburn, Joshua Guetzkow, Nissim Mizrachi, Hanna Herzog, and Elisa Reis. *Getting Respect: Responding to Stigma and Discrimination in the United States, Brazil, and Israel*. Princeton, NJ: Princeton University Press, 2018.

Langer, Emily. 'Franklin McCain, Who Helped Inspire Sit-Ins for Civil Rights as Part of Greensboro Four, Dies.' *The Washington Post*, 13 June 2014. https://www.washingtonpost.com/national/franklin-mccain-who-helped-inspire-sit-ins-for-civil-rights-as-part-of-greensboro-four-dies/2014/01/13/8c39840e-7c6e-11e3-9556-4a4bf7bcbd84_story.html

LeFrançois, Brenda A., Robert Menzies, and Geoffrey Reaume, eds. *Mad Matters: A Critical Reader in Canadian Mad Studies*. Toronto: Canadian Scholars' Press, 2013.

Lentin, Alana. 'Learning from Lisa Lowe,' 2017. http://www.alanalentin.net/2017/03/03/learning-from-lisa-lowe/

Lethbridge, Lucy. *Servants: A Downstairs View of Twentieth-Century Britain*. London: Bloomsbury, 2013.

Levi, Primo. *If This Is a Man*. Edited by Stuart Woolf. New York: The Orion Press, 1959.

Levi, Primo. 'Primo Levi's Heartbreaking, Heroic Answers to the Most Common Questions He Was Asked About "Survival in Auschwitz".' *New Republic*, 17 February 1986. https://newrepublic.com/article/119959/interview-primo-levi-survival-auschwitz

Leys, Ruth. *From Guilt to Shame: Auschwitz and After*. Princeton, NJ: Princeton University Press, 2007.

Linebaugh, Peter. *The Magna Carta Manifesto: Liberties and Commons for All*. Berkeley: University of California Press, 2009.

Link, Bruce G., and Jo Phelan. 'Stigma Power.' *Social Science & Medicine*, Structural Stigma and Population Health, 103 (2014): 24–32.

Loh, Lucienne. 'Comparative Postcolonial Ruralities and English Heritage: Julian Barnes's *England, England* and Kiran Desai's *The Inheritance of Loss*.' *The Journal of Commonwealth Literature* 51, no. 2 (June 2016): 302–15.

Loh, Lucienne. 'Rural Heritage and Colonial Nostalgia in the Thatcher Years: V.S. Naipaul's The Enigma of Arrival.' In *Thatcher & After*, edited by Louisa Hadley and Elizabeth Ho, 96–114. London: Palgrave Macmillan UK, 2010.

Lombroso, Cesare. *Criminal Man*. New York: G.P. Putnam's & Sons, 1911.

Longazel, Jamie. 'Moral Panic as Racial Degradation Ceremony: Racial Stratification and the Local-Level Backlash against Latino/a Immigrants.' *Punishment and Society* 15, no. 1 (2013): 96–119.

Lorde, Audre. 'Learning from the 60s.' Harvard University, February 1982. https://www.blackpast.org/african-american-history/1982-audre-lorde-learning-60s/

Lorde, Audre. *The Collected Poems of Audre Lorde*. New York: W.W. Norton, 2002.

Loury, Glenn. *The Anatomy of Racial Inequality*. Cambridge, MA: Harvard University Press, 2013.

Love, Heather. 'Close Reading and Thin Description.' *Public Culture* 25, no. 3 71 (2013): 401–34.

Love, Heather. 'Feeling Bad in 1963.' In *Political Emotions*, edited by Janet Staiger, Ann Cvetkovich, and Ann Reynolds. London: Routledge, 2010.

Loyd, Jenna, and Anne Bonds. 'Where Do Black Lives Matter? Race, Stigma, and Place in Milwaukee, Wisconsin.' *The Sociological Review* 66, no. 4 (2018): 898–918.

Lukachko, Alicia, Mark L. Hatzenbuehler, and Katherine M. Keyes. 'Structural Racism and Myocardial Infarction in the United States.' *Social Science & Medicine*, Structural Stigma and Population Health, 103 (February 2014): 42–50.

Lynch, Mona. 'Supermax Meets Death Row: Legal Struggles Around the New Pun.' In *The New Punitiveness: Trends, Theories, Perspectives*, edited by John Pratt, David Brown, Mark Brown, Simon Hallsworth, and Wayne Morrison. Cullompton, Devon: Willan Pub, 2005.

Madden, David, and Peter Marcuse. *In Defence of Housing: The Politics of Crisis*. London: Verso, 2016.

Major, Andrew. 'State and Criminal Tribes in Colonial Punjab: Surveillance, Control and Reclamation of the Dangerous Classes.' *Modern Asian Studies* 33, no. 3 (1999): 657–88.

Marable, Manning. *How Capitalism Underdeveloped Black America: Problems in Race, Political Economy, and Society*. London: Pluto Press, 2000.

Marsh, Sarah. 'British Children Living in Poverty "Could Hit Record High" – Report.' *The Guardian*, 20 February 2019. https://www.theguardian.com/society/2019/feb/20/british-children-living-in-poverty-could-hit-record-high-report

Marx, Gary. 'Role Models and Role Distance: A Remembrance of Erving Goffman.' *Theory and Society* 13, no. 5 (1984): 649–62.

Marx, Karl. *Capital: A Critique of Political Economy*. 1st English edition. Moscow: Progress Publishers, 1887. https://www.marxists.org/archive/marx/works/download/pdf/Capital-Volume-I.pdf

Marx, Karl. *Grundrisse: Foundations of the Critique of Political Economy*. Translated by Martin Nicolaus. London: Penguin, 1973. https://www.marxists.org/archive/marx/works/1857/grundrisse/

Matory, J. Lorand. *Stigma and Culture: Last-Place Anxiety in Black America*. Chicago: University of Chicago Press, 2015.

May, Theresa. 'Prime Minister Unveils Plans to Transform Mental Health Support', 2017. https://www.gov.uk/government/news/prime-minister-unveils-plans-to-transform-mental-health-support

Mayhew, Henry. *London Labour and the London Poor*. Oxford: Oxford University Press, 2012.

McCord, David. *The Statutes at Large of South Carolina: Acts Relating to Charleston, Courts, Slaves, and Rivers*. Vol. 7. Columbia, SC: A.S. Johnston, 1840.

McDaniel, Patricia. *Shrinking Violets and Caspar Milquetoasts: Shyness, Power, and Intimacy in the United States, 1950–1995*. New York: New York University Press, 2003.

McKittrick, Katherine. 'Yours in the Intellectual Struggle: Sylvia Wynter and the Realization of the Living.' In *Sylvia Wynter: On Being Human as Praxis*, edited by Katherine McKittrick, 1–8. Durham, NC: Duke University Press, 2015.

McWade, Brigit. 'Recovery as Policy as a Form of Neoliberal State Making.' *Intersectionalities: A Global Journal of Social Work Analysis, Research, Polity, and Practice* 5, no. 3 (2016): 62–81.

Meier, August, and Elliott M. Rudwick. *CORE: A Study in the Civil Rights Movement, 1942–1968*. New York: Oxford University Press, 1973.

Melamed, Jodi. *Represent and Destroy: Rationalizing Violence in the New Racial Capitalism*. Minneapolis: University of Minnesota Press, 2011.

Memmi, Albert. *The Colonizer and the Colonized*. London: Earthscan, 2003.

Mills, China. '"Dead People Don't Claim": A Psychopolitical Autopsy of UK Austerity Suicides.' *Critical Social Policy* 38, no. 2 (2018): 302–22.

Moody, Anne. *Coming of Age in Mississippi*. New York: Dial Press, 1968.

Morgen, Sandra, and Jeff Maskovsky. 'The Anthropology of Welfare "Reform": New Perspectives on U.S. Urban Poverty in the Post-Welfare Era.' *Annual Review of Anthropology* 32 (2003): 315–38.

Morris, Aldon. *The Scholar Denied: W.E.B. Du Bois and the Birth of Modern Sociology*. Oakland: University of California Press, 2015.

Mortram, Jim. *Small Town Inertia*. Liverpool: Bluecoat Press, 2017.

Mouser, Bruce. 'Iles de Los as Bulking Center in the Slave Trade, 1750–1800.' *Outre-Mers. Revue d'histoire* 313 (1996): 77–91.

Murch, Donna Jean. *Living for the City: Migration, Education, and the Rise of the Black Panther Party in Oakland, California*. Chapel Hill: University of North Carolina Press, 2010.

Murdoch, Jonathan, and Andy Pratt. 'From the Power of Topography to the Topography of Power: A Discourse on Strange Ruralities.' In *Contested Countryside Cultures: Otherness, Marginalisation, and Rurality*, edited by Paul J. Cloke and Jo Little, 51–69. London: Routledge, 1997.

Murray, Charles. 'Stigma Makes Generosity Feasible.' *AEIdeas: A Public Policy Blog from AEI* (blog), 30 November 2009. http://www.aei.org/publication/stigma-makes-generosity-feasible/

Neumeyer, Peter. 'Franz Kafka, Sugar Baron.' *Modern Fiction Studies* 17 (1971): 5–16.

Nigam, Sanjay. 'Disciplining and Policing the "Criminals By Birth", Part 1: The Making of a Colonial Stereotype – The Criminal Tribes and Castes of North India.' *The Indian Economic & Social History Review* 27, no. 2 (1990): 131–64.

Nijhar, Preeti. *Law and Imperialism: Criminality and Constitution In Colonial India and Victorian England*. London: Routledge, 2009.

Nilsen, Alf Gunvald. *Adivasis and the State: Subalternity and Citizenship in India's Bhil Heartland*. South Asia in the Social Sciences 7. Cambridge: Cambridge University Press, 2018.

Noble, Safiya. *Algorithms of Oppression: How Search Engines Reinforce Racism*. New York: NYU Press, 2018.

Northey, Anthony. *Kafka's Relatives: Their Lives and His Writing*. New Haven, CT: Yale University Press, 1991.

Nowicka, Magdalena. 'I Don't Mean to Sound Racist but…: Transforming Racism in Transnational Europe.' *Ethnic and Racial Studies* 41, no. 5 (2018): 824–41.

O'Hara, Mary. 'As a Jobcentre Adviser, I Got "Brownie Points" for Cruelty.' *The Guardian*, 4 February 2015. https://www.theguardian.com/society/2015/feb/04/jobcentre-adviser-play-benefit-sanctions-angela-neville

O'Hara, Mary. 'Mental Health and Suicide.' In *The Violence of Austerity*, edited by Vickie Cooper and David Whyte, 35–43. London: Pluto Press, 2017.

Olusoga, David. *Black and British: A Forgotten History*. London: Macmillan, 2016.

Olusoga, David. 'The History of British Slave Ownership Has Been Buried: Now Its Scale Can Be Revealed.' *The Guardian*, 15 July 2015. https://www.theguardian.com/world/2015/jul/12/british-history-slavery-buried-scale-revealed

Olusoga, David, and Casper Erichsen. *The Kaiser's Holocaust. Germany's Forgotten Genocide and the Colonial Roots of Nazism*. London: Faber and Faber, 2010.

Osborne, George. 'There Is a Dependency Culture', 28 February 2008. https://conservative-speeches.sayit.mysociety.org/speech/599696

Paine, Thomas. 'Reflections on the Life and Death of Lord Clive.' *Pennsylvania Magazine*. 1775. http://thomaspaine.org/questionable-authorship/reflections-on-the-life-and-death-of-lord-clive.html

Pakenham, Thomas. *The Scramble for Africa: 1876–1912*. London: Abacus, 1995.

Parker, Richard, and Peter Aggleton. 'HIV and AIDS-Related Stigma and Discrimination: A Conceptual Framework and Implications for Action.' *Social Science & Medicine* 57, no. 1 (July 2003): 13–24.

Parks, Gordon. 'Whip of Black Power.' *Life Magazine*, 19 May 1967.

Paton, Diana. *No Bond but the Law: Punishment, Race, and Gender in Jamaican State Formation, 1780–1870*. Next Wave. Durham, NC: Duke University Press, 2004.

Paton, Kirsteen. 'Beyond Legacy: Backstage Stigmatisation and "Trickle-up" Politics of Urban Regeneration.' *The Sociological Review* 66, no. 4 (2018): 919–34.

Patterson, Orlando. *Slavery and Social Death: A Comparative Study*. Cambridge, MA: Harvard University Press, 1982.

Paull, Jenny. 'The Scold's Bridle.' *Lancaster Castle* (blog), n.d. http://www.lancastercastle.com/history-heritage/further-articles/the-scolds-bridle/

Pavāra, Ja Vi. *Dalit Panthers: An Authoritative History*. Translated by Rakshit Sonawane. New Delhi: Forward Press, 2017.

Payne, Daniel. 'Bring Back The Welfare Stigma.' *The Federalist*, 21 August 2014. http://thefederalist.com/2014/08/21/bring-back-the-welfare-stigma/

Perera, Jessica. 'The London Clearances: Race, Housing and Policing.' Institute of Race Relations, 20 February 2019. http://www.irr.org.uk/news/the-london-clearances-a-background-paper-on-race-housing-and-policing/

Pescosolido, Bernice A., and Jack K. Martin. 'The Stigma Complex.' *Annual Review of Sociology* 41, no. 1 (14 August 2015): 87–116.

Peters, Paul. 'Witness to the Execution: Kafka and Colonialism.' *Monatshefte* 93, no. 4 (2001): 401–25.

Pinckard, George. *Notes on the West Indies: Written During the Expedition Under the Command of the Late General Sir Ralph Abercromby*. Vol. 3. 3 vols. London: Hurst, Rees and Orme, 1806.

Pinker, Robert. 'Stigma and Social Welfare.' *Social Work* 27, no. 4 (1970): 13–17.

Piven, Frances Fox, and Richard Cloward. *Regulating the Poor: The Functions of Public Welfare*. Updated edition. New York: Vintage, 1993.

Pleece, Warren. *Freedom Bound: Escaping Slavery in Scotland*. Glasgow: BHP Comics, 2018.

Plimmer, Gill. 'Virgin Care Sues NHS after Losing Surrey Child Services Deal.' *The Financial Times*, 2017. https://www.ft.com/content/297e7714-089f-11e7-97d1-5e720a26771b

Polanyi, Karl. *The Great Transformation: The Political and Economic Origins of Our Time*. Boston, MA: Beacon Press, 2001.

Povinelli, Elizabeth A. *Economies of Abandonment: Social Belonging and Endurance in Late Liberalism*. Durham, NC: Duke University Press, 2011.

Powell, Margaret. *Below Stairs*. New York: St. Martin's Press, 2012.

Pratt, John, David Brown, Mark Brown, Simon Hallsworth, and Wayne Morrison, eds. *The New Punitiveness: Trends, Theories, Perspectives*. Portland: Willan Pub, 2005.

Puppy, Vipin. 'Brand of Shame.' *India Legal*, 9 November 2016. http://www.indialegallive.com/special-story/brand-of-shame-15551

Rambani, Vishal, and Avtar Singh. '"Assume I Am a Thief, a Jeb Katri; Why Tattoo It on My Forehead?"' *Hindustan Times*, 9 October 2016. http://www.hindustantimes.com/punjab/assume-i-am-a-thief-a-jeb-katri-why-tattoo-it-on-my-forehead/story-z3uWxeuVAzfeQB6S4QxvUN.html

Rapport, Nigel. *Diverse World-Views in an English Village*. Edinburgh: Edinburgh University Press, 1993.

Ray, Arun. *National Human Rights Commission of India: Formation, Functioning and Future Prospects, Volume 1*. New Delhi: Khama, 2004.

Read, J., N. Haslam, L. Sayce, and E. Davies. 'Prejudice and Schizophrenia: A Review of the "Mental Illness Is an Illness like Any Other" Approach.' *Acta Psychiatrica Scandinavica* 114, no. 5 (1 November 2006): 303–18.

Rediker, Marcus. *The Slave Ship: A Human History*. New York: Viking, 2008.

Renton, Dave. *Never Again: Rock against Racism and the Anti-Nazi League 1976–1982*. Fascism and the Far Right. London: Routledge/Taylor & Francis Group, 2019.

Rice, Alan. 'The Cotton That Connects, the Cloth That Binds.' *Atlantic Studies* 4, no. 2 (2007): 285–303.

Richmond, Vivienne. *Clothing the Poor in Nineteenth-Century England*. Cambridge: Cambridge University Press, 2013.

Robinson, Cedric J. *Black Marxism: The Making of the Black Radical Tradition*. Chapel Hill, NC: University North Carolina Press, 2000.

Robinson, Cedric J. *Black Movements in America*. New York: Routledge, 2013.

Roy, Arundhati. 'The Doctor and the Saint.' In *Annihilation of Caste: The Annotated Critical Edition*, ebook, 23–337. London: Verso, 2014.

Roy, Arundhati. 'The Silence Is the Loudest Sound.' *New York Times*, 15 August 2019. https://www.nytimes.com/2019/08/15/opinion/sunday/kashmir-siege-modi.html

Rubin, Anne. 'Reflections on the Death of Emmett Till.' *Southern Cultures* 2, no. 1 (1995): 45–66.

Ryan, Frances. *Crippled: Austerity and the Demonization of Disabled People.* London: Verso, 2019.

Šabatová, Anna. 'Facility for Detention of Foreigners Bělá-Jezová: Evaluation of Systematic Visit.' Public Defenders of Rights, Ombudsman.' Public Defender of Rights, 9 September 2015. https://www.ochrance.cz/fileadmin/user_upload/ochrana_osob/ZARIZENI/Zarizeni_pro_cizince/Report_Bela-Jezova.pdf

Samuel, Raphael. 'Mrs. Thatcher's Return to Victorian Values.' *Proceedings of the British Academy* 78 (1992): 9–29.

Sandhu, Sukhdev. 'The First Black Britons.' BBC History, 2011. http://www.bbc.co.uk/history/british/empire_seapower/black_britons_01.shtml

Sarkin-Hughes, Jeremy. *Germany's Genocide of the Herero: Kaiser Wilhelm II, His General, His Settlers, His Soldiers.* Cape Town: UCT Press, 2010.

Saunders, Patricia. 'Fugitive Dreams of Diaspora: Conversations with Saidiya Hartman.' *Anthurium: A Caribbean Studies Journal* 6, no. 1 (2008): 1–16.

Savage, Michael, and Dulcie Lee. '"I Regularly See Rickets": Diseases of Victorian-Era Poverty Return to UK.' *The Guardian*, 23 December 2017. https://www.theguardian.com/society/2017/dec/23/poorer-children-disproportionately-need-hospital-treatment

Sayad, Abdelmalek. *L'Immigration Ou Les Paradoxes de l'altérité: L'illusion Du Provisoire.* Paris: Raisons d'agir, 2006.

Sayer, Andrew. *Why We Can't Afford the Rich.* Bristol: Policy Press, 2016.

Scambler, Graham. 'Heaping Blame on Shame: "Weaponising Stigma" for Neoliberal Times.' *The Sociological Review* 66, no. 4 (2018): 766–782.

Scheidel, Walter. 'The Comparative Economics of Slavery in the Greco-Roman World.' *Princeton/Stanford Working Papers in Classics*, 2005. https://papers.ssrn.com/sol3/papers.cfm?abstract_id=1096417

Scheper-Hughes, Nancy. 'Ire in Ireland.' *Ethnography* 1, no. 1 (7 January 2000): 117–40.

Scheper-Hughes, Nancy. *Saints, Scholars and Schizophrenics: Mental Illness in Rural Ireland.* Twentieth anniversary, updated and expanded edition. Oakland: University of California Press, 2001.

Schrecker, Ted, and C. Bambra. *How Politics Makes Us Sick: Neoliberal Epidemics.* Houndmills, Basingstoke : Palgrave Macmillan, 2015.

Schultheis, Silja. 'The Refugee Policy of the Visegrád Countries: "No One Invited You".' *Heinrich-Böll-Stiftung*, 15 September 2015. https://cz.boell.org/en/2015/09/15/refugee-policy-visegrad-countries-no-one-invited-you

Schweik, Susan. 'Stigma Management.' *Disability Studies Quarterly* 34, no. 1 (2014). http://dsq-sds.org/article/view/4014/3539

Scott, James C. *Weapons of the Weak: Everyday Forms of Peasant Resistance.* Nachdr. New Haven, CT: Yale University Press, 2000.

Sen, Amartya. 'Imperial Illusions.' *The New Republic*, 31 December 2007. https://newrepublic.com/article/61784/imperial-illusions

Sharpe, Christina. *In the Wake: On Blackness and Being*. Durham, NC: Duke University Press, 2016.

Shetty, Salil. 'Foreword, Amnesty International Report 2016/17: State of Human Rights,' 2017. https://www.amnesty.org/download/Documents/POL1048002017ENGLISH.PDF

Shilliam, Robbie. *Race and the Undeserving Poor: From Abolition to Brexit*. Newcastle: Agenda Publishing, 2018.

Sivanandan, Ambalavaner. 'Foreword. Racial Violence and the Brexit State.' Institute for Race Relations, 2016. http://www.irr.org.uk/app/uploads/2016/11/Racial-violence-and-the-Brexit-state-final.pdf

Skeel, David. 'Shaming in Corporate Law.' *University of Pennsylvania Law Review* 149, no. 6 (2001): 1811–68.

Skeggs, Bev. 'The Making of Class and Gender through Visualizing Moral Subject Formation.' *Sociology* 39, no. 5 (December 2005): 965–82.

Skeggs, Beverley. 'A Crisis in Humanity: What Everyone with Parents Is Likely to Face in the Future.' *The Sociological Review* (blog), 2019. https://www.thesociologicalreview.com/a-crisis-in-humanity-what-everyone-with-parents-is-likely-to-face-in-the-future/

Skeggs, Beverley. 'Imagining Personhood Differently: Person Value and Autonomist Working-Class Value Practices.' *The Sociological Review* 59, no. 3 (1 August 2011): 496–513.

Skeggs, Beverley. 'The Dirty History of Feminism and Sociology: Or the War of Conceptual Attrition.' *The Sociological Review* 56, no. 4 (2008): 670–90.

Skeggs, Beverley. 'The Forces That Shape Us: The Entangled Vine of Gender, Race and Class.' *The Sociological Review* 67, no. 1 (2019): 28–35.

Skeggs, Beverley, and Helen Wood. *Reacting to Reality Television: Performance, Audience and Value*. New York: Routledge, 2012.

Snyder, Timothy. *On Tyranny: Twenty Lessons from the Twentieth Century*. London: Bodley Head, 2017.

Sood, Aman. '"Jeb Katri" Tattoo Gone, but Scarred for Life.' *The Tribune*, 10 October 2016. https://www.tribuneindia.com/news/punjab/community/-jeb-katri-tattoo-gone-but-scarred-for-life/307407.html

Spicker, Paul. *Stigma and Social Welfare*. Creative Commons, 2011. http://openair.rgu.ac.uk

Spillers, Hortense. *Black, White, and in Color: Essays on American Literature and Culture*. Chicago: University of Chicago Press, 2003.

Stanziani, Alessandro. 'The Traveling Panopticon: Labor Institutions and Labor Practices in Russia and Britain in the Eighteenth and Nineteenth Centuries.' *Comparative Studies in Society and History* 51, no. 4 (2009): 715–41.

Steadman, Philip. 'Samuel Bentham's Panopticon.' *Journal of Bentham Studies*, 1 January 2012.

Steedman, Carolyn. *Landscape for a Good Woman: A Story of Two Lives*. New Brunswick, NJ: Rutgers University Press, 1987.

Steinberg, Stephen. *Race Relations: A Critique*. Stanford, CA: Stanford University Press, 2007.

Stewart, Mo. *Cash Not Care: The Planned Demolition of the UK Welfare State*. London: New Generation Publishing, 2016.

Stewart, Mo. 'State Crime by Proxy: Corporate Influence on State Sanctioned Social Harm.' *The Journal of Critical Psychology, Counselling and Psychotherapy* 18, no. 4 (2018): 217–27.

Stuckler, David, and Sanjay Basu. *The Body Economic: Why Austerity Kills: Recessions, Budget Battles, and the Politics of Life and Death*. New York: Basic Books, 2013.

Tamás, G.M. 'Anti-Immigration Referendum Sunday in Hungary.' *Open Democracy*, 2 October 2016. https://www.opendemocracy.net/en/can-europe-make-it/anti-immigration-referendum-sunday-in-hungary/

Tansel, Cemal Burak, ed. *States of Discipline: Authoritarian Neoliberalism and the Contested Reproduction of Capitalist Order*. Transforming Capitalism. Lanham, MD: Rowman & Littlefield International, 2017.

Taylor, Keeanga-Yamahtta. *From #BlackLivesMatter to Black Liberation*. Chicago: Haymarket Books, 2016.

Taylor, Steven J., Robert Bogdan, and Marjorie DeVault. *Introduction to Qualitative Research Methods: A Guidebook and Resource*. New York: John Wiley, 2015.

Taylor-Gooby, Peter. *The Double Crisis of the Welfare State and What We Can Do about It*. Basingstoke: Palgrave Macmillan, 2013.

Thatcher, Margaret. 'Pankhurst Lecture to the 300 Group.' Savoy Hotel, 18 July 1990. https://www.margaretthatcher.org/document/108156

Thatcher, Margaret. TV Interview for Walt Disney Corporation, 15 March 1989. https://www.margaretthatcher.org/document/107455

The Lambs Defence against Lyes. London: Giles Calvert, 1659.

Thompson, Edward Palmer. 'Rough Music Reconsidered.' *Folklore* 103, no. 1 (1992): 3–26.

Thompson, Edward Palmer. *The Making of the English Working Class*. New York: Vintage, 1963.

Todd, Nigel. 'A History of Labour in Lancaster and Barrow-in-Furness C. 1890–1920.' Lancaster University, 1976.

Todd, Selina. *The People: The Rise and Fall of the Working Class*. London: John Murray, 2015.

Tolia-Kelly, Divya. 'Fear in Paradise: The Affective Registers of the English Lake District Landscape Re-Visited.' *The Senses and Society* 2, no. 3 (2007): 329–51.

Torgalkar, Varsha. '69 Years After Independence, There Are Still Tribes That Are Considered "Born Criminal".' *Youth Ki Awaaz* (blog), 2016. https://www.youthkiawaaz.com/2016/08/denotified-tribes-discrimination-and-violence/

Townsend, Mark. 'Secret Plan to Use Charities to Help Deport Rough Sleepers.' *The Guardian*, 6 July 2019. https://www.theguardian.com/politics/2019/jul/06/home-office-secret-plan-charities-deport-rough-sleepers

Trilling, Daniel. 'What to Do with the People Who Do Make It Across?', 8 October 2015. https://www.lrb.co.uk/v37/n19/daniel-trilling/what-to-do-with-the-people-who-do-make-it-across

Trimble, Jennifer. 'The Zoninus Collar and the Archaeology of Roman Slavery.' *American Journal of Archaeology* 120, no. 3 (2016): 447–72.

Trouillot, Michel-Rolph. *Silencing the Past: Power and the Production of History.* Boston: Beacon Press, 1995.

Turner, Fred. 'Machine Politics: The Rise of the Internet and a New Age of Authoritarianism.' *Harper's Magazine*, 2019. http://fredturner.stanford.edu/wp-content/uploads/Turner-Machine-Politics-Harpers-Magazine-2019-01.pdf

Turvill, William. 'Journalists "Pushed Away" from "Distressing Scenes" Involving Migrants at Hungarian Train Station.' *Press Gazette UK*, 3 September 2015. https://www.pressgazette.co.uk/journalists-pushed-away-distressing-scenes-involving-migrants-hungarian-train-station/

Twain, Mark. *King Leopold's Soliloquy: A Defense of His Congo Rule.* Boston, MA: The P.R. Warren Co., 1905.

Tyler, Imogen. 'Deportation Nation.' *Journal for the Study of British Cultures* 25, no. 1 (2018): 25–41.

Tyler, Imogen. *Revolting Subjects: Social Abjection and Resistance in Neoliberal Britain.* London: Zed, 2013.

United Nations. 'Zeid Urges Czech Republic to Stop Detention of Migrants and Refugees', 22 October 2015. http://www.ohchr.org/EN/NewsEvents/Pages/DisplayNews.aspx?NewsID=16632&LangID=E#sthash.t6NZThkl.dpuf

Urry, John. *The Tourist Gaze: Leisure and Travel in Contemporary Societies.* Theory, Culture & Society. London: Sage Publications, 1990.

Vasdev, Kanchan. 'For 5 Women Branded on Their Foreheads, Verdict Too Little after 23 Years of Humiliation.' *The Indian Express*, 1 October 2016. https://indianexpress.com/article/india/india-news-india/amritsar-punjab-tattoo-women-forehead-humiliation-police-theft-jeb-katri-3090699/

Virdee, Satnam. "Racialized Capitalism: An Account of Its Contested Origins and Consolidation." *The Sociological Review* 67, no. 1 (2019): 3–27.

Virdee, Satnam. *Racism, Class and the Racialized Outsider.* Basingstoke: Palgrave Macmillan, 2014.

Virdee, Satnam. 'The Racialized Outsider as the Conscience of Modernity.' British Sociological Association Conference Keynote Lecture. Glasgow, 2019.

Vltchek, Andre. 'In Prague You Get Beaten for Defending Refugees.' *Counterpunch*, 30 October 2015. https://www.counterpunch.org/2015/10/30/in-prague-you-get-beaten-for-defending-refugees/

Wacquant, Loïc. 'Crafting the Neoliberal State: Workfare, Prisonfare, and Social Insecurity.' *Sociological Forum* 25, no. 2 (2010): 197–220.

Wacquant, Loïc. 'Scrutinizing the Street: Poverty, Morality, and the Pitfalls of Urban Ethnography.' *American Journal of Sociology* 107, no. 6 (2002): 1468–532.

Wacquant, Loïc, Tom Slater, and Virgílio Borges Pereira. 'Territorial Stigmatization in Action.' *Environment and Planning A: Economy and Space* 46, no. 6 (June 2014): 1270–80.

Wakefield, Edward. *England and America: A Comparison of the Social and Political State of Both Nations.* Vol. 1. 2 vols. London: Richard Bentley, 1883.

Walker, Robert. *The Shame of Poverty*. Oxford: Oxford University Press, 2014.

Walker, Robert, Grace Bantebya Kyomuhendo, Elaine Chase, Sohail Choudhry, Erika K. Gubrium, Jo Yongmie Nicola, Ivar Lødemel, et al. 'Poverty in Global Perspective: Is Shame a Common Denominator?' *Journal of Social Policy* 42, no. 02 (2013): 215–33.

Wallerstein, Immanuel Maurice. *Capitalist Agriculture and the Origins of the European World-Economy in the Sixteenth Century: With a New Prologue*. Berkeley: University of California Press, 2011.

Walters, William. *Governmentality: Critical Encounters*. London: Routledge, 2012.

Walvin, James. *Slavery in Small Things: Slavery and Modern Cultural Habits*. Chichester: Wiley Blackwell, 2017.

Warde, Alan. 'Conditions of Dependence: Working-Class Quiescence in Lancaster in the Twentieth Century.' *International Review of Social History* 35, no. 1 (1990): 71–105.

Weale, Sally. 'Tired, Hungry and Shamed: Pupil Poverty "Stops Learning".' *The Observer*, 14 April 2019. https://www.theguardian.com/education/2019/apr/14/tired-hungry-shamed-pupil-poverty-stops-learning

Weheliye, Alexander. *Habeas Viscus: Racializing Assemblages, Biopolitics, and Black Feminist Theories of the Human*. Durham, NC: Duke University Press, 2014.

Werrett, Simon. 'Potemkin and the Panopticon: Samuel Bentham and the Architecture of Absolutism in Eighteenth Century Russia.' *Journal of Bentham Studies* 2 (1999): 1–25.

West, Cornel. *Race and Social Theory: Towards a Genealogical Materialist Analysis* (blog), 2016. http://www.versobooks.com/blogs/2568-race-and-social-theory-towards-a-genealogical-materialist-analysis

Whitman, James. 'What Is Wrong with Inflicting Shame Sanctions.' *Yale Law Journal* 107, no. 4 (1998): 1055–92.

Wickware, Carolyn. 'CCGs Cutting Spending on Mental Health despite NHS Pledges.' *Pulse*, April 25, 2017. http://www.pulsetoday.co.uk/clinical/mental-health/ccgs-cuttingspending-on-mental-health-despite-nhs-pledges/20034293.article

Wildenthal, Lora. *German Women for Empire, 1884–1945*. Politics, History, and Culture. Durham, NC: Duke University Press, 2001.

Wildenthal, Lora. '"When Men Are Weak": The Imperial Feminism of Frieda von Bülow.' *Gender & History* 10, no. 1 (April 1998): 53–77.

Wilkinson, Kate. *Women and Modesty in Late Antiquity*. Cambridge: Cambridge University Press, 2015.

Williams, Eric. *Capitalism and Slavery*. Chapel Hill: University of North Carolina Press, 1944.

Williams, Patricia. 'Metro Broadcasting, Inc. v. FCC: Regrouping in Singular Times.' *Harvard Law Review* 104, no. 2 (1990): 525–46.

Woodcock, Andrew. 'Benefit Cheats Are "Mugging Taxpayers" Says Osborne.' *The Independent*, 17 October 2010. https://www.independent.co.uk/news/uk/politics/benefit-cheats-are-mugging-taxpayers-says-osborne-2109134.html

Wright Mills, Charles. *The Sociological Imagination*. Harmondsworth: Penguin, 1959.

X, Malcom. 'Malcom X in Cairo Urges African Aid to U.S. Negroes.' *The Militant*, 1964. http://hierographics.org/malcolmX.htm

Yang, Anand. 'Dangerous Castes and Tribes: The Criminal Tribes Act and the Magahiya Doms of Northeast India.' In *Crime and Criminality in British India*, edited by Anand Yang, 108–27. Tucson: University of Arizona Press, 1986.

Younge, Gary. '1963: The Defining Year of the Civil Rights Movement.' *The Guardian*, 7 May 2013. http://www.theguardian.com/world/2013/may/07/1963-defining-year-civil-rights

Younge, Gary. *No Place like Home: A Black Briton's Journey through the American South*. London: Picador, 1999.

Zelený-Atapana, Mnislav. 'Je Na Řadě Genocida Bělochů v Evropě?' *Lidové Noviny*, 18 July 2016. http://www.lidovky.cz/diskuse-je-na-rade-genocida-belochu-v-evrope-fe0-/nazory.aspx?c=A160718_135549_ln_nazory_mct

Zilcosky, John. *Kafka's Travels: Exoticism, Colonialism, and the Traffic of Writing*. New York: Palgrave, 2004.

Zimmerer, Jürgen. *From Windhoek to Auschwitz: On the Relationship between Colonialism and the Holocaust*. London: Routledge, forthcoming 2021.

Acknowledgements

This has proved a difficult to book to write, and I am grateful to everybody who has supported me in ways large and small. I would particularly like to acknowledge my friends and colleagues at Lancaster University, especially Chris Grover who so kindly stood in as acting Head of the Sociology Department so I could finish this book, our Departmental Officer Francesca Stephenson who kept everything running smoothly, Karen Gammon for keeping everybody in check, Hannah Morgan for the espressos, Joanna Kosta for the Polish cigarettes, Yang Hu for sitting in the front row to cheer me on when I gave one of the British Sociological Association keynotes in 2019. A big thank you also to Brigit McWade who worked as a research assistant during the first year of this project and gathered together an initial bibliography of the existing social scientific literature on stigma. My early conversations with Brigit were formative and I learnt a lot from her about the history of mental health, 'mad' activism and stigma power.

During the research for this project I have been part of a wider stigma research network, and learnt from others researching 'stigma power': thanks especially to Tom Slater, Gareth Thomas, Kirsteen Paton, Lisa Morriss, Jenna Loyd, Tracy Shildrick, Joanna Latimer and Graham Scambler. Thanks also to all my colleagues and friends at the Sociological Review Foundation, which has been such an inspiring intellectual community to be a part of, especially Bev Skeggs, Michaela Benson, Mark Carrigan, Jenny Thatcher, Attila Szanto, Marie-Andree Jacob, Emma Jackson, Steve Brown, Robin Smith, Ben Carrington, Gurminder Bhambra, Laurie Hanquinet, Sarah Green. I would also like to thank everybody who invited me to give talks and lectures during the period I was researching and writing this book, including friends and colleagues at York, Birmingham, Liverpool, Morecambe, Warwick, Leeds, Glasgow, Cardiff, London, Berlin, Dortmund and Cork, the British Sociology Association, and Impact Scotland. I have been overwhelmed with hospitality and generosity from the academic communities of which I am so grateful to be a part. A shout out also to the Surviving Society group, Chantelle Lewis, Tissot Regis, Saskia Papadakis and George Ofori-Addo for our podcast conversation about this project.

A massive thank you to everybody at the Morecambe Bay Poverty Truth Commission (and those in the wider UK Poverty Truth Movement), it has been such an honour to work with you all over the last few years. I am especially grateful to Roger Mitchell, Sue Mitchell, Andy Knox, Ally Mackenzie, Karen Wheeler, Emily Wheeler, Mark Thomas (Dusty), Alex Campbell, Annette Smith, Helen Greatorex, Patrice Van Cleemput, Suzanne Lodge, Daniel Burba, Mary Kinane, Heather Fowler, Caroline Jackson, Ann Marie Gavin, Krissie McGeogh, Andrew Bennett, Andy Maddox, Emily Tubitt, Angela Young, Mark Hutton, Steve Charman, Janey Todd, James Martin, Ian Cooper and Steven Wong.

Thanks also to the Elizabeth Roberts Working Class Oral History Archive at the Regional History Centre, Lancaster University, and especially to Sam Riches for reading sections of the book and offering historical advice on my interpretation of the data, and referencing thereof. Also to Jan Čulík at Glasgow University who assisted with some information about Czechia, and whose useful articles I drew on in my account of racism and responses to the refugee crisis.

While I was working on this book, I collaborated with two amazing young artists; Charlotte Bailey, with whom I produced a graphic essay based on one of the chapters of this book, and the graphic artist Tom Morris, whom I worked with to make an animated 'stigma machine' – thanks to both for your energy, input and creativity. To Kim Walker, my editor at Zed Books, and Sue Lascelles, the editor I worked closely with on the final manuscript, thanks both for advice, feedback and encouragement.

Friendship has given me sustenance throughout, and I would especially like to thank Sean Arnold, Jenn Ashworth, Brain Baker, Lisa Baraitser, Michaela Benson, Sarah Beresford, Laura Clancy, Caroline Falkus, Anne-Marie Fortier, Tracey Jensen, Paul Johnson, Kat Jungnickel, Bob Kemp, Jenna Loyd, Fiona Macleod, Maria Piacentini, Alison Rooke, Annette Smith, Bev Skeggs, Rachel Thomson, Deb Tyler, Karen Wheeler, Helen Wood and Satnam Virdee. An extra loud shout out to Bev for reading the manuscript and offering valuable comments, Satnam for ongoing intellectual dialogue, and Michaela, Jenn, Maria, Tracey and Fiona for everyday kindnesses, love and care.

Thanks also to my family, especially my six parents Jane and Mohamed, John and Liz, Barbara and Richard, my siblings, Jim & Taryn, Matt, Deb, Gavin & Nic, Sarah & Tony, Lamia & Rich, and Ibtissam. I am especially grateful to my children, the talented artist Louis Bennett and teenage freedom fighter Bella Tyler for challenging and inspiring me, I am so proud to be your mum. Finally, Bruce Bennett, my best friend, my rock and the love of my life, who has so patiently listened, read and given feedback throughout, thank you.

Index